The Routledge Companion to Accounting and Risk

To date, there has been little consideration of the many different ways in which accounting and risk intersect, despite organisations being more determined than ever to build resilience against potential risks. This comprehensive volume overcomes this gap by providing an overview of the field, drawing together current knowledge of risk in a wide range of different accounting contexts.

Key themes such as corporate governance, trust, uncertainty and climate change are covered by a global array of contributing scholars. These contributions are divided into four areas:

- The broader aspects of risk and risk management
- Risk in financial reporting
- Risk in management accounting
- Risk monitoring

The book is supported by a series of illustrative case studies which help to bring together theory and practice. With its wealth of examples and analyses, this volume provides essential reading for students, scholars and practitioners charged with understanding diverse facets of risk in the context of accounting in the business world.

Margaret Woods is Emeritus Professor of Accounting and Risk at Aston Business School, Aston University, UK. Founder of the European Risk Research Network, her extensive publications on risk particularly have attracted international media interest. Her book of case studies, *Risk Management in Organizations*, was published in 2011.

Philip Linsley is Professor of Accounting and Risk at the York Management School, University of York, UK. His research interests are risk-related and include investigating risk disclosure, and risk and culture. He is particularly interested in applying the ideas of Mary Douglas to the accounting field.

Routledge Companions in Business, Management and Accounting

Routledge Companions in Business, Management and Accounting are prestige reference works providing an overview of a whole subject area or sub-discipline. These books survey the state of the discipline including emerging and cutting edge areas. Providing a comprehensive, up to date, definitive work of reference, Routledge Companions can be cited as an authoritative source on the subject.

A key aspect of these Routledge Companions is their international scope and relevance. Edited by an array of highly regarded scholars, these volumes also benefit from teams of contributors which reflect an international range of perspectives.

Individually, Routledge Companions in Business, Management and Accounting provide an impactful one-stop-shop resource for each theme covered. Collectively, they represent a comprehensive learning and research resource for researchers, postgraduate students and practitioners.

Published titles in this series include (for a complete list of titles in this series, please visit www.routledge.com/business/series/RCBMA):

The Routledge Companion to Contemporary Brand Management
Edited by Francesca Dall'Olmo Riley, Jaywant Singh and Charles Blankson

The Routledge Companion to Banking Regulation and Reform
Edited by Ismail Ertürk and Daniela Gabor

The Routledge Companion to the Makers of Modern Entrepreneurship
Edited by David B. Audretsch and Erik E. Lehmann

The Routledge Companion to Business History
Edited by Abe de Jong, Steven Toms, John Wilson and Emily Buchnea

The Routledge Companion to Qualitative Accounting Research
Edited by Zahirul Hoque, Lee D. Parker, Mark A. Covaleski and Kathryn Haynes

The Routledge Companion to Accounting and Risk
Edited by Margaret Woods and Philip Linsley

The Routledge Companion to Accounting and Risk

Edited by Margaret Woods and Philip Linsley

Routledge
Taylor & Francis Group
LONDON AND NEW YORK

First published 2017
by Routledge
2 Park Square, Milton Park, Abingdon, Oxon OX14 4RN

and by Routledge
711 Third Avenue, New York, NY 10017

Routledge is an imprint of the Taylor & Francis Group, an informa business

British Library Cataloguing in Publication Data
A catalogue record for this book is available from the British Library

Library of Congress Cataloguing in Publication Data
Names: Woods, Margaret, 1954–editor. | Linsley, Philip, editor.
Title: The Routledge companion to accounting and risk / edited by Margaret Woods and Philip Linsley.
Description: Abingdon, Oxon; New York, NY: Routledge, 2017. | Includes bibliographical references and index.
Identifiers: LCCN 2016045312| ISBN 9781138860124 (hardback) | ISBN 9781315716756 (ebook)
Subjects: LCSH: Managerial accounting. | Financial risk management.
Classification: LCC HF5657.4 .R685 2017 | DDC 658.15/11–dc23
LC record available at https://lccn.loc.gov/2016045312

ISBN: 978-1-138-86012-4 (hbk)
ISBN: 978-1-315-71675-6 (ebk)

Typeset in Times New Roman
by Deanta Global Publishing Services, Chennai, India

MIX Paper from responsible sources FSC® C013056 FSC www.fsc.org

Printed and bound in Great Britain by
TJ International Ltd, Padstow, Cornwall

Contents

Figures

Tables

Contributors

Mark Billings is Senior Lecturer in Accounting and Business History at the University of Exeter Business School, UK. He previously held various administrative and financial management positions in investment banking and business, and academic posts at the City University Business School, London, Sheffield Hallam University and Nottingham University Business School. He holds degrees in economics and financial management from the Universities of Sheffield and London, and has been a member of the Institute of Chartered Accountants in England and Wales since 1985. His research interests are in banking, financial and accounting history and financial reporting, and he currently teaches undergraduate courses on corporate governance and auditing.

Binh Bui is a Senior Lecturer in Accounting at the School of Accounting and Commercial Law at the Victoria University of Wellington, New Zealand. Her research interests include the interface between strategy and management control systems, climate change and emission trading, risk management and accounting education. She has published papers in top-ranking accounting journals, including *Management Accounting Research*, *Behavioral Research in Accounting*, *Accounting Education: an International Journal*, and *Accounting History*. Her PhD thesis investigates changes in electricity generators' strategies and management control to manage business risks in the context of New Zealand Emissions Trading scheme. Continuing from her PhD, her current projects examine carbon accounting and assurance, and the role played by accounting in reducing carbon emissions within organisations in New Zealand and around the world.

Carolyn Cordery is an Associate Professor at Victoria University of Wellington, New Zealand. Her research focuses on not-for-profit organisations' accounting and accountability. She is interested in how these organisations are resourced and the resource constraints that cause many of these organisations to be financially vulnerable. As a member of the New Zealand Accounting Standards Board, she is also interested in improving the regulation of, and accounting in, these organisations. Carolyn is Joint Editor of *Third Sector Review*, on the editorial board of *Accounting History*, and *Accounting, Auditing and Accountability Journal*, and the Lotteries Community Sector Research Committee. Her teaching areas include accounting information systems and financial accounting.

Marie Gemma Dequae served as Group Risk & Insurance manager of the large Belgian multinational NV Bekaert SA for more than 20 years. In that role she designed, coordinated and managed the worldwide risk management programme, including risk treatment, transfer and risk awareness and culture. She is currently a board member of several Belgian companies. After serving as president and a board member of FERMA (the Federation of European Risk Management Associations) she still acts as an advisor, and is also active in the Belgian Association of Risk Management (BELRIM). She teaches economics and finance and, more recently, risk management at several universities and business schools.

Anthony Devine is a Graduate Tutor at Northumbria University, UK. He is completing his PhD which examines succession planning in family businesses. Anthony has experience in working in a family business in a senior capacity and has completed qualifications with the Family Firm Institute in Boston, Massachusetts, where he also acts as mentor and online tutor. He is on the board of a charity and has substantial teaching experience in teaching Accounting. He manages the Accounting degree programme at Northumbria, acts as examiner for the Association of International Accountants and is an external examiner at Sheffield Hallam University.

See Liang Foo is Associate Professor at the Singapore Management University where he teaches governance, risk management and assurance courses. He has worked in professional accounting firms in London and Singapore, and in the commercial sector, serving as co-chairman of the board of directors and chairman of the Audit Committee. He is a Fellow of the Institute of Chartered Accountants in England and Wales and the Institute of Singapore Chartered Accountants.

Kirstin Gillon is responsible for the ICAEW IT Faculty's thought leadership programme, Making Information Systems Work. In this role, she researches, writes and presents on a wide variety of issues related to digital technology, business and the accountancy profession. She liaises with the academic and policy community on technology issues, and organises events which bring together representatives from these communities and business. She joined ICAEW from PwC's IT consultancy practice and previously worked at IBM as a project manager and business analyst. She has a Master's degree in International Law from McGill University, Canada.

Nunung N. Hidayah is a lecturer at Aston Business School, Aston University, UK. She received sponsorship from the Islamic Research and Training Institute—Islamic Development Bank—for her PhD at Aston Business School, Aston University. Her research interests include governance and audit in Islamic financial institutions, organisation studies and critical finance studies. She was involved in curriculum development in Islamic Finance and Islamic Accounting, including the curriculum for the Postgraduate Islamic Finance Program of Al Maktoum Institute Dundee, and the University of Al Azhar Indonesia. She has been presented her working papers in European Organization Studies (EGOS) conferences, European Risk Research Network Conference and European Accounting Association Conference.

Christopher D. Ittner is the EY Professor and Chair of the Accounting Department at the Wharton School of the University of Pennsylvania, USA. He received his Doctorate in Business Administration from Harvard University. His research focuses on the design, implementation and performance consequences of performance measurement, cost management and enterprise risk management systems. He is an editor for *The Accounting Review* and serves on the editorial boards for several accounting and operations journals. His research has been published in leading accounting, labour economics, marketing and operations journals, and has received the American Accounting Association's Notable Contribution to Management Accounting Literature Award.

Katarina Kaarbøe is Professor at the Norwegian School of Economics in the Department of Accounting, Auditing and Law. Her research focuses on management control, most recently focused on Beyond Budgeting and Enterprise Risk Management. She has published a number of articles and book chapters within the area. She is project manager for the research programme ACTION—Accounting, Change and Tool Implementation in Organizations at NHH/SNF.

Thomas Keusch is an Assistant Professor of Accounting and Control at INSEAD. Prior to joining INSEAD he worked at Erasmus University Rotterdam and received his PhD at Maastricht University. His board research interests include risk management, CEO personality traits and various corporate governance issues, such as shareholder activism, executive compensation and boards of directors.

Beth Kewell is an author and academic who specialises in the study of risk comprehension, risk mitigation and risk governance. Her research critically evaluates the links between risk, science, technology and business, and has also focused on evaluating the links between language, organisational culture and decision-making in contexts typified by high levels of uncertainty. She has worked as an academic in the UK and Norway, and is currently affiliated to the Research Degrees Programme at the London School of Commerce, UK. She is co-author of *Risk: A Study of Its Origins, History and Politics* (with Matthias Beck).

Gillian Lees is Director of Governance and Risk Research, CIMA. She is responsible for developing CIMA's thought leadership and policy responses on governance and risk across all its key global markets. She has written and presented widely on the subject, particularly in respect of how boards can oversee strategy and risk effectively by understanding their business model within the context of a changing external environment. She is also CIMA's Technical Lead on a wide range of CGMA projects and authored the flagship report for the 2014 World Congress of Accountants, *New Ways of Working—managing the open workforce.*

Chu Yeong Lim is Associate Professor at the Singapore Institute of Technology where he teaches Advanced Company Accounting and Corporate Reporting courses. He has taught similar courses at the Singapore Management University (SMU) School of Accountancy. He has 15 years of industry experience in treasury, financial accounting and management accounting positions, primarily within the financial sector. His experience spans major companies including Credit Suisse, Citibank, Shell, Standard Chartered Bank, the Government of Singapore Investment Corporation and the Development Bank of Singapore. He holds a PhD from Manchester Business School, an MBA from the University of Warwick and is a CA (Singapore).

Philip Linsley is Professor of Accounting and Risk at the York Management School, University of York, UK. He has significant experience as an academic lecturer and researcher and teaches in the areas related to finance, accounting and risk. His research interests are risk-related and include investigating risk disclosure within the annual reports of financial and non-financial firms, risk and culture, risk management and risk systems. He is particularly interested in the ideas of Professor Dame Mary Douglas and in applying Douglas's cultural theory of risk to the accounting and finance field.

Mahmoud Marzouk is a Doctoral Researcher at the York Management School, University of York, UK. Mahmoud also completed his master's degree (MRes in Management) at the University of York in 2013. He has nine years of academic experience as a researcher and graduate teaching assistant at Menoufia University in Egypt and the University of York. His research interests lie primarily in the area of corporate risk disclosure. He is also interested in disclosure practices in emerging and developed market economies. He is currently a reviewer of both the *Journal of Applied Accounting Research* and *Journal of Financial Regulation and Compliance*.

Anita Meidell is Assistant Professor at the Department of Accounting, Auditing and Law at the Norwegian School of Economics. At the time of writing she was a PhD candidate in management control at the Norwegian School of Economics where she received her PhD in June 2016. She was a partner in Ernst & Young, where she was head of the Advisory practice in Bergen, Norway. Her research interest is in management control, with specific emphasis on enterprise risk management. She has published several articles within the area.

Tommaso Palermo is a Lecturer in Accounting at the London School of Economics and Political Science. Tommaso obtained a PhD in Management, Economics and Industrial Engineering at the Politecnico di Milano, Italy. His main research interests include the design and use of risk and performance management systems, risk culture in financial sector organisations and risk reporting and analysis in the aviation sector. Tommaso is also involved in a project that examines how accounting is implicated in the creation of markets for contested commodities, such as cannabis.

Philip Shrives is a Chartered Accountant and Professor in Accounting and Corporate Governance at Newcastle Business School, Northumbria University, UK. He has a degree from Newcastle University, a Master's degree from Glasgow University and a PhD in Accounting and Corporate Governance from University College Dublin. He has published articles with co-authors in a number of journals including *The British Accounting Review*, *Accounting, Auditing and Accountability Journal* and *Critical Perspectives on Accounting.* He has research interests in corporate disclosure, corporate governance, risk reporting and cultural theory. He has examined doctorates at UK and overseas universities and is currently an external examiner at University College Dublin.

Regine Slagmulder is a Partner and Full Professor of Accounting & Control at Vlerick Business School and a visiting professor at Ghent University, Belgium. Regine joined Vlerick Business School after an international career at various other institutions, including INSEAD, Tilburg University and McKinsey & Company. Her research and teaching activities focus on the link between performance and risk management systems, company strategy and corporate governance. She has published several books and numerous articles in both academic and practitioner journals on strategic costing and performance management. Her most recent work explores the interface between enterprise risk management and board effectiveness. In particular, she studies how risk governance and risk reporting are organised at senior management and board level to enable effective risk oversight. Regine regularly serves as invited speaker to both business and academic audiences.

Ying Kei Tse (Mike) is a Lecturer in Operations Management at the University of York, UK, based in the York Management School. Before taking up this post, he worked as a researcher at Nottingham University Business School and the Hong Kong Polytechnic University. His research crosses over different disciplines, including empirical research in risk management and supply chain management, data-mining of big social data, decision support in supply chain management, and development of OM educational simulation platforms.

Peter Verhezen is a Visiting Professor in Strategy and Business in Emerging Markets at the University of Antwerp/AMS, Belgium, and Adjunct Professor for Strategy, Ethics and Governance and Business in Asia at the Melbourne Business School, Australia. As the Principal of Verhezen & Associates Ltd and Senior Consultant for IFC-World Bank he advises boards on risk management, strategy and governance in the Asia-Pacific region. He studied International Relations and Applied Economics (MA), Management-Finance (MBA) and Philosophy (MA & PhD) and regularly publishes in the field of governance, business ethics and business in Asia.

Shraddha Verma is a Senior Lecturer at the Open University, having held previous academic positions at Birkbeck College and the University of York, UK. Shraddha has research interests in accounting and business history and in risk-related research. Her particular areas of interest are the professionalisation of accounting in India, the changing practices of oil companies in post-independence India and risk assessment, management and disclosure in both the public and private sector.

Gregory B. Vit is Associate Professor (Clinical) of Strategy & Organization at McGill University, Canada, where he teaches Strategy, Managing Innovation & Entrepreneurship. His industry experience spans three decades and includes working as Vice President with the Bank of America's Global Corporate and Investment Banking Group, where he specialised in international capital raising and corporate finance. He also worked as a financier in sales and structuring at TD Securities Inc.'s Capital Markets and Derivative Products Group Desk. As the Director of the McGill University Dobson Centre for Entrepreneurship, he continues to research and write about entrepreneurial fraudsters within large organisations.

Margaret Woods is Emeritus Professor of Accounting and Risk at Aston Business School, Aston University, UK. Founder of the European Risk Research Network, her extensive publications on risk particularly have attracted international media interest. Her book of case studies, *Risk Management in Organizations*, was published in 2011.

Minhao Zhang is a PhD candidate in the York Management School at the University of York, UK. He holds a master's degree in Management with Business Finance also from University of York. His doctoral research focuses on managerial risk perception, supply chain risk management, quality management and the social media analytics. He has published in *Supply Chain Management: An International Journal* and *Industrial Management & Data System*.

1
Introduction

Philip Linsley and Margaret Woods

Risk is a difficult concept. Individually, we have an intuitive sense of what is meant by 'risk'. We understand the world contains risks for this is evident in our daily lives where we continually encounter a variety of risks at work, in the home or outdoors. Some of these risks we may accept, and some we may try to manage or avoid; some give us cause for concern and others we barely think about. However, if we are asked to define what we mean by 'risk' then things become more challenging. We might resort to defining risk by reference to approximate synonyms such as 'harm' or 'hazard', and often any definition of risk will get bound up with discussions of 'uncertainty'. Hence, whilst we instinctively feel we know what risk is, it is awkward to articulate precisely what we mean by it. Similarly, if we are asked about the relative risk of different activities (say, using a mobile phone in comparison to fracking) we may have an opinion as to which we judge to be more risky but cannot always explain what has led us to make that assessment.

The complexities of risk have made it an appropriate subject for study. Over the last 30 years or so risk has been a major research theme across a wide range of academic disciplines. It challenges researchers to develop theories that can explain, for example, what factors influence our risk perceptions. Thus, anthropologists, sociologists, economists, psychologists, engineers and philosophers have all engaged in the task of furthering our understanding of risk and of relating it to concepts such as trust and blame. But risk has become a subject of major study not solely because its complexities are intellectually interesting to unravel; a further motivator for the study of risk is its importance to society. It is common to see tables listing major world risks published in the media and by consultancy firms. Current examples of these major risks relate to civil conflicts, Zika virus disease, terrorism, migration of refugees, climate change and the splintering of the European Union. It is common to want to categorise these significant risks. Hence, we may decide to label risks as political, health, societal, environmental, financial or whatever. The process of categorisation may provide a degree of reassurance that we understand the risk; however, such categorisations can be simplistic and misleading. These major risk issues often result in multiple risks which, in turn, lead to other risks. For example, climate change has been connected to risks of drought, famine and conflict. Further, such categorisations may not help us in understanding the causes of the risks nor how to address these risks to minimise their impacts. However, the severity of the impacts of these risks (as well as the accompanying fears they can provoke) ensures they warrant our attention and that they should be researched.

In respect of the accounting profession, risk and risk management discussions have been to the fore over the last decade. The Chartered Institute of Management Accountants (CIMA) and the Institute of Chartered Accountants in England and Wales (ICAEW), for example, have published a range of discussion papers and Thought Leadership reports in the risk area (see, for example, ICAEW, 2015). In the USA, the Committee of Sponsoring Organizations of the Treadway Commission (COSO)[1] has developed important and influential Internal Control and Enterprise Risk Management (ERM) frameworks. A growing awareness of, and focusing of attention upon, risk has resulted in significant numbers of companies and organisations implementing risk management systems and it is common for accountants to have some responsibility in respect of these systems. A consequence of these risk-focused debates in the accounting field is that 'risk governance' has been added to corporate governance terminology (see, for example, OECD, 2014; ICGN, 2015). Risk governance emphasises the now commonly held view that good governance implies that boards of directors will be proactive in identifying and acting upon risks, and will embed robust risk management systems.

Given that risk has emerged latterly to become a preoccupation in the accounting profession, in addition to being a major research topic in many academic disciplines, it is an apposite time to prepare an edited volume focused on accounting and risk. Accounting, in its broadest sense, encompasses roles in external and internal auditing, and financial and management accounting. The activities that these roles encompass are broad and, given its ubiquity, risk is inevitably pertinent to all these roles in myriad ways. In the conclusion to this edited volume we review potential areas for research.

To provide a structure for the volume, the chapters have been organised under four themes. Inevitably, different themes could have been selected, but those chosen provide the opportunity to explore and analyse topics that have a current relevance in risk debates. Part 1 provides some contextualisation by exploring some broader aspects of risk and risk management. Part 2 focuses upon risk in the context of financial reporting, and Part 3 in the context of management accounting. Part 4 then examines topics that have specific relevance to the monitoring of risk. The final chapters in each of Parts 2, 3 and 4 are case studies, as these are valuable in bringing out the complexities of risk and risk management.

We very much hope that this volume stimulates further interest in risk within an accounting context and encourages further research. We have already noted that risk is of concern to all of us and, therefore, the potential for undertaking research in this area that can have impact beyond the academy is great.

Note

1 The five organisations that sponsor COSO are all accounting and finance-related. They are: the American Accounting Association, American Institute of CPAs, Financial Executives International, Association of Accountants and Financial Professionals in Business, and Institute of Internal Auditors.

References

ICAEW (2015). Risk management: mindfulness and clumsy solutions. Prepared by P. Linsley and B. Kewell. ICAEW: London.

ICGN (2015). Corporate risk oversight. ICGN: London.

OECD (2014). Risk management and corporate governance. OECD Publishing.

Part I
Risk in context

2
A historical perspective on risk management

Mark Billings

The management of risk is inherent in all business enterprise, but it is only in, say, the last fifty years that risk management (RM) has emerged as a recognized management discipline, and only in the last twenty years or so that businesses other than financial institutions have begun to establish formal RM functions. The rise of 'formal' RM in business has manifested itself in numerous and familiar ways, many of which are explored in other contributions to this book: the routine risk assessments which are now part of strategic and operational reviews in many organizations; considerable increases in the formal reporting of risk and RM activities, both internally and externally; the adoption of enterprise-wide risk management (ERM), however this is defined; the appointment of chief risk officers (CROs) and formation of specific committees to manage risk; the development of formal RM standards or regulations in many countries and industries; the wider range and increased use of financial instruments and markets available to manage risk; and changed stakeholder expectations and a more intrusive role for government in organizational RM as attitudes to risk have evolved in our 'risk society' (Beck, 1992).

Readers will be well aware that the concepts of risk and RM in the business context have many potential meanings and the contributions to this book reflect this diversity from a range of perspectives. Businesses, governments, international organizations and not-for-profits must all manage their risks, and there are many providers of RM products and services to assist them, from insurers, to banks, to consultancy firms with their own packaged solutions. Professional bodies view RM as a specialism which gives their members a competitive advantage.

Much RM literature emphasizes the modernity of RM. For example, the insurance economist Georges Dionne claims that '[m]odern risk management started after 1955' (Dionne, 2013, p. 149). He identifies only six RM developments before that date, all of which relate to the development of theoretical concepts or of futures contracts on agricultural products, or the launch of academic journals (Dionne, 2013, p. 151, Table 1). James Lam has highlighted his appointment as the first-ever CRO in 1993 (Lam, 2014). But we must be sceptical of claims for the superiority of 'modern' RM. Arguably it failed its biggest test in 'our' financial crisis (Stulz, 2008), and some authors acknowledge that ERM has failed to realize its full potential (for example, Servaes *et al.* 2009).

Another assumption or assertion to be challenged is that our current era of globalization and the risks that arise from this and require management are unprecedented. Arguably, comparable integration of the global economy and financial markets, with high levels of mobility of goods, capital and labour, had been achieved at the outset of World War One, only to be suspended during the war years and then disintegrate under the pressures of the Great Depression (Rajan and Zingales, 2003). Unlikely as it may now seem, it would be unwise to assume that such a breakdown could not happen again.

Individuals and organizations have been coping with risk for hundreds, or even thousands, of years prior to the emergence of RM as a distinct management discipline. Businessmen (and historically they were almost invariably men, so it is not anachronistic to use this term) had to find ways to identify, assess and manage risks, even if they did not describe or consider such methods as RM. They were helped by the study of risk and the diffusion of resulting innovations in areas such as actuarial science and finance theory (Bernstein, 1996). Historians of business have not ignored RM, but it features in their work more often implicitly than explicitly. Witzel (2009), for example, explicitly recognizes RM in his management history, and some historians go further, viewing the history of risk as inextricably linked with the history of capitalism (for example, Levy, 2012).

None of this will surprise those advocates of ERM who view it as more than a mechanical process and acknowledge the complexity and diversity of real-world decisions under risk and highlight the relationship between RM and commercial strategy (and often governance). Indeed, much historical literature demonstrates how business risks defy simple classification and treatment, and the difficulty of disentangling risks and RM from strategic decisions, a view shared by some management scholars (see, for example, Grant and Visconti, 2006; and Hamilton and Micklethwait, 2006).

A familiar central problem in RM is that of asymmetric information. Historians have investigated the numerous ways businesses have found to acquire or exchange valuable information, skills and knowledge. Organizational form, discussed in more detail below, has played a central role. In the medieval period, for example, transactions and business relationships were structured to manage problems of risk and asymmetric information through diversification and self-contained partnerships (Baskin and Miranti, 1997, pp. 51–54).

Another method of overcoming information asymmetries is to build reputation and trust through repeated transactions, developing social capital through formal and informal networks. Economists sometimes view bodies such as guilds, chambers of commerce, trade protection societies and related organizations as evidence of 'rent-seeking' by their members. But this is only a partial explanation of their behaviour, as such bodies have for centuries provided formal networks offering services related to RM such as the dissemination of knowledge and expertise, the arbitration of commercial disputes, consultancy services, and lobbying of and partnerships with government (Bennett, 2011).

Business historians have explored numerous other methods of reducing information asymmetries. In the nineteenth century US traders exchanged information through personal networks before more formalized methods and institutions developed, eventually leading to the creation of credit reporting agencies such as Dun and Bradstreet (Olegario, 2006). Other methods used include economic forecasting (Friedman, 2013), market research (Schwarzkopf, 2016) and due diligence in corporate transactions (Billings *et al.* 2016).

Businesses have also sought to mitigate risk and uncertainty through their recruitment practices, for example the creation of management cadres and alumni networks in corporations such as General Electric and the consultants McKinsey. This can extend to the 'revolving door' between business and government, a practice often associated with the US, but also found in other countries (Billings, 2007; Denton, 2016). Other mechanisms facilitating interactions between business and government exist, for example the high-level Sunningdale conferences in the UK, where senior businessmen and government officials met annually to discuss topics of mutual interest (Rollings, 2014).

The literature on financial innovation and financial market development charts the evolution of modern financial systems, and generally emphasizes innovations in Italy in the thirteenth and fourteenth centuries and the role of Amsterdam and London in the seventeenth and eighteenth centuries (Baskin and Miranti, 1997; Murphy, 2009; Neal, 1990, 2016). The history of insurance is especially well-documented (for excellent recent examples see: Pearson, 2010; Borscheid and Haueter, 2012; and James, 2013). Derivatives, another important RM tool, are often treated as a recent innovation but can be dated back to at least seventeenth century Holland, where futures markets in tulips contributed to 'tulipmania' in the Dutch 'Golden Age'.

Economists' assessments of financial innovation are usually positive (for an example from a Nobel prize-winner, see Miller, 1992), although some also note the role of government in 'taking and mitigating risks' (Gordon, 2016, pp. 288–318). Historians tend to caution. They acknowledge that the development of financial markets and more sophisticated RM tools which have created opportunities for RM are associated with raised incomes and economic growth and have benefits for entrepreneurship. But these developments have also created tensions and new sources of risk, uncertainty and insecurity, and sometimes led to greater risk-taking and the disruptions associated with financial crisis (Neal, 2016; Sylla, 2003). Levy (2012), for example, argues that in the US the spread of commerce, the end of slavery, the Industrial Revolution, westward expansion and the rise of the corporation were associated with lack of trust in financial institutions and markets, which led to a retreat from markets for RM and increased reliance on mutual arrangements which enhanced trust. Nor are apparently useful innovations always successful—notwithstanding the vulnerability of the agricultural economy to climate and disease, Hamilton (2016) documents the chequered record of 'all-risks' crop insurance in US agriculture.

Although some RM revolves around the use of financial instruments and markets, much involves trying to shape or subvert market mechanisms through lobbying or political capture, or various types of collaboration such as the formation of cartels, mergers, strategic alliances, inter-firm networks, joint ventures or other constraints on competition. This leads us to consideration of organizational forms, which have proved highly adaptable over time to the needs of business. Most legal codes now offer a lengthy menu of different organizational forms that offer choices in reconciling the interests of different stakeholder groups to provide solutions to ownership, governance, financing and risk problems. The most prominent among the alternatives is the joint-stock company (JSC), considered the 'natural' form for many businesses, and an effective protection against risk, particularly of expropriation.

Although there are earlier antecedents, the VOC (Dutch East India Company) emerged as the first modern-style corporation in early seventeenth century Holland as a solution to the problem of liquidity in merchant ventures (Gelderblom *et al.* 2013). Limited liability came later, and the process of evolution of JSCs has been widely studied (for example: Alborn, 1998; Micklethwait and Wooldridge, 2003; Taylor, 2006; Wright, 2014). JSCs have many potential attractions from the perspective of RM, notably the ability to concentrate capital, the absolute or relative anonymity of ownership, and the 'corporate veil' to limit legal liabilities. But 'our' financial crisis has led some to question the dominance of the JSC as a business form. In part this reflects concerns over the balance between the interests of shareholders and other stakeholders (Haldane, 2015), but also the implications of limited liability in banking for risk-taking (Turner, 2014), including the transition of investment banks from (unlimited liability) partnerships to public companies.

Legal risk, of course, is ever-present for business, in the form of regulation or legislation, and judicial intervention. Legal and financial risks may interact, for example through innovations which emasculate prior contractual arrangements (Tufano, 1997). But businesses may have some freedom in this area, in their ability to choose the legal jurisdictions in which they incorporate or operate, their choice of organizational form, and their influence over corporate law.

Several organizational forms whose characteristics are strongly linked to RM have drawn particular attention from business historians. Baskin and Miranti (1997) charted the rise of conglomerates and their demise—originally a vehicle for diversification, their 'lack of focus' rendered them unfashionable when 'shareholder value' came to dominate in the 1980s and 1990s. Another much-studied form is the 'free-standing' company, legally-independent, typically operating outside its home country in a single economic sector, with most directors based in the home country but monitoring management overseas. The promoters, directors, bankers and professional advisers of such companies were usually heavily networked, an effective form of RM, and yet for reasons which remain to be researched fully, free-standing companies have largely disappeared and are now viewed as a historical phenomenon (Wilkins and Schröter, 1998). A final organizational form worthy of mention is the 'business group'. These are a means of risk-sharing particularly associated with emerging economies where markets or bureaucracies are ineffective. Such groups are composed of legally-independent companies and diversified businesses tied together by interlocking directorships, shareholdings and other extensive interconnections (Barbero and Puig, 2016; Colpan *et al.* 2010). They may be, but are not necessarily, family-based. The advantages and disadvantages of family business are a particularly rich area for business historians (Fernández Pérez and Colli, 2013).

The recent and rapid (re-)globalization of business has stimulated much reflection on the management of risks in international business. Businesses which choose to operate outside their home countries frequently face a wider range of risks than those with a narrower geographical focus, although international operations are often a means of mitigating or diversifying away from risks arising in the home country. Distance and politics generate risks that have to be managed. Sometimes these arise in principal-agent relationships, with information asymmetries exacerbated by distance and problems in the exercise of control in cross-border activities. There are also risks arising from technical and natural hazards, which we now label supply chain risks, and the 'liability of foreignness', such as the lack of familiarity with cultural norms when doing business in new markets. Political risk can arise when countries or regions become hostile to business in general, or to foreign-owned or -managed business in particular, with expropriation the most extreme outcome. In such circumstances political and financial risks become inextricably linked.

Casson and da Silva Lopes (2013) identify historical evidence of strategies to manage multiple and unexpected risks of foreign direct investment in high-risk environments. They focus on lobbying to secure home government support for businesses with international operations, and the traditional RM choices of avoidance or withdrawal, prevention and mitigation.

In maritime commerce, with long-distance trade and slow and limited communications, RM strategies necessarily ranged widely. Insurance arrangements, which date back at least several hundred years and probably longer (Leonard, 2016), were combined with the benefits of incorporation of business ventures as JSCs, which allowed merchants to pool risks and information. Cargoes were divided across different vessels and products, ports and counterparties diversified. In the eighteenth and nineteenth centuries, for example, British and American merchants built transatlantic networks that endured over time, even during wartime (Buchnea, 2014; Haggerty, 2009, 2012). In the twentieth century, British shipping lines reoriented their business to Europe and adopted containerization to manage political risk associated with the decline of Empire (White and Evans, 2015).

Business historians view World War One as a watershed for international business in many ways. Inward and outward international business operations became significantly more difficult with, for example, disruption to financial systems and shipping and distribution networks, loss of markets and difficulties in the procurement of all factors of production.

In interwar Germany, domestic companies developed strategies to manage the risks of their own international business, and non-German companies were forced to adapt to the risks of operating in the country's 'uniquely difficult' conditions (the focus of Kobrak *et al.* 2004). After World War One German businesses replaced foreign direct investment in Scandinavia with cartels and long-term contracts to offset the loss of overseas holdings, whether through financial failure or confiscation (Schröter, 1988). In addition to the intensifying pressures of nationalism there were 'stringent restrictions on foreign exchange, capital exports, goods imports, remittances of profits and royalty payments' from the early 1930s (Wilkins, 2004, p. 26). Multinational enterprises operating in Germany, such as Unilever, were obliged to reinvest in the country, or use unusual means to extract their funds, for example investing profits in physical assets such as ships (Forbes, 2007; Wilkins, 2004, p. 29; Wubs, 2008). German companies were forced to explore RM solutions to their own problems (see, for example, Jones and Lubinski, 2012, on the skincare and pharmaceutical company Beiersdorf; and Kobrak and Wüstenhagen, 2006). Corporate control was often 'cloaked' to limit unwelcome attention, for economic as well as political reasons, at home and abroad. From 1931 Beiersdorf adopted a 'ring' structure with foreign affiliates managed from Amsterdam to 'warehouse' ownership and mitigate the effects of German policy for its largely Jewish ownership and management. Its foreign affiliates also engaged in direct mutual lending to bypass German exchange controls. This strategy was unsuccessful in the long run, and the company suffered asset seizures, exclusion from important markets and trust problems with foreign partners.

If Germany is a classic country case, the motor manufacturer Ford is a classic case of a multinational business obliged to respond to changes in its environment, taking steps which were both 'good business' and effective RM. During the 1920s it expected its European subsidiaries to fund investment in plant and equipment out of their own profits, and increase local content to minimize freight costs and improve acceptability to national governments and consumers (Tolliday, 2003). Its German subsidiary moved in 1926 from an assembly plant with all components and materials imported, to a manufacturing plant in 1931 with 60 per cent of components and materials imported, 30 per cent purchased locally and 10 per cent manufactured by Ford, to '100 per cent German' vehicles in 1934 (Wilkins, 2004, pp. 30–31). During World War Two collaboration with the Vichy government became a survival strategy for the French subsidiary (Imlay and Horn, 2014). In the 1950s Ford prioritized the remittance of profits to the parent company, to minimize the local accumulation of funds to protect against exchange rate risk and blocked remittances (Tolliday, 2003). Ford's international experiences are representative of those of other companies, such as the similar financing practices among British manufacturing businesses in Latin America documented by Miller (2013).

War brings risks beyond those already discussed. Governments recognize the importance of maintaining maritime insurance in wartime and have frequently intervened to bolster such arrangements (Lobo-Guerrero, 2012). Modern wars have brought greater government intervention in areas of business such as working and employment practices, the supply of raw materials, production targets, output prices and profits. In many countries, including some non-combatants, World War One brought an unwelcome new risk to manage: the increased burden of taxation on corporate profits (Arnold, 2014; Billings and Oats, 2014). Businesses sought to mitigate its effects through lobbying and tax planning, and—especially those with international operations exposed to double taxation—in the longer run adapted their structures to reduce the impact of higher taxation (Mollan and Tennent, 2015).

The role of corporate reputation is recognized in business history (Kobrak, 2013; McKenna and Olegario, 2012), and legitimacy and reputation assume even greater importance in wartime. Smith (2016) argues that the ability of the Hongkong and Shanghai Banking Corporation (HSBC) to survive World War One was due, in part, to its ability to manage political risk in its 'home' markets, Hong Kong and the UK, by maintaining legitimacy in the eyes of stakeholders, particularly government. This required a wartime pivot from the bank's peacetime 'world citizen' identity to one more closely aligned with that of its home nation, which involved the termination of relationships with clients and employees associated with enemy nations. More generally, external risk reporting and communication can play an important role in RM through heading off disputes and managing expectations to avoid the breakdown of communications with stakeholders (Abdelrehim *et al.* 2015), although this can entail risks in itself when such reporting becomes 'impression management' (Brennan and Merkl-Davies, 2012; O'Connell *et al.* 2016).

It is for other contributors to this volume to debate how businesses manage risk now, and the role of accounting in that. The links between risk, accounting and governance, including internal control and the role of financial reporting standards in promoting transparency and reliability, are often stressed (van de Ven, 2010, p. 7). But the historical contributions of accounting and accountants to RM are wider than is sometimes suggested. The development, application and diffusion of more sophisticated accounting techniques are part of this story. This embraces, for example, the use of discounted cash flows in internal investment appraisal from the beginning of the nineteenth century (Brackenborough *et al.* 2001), investment analysis from later in that century (Rutterford, 2004), more systematic use of statistics in forecasting, budgeting and planning in early twentieth century business (Chandar and Miranti, 2009), and developments in management accounting (Edwards and Boyns, 2013). There is also abundant evidence of the central contribution of accountants in the development of the financial management and corporate treasury functions in businesses, embracing cash management, the management of financial risks, and the operation of internal capital markets, a substitute for or complement to undeveloped external capital markets (see, for example, Billings, 2007; Hiebl *et al.* 2015; Matthews *et al.* 1997, 1998; Pearcy, 2001).

Conclusion

This chapter implicitly argues that to some extent we should consider that 'all management is risk management', and suggests that history offers many insights into RM. The professionalization of management, whether generally or of RM, cannot provide solutions to all risk problems, particularly where information asymmetries and weak institutional protections persist in imperfect markets. The importance of diversification is apparent, as are the benefits of organizational flexibility, adaptability and resilience, and the willingness to adopt multiple approaches to RM, including reliance on natural hedges and local financing. The experiences of international business in the twentieth century point to potential challenges and responses in the event of another retreat from globalization. Attempts to classify risks too neatly are probably unhelpful in their management. We should also acknowledge the merit of some 'folk wisdom' on RM, such as the comment (almost certainly mis-) attributed to John Maynard

Keynes that 'it is better to be roughly right rather than precisely wrong'. The much-mocked 2002 comments of the US Secretary for Defense, Donald Rumsfeld, on 'unknown unknowns, the ones we don't know we don't know' also seem more comprehensible on historical reflection. The historical focus of RM differs from much 'modern' RM, which often appears to place greater emphasis on accountability and securing legitimacy, with adverse and sometimes unintended consequences for innovation and entrepreneurship and greater risk aversion on the part of shareholders (see, for example, the critiques of Hunt, 2003, and Power, 2007). Without the input of history, institutional memory and imagination, ERM or rules-driven RM are likely to offer only false comfort, a message 'our' financial crisis reinforced painfully.

References

Abdelrehim, N., J. Maltby and S.J. Toms (2015), 'Narrative Reporting and Crises: British Petroleum and Shell, 1950–1958', *Accounting History*, 20(2), May, pp. 138–157.

Alborn, T.L. (1998), *Conceiving Companies: Joint-Stock Politics in Victorian England*, London: Routledge.

Arnold, A.J. (2014), '"A Paradise for Profiteers"? The Importance of the Treatment of Profits during the First World War', *Accounting History Review*, 24(2–3), July–November, pp. 61–81.

Barbero, M.I. and N. Puig (2016), 'Business Groups Around the World: An Introduction', *Business History*, 58(1), pp. 6–29.

Baskin, J.B. and P.J. Miranti (1997), *A History of Corporate Finance*, Cambridge: Cambridge University Press.

Beck, U. (1992), *Risk Society: Towards a New Modernity*, London: Sage.

Bennett, R.J. (2011), *Local Business Voice: The History of Chambers of Commerce in Britain, Ireland and Revolutionary America, 1760–2011*, Oxford: Oxford University Press.

Bernstein, P.L. (1996), *Against the Gods: The Remarkable Story of Risk*, New York: John Wiley and Sons.

Billings, M. (2007), 'Corporate Treasury in International Business History', *Business and Economic History On-Line*, 5, http://www.thebhc.org/sites/default/files/billings.pdf

Billings, M. and L. Oats (2014), 'Innovation in Tax Design: Excess Profits Duty in the United Kingdom during World War One', *Accounting History Review*, 24(2–3), July–November, pp. 83–101.

Billings, M., A. Tilba and J.F. Wilson (2016), '"To Invite Disappointment or Worse": Governance, Audit and Due Diligence in the Ferranti-ISC Merger', *Business History*, 58(4), pp. 453–478.

Borscheid, P. and N.V. Haueter (eds.) (2012), *World Insurance: The Evolution of a Global Risk Network*, Oxford: Oxford University Press.

Brackenborough, S., T. McLean and D. Oldroyd (2001), 'The Emergence of Discounted Cash Flow Analysis in the Tyneside Coal Industry, c. 1700–1820', *British Accounting Review*, 33(2), June, pp. 137–155.

Brennan, N. and D. Merkl-Davies (2012), 'Accounting Narratives and Impression Management', in L. Jack, J. Davison and R. Craig (eds.), *The Routledge Companion to Accounting Communication*, London: Routledge, pp. 109–132.

Buchnea, E. (2014), 'Transatlantic Transformations: Visualizing Change Over Time in the Liverpool-New York Network, 1763–1833', *Enterprise and Society*, 15(4), December, pp. 687–721.

Casson, M. and T. da Silva Lopes (2013), 'Foreign Direct Investment in High-Risk Environments: An Historical Perspective', *Business History*, 55(3), pp. 375–404.

Chandar, N. and P.J. Miranti (2009), 'Integrating Accounting and Statistics: Forecasting, Budgeting and Production Planning at the American Telephone and Telegraph Company During the 1920s', *Accounting and Business Research*, 39(4), pp. 373–395.

Colpan, A.M., T. Hikino and J.R. Lincoln (2010), *The Oxford Handbook of Business Groups*, Oxford: Oxford University Press.

Denton, S. (2016), *The Profiteers: Bechtel and the Men Who Built the World*, New York: Simon and Schuster.

Dionne, G. (2013), 'Risk Management: History, Definition and Critique', *Risk Management and Insurance Review*, 16(2), pp. 147–166.

Edwards, J.R. and T. Boyns (2013), *A History of Management Accounting: The British Experience*, London: Routledge.

Fernández Pérez, P. and A. Colli (eds.) (2013), *The Endurance of Family Businesses: A Global Overview*, Cambridge: Cambridge University Press.
Forbes, N. (2007), 'Multinational Enterprise, "Corporate Responsibility" and the Nazi Dictatorship: The Case of Unilever and Germany in the 1930s', *Contemporary European History*, 16(2), May, pp. 149–167.
Friedman, W.A. (2013), *Fortune Tellers: The Story of America's First Economic Forecasters*, Princeton: Princeton University Press.
Gelderblom, O., A. de Jong and J. Jonker (2013), 'The Formative Years of the Modern Company: The Dutch East India Company VOC, 1602–1623', *Journal of Economic History*, 73(4), December, pp. 1050–1076.
Gordon, R.J. (2016), *The Rise and Fall of American Growth: The US Standard of Living Since the Civil War*, Princeton: Princeton University Press.
Grant, R.M. and M. Visconti (2006), 'The Strategic Background to Corporate Accounting Scandals', *Long Range Planning*, 39(4), pp. 361–383.
Haggerty, S. (2009), 'Risk and Risk Management in the Liverpool Slave Trade', *Business History*, 51(6), November, pp. 817–834.
Haggerty, S. (2012), *'Merely for Money'? Business Culture in the British Atlantic, 1750–1815*, Liverpool: Liverpool University Press.
Haldane, A.G. (2015), *Who Owns a Company?*, speech, 22 May 2015, London: Bank of England.
Hamilton, S. (2016), 'Precisely How Risky is Agriculture? The Fall and Rise of Crop Insurance', working paper presented at the Annual Meeting of the Business History Conference.
Hamilton, S. and A. Micklethwait (2006), *Greed and Corporate Failure: The Lessons from Recent Disasters*, Basingstoke: Palgrave Macmillan.
Hiebl, M., M. Quinn and C. Martinez Franco (2015), 'An Analysis of the Role of a Chief Accountant at Guinness c. 1920–1940', *Accounting History Review*, 25(2), July, pp. 145–165.
Hunt, B. (2003), *The Timid Corporation: Why Business is Terrified of Taking Risk*, Chichester: Wiley.
Imlay, T. and M. Horn (2014), *The Politics of Industrial Collaboration During World War II: Ford France, Vichy and Nazi Germany*, Cambridge: Cambridge University Press.
James, H. (2013), 'Introduction: The Insuring Instinct', in H. James, P. Borscheid, D. Gugerli and T. Straumann (eds.), *The Value of Risk: Swiss Re and the History of Reinsurance*, Oxford: Oxford University Press, pp. 1–20.
Jones, G. and C. Lubinski (2012), 'Managing Political Risk in Global Business: Beiersdorf, 1914–1990', *Enterprise and Society*, 13(1), March, pp. 85–119.
Kobrak, C. (2013), 'The Concept of Reputation in Business History', *Business History Review*, 87(4), Winter, pp. 763–786.
Kobrak, C. and J. Wüstenhagen (2006), 'International Investment and Nazi Politics: The Cloaking of German Assets Abroad', *Business History*, 48(3), July, pp. 399–427.
Kobrak, C., P.H. Hansen and C. Kopper (2004), 'Business, Political Risk and History', in C. Kobrak and P.H. Hansen (eds.), *European Business, Dictatorship and Political Risk, 1920–1945*, New York: Berghahn, pp. 3–21.
Lam, J. (2014), *Enterprise Risk Management: From Incentives to Controls*, 2nd ed, Hoboken, NJ: John Wiley.
Leonard, A. (ed.) (2016), *Marine Insurance: Origins and Institutions, 1300–1850*, Basingstoke: Palgrave Macmillan.
Levy, J.S. (2012), *Freaks of Fortune: The Emerging World of Capitalism and Risk in America*, Cambridge, MA: Harvard University Press.
Lobo-Guerrero, L. (2012), *Insuring War: Sovereignty, Security and Risk*, London: Routledge.
McKenna, C. and R. Olegario (2012), 'Corporate Reputation and Regulation in Historical Perspective', in M.L. Barratt and T.G. Pollock (eds.), *The Oxford Handbook of Corporate Reputation*, Oxford: Oxford University Press, pp. 260–277.
Matthews, D., M. Anderson and J.R. Edwards (1997), 'The Rise of the Professional Accountant in British Management', *Economic History Review*, 39(3), pp. 407–429.
Matthews, D., M. Anderson and J.R. Edwards (1998), *The Priesthood of Industry: The Rise of the Professional Accountant in British Management*, Oxford: Oxford University Press.
Micklethwait, J. and A. Wooldridge (2003), *The Company: A Short History of a Revolutionary Idea*, London: Weidenfeld and Nicolson.
Miller, M.H. (1992), 'Financial Innovation: Achievements and Prospects', *Journal of Applied Corporate Finance*, 4(4), Winter, pp. 4–11.

Miller, R. (2013), 'Financing British Manufacturing Multinationals in Latin America', *Business History*, 55(5), pp. 818–839.

Mollan, S. and K.D. Tennent (2015), 'International Taxation and Corporate Strategy: Evidence from British Overseas Business, circa 1900–1965', *Business History*, 57(7), pp. 1054–1081.

Murphy, A.L. (2009), *The Origins of English Financial Markets: Investment and Speculation before the South Sea Bubble*, Cambridge: Cambridge University Press.

Neal, L. (1990), *The Rise of Financial Capitalism: International Capitalism in the Age of Reason*, Cambridge: Cambridge University Press.

Neal, L. (2016), *A Concise History of International Finance: From Babylon to Bernanke*, Cambridge: Cambridge University Press.

O'Connell, B., P. de Lange, G. Stoner and A. Sangster (2016), 'Strategic Manoeuvres and Impression Management: Communication Approaches in the Case of a Crisis Event', *Business History*, 58(6), pp. 903–924.

Olegario, R. (2006), *A Culture of Credit: Embedding Trust and Transparency in American Business*, Cambridge, MA: Harvard University Press.

Pearcy, J. (2001), *Recording an Empire: An Accounting History of Imperial Chemical Industries Ltd 1926–1976*, Edinburgh: Institute of Chartered Accountants of Scotland.

Pearson, R. (2010), 'Introduction: Towards an International History of Insurance', in R. Pearson (ed.), *The Development of International Insurance*, London: Pickering and Chatto, pp. 1–23.

Power, M. (2007), *Organized Uncertainty: Designing a World of Risk Management*, Oxford: Oxford University Press.

Rajan, R.G. and L. Zingales (2003), 'The Great Reversals: The Politics of Financial Development in the Twentieth Century', *Journal of Financial Economics*, 69(1), July, pp. 5–50.

Rollings, N. (2014), 'The Twilight World of British Business Politics: The Spring Sunningdale Conferences Since the 1960s', *Business History*, 56(6), pp. 915–935.

Rutterford, J. (2004), 'From Dividend Yield to Discounted Cash Flow: A History of UK and US Equity Valuation Techniques', *Accounting, Business and Financial History*, 14(2), July, pp. 115–149.

Schröter, H. (1988), 'Risk and Control in Multinational Enterprise: German Business in Scandinavia, 1918–1939', *Business History Review*, 62(3), pp. 420–443.

Schwarzkopf, S. (2016), 'In Search of the Consumer: The History of Market Research from 1890 to 1960', in D.G.B. Jones and M. Tadajewski (eds.), *The Routledge Companion to Marketing History*, Oxford: Routledge, pp. 61–83.

Servaes, H., A. Tamayo and P. Tufano (2009), 'The Theory and Practice of Corporate Risk Management', *Journal of Applied Corporate Finance*, 21(4), Fall, pp. 60–78.

Smith, A. (2016), 'A LBV Perspective on Political Risk Management in a Multinational Bank During the First World War', *Multinational Business Review*, 24(1), pp. 25–46.

Stulz, R. (2008), 'Risk Management Failures: What Are They and When Do They Happen?', *Journal of Applied Corporate Finance*, 20(4), Fall, pp. 39–48.

Sylla, R. (2003), 'Financial Systems, Risk Management and Entrepreneurship: Historical Perspectives', *Japan and the World Economy*, 15(4), December, pp. 447–458.

Taylor, J. (2006), *Creating Capitalism: Joint-Stock Enterprise in British Politics and Culture, 1800–1870*, Woodbridge: Boydell.

Tolliday, S. (2003), 'The Origins of Ford in Europe: From Multidomestic to Transnational Company, 1903–1976', in H. Bonin, Y. Lung and S. Tolliday (eds.), *Ford, 1903–2003: The European History*, vol. 1, Paris: P.L.A.G.E, pp. 153–241.

Tufano, P. (1997), 'Business Failure, Judicial Intervention and Financial Innovation: Restructuring U.S. Railroads in the Nineteenth Century', *Business History Review*, 71(1), Spring, pp. 1–40.

Turner, J.D. (2014), *Banking in Crisis: The Rise and Fall of British Banking Stability, 1800 to the Present*, Cambridge: Cambridge University Press.

van de Ven, A. (2010), 'Risk Management from an Accounting Perspective', in M. Van Daelen and C. Van der Elst (eds.), *Risk Management and Corporate Governance: Interconnections in Law, Accounting and Tax*, Cheltenham: Edward Elgar, pp. 7–55.

White, N.J. and C. Evans (2015), 'Holding Back the Tide: Shipping, Gentlemanly Capitalism and Intra-Asian Trade in the Twentieth Century', in U. Bosma and A. Webster (eds.), *Commodities, Ports and Asian Maritime Trade Since 1850*, Basingstoke: Palgrave Macmillan, pp. 218–240.

Wilkins, M. (2004), 'Multinationals and Dictatorship', in C. Kobrak and P.H. Hansen (eds.) (2004), *European Business, Dictatorship and Political Risk, 1920–1945*, New York: Berghahn, pp. 22–38.

Wilkins, M. and H.G. Schröter (eds.) (1998), *The Free-Standing Company in the World Economy, 1836–1996*, Oxford: Oxford University Press.
Witzel, M. (2009), *Management History: Texts and Cases*, London: Routledge.
Wright, R.E. (2014), *Corporation Nation*, Philadelphia: University of Pennsylvania Press.
Wubs, B. (2008), *International Business and National War Interests: Unilever between Reich and Empire, 1939–45*, London: Routledge.

3

Risk tools and risk technologies

Beth Kewell and Philip Linsley

Introduction

The ability to assess risk, instil trust, and foster reassurance represent timeless, quintessentially human properties, which have proven essential to species survival. Few social processes can take place without recourse to these interrelated considerations (Kydd, 2000). The theory and practice of accounting provides for some very sophisticated methods of risk assessment, many of which have been superlatively enhanced by the development of spreadsheet technologies and software simulations (Gibson, 1997; Togo, 2004; Green and Calderon, 2005). A process of sociotechnical change, which began with the invention of the electronic calculator, is presently leading the way towards a fully integrated culture of cyber-accountancy. This revolution means that the future practice of today's accounting students will seem very different from the current era, in which old and new accounting technologies—that is to say, ledgers, calculators and computer spreadsheets—enjoy a complementary relationship. Advanced Risk Management Software Solutions (ARMSS) are already revolutionizing the risk assessment and compliance environment at large-scale corporate accounting firms. The diffusion of these technologies to other niches of the accounting, auditing and actuarial industries can be regarded as inevitable. Impact studies are beginning to identify the likely long-term effects of this shifting orientation, including the manner in which it is reformulating numerical classifications of risk and allied working practices (Wagner, *et al.*, 2006; Scott and Perry, 2006; Bamberger, 2010; Racz, *et al.*, 2010). Risk is not the sole factor to be affected by the transition to a new era of 'cyborg' accountancy. This chapter considers how the quintessentially human property of reassurance is likely to be transfigured by moves that will put intelligent machines in command of the kinds of compliance and reporting work traditionally performed by accountants.

From risk-instincts to risk-cyborgs and risk-panopticans

Thousands of students enrol at universities and colleges each year, in the hope of securing a future career in accounting or finance. Accounting and finance remain steadfastly popular options among university applicants because they are thought to offer a relatively secure professional career path with good earning potential. The financial crisis of 2007–2009 tested the salience of such received wisdom, by placing many accounting and finance employees at risk of redundancy. In keeping with many other industries facing hard times, the financial services sector adopted a recovery strategy that complemented workforce downsizing with the introduction of compliance software programmes, designed specifically to help finance companies manage the transition toward a much tougher global regulatory environment (Scott and Perry, 2006; Racz, *et al.*, 2010; Bamberger, 2010; Baldvinsdottir, *et al.*, 2010; Scott and Zachariadis, 2014). Advanced Risk Management Software Solutions (ARMSS) emerged from this period with a strong reputation for reliability, having helped many of the world's financial centres to regain lost reputational capital, and rebuild consumer trust (Bamberger, 2010; Baldvinsdottir, *et al.*, 2010; Racz, *et al.*, 2010). ARMSS platforms are now a firm feature of the business compliance landscape, having latterly taken on much of the responsibility for brokering risk, trust and reassurance within markets—and among client groups and regulators—that once rested solely on human shoulders.

This evidence seems to suggest that society trusts machines more than humans to manage financial and enterprise risks in the post-crisis era. This reorientation of accountability also represents an important example of 'social-cybernetic transference', wherein machines and devices take centre stage, becoming the primary catalysts for activities that human beings feel they can no longer perform effectively. When set into motion, this process of surrendering responsibilities, skills, and aptitudes to machines tends to be one way and irreversible, such that a return to the old ways of doing things is rarely entertained thereafter, except by way of nostalgia (Verbeek 2002, developing Borgmann, 1999; see also Mitcham, 1994; Higgs, *et al.*, 2000; Ihde, 2004; Scharff and Dusek, 2014).

If this lesson applies as readily to ARMSS (as it does to other processes of technology adoption) then the future of financial risk management seems locked on-course for an inevitable outcome, in which many old methods of assessment based on simple technologies—for example, the *Risk Register* imprinted on paper—will be abandoned in favour of interactive and multi-dimensional alternatives. This, in turn, will complete a process that has extracted, synthesized and re-engineered *risk instincts* honed from natural biological sources into metallic precision instruments. ARMSS symbolize the ultimate separation or 'distancing' of our late-modern hyper-risk-cognisant selves from our natural selves, and the instinctual reading of 'natural signs' that guaranteed our earliest survival (Borgmann, 1999, pp. 1–7).

Being alert to the presence of risk is an ecological necessity, which is said to transcend boundaries, including those that exist between species. Plants, animals, and humans maintain complex defence mechanisms that ensure survival against the ever-present threat of predation. Camouflage represents one of nature's best answers to the problem of risk mitigation in the wild, permitting some chameleons to change colour, and some spiders to play dead. Evolution has correspondingly provided many species of reptiles, mammals and aquatic life with enviable powers of surveillance and threat-detection or *Umwelt* (Partman and Marler, 2002). Whilst often conceived as an act of individual watchfulness, the performance of biological *Umwelt* among certain plants species and animal (thus defined as an ability to detect, interpret, and avoid hazard) represents a collaborative act, necessitating mutual recognition, group interaction, reciprocity and a good measure of trust (Giddens, 1991; Partman and Marler, 2002; Adams, 2004). The instinctual world of plants and animals is full of examples of 'risk communication' that create 'instant alerts', using sound, scent and gesture to warn others and ward off expectant foes (Partman and Marler, 2002). Human processes of risk identification and risk communication similarly make prodigious use of our natural ability to tacitly identify, and then emote, appropriate responses to danger (see especially Adams, 2004).

Crucially, human risk-cognisance, risk-interpretation and risk-calculation combine this biologically foregrounded capacity for *Umwelt* with an equally strident aptitude for shaping constructs and making technology. A long-running process of convergence between the 'natural-born' (adapting Clark 2003) elements of human *Umwelt* and science, technology, design, and engineering has arguably reached a critical point of fruition in our own time, with the advent of software products and computer simulations, which aim to maximize individual and collective aptitudes for risk-vigilance. Expectations of an imminent revolution in Artificial Intelligence (AI) are hastening the sense in which *Umwelt* is fast becoming a 'cyborg property'—that is to say a special type of cerebral capacity, which can only be reproduced by fusing human and machine intellects together (Mitcham, 1994; Lenk, 1998; Verbeek, 2002; Clark, 2003; Ihde, 2004; Bamberger, 2010; Scharff and Dusek, 2014). Should they be perfected, AI solutions for risk forecasting could well achieve the panoptical aggrandizement of foresight that many institutions, organizations, and individuals yearn for; granting purchasers an unencumbered and resplendent view of their surroundings. Collective want for the invention 'Panopticans', or buildings and devices that 'make it possible to see constantly' represents a longstanding desire on the part of humanity to gain total power and mastery over the visual terrain (Foucault, abridged in Schraff and Dusek 2014, p. 656). Whether applied, as in its original Benthamite conception, to create prisons with no hiding places or in its more contemporary form, as horizon-spanning computerized mapping, surveillance, and monitoring systems, which yield perfect information, the panoptican epitomizes both the desire for control and the desire for reassurance. Thanks to the efforts of social scientists, control, and the concomitant relationship it shares with 'reward and punishment', signifies the most widely documented and comprehended of these two desired states (Foucault, abridged in Schraff and Dusek 2014, p. 656). To evince control within an organizational or social setting can also, under certain special circumstances, elicit genuine reassurance when the cultural climate is positive, encouraging, motivating and rewarding. Conversely, control leads to insecurity, instability, and discouragement where it is administered in an environment of cultural coercion, recrimination, aggression, and punishment.

'Risk-Panopticans', of the kind being marketed to business by the software industry, combine a desire for optical mastery with the desire for optimal *Umwelt*; the want for unhindered control of organizational contingencies; and the power to dictate the terms upon which risks are calculated. It is perhaps no surprise to learn that the accounting and finance professions occupy one of the most sought-after niche markets for software products that offer an optimal solution to the demands of modern financial and general risk management (Wagner, *et al.*, 2006; Scott and Perry, 2006; Baldvinsdottir, *et al.*, 2010; Racz, *et al.*, 2010; Bluemner, n.d.; Cau, n.d). In the main, the sales and marketing messages being sent to potential purchasers, including chartered accountants, data analysts, and financial managers are on the basis that the 'spreadsheet is dead' (Rasmussen, n.d.). The supporting narrative in which is this message is anchored emphasizes the redundancy of the spreadsheet as an obsolete tool that once revolutionized accounting practice and corporating reporting, in the face of a new breed of software products that promise enhanced interoperability, custom-built decision-support facilities, real-time supply-chain analysis and market forecasts that constantly update themselves (Gibson, 1997; Scott and Perry, 2006; Wagner, *et al.*, 2006; Racz, *et al.*, 2010; Baldvinsdottir, *et al.*, 2010; Bamberger, 2010; Bluemner, n.d.).

Though initially developed to aid compliance management in the financial sector, following the introduction of COSO (Committee of Sponsoring Organizations) recommendations and Sarbanes-Oxley (SOX) regulation in the United States (Forrester Research Inc., 2014; Baldvinsdottir, *et al.*, 2010; Bamberger, 2010; Rasmussen, n.d.). During more recent times, fresh markets for risk-panoptic software have been created in the fields of supply-chain management and enterprise risk mitigation, widening the scope of support provided by the software and software vendors to include key aspects of non-financial business-management (Baldvinsdottir, *et al.*, 2010). Whilst greatly improving the quality of the 'risk-viewfinder' that companies may hold up to reality, they require far greater information-systems maintainance and vendor-support than is the case for the humble spreadsheet or stand-alone risk management programmes of old. They also require, more human capital, pose greater depreciation risks, and in some cases, cause change-management misalignments, initiate technology dependency, foster organizational memory loss, and encourage the dissolution of tacit expertise and the 're-categorization' of knowledge in ways that increase rather than decrease risk opacity (Scott and Perry, 2006, pp. 4–9; Wagner, *et al.*, 2006; Baldvinsdottir, *et al.*, 2010; Bamberger, 2010).

This depiction of upheaval implies that risk-panoptic software has yet to deliver the full functionality, ease-of-use, perfect foresight and control leverage suggested by its most zealous marketeers (Bamberger, 2010). Set against developments in the 2000s, Scott's work and that of Bamberger, argues in favour of a 'Research Agenda' examining the organizational, systems and labour process implications that are beholden to next generation risk-software. In the remaining sections of the chapter, we argue for a complementary Research Agenda within which it is possible to evaluate the long-term cultural effects of abandoning responsibility for the types of risk, trust and reassurance that have previously been managed by flesh and blood accounting professionals to intelligent machines.

Risk, trust and reassurance as human properties

Risk, trust and reassurance are familiar human properties that we may experience without the need for simulation on a computer screen as our window on the world. We have nevertheless arrived at a point in human history when it can be thought best to channel these properties through internal portals and mobile devices, so that they do the protecting (Scharff and Dusek, 2014, pp. 582–587). This does not mean that physical forms of reassurance have disappeared from social life. Indeed, they remain essential to daily living. Whilst appearing mundane and commonplace aspects of domestic life—for example, the perimeter fence, the lockable door, the combination safe, and the spyglass—they afford levels of basic safeguarding that were revolutionary at the time of their invention. Each represented a vital new addition to an increasingly *automated Umwelt.* What makes computers special is their ability to combine the physical safeguarding of life and property represented in and by fences and locks, with a range of predictive tools that tells us if and when we should expect to see barbarians at the gate. Computerized safeguarding achieves results by dovetailing the material with the simulcra (Verbeek, 2002). For example, computers can at one and the same time lock doors and launch missiles in the physical universe; display images of the warhead in flight; and prepare estimates of how successful these defensive measures will be.

Computer-borne simulations of risk engage with *Umwelt* on a multi-dimensional basis, reaching far outside the perimeters of individual cognisance and human visual proficiency. The latest versions of these programmes extend the boundaries of what is observable in the *Umwelt*, penetrating deep below the perceptual surface, and extending the horizon to its conceivable limits. They do so using art, logic and engineering to dextrously recreate and interact with a spatial enviroment that incorporates numerous kinds of real and imagined, or hypothetical, 'risk-objects' (see Scott and Perry, 2006, pp. 4–9). ARMSS programmes exist, therefore, to 'extend minds', beyond the limitations of grey-matter and human 'skin-bags' (adapting

Clark, cited in Selinger and Engstrom, 2014, p. 636). Software *is us*: human hands build circuit boards, write code, and implant logorithms that 'mimetically' (see Rees and Richardson, 2013) replicate human thoughts, feelings and experiences (see Mitcham, 1994; Clark, 2003; Ihde, 2004; Scharff and Dusek, 2014). Many of these thoughts, feelings and experiences will relate to risk. Upon transfer, they will become part of an 'alteritous' hyper-magnified simulation of the human countenance, which attempts to make good its many imperfections (Ihde reprinted in Scharff and Dusek, 2014; Borgmann cited in Verbeek 2002; Rees and Richardson, 2013).

In so doing, computer-aided risk analysis populates *Umwelt* with existential threats, and potentially menacing actors, who may never cross the threshold of a physical universe. Aside from the efficiency arguments asserted by manufacturers and vendors (Baldvinsdottir, *et al.*, 2010), the success of risk-software product-marketing, in the late modern age, is partly explained by this propensity for representing and illuminating, in Borgmann's terms, a 'hyper-real' version of *Umwelt* (adapting Verbeek, 2002), which is capable of staging and synchronizing every possible version of events that computer programmers and data analysts can think of. Why then, might such an aptitude seem attractive and necessary to purchasers of this software? What old and new desires might be satiated by such a purchase?

The decision to buy risk management software is a major capital expense for the organizations and individuals seeking automated solutions for the risk management problems they adduce (Wagner, *et al.*, 2006; Scott and Perry, 2006; Bamberger, 2010). Considerable change-efforts may be required to ensure the proper integration of ARMSS systems into existing operational infrastructures and a reorientation of organizational culture may be necessary (Racz, *et al.*, 2010; Baldvinsdottir, *et al.*, 2010; Wagner, *et al.*, 2006; Scott and Perry, 2006; Rikhardsson, *et al.*, 2006). On first inspection, the motivations for making an investment choice of this kind seem to mostly correspond with the desires identified by markeeters of a yearning for complete organizational mastery and fault-free logisitics (Racz, *et al.*, 2010; Baldvinsdottir, *et al.*, 2010; Wagner, *et al.*, 2006; Scott and Perry, 2006; Rikhardsson, *et al.*, 2006). Computer simulations of risk intimate that this future is obtainable and within reach, offering a much vaunted release from the very modern-seeming problem of workplace inefficiency.

The quest for ever-greater control over hazardous risks, and their unwanted infiltration into social and organizational life, can be therefore seen as one type of carthartic gain to be acquired from automation. Yet there has always been more to life than struggles with inefficiency, which are, in themselves, a symptom of much deeper dissatisfaction with human frailty, malaise and imperfection (Verbeek, 2002). By promising to both simulate and manage risks computers may provide us with the vital resources and panoptic capabilities we need to plug cognate gaps in our ability to read *Umwelt*. They could, in this respect, turn out to be a panacea or 'cure-all' for the double delinquencies of 'bounded rationality' and 'imperfect information (see Bammer and Smithson, 2009). Independent evaluations of their capabilities suggest that, while risk software solutions cultivate better assessment, coordination and preparedness for risk events (Racz, *et al.* 2010), they do not represent a faultless solution to the pervasive (existential) problem of 'foresight failure' (Turner, 1976). Not every risk may be accounted for, even by the most sophisticated human or artificial intellegence (or cyborg combination thereof). The engineering behind risk software solutions may falter or succumb to viruses. Vendors and operators of these systems may find ourselves without the internet or electricity, at which point such solutions become useless.

The desire for perfect foresight and unfettered knowledge can be seen as part and parcel of an unrequited aspiration or dream of technological deliverance that typifies 'late modernity' (Giddens, 1991). Technology rarely lives up to either these sublime expectations or the more mundane hope that automated devices will alleviate the challenges they were designed to resolve without raising new skirmishes, pathologies and dependencies (Scharff and Dusek, 2014; Bamberger, 2010; Ankiewicz and de Swardt, 2006; Verbeek, 2002; Higgs, *et al.*, 2000; Lenk, 1998; Ihde, 1995). Technological innovations become overburdened with a weight of expectation they cannot meet (Higgs, *et al.*, 2000; Scharff and Dusek, 2014). When they fail, technologies and, by extension, the information experts, scientists, engineers and graphic designers who put them together, can become scapegoats for failure (Higgs, *et al.*, 2000). This rather bleak view of the place of technology suggests that it is inevitable that manmade inventions will always be incapable of delivering 'the good life' we seek, because of the intractable complications their introduction often incurs (Higgs, *et al.*, 2000). Even if they cannot deliver a lasting version of the utopian good life, technological innovations do supply fleeting forms of satisfaction that include the sense of relief to be obtained from adverse risk-avoidance.

If efficiency and hazard control are the first and second reasons companies give for purchasing risk software, then trust-building and reassurance seeking are the third and fourth motivating factors they are likely to put forward. Many 'advertorials' for risk management software solutions entertain reassuring language as part of a sales pitch (see by way of example Bluemner, n.d.). Thus, for instance, the sales materials, brochures and vendor comparison sites aimed at accounting and finance professionals impress upon their readers the reassuring benefits to be gained from allowing an automated system (that can be trusted not to produce errors) to manage compliance and reporting requirements (Racz, *et al.*, 2010; Ankiewicz and de Swardt, 2006; Rikhardsson, *et al.*, 2006; Bluemner, n.d.; Rasmussen, n.d.). Notwithstanding its powerful influence, and selling-power, the links between organizational decision-making, technological change, and reassurance-seeking are seldom discussed with the same candour and rigour as efficiency, creating a knowledge deficit of considerable scope and size. How reassurance affects practices in the accounting and finance domain is an especially important issue, given the many ways in which accounting and finance professionals must reassure, conciliate, soothe and placate clients, regulators and shareholders.

Reassurance-giving (and receiving) is one of the most important heuristics (cognitive shortcuts) allied to processes of risk decision-making, wherein its function is to help move deliberations into a decisive end-state that closes or creates an exit-point for the discussion. Reassurance mechanisms achieve this departure/culmination by enabling 'sufficing' behaviours to emerge. While not all sufficing behaviours are positive, some exist to mark the satisfactory consideration of equally poor or damaging options for which there can be no enlightened outcome (Hobson's Choice), many engage with the 'pursuit of happiness', even if they do so by small measures and increments. Reassurance heuristics are thereby responsible for the temporary relief and catharsis that risk analysis and assessments of probability/possibility provide. They are an extremely important esoteric resource that puts the mind at ease—the social, cognitive and emotional attributions of which are outlined to best effect within the nursing and medical literatures (Schwartz, 1966; Farced, 1994) and which cast reassurance as a naturally occurring didactic phenomenon, performed by a caregiver, for the benefit of a receiver. The receiver in question must be ready to accept the reassurance they are given as appropriate and valid, suggesting that reassurance does not work as a psychosocial construct, unless 'trust' and 'attachment' are already present (Schwartz, 1966; Farced, 1994).

Elementary definitions of this kind emphasize the dispensatory nature of reassurance, the extent to which it is foreground by benevolent gestures, conferred for reasons of honourable intent. Conventional wisdom promotes the idea that reassurance-giving is primarily an act of compassion, empathy and catharsis, extended by enlightened individuals, who believe themselves capable of vanquishing fear and anxiety in another person. The giving and receiving of reassurance is such a normal part of life that the dynamics it involves can be all too easily taken for granted as a moral impetus and force for good that exerts benign and innocuous influence. Yet, in truth, the art of giving and receiving reassurance hinges on an unequal power-balance, tilted in favour of the 'giver', 'reassurer' or 'dispenser' of consolation and solace. To seek reassurance is to acknowledge deference to the expertise, knowledge and practical wisdom acquitted by a reassurance-giver. When dispensing reassurance, the person (or persons) concerned has the power and, sometimes, the official authority to take away a person's concerns and alleviate them of burdensome tribulations. Reassurance can be seen, in this respect, as a powerful means of acquittal, the deployment of which affirms the status, authority, verisimilitude, and legitimacy of those permitting and/or undertaking such exoneration. This interpretation of what reassurance is and does promotes a didactic conception of the term, allying reassurance-giving with the consoling and solacing intentions of sagacious authority figures, whose knowledge and expertise is considered more befitting of the task than that of a layperson (Farced, 1994; Stark, *et al*., 2004; Pascoe, 2006; Wain, 2006). Characteristically, persons cast in the role of expert reassurer include parents reassuring their children, spiritual guides reassuring convert and pilgrims, teachers reassuring their pupils, and doctors and nurses reassuring their patients (Farced, 1994; Stark, *et al*., 2004; Pascoe, 2006; Wain, 2006). These archetypal illustrations serve to demonstrate that traditional notions of reassurance-seeking and reassurance-giving correspondingly emphasize pedagogical instruction, and inter alia, the need to demonstrate to, or even 'teach', the receivers of advice that they need not be unduly fearful (Farced, 1994; Stark, *et al*., 2004; Pascoe, 2006; Wain, 2006).

Notwithstanding these claims to virtuous intent, it may also be the case that givers provide false reassurance, either deliberately if they are engaging in a deception, or inadvertently if their words and actions are subject to misinterpretation (Farced, 1994; Stark, *et al*., 2004; Pascoe, 2006; Wain, 2006). Faux catharsis-giving is a staple of the con artist, the fraudster and the predatory individual, and its achievement, a principal behavioural repertoire, tactic or schemata that has come to be associated with disreputable occupations. Genuine, sagacious, and morally enlightened uses of reassurance tend to go hand-in-hand with 'angelic' professional archetypes: nurses, doctors, teachers, social workers, pastoral advisors, environmental protection officers, and veterinarians, and represent the professional cadres whom we perceive most readily to signify the pursuit of an ennobled 'higher purpose' of protecting, shielding and safeguarding. The value constructs allied to archetypes of work performed by police and the legal system similarly foster reassurance by 'maintaining the peace', preventing harm, ensuring justice is upheld and encouraging redress. These acts of safeguarding embody different yet related forms of reassurance to those enacted by emergency response teams and the armed services we rely on to rescue and provide security in situations of extremis, saving persons, animals, buildings, cities, crops and vital infrastructures from certain disaster. Respectively, each occupational group in society has its own reassuring role to fulfil, even if the professions sometimes seem to 'do reassurance' differently.

The evidence provided by medicine and nursing suggest that reassurance is an exceptionally important facet of professional practice, performed routinely within professional occupations that pledge to protect and prevent vulnerable persons, assets and environments from harm. A definitive list of the reassuring professions would not be complete without the addition of safety specialists, engineers, and accounting professionals, whose roles within organizations and institutions is no less protective. The 'psychological contracts' upheld between accounting and finance experts and their clients are emboldened by pledges, which carry the imprint of reassurance, encoded with a stridently propitious moral message. For example, in audit, the 'true and fair' opinion is just such a form of pledge and is an emblem reassuring the reader of financial statements. Despite its heuristic significance, as a force that shapes many of the behaviour codes we adhere to, reassurance is—regrettably—often the forgotten contributor to trust relations, the actor who rarely appears on stage, despite being central to the dramaturgy of a scene. Reassurance epitomizes the silent (taken-for-granted) partner in the psychological contract upon which most financial services agreements and business transactions are agreed. Though equal at least in importance to risk, reassurance is less frequently considered as a suitable debating point in social dialogues about hazard and trust. Thus, we have come to know a great deal about the dangers we hope to mitigate, whilst failing to consider fully how we intend to exploit, enjoy and make the most of the purgative and remedying effects risk prevention work achieves, including the sensory state of feeling reassured. It is as if risk prevention is an end itself, a relieving circumstance that prevented something bad from happening. Our gut reaction is to want to 'move on' from this real or hypothetical 'unpleasantry' as swiftly as possible, without stopping to consider what we have gained from experiencing this new-found sense of release and contentment. We do not linger over reassurance partly because we feel we cannot afford to, in an unreliable and sometimes terrifying late modern age, outwardly governed by incertitude (Beck and Kewell, 2014).

Risk software solutions and the delivery of reassurance (a Research Agenda)

When seen in these terms, reassurance affords both a brief spell of the 'good life, and in terms of Kantian philosophy, a glimpse of what a better, more enlightened world might resemble (Scharff and Dusek, 2014; Higgs, *et al.*, 2000; Mitcham, 1994). The sensory experience of reassurance is implicity pleasurable because it is moral, nurturing and protecting. In early societies, reassurance arose from the bonds of kinship and trust that form between members of clans (Kydd, 2000; Granovetter, 1985). Expert-client relationships framed in the modern age replicate this intimacy, if within the context of 'disembedded' market societies that are increasingly typified by 'faceless transactions' (Kydd, 2000; Granovetter, 1985; Pinch and Swedberg, 2008). While it is a 'social capital', with antiquarian origins, reassurance arguably remains one of the most valuable assets affecting client management in the twenty-first century economy, forming an implicit part of notions of good service and customer satisfaction that secure repeat business and cement commercial reputations (Rhett and Walker, 2009). The trust relations behind client management would arguably cease to function without the dynamic of reassurance. Some industries, such as insurance and pharmaceuticals, have come to understand the 'commodity value' of reassurance, and its key antonyms of insecurity and dissatisfaction, building business and corporate empires around the consumer influences these sense states bring to bear. 'Reassurance analysis' could potentially move beyond its traditional focus (of the clinic) by examining the patina of reassurance giving in key sectors of the commercial world where interpersonal trust remains exceptionally important, such as in the fields of accountancy and finance; or where the marketing of an industry calls upon dual narratives of insecurity and comfort to acquire custom. An alternative line of inquiry could evaluate the role reassurance plays in the agreement and textual contracts (both ancient and modern) to see how this medium of agreement brings a mutual sense of accord to signing parties.

Philosophers of technology might argue in favour of hermeneutic research that inspects the emotion and psychosocial investment we had made in technology, as a giver of reassurance, and how a growing dependence relationship between ourselves and machines is reshaping the social construction of this all-important value nexus. The late modern age (see Giddens, 1990, p. 150) has been typified by the 'transference' of many responsibilities to the machine-world, beginning with the task of calculation (Bamberger, 2010; Pinch and Swedberg, 2008; Stark, *et al.* 2004; Clark, 2003; Verbeek, 2002; Borgmann, 1999; Lenk, 1998; Ihde, 1995; Mitcham, 1994). At the outset of this process, machines were ancilliary/adjunct devices, such as the abacus, which helped automate arithmetical processes of tallying and counting (Borgmann, 1999, pp. 40–43; Beck and Kewell, 2014, chap. 1). Though they have always retained a 'reassuring function', simple adding machines did not bear any responsibility for our hopes and dreams of escape and enlightenment. Machines started to take partial custody of reassurance-giving responsibilities with the onset of the Industrial Revolution (adapting Borgmann, 1999), at which point they became responsible for delivering crops, mining ores and minerals, building infrastructures, conducting wars, manufacturing products, and managing stock-market transactions (for the latter, see especially Pinch and Swedberg, 2008). Since their invention, computers, including the Enigma machine, have been imparted with the grave responsibility of safeguarding humanity by deciphering risks, estimating their impact, and providing us with the raw data to make judgements about them. This process can be seen as a 'slow-fusion' of human qualities with those of machines, and thus, a steady closing of the gap between 'actors and networks (Hilgartner, 1992). The latest generation of risk software solutions cements this union even further by providing both a 'one best (panoptic) solution' to the problems of *Umwelt* and a much desired means for coordinating human and machine activities across spatial, organizational, and intellectual frontiers (Baldvinsdottir, *et al.*, 2010; Racz, *et al.*, 2010; Rikhardsson, *et al.*, 2006; Wagner, *et al.*, 2006; Scott and Perry, 2006).

Most professions are built on a combination of 'techniques'—which need not require any technology input; 'technics' for establishing, designing and assembling technologies; and the physical output of this process, that is to say, usable 'technologies' (Mitcham, 1994; Ihde, 1995; Lenk, 1998; Higgs, *et al.*, 2000; Verbeek, 2002; Clark, 2003; Ankiewicz and de Swardt, 2006; Pinch and Swedberg, 2008; Scharff and Dusek, 2014). As is the norm in many contemporary fields of expertise, the practice of modern-day accounting and finance combines elements of technique, technics and technology. For instance, it is still an essential prerequisite, even in this advanced era of statistical computing, that trainee accountants should have a facility for mental arithmetic as a pivotal technique that requires no technological interaction (adapting Borgmann, 1999, pp. 40–43). These same trainees must simultaneously acquire the ability to work fluently with technologies for writing down accounting information and keeping tally with pens, pencils and paper that are much closer to nature than software products (Borgmann, 1999, pp. 40–43). In some cultures, this education process starts at a very young age with the first introduction of the abacus, as a venerated antiquarian technology that brings speed to the art of calculus without the need for silicon chips and battery power. Accounting practitioners and financial analysts must also be able to supplement an ability for calculation with equal knowledge of the advanced symbolic and visual language of mathematics, such that they should, by the time of their final exams, be able to replicate and work interchangeably between specialist accounting models, diagrams, graphs, and formulae. Crucially, someone who is ready to enter the profession will also know how to read the *Umwelt* and remediate risk. Most, if not all, of these areas of practice may be performed without recourse to higher technologies, computer simulations and risk software solutions of the coming world of accounting AI. Each area of skill outlined above may engender its own unique social construct of reassurance and, hence is worth investigating, with a view to better ascertaining how the marriage of techniques, tacit skills and traditional technologies produces enough trust to be reassuring.

The push toward the automation of accounting and finance is linked to a very strong desire, on the part of many contributors to the profession, for the achievement of technological transcendence (Scott and Zachariadis, 2014; Baldvinsdottir, *et al.*, 2010; Bamberger, 2010; Wagner, *et al.*, 2006; Scott and Perry, 2006). The 'technics' of accounting have provided highly favourable conditions within which to achieve this aim, whilst simultaneously producing a counterculture that would prefer the profession to maintain a clear separation between the human and technological elements of accounting labour, fearing a future in which key tacit financial skills, and the power to use them, become 'lost in the machine'. This counterthetical viewpoint identifies a boundary through which the profession should not pass. It is one thing to input data into spreadsheets and simulations, and quite another to let machines, and any future cyborgs, choose how to use and coordinate this data. Such a perspective regards tradition as a safe and trustworthy source of reassurance, whilst viewing any future cyborg accountant as a unit of potential threat and dictatorship, akin to the *HAL 9000* computer envisioned in Arthur C. Clarke's *2001: A Space Odyssey* (see Ihde abridged in Scharff and Dusek, 2014, p. 559). The existence of such a diametrically opposed set of opinions suggests that future disagreements about what direction the professions should take are likely to have a strong technological angle to them. As we have seen, several commentators already see risk software solutions as heavily implicated in this controversy (Baldvinsdottir, *et al.*, 2010; Bamberger, 2010; Racz, *et al.*, 2010; Rikhardsson, *et al.*, 2006; Wagner, *et al.*, 2006; Scott and Perry, 2006).

We would seek, in contributing to an already lively discussion on this topic, to highlight a number of questions related to Science and Technology Studies (STS) about how risk software solutions, including those with AI capabilities, will be utilized by their purchasers to engage in reassurance-giving. What forms of reassurance-giving will they take on? Will their design include reassuring voices and visuals? Whom will they aim to reassure most: the accountant and financial analyst, the general manager, the client, the regulator or all of these groups?

Conclusion

The construction of reassurance mechanisms in one-to-one professional relationships is perhaps best outlined in relation to doctors and nurses and their patients, and the fragile negotiation of human frailties, hopes and expectation this involves. Accounting and finance professionals who work with clients may recognize some of the social dynamics of trust to which the above alludes, particularly in relation to client management, and the ability they possess to safeguard from harm and ensure financial security. Accountants have a psychological contract with clients that is dependent upon reputation (of the person and the profession/institution/company to which they belong), personal trust that only a good reputation can bestow. Reassurance, given by a trusted professional (whether a doctor, lawyer, educator, financial adviser or accountant), is a reputation-dependent symbolic commodity or 'capital'. Reputation and reassurance arguably reinforce one another. Reassuring advice is more likely to be accepted and believed by someone we trust, know personally or have faith in than by someone we regard (as yet) still to merit trust. Reassurance given by someone we do not know, have yet to bond with, or hold in disrepute, is likely to be rejected, treated with scepticism and even derision if it is given by a doubtful person, or person allied to doubtful institutions, agencies and professions. Esteem factors and signals are essential prerequisites to both the trust relations we share with others and our ability to accept or be guided by reassurance from them. Individual trust relationships and those that are closely 'embedded' through personal knowledge, kinship and past dealings are cast within cultural microcosms of just a few people. The trust nexus 'binding' social actants to one another in these small networks substantiate lasting forms of reassurance that arise as an outcome of close 'mutuality'—and the protection this affords against uncertainty and harm.

Disembedded societies rely more and more on technology as a substitute for interpersonal trust relations (Kydd, 2000; Granovetter, 1985). The dangers inherent in 'technological over-dependency' frequently become manifest during these periods of transformation, when they are likely to be accompanied by regret and lament at the loss of tradition, craft skills and the way of life to which a recently superseded occupation or technical art was formerly wedded (ibid). In banking and finance there is great nostalgia for the 'local bank manager' and, thus, a 'pillar of the community' who have become the sacrificial lambs of an electronic banking revolution. Much like the chartered accountant to whom we might be referred by a friend or neighbour, the archetype of the local bank manager epitomized the last gasp of an age of interpersonal trust that was blown away by the 'white heat' of automation in the 1960s and 1970s (Scott and Zachariadis, 2014).

When automated, simulated and computer-generated accounting technologies first emerged, they were marketed as efficiency tools that would improve organizational coordination and business-to-business efficacy between corporations and their logistical partners (Baldvinsdottir, *et al.*, 2010). The emphasis of contemporary product marketing for Risk Management Information Systems (RMIS), Governance, Risk and Compliance Services (GRCS) and enterprise risk management (ERM) juxtaposes traditional efficiency messages with those allied to safeguarding, protection, and the sense of reassurance to be gained from restructuring the business around an ever watchful, panoptic 'electronic sentinel' capable of managing a thousand different risks in one go. To this end, integrated risk software solutions are a step toward a future in which computers take over as the true 'brains of the firm' fulfilling a prediction made by Stafford Beer in 1972. The future of the accounting profession, and its preferred training and teaching methods, are likely to be up for grabs as the cyborg incursion gathers pace. Will the accounting profession and accounting education have to change in order to accommodate integrated risk software solutions and AI before they arrive?

References

Adams, M., (2004), 'Whatever Will Be Will Be: Trust, Fate and The Reflexive Self', *Culture and Psychology*, 10, pp. 387–408.

Adriaans, P. and J. van Benthem (2008), *Handbook of Philosophy of Information.* Amsterdam: Elsevier.

Ankiewicz, P. and E.d.V.M. de Swardt (2006), 'Some Implications of the Philosophy of Technology for Science, Technology and Society (STS) Studies', *International Journal of Technology and Design Education*, 16, pp. 117–141.

Baldvinsdottir, G., J. Burns, H. Nørreklit, and R. Scapens (2010), *Risk Manager or Risque Manager? The New Platform for the Management Accountant*, London: Chartered Institute of Management Accountants.

Bamberger, K. (2010), Technologies of Compliance: Risk and Regulation in a Digital Age. *Texas Law Review*, 88(4), pp. 669–739.

Bammer, G. and M. Smithson (eds.) (2009), *Uncertainty and Risk.* London: Earthscan.

Beck, M. and B. Kewell (2014), *Risk: A Study of Its Origins, History and Politics.* London: World Scientific/Imperial College Press.

Beer, S. (1972), *Brain of the Firm.* Herder and Herder.

Bluemner, A. (n.d.), Enterprise Risk Management Software Guide.: Find Accounting Software.

Borgmann, A. (1999), *Holding On to Reality: The Nature of Information at the Turn of the Millenium.* Chicago: University of Chicago Press.

Cau, D. (n.d.) Governance, Risk and Compliance (GRC) Software, Business Needs and Market Trends. https://www2.deloitte.com/content/dam/Deloitte/lu/Documents/risk/lu_en_ins_governance-risk-compliance-software_05022014.pdf

Clark, A. (2003), *Natural-Born Cyborgs: Minds, Technologies and the Future of Human Intelligence.* Oxford: Oxford University Press.

Farced, A. (1994), 'A Philosophical Analysis of the Concept of Reassurance and its Effect on Coping', *Journal of Advanced Nursing,* 20(5), pp. 870–873.

Forrester Research Inc. (2014), *The Forrester Wave(TM): Governance, Risk and Compliance Platforms, Q1 2014.* Cambridge, MA: Forrester Research Inc.

Gibson, M. (1997), *Information Systems for Risk Management.* Washington DC: Federal Reserve Board.

Giddens, A. (1990), *On the Consequences of Modernity.* Cambridge: Polity Press.

Giddens, A. (1991), *Modernity and Self-Identity: Self and Society in the Late Modern Age.* Cambridge: Polity Press.

Granovetter, M. (1985), 'Economic Action and Social Structure: The Problem of Embeddedness', *The American Journal of Sociology*, 91, November, pp. 481–510.

Green, B. and T. Calderon (2005), 'Assessing Student Learning and Growth Through Audit Risk Simulations', *Advances in Accounting Education,* 7, pp. 1–25.

Higgs, E., A. Light and D. Strong (eds.) (2000), *Technology and the Good Life.* Chicago: University of Chicago Press.

Hilgartner, S. (1992), 'The Social Construction of Risk Objects: Or How to Pry Open Networks of Risk. In J. J. C. L. Short, ed. *Organizations, Uncertainties, and Risk.* Boulder: Westview.

Ihde, D. (1995), 'Philosophy of Technology, 1975–1995', *Society for Philosophy of Technology*, 1(1–2), pp. 8–12.

Ihde, D. (2004), 'Has the Philosophy of Technology Arrived? A State of the Art Review', *Philosophy of Science*, 71, pp. 117–131.

Kydd, A. (2000), 'Trust, Reassurance and Cooperation', *International Organization*, 54(2), pp. 325–357.

Lenk, H. (1998), 'Advances in the Philosophy of Technology: New Structural Characteristics of Technologies', *Society for Philosophy of Technology*, 4(1), pp. 93–103.

Mitcham, C. (1994), *Thinking through Technology: The Path between Engineering and Philosophy.* Chicago: University of Chicago Press.

Partman, S. and P. Marler (2002), 'The *Umwelt* and Its Relevance to Animal Communication: Introduction to Special Issue', *Journal of Comparative Psychology*, 116(2), pp. 116–119.

Pascoe, E. (2006), 'The Value to Nursing Research of Gadamer's Hermeneutic Philosophy', *Journal of Advanced Nursing*, 24(6), pp. 1309–1314.

Pinch, T. and R. Swedberg (2008), *Living in a Material World.* Cambridge, MA: MIT Press.

Racz, N. Panitz, J. C., Amberg, M., Weippl, E. and Senfert, A. (2010), Governance, Risk and Compliance (GRC) Status Quo and Software Use: Results from a Survey among Large Enterprises. Brisbane, n.p.

Rasmussen, M. (n.d.), Sarbanes-Oxley Technologies: GRC Technology vs. Spreadsheets. http://searchdata-management.techtarget.com/answer/Sarbanes-Oxley-compliance-GRC-technology-vs-spreadsheets

Rees and Richardson (2013), We ask the experts: Will robots take over the world? http://www.cam.ac.uk/research/discussion/we-ask-the-experts-will-robots-take-over-the-world

Rhett, H. and L. Walker (2009), 'Johnson Signaling Intrinsic Service Quality and Value via Accreditation and Certification', *Managing Service Quality: An International Journal*, 19(1), pp. 85–105.

Rikhardsson, P., P. Bst, P. Green and M. Rosemann (2006), *Business Process Risk Management, Compliance and Internal Control: A Research Agenda.* Aarhus: n.p.

Scharff, R. and V. Dusek (eds.) (2014), *Philosophy of Technology: The Technological Condition (An Anthology).* Malden, MA: Wiley Blackwell.

Schwartz, L. (1966), 'Some Notes on Reassurance in Medical Practice', *Psychosomatics*, 7(5), pp. 290–294.

Scott, S. and N. Perry (2006), 'The Enactment of Risk Categories: Organizing and Re-organizing Risk Management Practices.' September ed. London: Department of Management, Information Systems Group.

Scott, S. and M. Zachariadis (2014), *The Society for Worldwide Interbank Financial Telecommunication (SWIFT).* London: Routledge.

Selinger, E. and T. Engstrom (2014), 'A Moratorium for Cyborgs: Computation, Cognition and Commerce', in R. Scharff and V. Dusek (eds.), *Philosophy of Technology.* Chichester: Wiley Blackwell, pp. 631–640.

Stark, D., Kiely, M., Smith, A., Morley, S., Selby, P. and House, A. (2004) 'Reassurance and the Anxious Cancer Patient', *British Journal of Cancer*, 91, pp. 893–899.

Togo, D. (2004), 'Risk Analysis for Accounting Models: A Spreadsheet Simulation Approach', *Journal of Accounting Education*, 22, pp. 153–163.

Turner, B. (1976), 'The Organizational and Interorganizational Development of Disasters', *Administrative Science Quarterly*, 21(3), pp. 378–397.

Verbeek, P. (2002), 'Devices of Engagement: On Borgmann's Philosophy of Information and Technology', *Techne: Research in Philosophy and Technology*, 6(1), pp. 69–92

Wagner, L. S. Scott and R. Galliers (2006), 'The Creation of Best Practice Software: Myth, Reality and Ethics', *Information and Organization*, 16(3), pp. 251–275.

Wain, K. (2006), 'Contingency, Education and the Need for Reassurance', *Studies in the Philosophy of Education*, 25(1–2), pp. 37–45.

4

Insights into corporate governance and risk

Exploring systems from Germany, the United States and the United Kingdom

Anthony Devine and Philip Shrives

Introduction

Prior to the 1980s few people had heard of the term 'corporate governance', then suddenly it became the phrase of the moment. One key reason for this was a number of scandals that occurred around this time such as Polly Peck International (a textile company which grew very rapidly in the 1980s) and Maxwell Communications (a newspaper and printing company). Up to this point, if scandals occurred and companies collapsed, people tended to think auditors were to blame (as well as directors). One of the reasons for this was that everyone knew auditors carried insurance. However, auditors have always made it clear that they could not be responsible for fraud. This has applied ever since the infamous 1898 'Kingston Cotton Mill' case where the auditor was described as 'a watchdog and not a bloodhound' but more recently in the Caparo case (*Caparo Industries plc v. Dickman and others 1990*), where it was held that no duty of care was owed to individual investors by auditors. Auditors have emphasised that it was particularly difficult to audit management assurances especially those dealing with sensitive management issues and estimates. Thus, if auditors were not to blame, who was? Was it the board of directors?

In the late 1980s the Bank of England felt that governance was possibly better in other competitor countries such as Germany and Japan which operated the two-tier board system. Accordingly, in 1991, the Financial Reporting Council, the London Stock Exchange and the accountancy profession commissioned the Cadbury committee to conduct a review of UK corporate governance. This committee was chaired by Sir Adrian Cadbury.[1] His committee went on to produce the Cadbury Report (entitled the Financial Aspects of Corporate Governance). From there corporate governance with its 'comply or explain' approach came into being in the UK and was subsequently imitated in a number of countries around the world (Seidl *et al.* 2013). Table 4.1 summarises the key principles which emerged from the original report. The purpose of these recommendations was to improve controls within companies, both at board level and throughout the business. Not all of these recommendations have been implemented and inevitably this may expose companies to further risk. And of course companies do not have to comply providing they can supply an explanation (Shrives and Brennan, 2015).

Table 4.1 Summary of the Cadbury Report recommendations (1992)

Companies should make a statement about compliance with the code, giving reasons for any areas of non-compliance—this is the birth of the 'comply or explain' system
Auditors should review only those parts of the compliance statement that can be objectively verified; the auditors practicing board is to provide guidance
Institutional shareholders should encourage compliance
A new committee should be appointed to monitor compliance/update the code
Director's service contract should not exceed three years without shareholders' approval
Suggestions on interim reporting
Non-audit fees should be disclosed
Guidelines on audit partner rotation
Directors should report on going-concern with auditors commenting
Legislation to back internal controls and going-concern
Legislation on fraud reporting
Accounting profession should consider improving the standing of auditors
References made to expanded audit report
Various other items

In the US similar scandals occurred to those in the UK. The hugely successful energy giant Enron, which had outperformed the market on just about every metric, was suddenly in serious trouble—this becoming apparent to the outside world in October 2001. Income related to future years was initially being recognised in the current year on a number of projects. This process continued requiring more and more fictitious revenue recognition to occur until the bubble burst and the performance could be faked no longer. George Bush's US government did not take the same 'softly softly' approach adopted in the UK (Sir Adrian Cadbury later stated that 'he that governs sits quietly at the stern and scarce is seen to stir' (Cadbury, 2002, p. 1)). Instead, the Sarbanes Oxley Act of 2002 was enacted with its 'zero tolerance' approach to non-compliance. Company officials whose organisations did not comply could, in theory, be sent to prison for up to seven years (note though that in practice this has not transpired). Despite the emphasis on corporate governance and its ally risk management, companies still face problems and scandals. Thus there remain many unanswered questions. Corporate governance is part of risk management but risk management is also part of corporate governance, so the relationship between the two is fascinating and worth exploring.

In this chapter we explore aspects of corporate governance and its relation to risk. Poor corporate governance can lead to increased organisational risk. In discussing corporate governance the chapter explores three different countries: the UK, the US and Germany.

The structure of the chapter is as follows: first we explore the background to corporate governance, emphasising why corporate governance is needed. Next we examine the theory that underpins corporate governance. The key theory in this area is agency theory, but in recent years other theories have emerged offering different perspectives. The chapter continues by exploring the various types of board structures which exist and what is meant by 'comply or explain'. Where companies fail, to what extent does that result in increased risk? In answering this question we also examine non-compliance in the UK and Germany, making suitable comparisons with the US system, governed by the Sarbanes Oxley Act of 2002 (henceforth referred to as 'SOX').

Corporate governance background

The UK

Up to the 1980s corporate governance was relatively straightforward. Companies had boards of directors (sometimes with a separate CEO and Chair, other times these roles were combined). Typically these companies had non-executive directors and the possibility of subcommittees, most notably, audit committees. Companies were of course subject to external audit. Following the Cadbury Report recommendations a number of subsequent reports were produced including Hampel, Greenbury, Smith, Higgs, Turnbull (with later revisions), and (more recently) Walker. These reports covered directors' remuneration, internal controls and risk and most notably, subcommittees of the board. It is interesting that many of these issues from twenty years ago are still not resolved and that applies particularly to directors' pay (see Shrives and Welch, 1997).

These reports formed the basis of the Combined Code (although not every recommendation was implemented), and corporate governance arrangements became much more formalised. A key aspect was non-executive directors (or NEDs), and those referred to as 'independent non-executive directors'. The first Combined Code was the 1998 version which was followed by the 2003 version with significant reforms. From 2006 onwards, every two years there were subsequent iterations of the Code, the most recent of which has been the 2014 Code. Recent amendments to the Code include the re-appointment of directors (now annually) and the appointment of an external reviewer for the board (at least every three years—see provision B.6.2). The Code is now typically updated every two years (since 2006) although recently (2016) the Financial Reporting Council (FRC) has announced that the 2014 Code will not be updated until 2019. This allows company directors to catch up with all the changes that have occurred and the FRC to properly evaluate all the changes.

Even large companies often do not comply with *all* aspects of the Code including important areas such as the number of non-executive directors and the composition of audit, remuneration and nomination committees.

Germany

Traditionally German accounting was very secretive. This was mainly because German banks provided much of the funding for companies and these banks were represented on the boards. Thus there was no need to disclose information to outsiders. In the 1990s German companies needed to raise capital from outside of the enterprise so as to compete in international markets. In order for German companies to obtain listings on overseas stock exchanges, they needed to become much more transparent and started to comply with, first, US Accounting Standards and, later, with International Accounting Standards. Since the late 1990s laws have been introduced that have had significant impact on the transparency of German accounting practice. The need for raising capital internationally coupled with changes in the laws on transparency (HGB and KonTraG) had heralded a new world of corporate transparency. German companies have had to adapt from an insider system of governance (focussing, for example, on creditors, employees and suppliers) to a much more open system in order to raise finance on (for example) the New York Stock Exchange. Special tax arrangements permitting tax-free capital gains were made, which helped split up the financial arrangements that block holders, banks and employees held in coalition. However, German companies have faced a number of scandals, notably those in the high-tech market (for example, the computer chip manufacturer Infineon Technologies, headquartered in Munich, where in 2005 employees were alleged to have taken substantial bribes[2]). Added to that, stock markets have had a difficult time since the global financial crisis from 2007 onwards (see Clarke, 2007). Some of these issues have led people to question the extent to which this new open form of governance is appropriate for German companies. However, the problems do not just relate to the new systems of governance. Recent events at Volkswagen involving emissions have also raised questions about the mechanisms by which supervisory boards (discussed later in the chapter) contribute to good governance.

The United States

As previously outlined, much of corporate governance regulation in the US largely came about as a result of various accounting scandals. These scandals involved a number of companies such as Waste Management, Global Crossing, Sunbeam and WorldCom (and many more which are covered in the detailed and entertaining account by Clikeman, 2013) but most significant of all was that of the Houston-based energy company, Enron. It is probably the most widely cited corporate scandal of our time. According to Brown (2005, p. 151): 'By 2000–2001, the stage was set for the "perfect storm" of corporate governance lapses'. The result of all these problems was the production of SOX (passed by the Senate as the 'Public Company Accounting Reform and Investor Protection Act 2002'). The key aspects of SOX are to:

- Strengthen independence of auditing firms
- Improve transparency of financial statements and disclosure
- Improve objectivity of analyst research
- Strengthen enforcement of the securities laws.

The introduction of SOX in 2002 was quite surprising given the background of American accounting and auditing. In terms of accounting standards, the Financial Accounting Standards Board (FASB) had been set up in 1973, some thirty years previously. Despite extensive development of accounting standards and over 150 years of auditing experience, extensive reform was still required. Whether SOX will be sufficient remains debatable but past evidence would, regrettably, suggest otherwise. Compliance costs are likely to cause unintended consequences which, in turn, may lead to future relaxation of the rules.

Theoretical background to corporate governance

Company risks often originate from events relating to corporate mismanagement and a lack of adequate controls. A lack of control and mismanagement means that these events often stem from the top of an organisation. Garrett (2010) uses a Chinese proverb as the title of his book: *The Fish Rots from the Head*, symbolising that individuals in the boardroom must be held accountable for organisational controls. Management can be in a position to override controls so it is essential that the culture of an organisation is set correctly by the board.

Management needs to establish adequate internal controls with risk management being a key part. Poor corporate governance is likely to significantly increase the risks faced by companies. A proper control system, incorporating segregation of duties, ensures that fraudulent or miscreant behaviour is likely to be prevented. An essential aspect of UK governance is the separation of the roles of CEO and Chair. Thus segregation of duties can go right to the top of the organisation. Too much control placed in the hands of one person is always a risk: This was demonstrated in a number of scandals, most notably that of Maxwell Communications.

The typical way to explain this is agency theory. Shareholders cannot run the company so they appoint managers to carry out this task. To reduce risks companies need to incur agency costs which typically would be boards of directors (and various sub-committees) and internal/ external audit. To some extent at least the growth of corporate governance has resulted from a failure of external audit.

Agency theory

Agency theory describes the possible problems which could arise from conflicting interests and information asymmetry between two parties of a contract (Berle and Means, 1932; Jensen and Meckling, 1976). In the case of listed firms, this conflict arises when the agent (manager), who is acting on behalf of the principal (owner), exerts a degree of opportunistic behaviour and thereby acts in his or her own interests rather than those of the owners (for example, the shareholders). The costs which are associated with the agency problem are known as 'agency costs' (Jensen and Meckling, 1976). These agency costs comprise two major areas. First, there is the cost of preventing agency problems, such as governance structures and control or incentive systems. The second area is the economic damage which can be caused by management behaving in an opportunistic way, such as free-riding and shirking (Siebels and zu Knyphausen-Aufseβ, 2011). The principal-agent problem, therefore, is underpinned by a fundamental assumption that, as separation of ownership and control increases, so too does the agency problem and therefore related costs (Ang *et al.*, 2000; Fama and Jensen, 1983; Schulze *et al.*, 2002).

Institutional theory

Theories often work better in concert with each theory explaining part of what is predicted or observed. Agency theory cannot, by itself, always explain corporate governance and a discussion of institutional theory can be beneficial. Institutional theory helps us understand why institutions and the people running them behave in the way they do. DiMaggio and Powell's (1983) work details three types of institutional isomorphism; namely coercive, mimetic and normative.

Coercive isomorphism is described by DiMaggio and Powell (1983, p. 150) as both, 'formal and informal pressures exerted by organisations upon which they are dependent by cultural expectations'. Coercive isomorphism is the practice of following rules or regulations. However, we also should take into consideration the informal pressures which may be apparent. If the norm is to comply with a particular provision of the Code then organisations are likely to be coerced into this 'norm' by an informal pressure. In the UK and Germany the expectation is that companies will comply with the Code, if they do not comply then they are expected to provide an explanation which is equivalent in 'value' to compliance. A study by Shrives and Brennan (2015) in the British Accounting Review showed that the quality of explanations for non-compliance was variable. It may be that this is because the inclusion of explanations can draw attention to the fact of non-compliance, whereas companies might prefer that their non-compliance was 'dressed up' to look like compliance.[3] In particular, some companies only provide an 'assertion of difference' rather than providing a full and bespoke explanation which is consistent with the principle of 'comply or explain'.

Isomorphism in mathematics is used to transfer one phenomenon to another, emulating properties in one mathematical problem and equation to help solve a problem in another. In essence, *mimetic isomorphism* is the practice of organisations seeking to be equal to one another. When organisations (or their directors) are unsure of what action to take, following others (termed 'mimetic' or 'isomorphic' behaviour) provides a sense of security. In terms of corporate governance, we sometimes find that when organisations perceive others to be more legitimate than themselves (DiMaggio and Powell, 1983) they will have a tendency to copy. Consider for example the situation where a company does not want to comply with the Corporate Governance Code. Although companies may not typically copy the exact explanation used in another company (although they are quite likely to copy their own explanations from year to year, which may suggest they become boilerplate), they may be tempted to copy the actual act of non-compliance. Consequently, many companies, even within the FTSE 350 in the UK, fail to comply with some of the tenets of corporate governance (such as proportion of independent non-executive directors or constitution of the various subcommittees of the board). Directors who see one company not complying may be tempted to do likewise, especially when they see non-compliance has no sanctions either from the Financial Reporting Committee or from auditors or investors. Investors can of course question non-compliance (and occasionally do so such as in the case of Marks and Spencer—see side panel 1) but often are more concerned about performance. In some respects the current UK system may be more aligned to 'comply or perform'.

Normative isomorphism

The final part of institutional theory concerns normative behaviour. Normative isomorphism is the concept that company directors or managers may come from the same educational training or professional background and therefore react to outside stimuli in a similar way (DiMaggio and Powell, 1983). This normative isomorphism is closely linked with the 'bandwagon' effect (Abrahamson and Rosenkopf, 1993). Although Abrahamson and Rosenkopf (1990) focus mainly on the bandwagon pressures to consciously align with others, an alternative view by scholars is that the bandwagon effect is not necessarily 'covertly copying' (Shrives, 2010, p. 120) but a result of following advice or best practice (Collins, 1979; DiMaggio and Powell, 1983; Larson, 1977). Thus, in essence managers or executives from the same background or training tend to behave in similar ways. Many finance directors of FTSE companies are Chartered Accountants and thus can be expected (according to normative isomorphism) to behave in similar ways. This can be quite risky for the markets as a whole because companies appear to be influenced by 'groupthink'. The aspects of institutional theory can all come together and the slippery slope then becomes expected practice. Instead of companies following good practice, pressure put upon them by shareholders and other stakeholders encourages them to behave in quite risky ways. For example, the slightly controversial practice of fair value accounting has become acceptable in this century and the old concept of prudence has faded. There is nothing wrong with this necessarily until it is taken to extremes and then other companies follow. It is not a huge step from there to creative accounting, a practice which considerably increases risk for company stakeholders.

Resource dependence theory

Another theory can also help understand corporate governance behaviour. Under resource dependence theory, companies act or react to maximise the resources (including directors) available to them. Resource dependence theory suggests that for companies there are advantages to non-compliance with certain provisions of the Code. From a practical stance, for instance, it suggests that outside or non-executive directors could provide advice (among other things) on legal aspects of business, banking or lines of credit (Stearns and Mizruchi, 1993),

Side panel 1

Marks and Spencer: looking through Rose coloured glasses?

In the UK one of the most frequently referenced cases regarding role duality is that of Sir Stuart Rose and Marks and Spencer (M&S). In 2008 Stuart Rose was appointed as CEO and Chair of M&S. At the time there was much discussion and criticism around the appointment, with Legal and General (L&G, an institutional shareholder) given only one hours' notice before Rose was appointed. At the time, L&G's head of equities, Mark Burgess, said, '[w]e believe strongly in the separation of the roles of Chairman and Chief Executive', and 'we believe [the] announcement is unwelcome' (Burgess *et al.*, 2008). Similarly a representative from the Association of British Insurers said, "[t]he appointment raises fundamental concerns for our members. M&S has a lot of work to do to persuade people this is the right approach' (Attwood, 2008).

The reason why so many people were against the controversial decision was due to the way Sir Stuart was appointed to the role. It had been thought that he would remain CEO until early 2009, but fear around stability was aroused by the strained relationship between Sir Stewart and Lord Burns, the incumbent Chair. The result was that Sir Stewart's tenure as CEO was fast approaching completion, but M&S wanted to keep him in the business. The only way to achieve this was to go against corporate governance best practice and for Lord Burns to step down.

There was a fear that Sir Stuart might step down if things didn't work out in the way he planned. Although Sir Stuart claimed he was building up strength from within, he was unable to identify a suitable successor. Sir David Michels (deputy Chair) admitted that no one likes flouting a rule (of course the Corporate Governance Code is not actually 'rules'), but that 'sometimes you have to do something a little skew whiff in the short term'.

Questions to consider

1 Sir Stuart Rose is thought to be one of Marks and Spencer's best CEOs. Did that justify him also being appointed as both CEO and Chair? Are there different skills attached to the different positions?
2 Assume a company which is to appoint a separate Chair and CEO: What are the problems associated with the previous CEO becoming Chair?
3 Does corporate governance affect the share price? During Stuart Rose's rule the share price fell from 750p to 375p at the time of the announcement.
4 Should we allow companies to engage in 'skew whiff' activities? What might be the consequences?

thereby enhancing firm performance and ultimately survival. Thus, non-executive directors provide a useful additional 'resource' to companies. These attributes (their knowledge and experience) are said to add value to the board. Compliance with the Code may impede these objectives because the Code focuses more on the 'second pair of eyes' control aspects rather than just their industry knowledge or experience.[4] Thus the business faces a dilemma—comply or obtain the necessary resources. Under 'comply or explain', of course, companies can choose not to comply in order to retain, for example, a non-executive director working beyond the nine-year maximum guidance suggested by the Code. The director, however, after working with a company for nine years will probably not be seen to be independent. The trade-off between expertise and independence is a difficult one. Non-executives with experience are very useful to a company but when they fail to act as the *crucial* 'second pair of eyes' as is intended by the Corporate Governance Code, they subject the company to increased risk.

These theories can be used to explain or predict relationships between company performance and corporate governance variables. For example, one might expect companies with good corporate governance to have better disclosure as governance is often linked to transparency. Similarly, companies with better compliance may exhibit lower levels of risk. Later in this chapter we explore the impact compliance may have on company risk. Before doing so, we take a look at board structures and these can vary according to country.

Board structures

The precise structure of boards may differ according to location but there are two main models. The US and the UK, for example, have a single-tier structure; this is in contrast to German companies who adopt a two-tier structure. In the UK companies are encouraged to separate Chairs and CEOs, whereas in the US role duality (combining the aforementioned roles) is commonplace, although decreasing. A key aspect of the UK system which was highlighted by the Cadbury report (and emphasised subsequently and throughout this chapter) is the role of the non-executive directors. These are usually termed outside directors in the US and in Germany the supervisory board acts in place of non-executive directors. Thus the supervisory board is responsible for overseeing the executive or management board.

In the UK there is emphasis placed on the need for non-executive directors (NEDs) to be independent.[5] According to the Code, 50 per cent or more members of the board should be independent non-executive directors. In the US, SOX required an increase in the numbers of non-executive directors. For example, just as in the UK, all members of the audit committee are required to be independent, the only difference being that UK companies can choose not to comply if they provide an explanation (as outlined above). As in the UK, over the last ten years the number of outside directors on US boards has increased significantly (Krause *et al.*, 2014).

In Germany the two-tier board consists of a supervisory board and management (or executive) board. The supervisory board appoints the management board and decides on directors' remuneration. The management board typically consists of executives from core business functions. Membership of the supervisory board consists of elected representation from both shareholders and employees and is dependent upon the number of employees in the company. If a company has more than 500 (2000) employees, a third (a half) of the supervisory board would be represented by employees. In the UK something similar was considered by the Bullock report in the 1970s. In German multi nationals the supervisory board members are typically German, thus possibly raising questions as to their independence when reviewing the strategic decisions of the executive board. German workers are unlikely to recommend the closure of a German factory.

'Comply or explain' … increased risk?

The UK and Germany both adopt a similar approach to compliance. In the UK companies either comply with the Code provisions or provide an explanation for non-compliance. In Germany the system is slightly different, provisions are split into suggestions and recommendations. A 'comply or explain' approach is expected against the recommendations where companies are legally obliged to follow or provide an explanation. There is no obligation to report compliance with suggestions as these are optional. Provisions which are classified as recommendations are preceded with the word 'shall' whereas suggestions are preceded with 'should'.

The 'comply or explain' system is based on the philosophy that 'one size does not (necessarily) fit all'. The German Corporate Governance Code states (2015, p. 2) that companies are able to 'reflect sector and enterprise specific requirements' in their corporate governance procedures. It goes on to state: 'A well justified deviation from a code recommendation may be in the interest of good corporate governance. Thus, the Code contributes to more flexibility and more self-regulation in the German corporate constitution'. We should not necessarily assume that companies that do not comply with the Code are riskier than those that do. Indeed, it could well be that those who do not comply have thought more about the type of governance that is appropriate to their company and those who claim compliance are simply 'ticking a box'. However, where companies fail to comply and fail to provide an adequate and bespoke explanation, readers of annual reports should be wary. If they are shareholders they should be prepared to evaluate explanations and if necessary raise questions at the Annual General Meeting.

Corporate governance risks

This section of the chapter discusses the links between corporate governance and risk. In particular, we examine specific characteristics of corporate governance (for example CEO duality, independence of non-executive directors and constitution of committees) which we believe may have an impact on business risk.

CEO duality

A key aspect of corporate governance is role duality. If one person is both CEO and Chair this means too much power is vested in one place. Corporate governance concerns itself with providing a 'second pair of eyes', which scrutinise decisions made by others. In so doing, the risk that one person will make the wrong decision or take the wrong action is much reduced. The independence of the Chair provides a balance to the board and also offers a cushion for the possibility of over-ambitious plans of the CEO (Stiles and Taylor, 1993). Monks and Minow (2008, p. 304) state that, 'the board exists to keep management accountable for the vast discretionary power it wields, thus, when the Chairman of the board is also the CEO, it makes management accountable to a board lead by management'.

Despite the discouragement of duality within much of corporate governance writing, some academics and practitioners take a different view. Proponents of duality argue that it could lead to superior firm performance as it permits clear-cut leadership for purposes of strategy formulation and implementation (Baliga *et al.*, 1996; Anderson and Anthony, 1986; Stoeberl and Sherony, 1985). It should not be assumed that separating the two positions *necessarily* lowers company risk. Some writers argue that the circumstances or context may have an impact, particularly in industries such as technology and other such markets which require rapid decision-making (Anderson and Anthony, 1986). It is possible to argue that in those industries operational risk may be lowered when the roles are effectively combined. Indeed, the UK Code allows for this and companies can combine the roles and provide a good explanation for the reasons for so doing while maintaining a high standard of governance. Notably, CEOs who support duality state four key principles which highlight how the separation approach erodes their ability to provide effective leadership (Dahya and Travlos, 2000). Arguments that could be made against role separation include:

- It creates rivalry between the chairperson and the CEO;
- It creates conflict between the management and the board;
- It creates confusion due to the existence of two public corporate spokespersons;
- It curtails innovation.

Anderson and Anthony (1986) contend that '[Chair and CEO] combined provides a single focal point for company leadership. There is never any question about who is boss or who is responsible'. A further benefit of dual structures is the cost saving element of knowledge transfer between the two roles, and, of course there are financial savings in terms of remuneration.

In UK duality caused some concern at Marks and Spencer. Questions were raised about the legitimacy of Sir Stuart Rose to hold the two senior positions in 2008 (Chair and CEO). The institutional investors Schroders complained that appointing Stuart Rose to the combined position was 'appalling' (Hosking and Hawkes, 2008). In the UK it is now comparatively rare for UK companies to have joint CEOs/Chairs, nevertheless some companies still have CEOs who go on to be the Chair, a practice frowned upon by the Code. Although some UK companies do still combine the roles (for example, the UK FTSE 100 company Antofagasta plc) the practice is very much in decline.

In the US it is commonplace for the two positions to be combined and this is not specified by SOX (i.e. it is permitted). In recent times, however, there have been a number of companies in the US who have separated the roles, for example, Apple, who appointed Tim Cook as CEO shortly before Steve Jobs' death, and subsequently appointed Arthur D. Levinson as Chair. In side panel 2 we examine a related case in the US involving the computer giant HP and its previous CEO Carly Fiorina (in early 2016 she was a republican runner for the president but subsequently withdrew).

Side panel 2

Hewlett Packard: a case study of Carly Fiorina's reign

Throughout the 1980s Carly Fiorina rose through the ranks of AT&T and later the spinoff company Lucent, becoming the company's first female executive officer. In 1999 she was appointed CEO of Hewlett Packard (HP) and a year later, Chair. Some have commented that her six-year reign was the worst period in HP's history, while others have defended her leadership style (Gandel, 2015; Mitchell, 2015). In 2002 Fiorina oversaw the largest merger in technology history with HP making a $25 billion purchase of Compaq. Fiorina was the driving force behind a very unpopular merger with 49 per cent of the board opposing the bid. This opposition included the board member Walter Hewlett (son of HP co-founder; William Hewlett), who launched a failed proxy fight to overturn the merger. In 2002, HP Compaq became the world's largest personal computer manufacturer. By 2005, HP had reduced its workforce by 30,000, much to the dismay of the American public and employees of HP

(continued)

Compaq. During that time employees around the world felt disenfranchised with the situation and feared for job security.

Fiorina had a reputation of a glamorous CEO who flew around the world on private company jets with a three-person styling team. She received millions of dollars in salary, share options and other associate financial benefits, while at the same time employees at HP Compaq employees were losing their jobs. As a result Fiorina was widely unpopular with the board and with company staff: during her tenure, staff satisfaction at HP was at an all-time low. In early 2005 HPs, stock lost half its value, with the NASDAQ down 26 per cent as a result of the tech bubble. The board and shareholders asked Fiorina to step down as CEO and Chair.

Interestingly, the short-term view does not tell the whole story. If we think about HP today and the way it operates, much of its profit is based on the manufacturing of hardware. Without the Compaq merger during Fiorina's tenure, HP would not have as strong a hold in today's market. In addition, a few years after the merger HP employed more people than were previously employed by both companies.

The case is interesting in the discussion of role duality because Fiorina had almost total control over the direction of HP, during which time she executed widely unpopular decisions and deals with shareholders and employees—all of which, at the time, seemed damaging to the company. An independent chair may have questioned these decisions and, in turn, reduced the company's exposure to risk. But that argument is not clear-cut once one takes a longer term view. In 2016 we see a different HP, the company is a global giant and the largest producer of computer hardware. It can now (with the benefit of hindsight) be said with some confidence that if the roles of CEO and Chair had been separate, then Fiorina would have been unable to execute business decisions in the way that she did. Arguments for role duality often use the premise that speed of decision-making is key in industries such as technology (which change rapidly). Thus, having one person as both CEO and Chair enables the business to make fast decisive decisions which enable them to remain ahead of competition. So we must consider not just the risks associated with the dual role arrangement but also the potential for opportunity and how these can affect the success of a company. It may well be that for certain types of company, under certain conditions, that the two roles are best combined. On balance, it seems as if separating the two positions controls the risks better (because of the checks and balances that the second pair of eyes provides). But maybe that approach means opportunities (the opposite of risk) will be lost. Thus, this shows how the flexible 'comply or explain' approach can get the *very best* out of corporate governance. Rules are not always ideal. Non-compliance with a strong bespoke explanation is a very desirable approach to governance and is easily equivalent and may be *even better* than compliance.

Questions to consider

1 Typical corporate governance thinking would indicate that the roles of CEO and Chair should be separated. What are the advantages and disadvantages of role duality? What risks might be attached to an individual fulfilling both roles? Are there any risks attached to separating the roles? What about opportunities?
2 To what extent did Carly Fiorina contribute to the success or otherwise of HP today?

In Germany the roles are separated because of the two-tier board structure. Nevertheless, the effectiveness of the two-tier system only works if supervisory boards are well balanced, experienced and diverse. German companies have often been criticised for the construction of supervisory boards. Issues have included members serving on multiple boards; too many workforce representatives thus diluting the shareholders' voice; board membership being generally too big and the number of supervisory board meetings being one of the lowest in Europe. One of our major criticisms of German supervisory boards is that members are simply not sufficiently independent. Workforce representatives may make decisions based solely on their own interests and the multi national nature of some German companies is often not reflected in the composition of their supervisory boards. There are related risks to all these issues. If, for example, members serve on too many boards they are unlikely to be sufficiently focused and may fail to notice issues. Too few meetings can indicate key control issues being overlooked and problem areas not adequately discussed. The fact that multi national German companies supervisory boards are mainly comprised of German nationals may cause boards to focus more on local issues. Lack of independence may affect decisions made by the supervisory board. All these add up to increased risk for the business.

Independence of NEDs

A key aspect of governance for US and UK companies is the independence of non-executives. If NEDs are not sufficiently independent they will lack that critical approach needed to properly carry out their roles. In the UK Northern Rock (the northern building society turned floated bank) non-executives were criticised by the Treasury Committee for their ineffectiveness (Treasury Committee, 2008). In particular they appear to have failed to exercise the necessary judgement to limit the financial risks that the bank faced. They also found it difficult to stand up to the CEO, Adam Applegarth. Some of the similar backgrounds of executives and non-executives may also cause some to question the true independence of NEDs (and perhaps even the independence of the auditors) within Northern Rock at the time. Again, this shows that groupthink or normative behaviour may expose a company to unforeseen risks. These risks only come to light under certain special circumstances (particularly when 'unknown unknowns' occur or come to fruition) so it is difficult to identify them in advance. However, there are often warning signals. It is interesting that Arthur Anderson had been involved in a notable number of auditing scandals well before the problems at Enron came to light (Clikeman, 2013).

In order to ensure that organisational risks are adequately addressed, it is essential that NEDs are truly independent from the company. NEDs need to avoid personal and financial links with the company, have integrity and be willing to question decisions made by the executives if the risk management of the company is to be effective. In a study the authors undertook (Shrives and Devine, 2012) looking at non-compliance in the UK and Germany, they found that independence of NEDs in the UK was ranked number one in terms of non-compliance (for FTSE 100 companies). Despite being a key area for corporate governance, our findings suggest that UK companies are subjecting themselves to organisational risk, which could cause damage to the company. Our findings also show that the German companies' non-compliance areas tend to be less critical to governance and thus, arguably, expose the companies to lower levels of risk. Nevertheless, this is to some extent countered by the fact that non-compliance with governance regulations (sometimes termed soft law) is considerably more extensive in Germany than the UK (see Seidl *et al.*, 2013).

Several British companies are also facing issues when it comes to succession planning on boards of directors. Some companies are failing to adequately plan for the provision in the Code which recommends that NEDs leave the board after serving for a maximum period of nine years. This lack of planning leads to a company being inadequately prepared for the next generation of NEDs, resulting in questionable independent leadership and challenge.

In the US the role of NEDs or outside directors is similar to that in the UK. A well-known case was that of Disney where the non-executives were closely related to the CEO, Michael Eisner. The outside directors (who have been said to fail every corporate governance test) included the principal of the school attended by his children, his lawyer, his architect and the President of Georgetown University, Washington DC, an institution that had received considerable donations from Michael Eisner (Markham, 2015). They were clearly hand-picked and lacked independence. This lack of independence meant that the non-executives were effectively in the 'chair's pocket' with the associated risk that too much power was in one place. Decisions would not necessarily be subject to scrutiny by the NEDs. Ironically, after some disastrous decisions, members of the board were removed by Eisner on the basis that they were 'not independent'. Yet another of the outside directors was retained, despite their spouse earning considerable amounts of income from a Disney-linked project. A particular focus of independent non-executive directors is the part they play in the various subcommittees of the board. In this case that function would not be effective and again would expose the company to increased risk.

Constitution of committees

One of the key things to consider is that the subcommittees are staffed by members of the board and, in the case of Germany, the supervisory board. Thus, if there are issues regarding the independence and training of the board, this will inevitably lead to problems with composition of the various subcommittees. If these committees are inappropriately staffed they are unlikely to be effective.

In our study (Shrives and Devine, 2012), some of the top five ranked non-compliances in Germany include:

- Composition and training of the supervisory board (ranked third)
- Supervisory board members appointment of the management board (ranked equal fifth)
- Setting up the nomination committee correctly (ranked equally fifth).

In the UK they include:

- Constitution of the remuneration committee (ranked second)
- Constitution of audit committee (ranked fourth)
- Constitution of nomination committee (ranked equally fifth).

As is evident from the above, the construction of these committees in both British and German companies is somewhat questionable. These findings would seem to imply that the main committees making key decisions within the company are sometimes inadequately constructed. In terms of risk, a particular cause for concern is the audit committee that deals with the independence of the auditors and in most cases a consideration of business risk. A lack of independence can have 'knock-on' effects regarding the risks these companies face.

In the US a similar committee structure operates, albeit with slightly different names. For example, nominating committee in the US (termed nomination committee in the UK), compensation committee (remuneration committee) and risk committee (audit committee). In addition some companies also have disclosure committees. Under SOX all companies are required, by law, to comply with basic requirements of having three committees. Thus, it could be argued that, in principle, this legal requirement results in higher compliance and arguably less risk.

Discussion

Recent studies of corporate governance consider that non-compliance leads to an increase in risk faced by the company (Baker and Griffith, 2007). Although equal weighting appears to be given to all provisions in governance codes, there are sections thought to be particularly critical to good corporate governance practice (as discussed above). Non-compliance with these areas is likely to lead to increased organisational risk. Where companies fail to give adequate explanations, shareholders should see the need to question companies in these key areas.

In our study (Shrives and Devine, 2012) the majority of the UK items appear to relate to construction of the board and in particular the independence of non-executive directors (as discussed briefly in above). Within German companies listed on the DAX-30, the incidence of non-compliance appears higher in comparison to non-compliance in the UK. However, our study (Shrives and Devine, 2012) found that German companies tend to not comply with relatively minor provisions which do not significantly increase risks within the company. In the UK the reverse is true; the code provisions which are 'breached' refer to fundamental tenets of corporate governance, which could substantially increase risk placed upon the company, in particular to shareholders and other investors.

Given what we know about the US style of rules-based corporate governance, one could argue that the investor who wishes to place money in a market which is less risky in terms of corporate governance compliance has a clear choice to make. A rules-based market offers more confidence that corporate governance principles have been complied with, whereas a principle-based market does not offer this assurance. Those in favour of the 'comply or explain' approach would counter this by arguing that this assurance is indeed offered by markets which operate a principle-based approach (such as the UK and Germany) on the basis that explanation of non-compliance can be equivalent to compliance. In addition, rules-based systems are very expensive to administer, a cost which is ultimately borne by the shareholder. However, the extent to which the 'comply or explain' system offers good governance depends on the quality of the explanation. Shrives and Brennan (2015) find that the quality of UK corporate governance explanations can be poor and thus are unequal to compliance. Even large companies have a tendency to state only what they are not complying with, without providing a full explanation. Many companies provide a general explanation which does not relate to their specific circumstances. Interestingly, in Germany, a preliminary study that we carried out in 2012 finds that there is a relationship between the size (market capitalisation) of companies and the extent to which they employ mimetic isomorphic behaviour with regard to their own compliance statements. In simple terms, the smaller the company, the more likely they are to copy compliance statements from previous versions of their own annual report (Devine and Shrives, 2012). This is an important consideration in the discussion of risk, because those arguing that the explanation is equal to compliance are doing so on the basis that faith is placed in companies to re-visit their areas of non-compliance on an annual basis. While a copied explanation might be appropriate if the reason for non-compliance still applies, it may suggest that companies are cutting and pasting in the same way as other research has shown companies cut and paste their risk statements (see the discussion in Abraham and Shrives, 2014). Thus a key question needs to be considered: are the key areas of governance risk being addressed in an adequate way? Again, this is something that a properly constituted audit committee should be considering. In some ways the audit committee is the most crucial of the board subcommittees. Even then the UK's Code only requires one person to have recent and relevant financial experience and in the fairly recent past FTSE 350 companies have been found wanting with this (this also applies in SOX, although in the US it is a requirement and cannot be 'explained').

We believe that neither a rules-based system nor a 'comply or explain' principles-based system is ideal. The debate around hard and soft regulation has always been present, not just in this context but also others such as within financial reporting.

Concluding comments

Each approach to governance has its deficiencies. Accounting and governance scandals seem to continue to be unstoppable even in seemingly well constituted companies. Often issues are related to finance and the financial stability of businesses. Linking directors' pay to performance was originally thought to align pay with share price performance and hence shareholders' returns. But the setting of such targets (or KPIs—key performance indicators) can give rise to other unintended consequences. Managers may be (inevitably perhaps) tempted to manipulate accounting numbers especially where their own remuneration is concerned. Over the years, typically accounting issues have arisen concerning over-optimistic revenue recognition, under-recording of expenses and incorrect treatment of assets and liabilities.

Corporate governance issues are not purely restricted to financial misdemeanours. The recent case of the emissions scandal concerning Volkswagen (discussed in Adams, 2015) emphasises this. Similar other unresolved examples in the car industry such as Toyota (unintended acceleration) and General Motors (the ignition switch controversy) also raise pertinent questions. Did their board (or boards in the case of Volkswagen) know? Were these risks adequately discussed? If the board members didn't know, exactly why was that, when these incidents can cause catastrophic damage to company reputation, customers and critically, in the case of Volkswagen, the environment. One thing is clear, boards have to take their responsibilities very seriously and it is entirely reasonable, for instance, for Volkswagen customers to raise questions about the validity or otherwise of the boards, their make-up and their abilities (see Adams, 2015).

Regulation such as SOX in the US has proved to be very expensive and ultimately can even 'price' companies out of their markets. The risk that regulation can have undesirable consequences is a very real one. Even the regulators themselves admit that perhaps regulation has gone too far and has become too expensive. Nevertheless, it would be wrong to think that a totally flexible approach is necessarily the complete solution. In the UK and Germany, as in many other countries (such as Sweden, the Netherlands or Denmark), there is no official follow-up or checks carried out on voluntary compliance, except perhaps by academics or other corporate governance researchers (Galander *et al.*, 2015). If there is no follow-up then to what extent can we rely on corporate governance in non-compliant or even compliant companies? The authors of this chapter maintain that non-compliance is quite acceptable (and can be equivalent to compliance) but this has to be matched with adequate and bespoke explanations. Research by Shrives and Brennan in 2015 showed that explanations are often incomplete, lack specificity and sometimes only amount to an 'assertion of difference' with no real explanation at all. The so-called 'slippery slope' begins when companies fail to provide adequate explanations and take advantage of, or abuse, the flexibility that the Code offers. Directors' behaviour at one company can often imitate that at another in line with institutional theory. In the UK some FTSE companies are, perhaps surprisingly, still not complying with basics such as proper constitution of boards and committees and this, in turn, exposes companies to considerable risk. A key aspect is the appointment of directors, and boards need to step up their succession planning.

To move forward on corporate governance different stakeholders must *all* play their part. Auditors must continue to take responsibilities seriously, challenge directors rigorously and, where necessary, qualify audit reports and be willing to consider resignation. Non-executives must be appropriately independent and skilled (sometimes in technical areas) and be willing to challenge and question executives. Non-executives and auditors who lack independence are rather like lifeguards who cannot swim (Clikeman, 2013). Shareholders must be willing to speak up at AGMs and recent evidence has shown that shareholder activism is certainly on the increase in a number of countries. Finally, regulators—even under a 'comply or explain' system—need to be willing to step in. They cannot just rely on shareholders who typically are mainly interested in returns. Other stakeholders need to be considered. Corporate governance can help reduce risk for all stakeholders but each stakeholder must play their part.

Notes

1 Sir Adrian Cadbury, a former British Olympic rower, passed away in September 2015, aged 86, after a long and distinguished career. He was Chair of Cadbury from 1965 and retired in 1989. Cadbury was purchased by Kraft Foods in 2010; subsequently the confectionery/snack business was spun off into Mondēlez International.

2 Also at that time there was a scandal at Volkswagen over payments to executives and in 2009 an issue concerning a member of the supervisory board at Škoda (a Volkswagen Audi Group subsidiary). Other German companies (allegedly BMW, Mercedes, Commerzbank and Siemens just to name a few) have all been affected by employees accepting questionable payments in return for business favours. Recent events at Volkswagen (2015) are discussed later on in the chapter but questions are being constantly being raised about their governance and in particular the supervisory board. Over the years VW scandals have concerned prostitution, questionable payments and now (2015–2016) environmental issues where around 11million cars (584,000 in the US alone) at VW and Audi (possibly Porsche and Skoda too) were fitted with an emissions 'cheat device'. This recent event is said to have reduced the value of the company by billions of Euros. Under the US Clean Air Act (originally enacted in 1963) the company could be fined up to $37,500 per vehicle and there is the possibility of having to buy back affected cars.

3 As is emphasised throughout this chapter an explanation is not something to be thought of as a defect. Non-compliance and a bespoke explanation can be *fully* equivalent to compliance. This is because providing an explanation can still show that a company is complying with the overarching principles, even though there may be non-compliance with an individual provision. Companies should not be forced into an act of compliance because an essence of corporate governance is that 'one size does not (necessarily) fit all'. Companies which do not provide bespoke explanations or misstate their compliance are affecting the viability of the 'comply or explain' system. In the UK, the Financial Reporting Council (FRC) believes it is for shareholders to evaluate these explanations, but shareholders are often much more concerned about financial performance so the authors do not wholly accept this view. Other stakeholders including regulators and auditors need to be willing to question company directors and audit committees, particularly where the explanation is woefully inadequate or, perhaps worse, compliance is wrongly stated.

4 In truth, companies are often looking for both of these characteristics in non-executives. However, these can conflict. A non-executive director who knows the industry will be useful but if he or she has worked closely with the executive directors before (or for a long period of time) may fail to be (or cease to be) independent. Similarly, a non-executive director who is independent but lacks the industry knowledge is unlikely to be effective. Recent scandals (for example in the UK Northern

Rock Bank) have emphasised the importance of directors having appropriate knowledge and skills in addition to other characteristics such as integrity and confidence.

5 Non-executives who are not independent can still be appointed but are referred to as 'grey directors'.

References

Abraham, S. and P.J. Shrives (2014), 'Improving the Relevance of Risk Factor Disclosure in Corporate Annual Reports', *The British Accounting Review.* [Online]. 46(1), pp. 91–107. Available from: http://www.sciencedirect.com/science/article/pii/S0890838913000838 [Accessed: 01/03/16].

Abrahamson, E. and L. Rosenkopf (1990), When Does Bandwagon Diffusion Roll? How Far Do They Go? And When Do They Roll Backwards: A Computer Simulation', *Academy of Management proceedings.* [Online]. 1990(1), pp. 155–159. Available from: http://proceedings.aom.org/content/1990/1/155.short [Accessed: 10/08/2015].

Abrahamson, E. and L. Rosenkopf (1993), 'Institutional and Competitive Bandwagons: Using Mathematical Modelling as a Tool to Explore Innovation Diffusion', *Academy of Management Review.* [Online]. 18(3), pp. 487–517. Available from: http://amr.aom.org/content/18/3/487.short [Accessed: 10/08/2015].

Adams, C. (2015), 'Ethics Versus Profit', *Economia.* [Online]. 44, pp. 64–65. Available from: http://economia.icaew.com/business/december-2015/ethics-versus-profit [Accessed: 01/03/16].

Anderson, C.A. and R.N. Anthony (1986), *The New Corporate Directors: Insights for Board Members and Executives.* New York: Wiley.

Ang, J.S., R.A. Cole and J.W. Lin (2000), 'Agency Costs and Ownership Structure', *The Journal of Finance.* [Online] 55(1), pp. 81–106. Available from: http://onlinelibrary.wiley.com/doi/10.1111/0022-1082.00201/abstract [Accessed 10/08/2015].

Attwood, K. (2008), 'Investors Attack M&S Plan to Make Rose Chairman', *Independent.* [online] Available at: http://www.independent.co.uk/news/business/news/investors-attack-ms-plan-to-make-rose-chairman-794061.html [Accessed 02/03/2016].

Baker, T. and S.J. Griffith (2007), 'Predicting Corporate Governance Risk: Evidence from the Directors' and Officers' Liability Insurance Market', *Chicago Law Review.* [Online]. 74, p. 487. Available from: http://heinonline.org/HOL/PrintRequest?collection=journals&handle=hein.journals/uclr74&div=26&id=497&print=section&format=PDFsearchable&submit=Print%2FDownload [Accessed: 02/03/16].

Baliga, R.B., R.C. Moyer and R.S. Rao (1996), 'CEO Duality and Firm Performance: What's the Fuss?' *Strategic Management Journal.* [Online]. 17(1), pp. 41–53. Available from: http://www.jstor.org/stable/pdf/2486936.pdf?seq=1#page_scan_tab_contents [Accessed: 25/02/16].

Berle, A. and G. Means (1932), *The Modern Corporation and Private Property.* New York: Macmillan.

Brown, G.M. (2005), 'Changing Models in Corporate Governance: Implications of the US Sarbanes-Oxley Act', in K.J. Hopt, E. Wymeersch, E.H. Kanda and E.H. Baum (eds.), *Corporate Governance in Context.* Oxford: Oxford University Press. pp. 143–162.

Burgess, K., E. Rigby and T. Braithwaite (2008), 'Investor Fury at M&S Role for Rose', *Financial Times.* [Online]. Available at: http://www.ft.com/cms/s/5fe56f18-ef0b-11dc-97ec-0000779fd2ac,Authorised=false.html?siteedition=uk&_i_location=http%3A%2F%2Fwww.ft.com%2Fcms%2Fs%2F0%2F5fe56f18-ef0b-11dc-97ec-0000779fd2ac.html%3Fsiteedition%3Duk&_i_referer=&classification=conditional_standard&iab=barrier-app#axzz416WAVBwk [Accessed 02/03/2016].

Cadbury, A. (1992), *The Financial Aspects of Corporate Governance: A Report of the Committee on Corporate Governance.* London: Gee and Co.

Cadbury, A. (2002), *Corporate Governance and Chairmanship: A Personal View.* Oxford: Oxford University Press.

Clarke, T. (2007), *International Corporate Governance: A Comparative Approach.* London: Routledge.

Clikeman, P. (2013), *Called to Account, 2/E.* New York: Routledge.

Collins, R. (1979), *The Credential Society.* New York: Academic Press.

Dahya, J. and N. Travlos (2000), 'Does the One Man Show Pay? Theory and Evidence on the Dual CEO Revised', *European Financial Management.* [Online]. 6(1), pp. 85–98. Available from: http://onlinelibrary.wiley.com/doi/10.1111/1468-036X.00113/epdf [Accessed: 25/02/16].

Devine, A. and P. Shrives (2012), 'Comply or Copy: The Extent of Mimetic Isomorphism in German Corporate Governance Compliance Statements'. *European Accounting Association 35th Annual Congress.* Ljubljana, Slovenia, May 2012.

DiMaggio, P. and W. Powell (1983), 'The Iron Cage Revisited: Institutional Isomorphism and Collective Rationality in Organizational Fields', *American Sociological Review*, 48(2), pp. 147–160.

Fama, E.F. and M.C. Jensen (1983), 'Separation of Ownership and Control', *Journal of Law and Economics*. [Online]. 26(2), pp. 301–325. Available from: http://www.jstor.org/stable/725104?seq=1#page_scan_tab_contents [Accessed: 10/08/2015].

FRC. (2014), *The UK Corporate Governance Code*. [Online]. Available from: http://www.ecgi.org/codes/documents/uk_cgcode_sept2014_en.pdf [Accessed: 23/02/16].

Galander, A., P. Walgenbach and K. Rost (2015), 'A Social Norm Perspective on Corporate Governance Soft Law', *Corporate Governance: The International Journal of Business in Society*, 15(1), pp. 31–51.

Gandel, S. (2015), 'Fact Check: Carly Fiorina Didn't Have a Great Run as CEO of Hewlett Packard', *Fortune Magazine*. [Online.] Available from: http://fortune.com/2015/09/17/carly-fiorina-business-record/ [Accessed: 29/10/15].

Garrett, B. (2010), *The Fish Rots from the Head: Developing Effective Board Directors*. London: Profile Books Ltd.

German Corporate Governance Code (2015) (THE) Commission Regierungskommission Deutscher Corporate Governance Kodex [Online]. Available from: http://www.ecgi.org/codes/documents/cg_code_germany_5may2015_en.pdf. [Accessed: 23/02/16].

Hosking, P. and S. Hawkes (2008), Schroders Say Marks and Spencer Move to Promote Sir Stuart Rose is Appalling. *The Times*. 29 March. [Online]. Available from: http://www.thetimes.co.uk/tto/business/industries/retailing/article2186059.ece [Accessed: 24/02/16].

Jensen, M. and Meckling, W. (1976), Theory of the Firm: Managerial Behaviour, Agency Costs and Ownership Structure. *Journal of Financial Economics*. [Online]. 3(4), pp. 305–360. Available from: http://www.sciencedirect.com/science/article/pii/0304405X7690026X3 [Accessed: 10/08/2015].

Krause, R., M. Semadeni and A.A. Cannella (2014), 'CEO Duality: A Review and Research Agenda', *Journal of Management*. [Online]. 40(1), pp. 256–286. Available from: http://jom.sagepub.com/content/40/1/256.full.pdf+html [Accessed: 25/02/16].

Larson, M.S. (1977), *The Rise of Professionalism: A Sociological Analysis*. Berkeley: University California Press.

Markham, J.W. (2015), *A Financial History of Modern U.S. Corporate Scandals: From Enron to Reform*. London: Routledge.

Mitchell, D. (2015), Here's Why Carly Fiorina is Such a Controversial Figure. *Time Magazine*. [Online]. Available from: http://time.com/3845767/carly-fiorina-hp/ [Accessed: 29/10/15].

Monks, R.A. and M. Minow (2008), *Corporate Governance*. 4th ed. Oxford: Blackwell.

Schulze, W.S., M.H. Lubatkin and R.N. Dino (2002), 'Altruism Agency and Competitiveness in Family Firms', *Managerial and Decision Economics*. [Online]. 23(4–5), pp. 247–259. Available from: http://onlinelibrary.wiley.com/doi/10.1002/mde.1064/abstract [Accessed: 10/08/2105].

Seidl, D., P. Sanderson and J. Roberts (2013), Applying the 'Comply or Explain' Principle: Discursive Legitimacy Tactics with Regard to Codes of Corporate Governance,' *Journal of Management and Governance*. [Online]. 17(3), pp. 791–826. Available from: http://link.springer.com/article/10.1007/s10997-011-9209-y [Accessed 07/09/14].

Shrives, P.J. (2010), *Disclosure in Disarray: Assessing Corporate Governance Explanations of Non-compliance*. Thesis submitted in partial fulfilment of requirements for degree of Doctor of Philosophy. Dublin: University College Dublin.

Shrives, P.J. and N.M. Brennan (2015), 'A Typology for Exploring the Quality of Explanations for Non-Compliance with UK Corporate Governance Regulations', *The British Accounting Review*. [Online]. 47(1), pp. 85–99. Available from: http://www.sciencedirect.com/science/article/pii/S0890838914000584 [Accessed: 23/02/16].

Shrives, P.J. and A. Devine (2012), To What Extent is Non-Compliance with Corporate Governance Codes an Operational Risk? *5th Annual European Risk Research Network Conference*. Luxembourg, September 2012.

Shrives, P.J. and C.J. Welch (1997), 'Another Day, Another Dollar: The Remuneration of Directors', *Management Accounting*, 7(6), pp. 42–48.

Siebels, J.-F. and D. zu Knyphausen-Aufseß (2011), 'A Review of Theory in Family Business Research: The Implications for Corporate Governance', *International Journal of Management Reviews*. [Online]. 14(3), pp. 208–304. Available from: http://onlinelibrary.wiley.com/doi/10.1111/j.1468-2370.2011.00317.x/abstract?userIsAuthenticated=false&deniedAccessCustomisedMessage= [Accessed: 10/08/2015].

Stearns, L.B. and M.S. Mizruchi. (1993), 'Board Composition and Corporate Financing: The Impact of Financial Institution Representation on Borrowing', *Academy of Management Journal.* [Online]. 36(3), pp. 603–618. Available from: http://amj.aom.org/content/36/3/603.short [Accessed: 10/08/2015].
Stiles, P. and B. Taylor. (1993), 'Maxwell: The Failure of Corporate Governance', *Corporate Governance: An International Review.* [Online]. 1(1), pp. 34–45. Available from: http://onlinelibrary.wiley.com/doi/10.1111/j.1467-8683.1993.tb00008.x/abstract;jsessionid=607A43AFA97DD81DD73E51464009AAE8.f03t02 [Accessed: 12/09/2015].
Stoeberl, P. A. and B.C. Sherony (1985), 'Board Efficiency and Effectiveness', in E. Mattar and M. Balls (eds.), *Handbook for Corporate Directors.* New York: McGraw-Hill, pp. 12.1–12.10.
Treasury Committee (2008), The Run on the Rock. *House of Commons Treasury Committee.* Volume 1. London: The Stationery Office.

Part II
Financial reporting and risk

5

Financial reporting risks in relation to financial instruments

Chu Yeong Lim and See Liang Foo

Introduction

Financial reporting is increasingly challenging in today's complex business environment. In recent years, the promulgations of new and enhanced financial reporting standards pose further pressure to an already demanding financial reporting regime.

Of specific interest is financial reporting in relation to financial instruments. A financial instrument is any contract that gives rise to a financial asset of one entity, and a financial liability or equity instrument of another entity. A contract is a legally binding agreement between two parties which accrues rights over assets to one party, and corresponding obligations over liabilities on the other party.

Financial instruments aim to reduce business risks faced by a corporation. They are used in a number of ways for hedging, trading and investment purpose. The cumulative fair value gains and losses of financial instruments are booked as financial assets and financial liabilities respectively. Some examples of financial assets include cash, a contractual right to receive cash or another financial asset from another entity, a contractual right to exchange financial assets or financial liabilities with another entity under conditions that are potentially favourable to the entity, and an equity instrument of another entity. Financial liabilities include borrowings with an obligation to deliver cash or another financial asset to another entity and an exchange of financial assets or financial liabilities with another entity under conditions that are potentially unfavourable to the entity. Examples of financial instruments are foreign exchange (FX) spot trades and foreign exchange (FX) forward trades. The financial instruments are recorded as financial assets and financial liabilities on the balance sheet.

Financial instruments are significant components in the financial statements. IFRS 9, the financial reporting standard on financial instruments, is a lengthy document. Although recently revised[1] and much improved, its principles and guidelines are relatively complex in practice. The nature of financial instruments is varied, ranging from the basic (e.g. cash) to the complex (e.g. derivative instruments). Assumptions are to be articulated and judgements must be exercised, more pertinently, in relation to recognition, classification and measurement of financial instruments. In fact, complex financial instruments may increase business risks, for example, where the methodology, assumptions and data used in the valuation model are not relevant or reliable. Consequently, from a financial reporting perspective, the risk of material misstatement in financial statement increases.

Financial statements are an integral part of a company's financial reporting. The objective is to provide financial information about the reporting entity that is useful to existing and potential investors, lenders and other creditors in making decisions. To be useful, financial information must be relevant and depict faithful representation of the economic phenomena, complete, neutral and free from error (IASB, 2015). In other words, financial statements must be free of material misstatement.

But what gives rise to the risk of material misstatement? How should the risks be managed? The objectives of this chapter are to examine these two questions in relation to financial instruments. In view of the wide scope of the subject matter, it focuses on the pertinent accounting issues, namely, recognition, classification and measurement concerns in the statement of profit or loss and the statement of financial position. To provide the appropriate context, this chapter commences with a discussion of the financial reporting eco-system by understanding the accounting process and the key stakeholders involved in financial reporting. Next, it provides a brief overview of IFRS 9, followed by the risks of material misstatements in financial assets and liabilities. Whilst there are many existing internal controls frameworks (e.g. COSO, Turnbull, etc.) being adopted by companies, this chapter focuses on those internal control measures over the recognition, classification and measurement concerns. Besides effective design, internal controls must be operationally effective for the financial statements to be relevant and reliable. The chapter ends with the challenges in sustaining effective internal controls and the limitations of this chapter.

Financial reporting eco-systems

Financial reporting supply chain

Each year, companies are required to present audited financial statements, subject to the relevant audit exemption threshold, to their shareholders and lodge them with the relevant regulatory agencies. The preparation of the financial statements or the accounting process comprises a set of activities in converting information about transactions into financial statements (see Figure 5.1). More importantly, an inherent part of the accounting process includes the establishment of a sound internal control framework over financial reporting as a regulatory imperative (e.g. Sarbanes-Oxley, etc.).

Whilst the preparation of financial statements may appear to be the domain of the companies, in particular, the preparers and management, in reality, the financial reporting supply chain involves a complex web of key stakeholders to enhance the quality of financial reporting (see Figure 5.2). These include the governing bodies (e.g. board of directors and audit committee, where appropriate), financial reporting standard setters, external auditors, regulators (e.g. listed companies and external audit regulators), analysts and investors.

The International Federation of Accountants (IFAC) advocates the notion of a financial reporting supply chain to embrace a 'more holistic view of financial reporting' (Choudhury, 2014). In other words, every key player has a part and should be involved in the improvement of financial reporting quality. The strength of the supply chain can be compromised by the weakest link (player).

Brief overview of IFRS 9

The classification of debt instruments into amortized cost and fair value depends on the business model and contractual cash flow characteristics of the financial instruments. The business

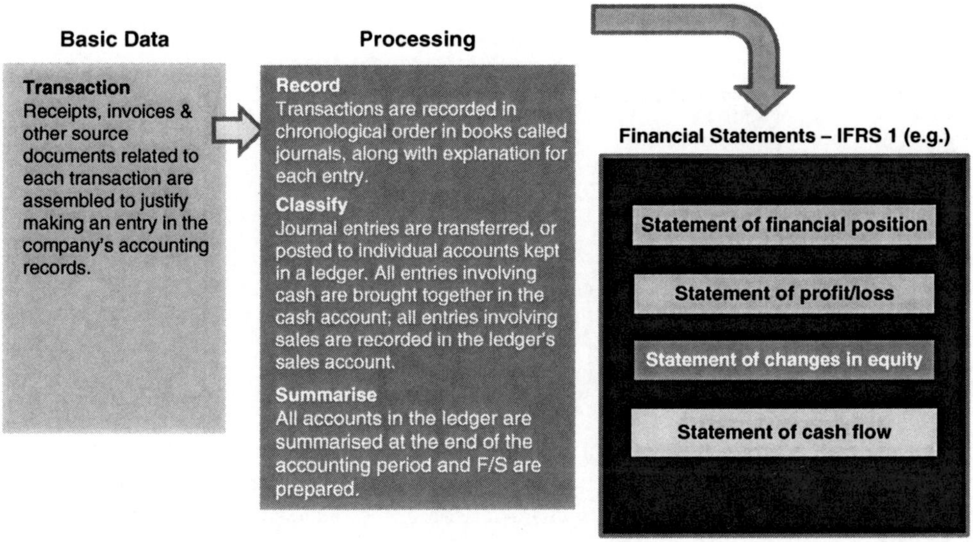

Figure 5.1 The accounting process.

Source: Adapted from Chapter 15, Understanding Accounting and Financial Statements. Retrieved from http://bus.msjc.edu/Portals/22/Caren/student%20ppt%2015ed/ch15ST15.pdf

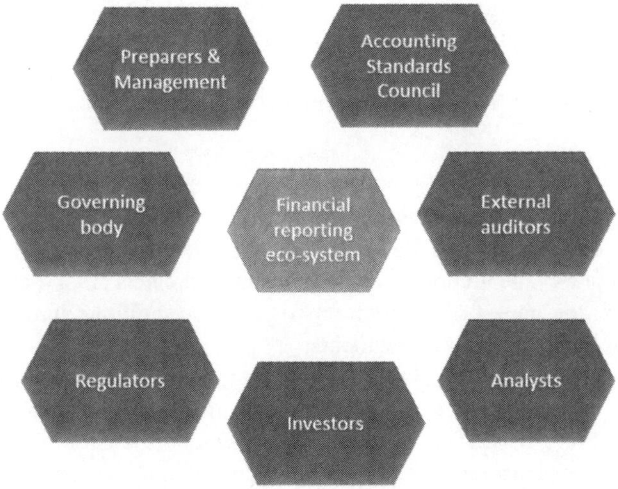

Figure 5.2 Components of the financial reporting supply chain.

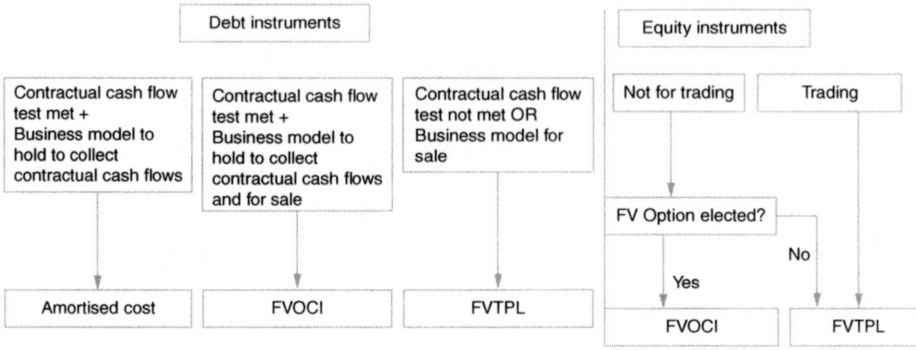

Figure 5.3 Overview of amended "IFRS 9" classification model for financial instruments.

models are 'held to collect contractual cash flows', 'held for sale' or 'held both to collect contractual cash flows and for sale'. The business model is determined at the business unit or legal entity level. The contractual cash flow characteristic of the financial instrument is satisfied if the cash flows are payments for time value of money and credit risks.

If the financial instrument does not satisfy the contractual cash flow characteristics the financial instrument is fair valued. If the financial instrument is held to collect contractual cash flows and the business model is to hold to collect contractual cash flows and for sale, the financial instrument is accounted for at fair value with fair value changes recognized in other comprehensive income (FVOCI). If the financial instrument is held to collect contractual cash flows and the business model is to hold to collect contractual cash flows only, the financial instrument is accounted for at amortized cost

Equity instruments that are not held for trading may be classified under FVOCI without recycling if elected by the entity or FVTPL if FVOCI is not elected. Equity instruments held for trading are classified at FVTPL.

Figure 5.3 provides an overview of the IFRS 9 classification model on financial instruments.

Accounting process for financial instruments

Figure 5.4, below, provides a diagrammatic representation of the key actors in the accounting process for the simplest trading environments in the banking sector, with arrows showing the possible permutations of interactions. The number of communication channels among the actors increases exponentially when the bank organization is structured in multiple dimensions: customer, functional, geographical and product segments.

The front office traders are typically grouped by desks according to the products, geography and customer segments they manage. The traders report to a desk head/trader manager, who in turn reports to an overall treasury head. The treasury heads may be responsible for a geographical region, product segment or customer segment. The organization of (or 'roll-up' in) the performance reporting process depends on the bank's strategic focus. A group of traders may face and provide treasury services to clients. Another group may trade on the bank's own account while yet another may create products to manage the risks of the banks.

The control functions interacting with the traders in the middle office and back office include operational/settlement staff, business controllers and accountants. The internal monitoring function includes compliance officers, internal auditors and risk managers. The accountants are traditionally grouped on the basis of the functions and the business groups they support (e.g. product control, business unit control group, middle office and corporate

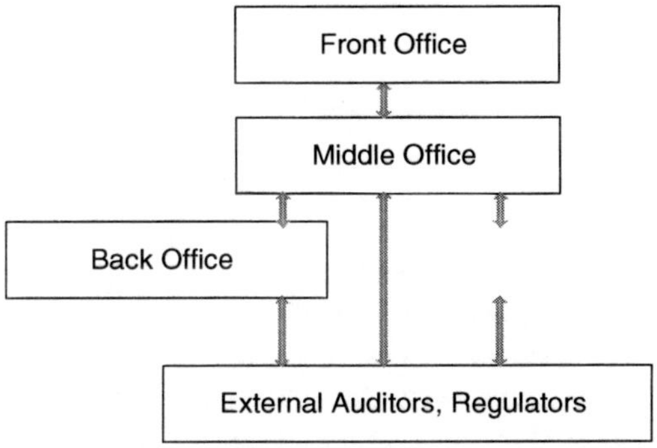

Figure 5.4 Communication flows among key players in a financial reporting environment.

reporting). This type of 'roll-up' is based on geography and business groupings—for example, there will be accountants in business unit control groups undertaking financial and management reporting in corporate banking and retail banking groups respectively. Controls external to the organization include bank regulators/ supervisors, external auditors and accounting and auditing standard setters.

The business process and information technology (IT) system infrastructure within the organization are areas of potential financial reporting risks. The accountants and auditors need to understand how the systems generate the financial numbers, how the accounting entries are generated under what events and conditions for each transaction.

The information systems cater to different products, geographical locations, functions, customer groups:

1 In terms of products: current account system (local currency and foreign currency), deposit system (retail and corporate, local currency and foreign currency), housing loan system, other retail loan systems (personal overdraft, car loans, renovation loans, student loans), credit card system, corporate loan system, and treasury systems (foreign exchange, equity, bonds, commodities, derivatives);
2 In terms of locations: global, regional (e.g. Asia Pacific, EMEA—Europe plus Middle East, US), local/country (largely to meet country-specific regulatory requirements); the booking of trades in different locations is for tax reasons and business decision-making purposes as the market liquidity/accessibility differs in different locations;
3 In terms of functions: front office (e.g. trader input), operations/settlements, risk management, valuation, accounting—product control, middle office, financial reporting groups; management information systems (MIS) versus general ledger (GL);
4 In terms of customer groups: private banking clients, corporate clients (split into government agencies, government-linked companies, multi national companies, local large corporate firms, small and medium sized enterprises), priority customers, mass market retail customers.

Trade processing systems consist of trade capture and static data maintenance by the reference data team, back office and operations teams.

Figure 5.5 shows the functions responsible for each stage of the deal flow from front office to operations, risk management, middle office and product control. Dealers first input the deals into the treasury front office system. The financial reporting risks include:

- Completeness whether dealers input their deals into the system,
- Timeliness of deal input,

- Accuracy of deal details input by traders, (deal details inputted include deal date, settlement date, nominal amount, contracted rate),
- Valuation of deals using external market prices or internal models.

The middle office and back office are responsible for deal confirmation, custodian operations, processing and settlements. The product controllers and accountants carry out price verification and valuation, financial accounting in general ledger (GL) and regulatory reporting. The GL structure and the accounting in GL are briefly described next (see also Figure 5.5).

There are risks in the financial reporting processes from the treasury systems to the GL. The unrealized foreign exchange (FX) P/L and fair value asset/liability account balances on the GL come from the fair valuation accounting entries posted by the treasury systems. The accuracy of the unrealized FX P/L entries to the correct accounts, on the correct posting date and for the correct amounts, depend on the deal input accuracy and the correct setup of accounting in the treasury system. Measurement accuracy also depends on the valuation method in the treasury system and accuracy of rate input for valuation purposes.

When cash has been settled, the foreign currency cash positions are valued by the GL. The GL contains all foreign currency cash positions of the bank generated from all the sub-systems (plus the manual postings to GL). Measurement accuracy depends on the contract rate input and the rate used to translate the foreign currency to functional currency.

The front office systems feed data to the accounting system to generate entries to GL in a straight-through processing (ERP) approach. Accounting entries are event-driven. For example, trade date of foreign-exchange spot trades triggers balance sheet entries, settlement date triggers cash entries, and revaluation date triggers fair value accounting entries. The internal accounts within the accounting module are translated and mapped to the accounts in the GL system. The classification and measurement accuracy of the transactions depends on the correct mapping of treasury system accounts to the GL. The GL is built to meet head office financial reporting requirements. The GL is further translated by Finance to meet local regulatory reporting requirements.

Each account is posted primarily from a single sub-system to avoid duplication of entries and confusion. Sub-ledger is set up for each business, legal entity/branch and currency.

The trial balance for each currency should reconcile (i.e. debits should equal credits). The revaluation of the foreign currency balances to functional currency will result in foreign exchange gain/loss.

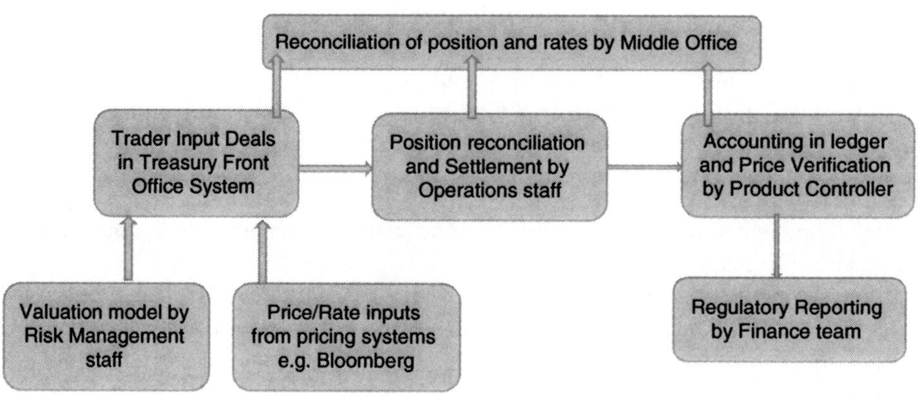

Figure 5.5 Treasury deal flow from front office system to general ledger system.

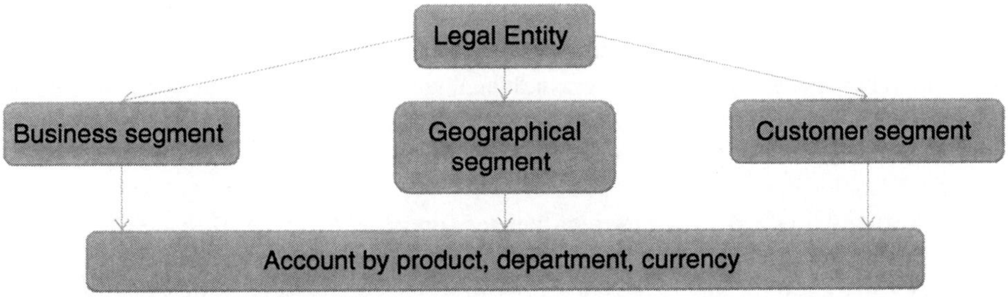

Figure 5.6 GL Tree structure.

The general ledger is set up by business entity, company/subsidiary/branch in a tree structure, described in Figure 5.6. Management information is at the business segment level. The accounting system usually adopts a multi-dimensional concept: business/customer segment/ legal entity. One GL account may 'belong' to a few business segments, for example, FX realised P/L account and unrealised P/L may be attributed to the treasury business which manages the FX risk. Business units and legal entities are different fields. A bank may decide to use different functional currencies for different legal entities. This creates very complex FX translation issues. For example, a USD position in legal entity X that uses SGD functional currency will show a USD/SGD FX profit/loss while the same position in legal entity Y that uses USD functional currency will not show any FX translation profit/loss.

The operations team maintains the static data on the counterparties. Examples of static data maintained include counterparty name, bank type (commercial bank, investment bank, etc.), country of residence and country of incorporation. The reference data setup in systems is done by the trade support and control or reference data team. Examples of static data requirements are as follows:

- Books/departments: mnemonic code, name of book, profit centre, entity, desk, GL (General Ledger) code, country/market,
- Instrument: FX forward/spot/swap, loans, deposits, MM/FI securities, issuance/contract code,
- Account of counterparty: name, type of account, owner of account,
- SSI: Account number, account name, bank identifier, beneficiary,
- Nostro/deposit account: name of agent bank, currency/security, external account number, associated sub-branches, interest charge, data account opened,
- Holiday calendars: date, name of holiday,
- Currency: currency code, decimal point, quotation (direct/indirect).

Any errors in static data maintenance such as the holiday calendars create financial reporting errors.

The currency should be a separate field tagged to the GL accounts. A new GL account is set up with multiple currencies and business units. An example is 'unrealized P/L – FX' account. When it is set up the account should cater for FX trading by different business units and across different currencies. This methodology avoids the use of different GL account numbers for similar accounts in different currencies.

The GL balance sheet account balances are reconciled against the sub-system balances. For example, the FX deals in sub-systems are reconciled against the GL accounts on unrealized P/L; cash accounts in GL are reconciled by settlement/nostro reconciliation team against the physical nostro accounts. The reconciliation is further segregated by currencies, business units and types of deposits. The GL control accounts are reconciled against the sub-ledgers. For example, the business segment numbers and legal entity numbers should be reconciled in total. Banks try to minimize system interfaces using a global GL that caters to both financial reporting and management information system (MIS) reporting requirements. This enhances data integrity/completeness.

If the same product is traded by different business units which own different systems, the different systems may generate fair value differences, for example, FX trades done between Sydney money market desk and Singapore Treasury offices and both offices use different systems to book/value the trade. There should be common rates used to value the FX trades booked in Singapore and Sydney offices.

The interest accrual calculation methodology in bank accounting information systems need to consider the following points:

- Accrual frequency: daily, revaluation dates set within system;
- Non-working day booking: Accrual amount to either include or exclude the next non-working days (e.g. on Friday, whether to include accrual for Saturday and Sunday);
- End of month non-working day: Where last date of month is not a working day, to determine if the non-working days should be included in the accrual calculations.

The above setting on organizational structure and accounting information systems and processes set the context to examine the risk of misstatements of financial instruments in the next section.

Risk of material misstatements in financial instruments

This section looks from the preparer perspective at the types of risks in financial reporting, and where they occurred. Financial instruments include forwards, swaps and options, including some complex structures such as mortgage-backed securities, asset-backed securities with Lehman case and structured products.

To be useful, financial statements must be fairly presented to show a true and fair view. For the statement of financial position, this means that all account balances (e.g. assets, liabilities and equity) satisfy the assertions of existence, completeness, valuation and rights/obligations as at the financial year-end. The pertinent assertions related to the transactions in statement of profit or loss are occurrence, accuracy, classification, completeness and cut-off.

A failure to abide with any one of these assertions can lead to misstatement(s) in the financial statements. A misstatement arises where there is a difference between the reported figures, and what is expected to be reported, in order for the financial statements to be fairly presented to show a true and fair view. Misstatements can be factual, in the case of a clear breach of a requirement of a financial reporting standard, or could be judgemental, arising from unsuitable estimation techniques or the selection of inappropriate accounting policies (ACCA, 2016). Information is materially misstated if omitting it or misstating it could influence decisions that users make on the basis of an entity's financial statements. The risk of material misstatement of financial statements can be due to error or fraud. Hence, proper internal controls should be put in place to minimize these exposures.

The high volume of transactions in financial instruments and their complexity make the preparation of financial statements challenging. The financial assertions of 'completeness and accuracy are essential if the accounting records are to provide an appropriate basis for the preparation of the financial statements' (Auditing Practices Board, 2009). As financial instruments are either accounted for at amortized costs or fair value, proper classification is an essential consideration under IFRS 9. Owing to the nature of financial instruments, their valuation in the financial statements, and the computing and treatment of profit or loss in the statement of profit or loss, require considerable effort and judgement. The potential risk of material misstatement in the statement of profit or loss (see Table 5.1) and statement of financial position (see Table 5.2) are listed below.

Table 5.1 Statement of profit or loss: transaction-level assertions and the risks of material misstatement in financial instruments

Assertion(a)	*What it means(b)*	*Risk of misstatement(b)*
Occurrence	The financial transactions occurred (or actually took place) giving the company a contractual right (or obligation) over the financial asset (or financial liability).	Financial transactions recorded in the absence of binding contracts.
Completeness	All financial transactions with binding contracts recorded.	Financial transactions with binding contracts are omitted or not recorded.
Classification	All transactions have been recorded within the correct accounts in the general ledger.	Financial transactions with binding contracts are erroneously classified under amortized costs (or fair values).
Accuracy	The full amounts of all transactions were recorded, without error.	The amounts of the financial transactions with binding contracts are erroneously recorded.
Cutoff	All transactions were recorded in the correct accounting period.	Financial transactions with binding contracts are recorded in the wrong accounting period.

Sources: (a) International Federation of Accountants (2012); (b) Adapted International Federation of Accountants (2012).

Table 5.2 Statement of Financial Position: account balance assertions and the risks of material misstatement in financial instruments

Assertion(a)	*What it means(b)*	*Risk of misstatement(b)*
Existence	All account balances exist at the year-end for assets, liabilities, and equity.	Financial instruments were included in the statement of financial position in the absence of legally binding contracts (i.e. they do not exist or are not real).
Completeness	All the asset, liability, and equity balances have been fully and completely reported.	All financial instruments with legally binding contracts are not completely reported in the statement of financial position.
Rights and obligations	The entity has the rights to the financial assets it owns, and has obligations for the financial liabilities.	Financial instruments reported asset amounts where the company has no right (e.g. in the case of trade receivables with factoring arrangements).
Valuation	All asset, liability, and equity balances have been recorded at their proper valuations.	The amounts of the financial instruments with binding contracts are erroneously valued.

Sources: (a) International Federation of Accountants (2012); (b) Adapted from International Federation of Accountants (2012).

Examples of internal controls over the risk of material misstatements in financial instruments

Whilst specific measures must be articulated to respond to the risks of material misstatement, a sound foundation of internal controls or a control environment is essential to ensure that the internal controls not only exist but are operating effectively. A sound control environment exists when the organization demonstrates commitment to integrity and ethical values; exercises oversight responsibility; establishes structure, authority and responsibility (e.g. the organizational structure and processes, as described above); demonstrates commitment to competence; and enforces accountability (COSO, 2013). The main thrust is to propagate and sustain a strong tone at the top and a control consciousness across the entity. These entity-level controls (for more information on entity level and transaction level controls, see EY, 2010) are

Table 5.3 Some examples of entity level controls in relation to the risk of material misstatement (RMM)

Entity level controls	*Implication on the RMM*
The level of knowledge and experience of management and those charged with governance(a)	The knowledge gap between accountants and front office traders may pose financial reporting risk as the accountants may rely on inputs from traders to value their positions. Third-party valuations bring their own risks as the entity management and accountants need to assess if the third party has the requisite expertise. The management and CFO will need to attest to and sign off the entity's financial statements even if they rely on third-party valuations of the derivative positions. Similarly, the auditors may rely on their own in-house or third-party valuation expertise so that they can provide an opinion on the truth and fairness of the client's financial statements. Without relevant knowledge and experience, there is little understanding of the financial instrument and the level of risk exposure may be higher than expected. Hence, this increases the RMM.(b)
Direction from management and those charged with governance(a)	Without clearly stated policies (include risk appetite) approved by those charged with governance, the purchase, sales and holding of financial instruments may not be aligned with management's risk appetite. More significantly, they may expose the company to speculative activities and threaten its liquidity position. Going concern may be affected which is a fundamental premise used in the preparation of financial statements.(b)
Segregation of duties and the assignment of personnel(a)	Proper segregation of duties should be in place for those personnel involved in dealing, settlements, sending out trade confirmations and checking replies from counterparties, and recording of all transactions correctly in the accounting records, including the valuation of complex financial instruments—without which the integrity of the financial statements will be at risk.(b)
Monitoring of controls(c)	The complex nature of financial instruments requires timely monitoring and responses to properly address the risk of material misstatement. There should be regular monitoring by those charged with governance and management of the risk management and internal control. Examples of entity level controls include management's monitoring of the front office controls over off-market rates, tape recording of trader deals over the phone, front to middle and back office system reconciliations, deal input controls via system verification, and compliance leave.

Sources: (a) Selection of elements from Auditing Standards (b) Extracted and adapted from Auditing Standards Board (2009); (c) IFAC (2011).

Table 5.4 Some examples of transaction level controls in relation to management assertions

Assertion	*Issue*	*Example of internal control*
Completeness of recording(a)	High volumes of transactions and their complexity can make confirming completeness very difficult.	• Record all binding contracts in the register to ensure that they are all accounted for in the financial year. • Reconciliation of transaction accounts with payments/receipts • Client/customer confirmation; Supervisory check/control • Periodic review of completeness controls Documents include trade/deal confirmations with counterparties and customers, records of trader deals in the system and on phone, and reconciliations between front and back office systems. Examples of the reconciliations have been explained above.
Accuracy of recording(a)	High volumes of transactions and their complexity can make confirming completeness very difficult.(a)	• Match/check of amount recorded with the transaction records/contracts. • Reconcile sub-ledgers with general ledger. • Reconciliation of records with external documents (e.g. bank statements, custodian statements, etc.) • Client/customer confirmation • Supervisory check/control • Periodic review of accuracy controls Documents include trade/deal confirmations with counterparties and customers, records of trader deals in the system and on phone, and reconciliations between front and back office systems. The verification of valuation method and rate input to control measurement accuracy has been explained above.
Valuation(b)	The varied judgement in valuation can contribute to the risk of material misstatement. The components of valuation risk may include:(c) 1 Model risk: the risk of imperfections and subjectivity of valuation models; 2 Price risk: relates to changes in the level of prices due to changes in interest rates, foreign exchange rates, or other factors related to market volatilities of the underlying rate, index, or price; 3 Liquidity risk: relates to changes in the ability to sell or dispose of the complex financial instrument; and 4 Basis risk: the risk associated with imperfect hedging where there is a difference between the fair values (or cash flows) of the hedged item and the fair values (or cash flows) of the hedging instrument. Further challenge occurred when information of the market price is not available or is limited.	Financial instruments are recorded at amortized cost or fair value. • There are proper policies related to the valuation of financial instructions and regular review to be aligned with the financial reporting framework. • There is proper check and review of valuation made for reliability and reasonableness. • There are regular review and stress testing of the valuation models to ensure relevance and robustness. • There is regular periodic review for impairment. • Hedge accounting is applied appropriately. • Leveraging on expertise of third party for valuation with proper due diligence for reliability and robustness. • For financial instruments accounted for at amortized cost, the amortization schedule details are periodically verified against the trade contract details. For financial instruments accounted for at fair values, the model assumptions are tested by risk management function and inputs are verified independently by the product control function.

(*continued*)

Table 5.4 Continued

Assertion	*Issue*	*Example of internal control*
Presentation and disclosure(d)	Presentation and disclosure may not be in accordance with the financial reporting frameworks.	Review by management and those charged with governance that the presentation and disclosure is in accordance with the financial reporting framework, the information is classified and summarized in a reasonable manner that is neither too detailed nor too condensed, and the financial statements reflect the underlying transactions and events in a manner that presents the financial position, results of operations, and cash flows. The general ledger accounts should be of sufficient level of detail to provide the necessary presentation and disclosure. The chart of accounts and the presentation and disclosure are centrally managed and reviewed by Finance.
Classification(e)	The complex nature of the financial instruments in classification between amortized cost and fair value may lead to potential risk of material misstatement as this also affects the recognition of gains and losses.	• There are proper policies related to the classification of financial instruments in accordance with the financial reporting framework. • There is proper check and review of classification for accuracy and in compliance with the financial reporting framework. • There are regular reviews and stress testing of the valuation models to ensure relevance and robustness. • There is regular periodic review for impairment. The general ledger accounts should be of sufficient level of detail to provide the classification of financial instruments. The chart of accounts and the presentation and disclosure are centrally managed and reviewed by Finance. The product control function reviews the classification of trades in the system to ensure adherence to financial reporting requirements.

Sources: (a) para. 21, (b) para. 22, (c) para. 59(B), and (d) para 23 of Auditing Standards Board (2009); and (e) International Federation of Accountants (2012)

set by those charged with governance and management. Some examples of entity level controls in relation to the risk of material misstatement of financial instruments are shown in Table 5.3.

Besides entity level controls, which are pervasive across the enterprise, transaction level controls are designed and implemented for each account in the financial statements. Essentially, at each stage of the accounting processes covered above, these control activities are carried out to reduce the risks of misstatements. Some examples of transaction level controls in relation to the risk of material misstatement of financial instruments are shown in Table 5.4.

Challenges in financial reporting

Information system and organization structure

A bank organization reporting structure is usually multi-dimensional: product, country/region, functions and customer groups. The information system has to be aligned to the organization reporting structure so that the revenue/cost/profitability data are available for performance evaluation purposes and other product/customer data are available for business decision making (an example is the launch of structured product in the priority bank customer segment).

One financial reporting risk is that the organization structure changes at a faster pace than the information system, so that the information systems cannot keep up with the organization structure and business. For example, a vendor treasury system could be used to book the FX option and FX spot and forward trades of the global FX option traders. The local FX traders use an in-house proprietary system to book their FX spot and forwards. This is because the in-house system can cater for a larger number of deals than the vendor system and local FX traders execute more FX trades than global FX option traders. The vendor system but not the in-house proprietary systems can handle FX option trades, thus the vendor system and the in-house proprietary system may record and value the FX trades differently. In such a case the information systems create financial reporting risks.

Global system versus local regulatory/market requirements

This is a global system versus local system issue. For consistency in valuation and accounting of trades across locations, for efficiency (elimination of reconciliation efforts, economies of scale) and for accuracy (avoiding system interface errors), the same system should ideally be used worldwide for the same products. The same system is typically used for front-to-back booking of trades (including settlement and accounting) for the same reasons. However, there may be local regulatory or local business requirements that the one global system is not able to handle. For example, the accounting rules differ between US and UK. In many cases, separate MIS or regulatory systems are used to meet the local needs. This creates system interface and data consistency issues. The local financial reporting staff may not have access to the global system for data security issues or the global system IT people may not have access to local customer information for regulatory (customer confidentiality) reasons. This creates operational difficulties because of access to incomplete information.

Despite globalization, specific country needs still differ widely. Banks try to meet specific local customer needs to be competitive and gain customers. The original intent of a global system is to standardize the data fields for efficiency purposes and the global system IT people resist adding data fields or functionality specific to a country. This leads to the growth of local systems and Excel spreadsheets to meet local business needs and so creates data inconsistency.

In the case of global systems used by various locations, the cut-off times for day-end, month-end and year-end closing needs to be determined and be consistently applied across different locations. One approach is to use the location on the latest time-zone as the cut-off time. This ensures that the trades are included in the ledgers of both locations and the same rates are applied for pricing the trades. If the trades are booked multiple times into different systems manually, financial reporting risk increases due to human errors.

Valuation in financial reporting

The interactions between various risk factors make measurement for valuation a challenge in financial reporting. Examples are the CVAs (credit valuation adjustments) and DVAs (debit valuation adjustments) which require consideration of both market risks and counterparty credit risks, which could switch between CVAs and DVAs depending on whether the transaction is in or out of money for the entity and counterparty.

CVAs are credit valuation adjustments. DVAs are debit valuation adjustments. It is counter-intuitive to record fair value gains/losses on own liability. As the credit risk of the reporting entity increases, the fair value of its liability decreases, and the entity records fair value gains in its income statement. A deterioration in an entity's financial condition gives rise to a gain for the entity. The difficulty is to measure CVAs and DVAs when credit spreads of publicly traded CDS (credit default swaps) are not available. In that case, internal models are used to estimate credit spreads. The factors considered in the models are portfolio size (larger portfolios increase CVA/DVA), current fair value (in or out of money increases CVA/DVA), duration to maturity (longer duration increases CVA/DVA), netting of positions (more netting decreases CVA/DVA), collaterals (more collaterals decreases CVA/DVA), and complexity of portfolio (greater complexity increases CVA/DVA). The International Valuation Standards Council (IVSC) provides guidance on the CVA and DVA measurement. Different methods are acceptable for CVAs and DVAs, and non-banks may not have the sophisticated systems in banks to consistently monitor and adjust the CVAs and DVA (International Valuation Standards Council, 2005).

Dealers may not share their valuations of the entity's positions due to the proprietary nature of information. The entity may need to obtain third-party valuations of the positions. There are also divergent practices on handling funding of uncollateralized derivative positions.

The volatile and complex market environment creates risks in valuations as the valuation numbers may vary significantly. Small changes in input assumptions can create significant changes in the valuations. Stress testing and scenario testing are useful tools to determine the degree of financial statement misstatements that can potentially arise from volatile market inputs and model changes.

Conclusion

Controls over financial reporting risks should include controls over business processes and information systems. This chapter provides an overview of financial reporting assertion and related risks of material misstatement in a wide spectrum of controls. Controls include hard controls on processes and systems and soft controls on culture and structure. Both elements are needed to ensure that risk management over financial reporting is effective and sustainable. In the case of financial instruments in a banking environment, significant judgement is required in their recording and valuation. We provide a few examples on the potential financial reporting risks in the business processes and information systems of financial instruments. Whilst by no means exhaustive, this chapter serves to provide guidance on key matters to consider in financial reporting risks, particularly in financial instruments.

Note

1 On 20 February 2014, the IASB voted that the effective date for IFRS 9 shall be 1 January 2018.

References

ACCA (Association of Chartered Certified Accountants) (2016, November 17) *Assessing the Risk of Material Misstatement*. Available from http://www.accaglobal.com/sg/en/discover/cpd-articles/audit-assurance/material-misstatement.html

Auditing Practices Board (2009, October) *Auditing Complex Financial Instruments – Interim Guidance*. Practice Note 23 (Revised). Available from https://www.frc.org.uk/Our-Work/Publications/APB/PN-23-(Revised)-Auditing-Complex-Financial-Instrum.pdf

Choudhury, Fayez (2014, September 2), *Making Financial Reporting Better: Strengthening the Financial Reporting Supply Chain*. Available from https://www.ifac.org/global-knowledge-gateway/viewpoints/making-financial-reporting-better-strengthening-financial

COSO (Committee of Sponsoring Organizations of the Treadway Commission) (2013) *Internal Control—Integrated Framework*. Available from http://www.coso.org/documents/990025p_executive_summary_final_may20_e.pdf

EY Ernest & Young (2010, November), *Internal Controls over Financial Reporting*. Available from http://www.fmi.ca/uploads/1/PIC_presentation_-_Session_1.pdf

IASB (International Accounting Standards Board) (2015, May) IFRS Conceptual Framework for Financial Reporting. Exposure Draft ED/2015/3. http://www.ifrs.org/Current-Projects/IASB-Projects/Conceptual-Framework/Pages/Conceptual-Framework-Summary.aspx

IFAC (International Federation of Accountants) (2011, December), *Special Considerations in Auditing Financial Instruments*. International Auditing Practice Note (IAPN) 1000. Available from https://www.ibr-ire.be/fr/reglementation/doctrine/circulaires/Documents/2012%2006%20-%202012%2006%2018%20Annexe%20Circulaire%20IAPN%201000.pdf

IFAC (International Federation of Accountants), IAASB (The International Auditing and Assurance Standards Board) (2012, March), *ISA 315 (Revised), Identifying and Assessing the Risks of Material Misstatement through Understanding the Entity and Its Environment*. Available from https://www.ifac.org/system/files/meetings/files/20130415-IAASB-Agenda_Item_5-D_Disclosures%20-%20ISA%20315%20(Revised)%20for%20reference%20ONLY.pdf

IVSC (International Valuation Standards Council) (2005), *Credit and Debit Valuation Adjustments*. Available from https://www.ivsc.org/files/file/download/id/99

6
Risk reporting

Mahmoud Marzouk, Philip Linsley and Shraddha Verma

Introduction

Today's business environment is often perceived as beset with risks and uncertainties with companies exposed to a wide range of internal and external risks. Thus, in this constantly changing business environment it is generally acknowledged that companies face many threats, challenges and uncertainties including (but not limited to) economic, political and social risks. Operating in a volatile and unpredictable business environment requires companies and other organisations to have an effective risk management system and strategies to contend with risks. These challenges may not only affect company performance but also endanger a company's survival. Therefore, as a part of good governance, firms should develop strategies to respond to such challenges and mitigate or take advantage of their potential impacts and outcomes. In this way they can protect and create wealth for shareholders.

It is also argued that it is incumbent upon companies to keep shareholders and other information users informed about their risk exposures and their risk management strategies, and that companies should also justify to investors in particular the rationale for taking particular risks. Accordingly, corporate risk disclosure (or risk reporting) is a means for investors and stakeholders to be better informed about the risks a firm faces and how these are being managed. It is generally assumed that corporate risk disclosure (CRD) is important as it aids stakeholders in assessing management performance by providing a picture of how well management manages risks and aids stakeholders in their decision-making by facilitating an assessment of the risk profile of the company.

The impetus for corporate risk disclosure

Academic studies identify the initial impetus for risk disclosures to be provided as deriving from the publication of discussion papers in the 1990s by professional accounting institutes recommending that companies provide risk information to investors (see, for example, Linsley and Shrives, 2006). The Institute of Chartered Accountants in England and Wales (ICAEW) has been at the forefront of these discussions and asserts that risk-related information is necessary as it facilitates the reader of the annual report in assessing the risk profile of the company which, in turn, enables the reader to make risk-informed decisions (see, for example, Institute of Chartered Accountants in England and Wales, 1997, 1999, 2002, 2011).

In its 1997 report on CRD, the Institute of Chartered Accountants in England and Wales (ICAEW, 1997) placed considerable emphasis on the importance of risk reporting and looked to motivate companies to provide risk information voluntarily by demonstrating the usefulness of enhanced CRD to companies and to shareholders. This is one of the first CRD reports published and it addresses the importance of providing risk-related information, setting out why CRD is needed and what it can achieve as follows (pp. 5–8):

1. *To provide practical forward-looking information*: investors need more future-oriented information on risks to make better decisions through enhancing their ability to predict the company's future cash flows and assess its possible future performance.
2. *To reduce the cost of capital*: the report claimed that companies might lower the cost of capital through enhanced CRD, otherwise investors would require a higher risk premium or higher rate of return for the uncertainty associated with their investments.
3. *To encourage better risk management*: the report proposed that improved risk reporting should enhance the company's ability to effectively manage the risks it faces. Improved CRD should also lead to increased cash flows and greater value for shareholders. Moreover, it improves the corporate image and produces an appealing picture of the company for investors.
4. *To provide other benefits to investors*: the report presented some benefits particularly to investors associated with enhanced CRD: first, to ensure that the same information is made available to all investors; second, to ensure that investors can evaluate the management performance in light of the risk and risk management information provided; and third, to protect investors through keeping them informed about the company risk exposure.

Following on from this, the ICAEW published two other reports, *No Surprises – The case for better risk reporting* and *No Surprises – Working for better risk reporting* in 1999 and 2002 respectively, to further emphasise the significance of CRD and risk-related information to companies and shareholders. More recently, the ICAEW has published another report in 2011. The report sheds light on the inadequate risk disclosure provided in corporate reports to shareholders and other users of information pre-crisis and puts forward suggestions for better risk reporting.

This indicates the significant role professional institutes and other regulatory bodies, such as the ICAEW and the U.S. Securities and Exchange Commission (SEC), have had in improving the level of CRD to enrich the annual reports and meet risk information needs of investors and stakeholders in general. These discussion papers have commonly argued that the disclosure of risk information in the annual report can be beneficial for the company as it may reduce the cost of capital and improve its risk management capabilities. More recent professional discussions have gone further and consider risk reporting as integral to the risk governance agenda (see, for example, Airmic, 2013). Risk governance is a term used to emphasise that board processes and structure must encompass risk management and was, for example, the focus of the 2014 update of the UK Corporate Governance Code.

In addition, a number of countries have enacted regulation which obliges companies to report on risks. For example, in the UK there are requirements to disclose risk information in a company's annual report set out in the UK Corporate Governance Code and the Companies Act 2006. Provision C.2.1 of the UK Corporate Governance Code states that in the annual report 'directors should describe those (principal) risks and explain how they are being managed or mitigated' whilst section 417 of the Companies Act 2006 requires that '(t)he business review must contain ... a description of the principal risks and uncertainties facing the company'. What is evident is that the 2006 Companies Act and UK Corporate Governance Code requirements permit management freedom to decide which risks will be disclosed as principal risks and what discussions will accompany these principal risks. It is understandable that the risk disclosure requirements of both the Companies Act and the UK Corporate Governance Code are broad as it is difficult to make specific prescriptions as to how a company should disclose its risks; namely, risks can differ markedly from company to company as can their management. The outcome is that there is considerable scope for managers to decide on the substance of the risk disclosures and on the accompanying narratives.

Similarly, companies operating in the USA are required to provide quantitative and qualitative information on risks within the form 10-K as Risk Factors under Item 1A. In Germany an accounting standard (German Accounting Standard—GAS 5) was published in 2001. This Accounting Standard has subsequently been withdrawn and the risk reporting requirements are now encompassed in GAS 20 (Group Management Report). GAS 20 addresses risks and risk reporting in more detail than UK requirements. The summary of GAS 20 provides further guidance stating:

> ... the report on expected developments and on opportunities and risks is designed to enable a knowledgeable user to obtain a suitable understanding of the expected development of the group and of the material opportunities and risks associated with this development. Forecasts must be made about the most important financial and non-financial key performance indicators that are also used for the internal management of the group. The forward-looking period must cover at least one year, starting from the most recent reporting date of the consolidated financial statements. Foreseeable special factors affecting the period after the forward-looking period must be presented and analysed ... The forecasts must contain disclosures about the expected change in the projected key performance indicators compared with the relevant actual figures for the reporting period, and must illustrate the direction and intensity of the change. Risk reporting encompasses disclosures on the individual risks and a summary presentation of the risk position, together with disclosures on the risk management system if the parent entity is publicly traded. It must report on material risks that could affect the decisions of a knowledgeable user of the group management report. The risks presented must be quantified if this is also done for internal management purposes and the quantitative disclosures are material for a knowledgeable user. To enhance the clarity and transparency of the risk report, the individual risks must either be ranked by their importance or combined into categories of similar risks. Opportunities must be treated in the same way as risks.

A key aspect of risk disclosure is that it is intended to improve risk reporting by overcoming the information asymmetry problem, reducing the information gap between management and shareholders through ensuring individual and institutional/major shareholders are provided with identical risk information. Generally, previous studies support this idea that risk reporting can assist investors to be better informed about the company risk profile (Abraham *et al.* 2012; Beretta and Bozzolan, 2004a; Cabedo and Tirado, 2004; Campbell *et al.* 2014; Deumes 2008; Linsley and Shrives, 2000; Linsley and Shrives, 2005a; Solomon *et al.* 2000). Further, it is argued that risk reporting should aid the capital markets to function more efficiently through promoting transparency and which, in turn, should stimulate economic development

(Abraham *et al.* 2012; Deumes, 2008; Linsley and Shrives, 2005b; Mousa and Elamir, 2013). Increased risk disclosure may also be important to the overall investment climate and national economic growth, as it contributes to the improvement and stability of the investment environment and capital accumulation (Rajab and Handley-Schachler, 2009). However, whilst it can be seen that GAS 20 is more comprehensive than, say, UK requirements, it still leaves considerable scope for companies to decide on what will constitute their risk disclosures.

What do prior studies tell us about corporate risk disclosure?

Introduction

CRD has grown as a topic of importance in accounting and there is a burgeoning literature. Whilst it is a distinct area of research it is also allied to other types of disclosure studies within the accounting domain. Extant research investigating risk reporting practices and potential determinants of risk disclosures is more prevalent in respect of developed countries; however, there is also a growing body of research on CRD in emerging economies. This section provides a summary of the results of prior CRD research and is organised according to the country that forms the basis for the different studies. Before presenting this research there are some general comments that can usefully be made in respect of these prior studies.

First, it is of note that the primary research methodology adopted in these prior studies is content analysis. The approach to undertaking the content analysis is either manual or computerised. The former is time-consuming; however, computerised textual analysis is problematic. Computerised textual analysis in CRD studies relies on searching for key words such as 'risk', 'risky, 'uncertainty' but there is a difficulty in knowing whether risk discussions have been fully identified. This is particularly so as 'risk' is a difficult concept to define. Second, the studies tend to attempt to identify the key characteristics of the risk disclosures or to identify any associations between the risk disclosures and a range of corporate governance characteristics. Typically, the types of characteristics being identified are whether the risk disclosures are: forward-looking or backward-looking; quantified (or monetary) or not; and providing good (or positive) news or bad (or negative) news. The rationale for examining these characteristics is that it is more useful if risk disclosures are forward-looking and quantified, and that managers are willing to be honest in their assessments of risk and will, therefore, provide bad news and not seek to skew their discussions towards good news. When looking to test for associations between amounts of CRD (often measured by the number of risk disclosure sentences provided in the annual report) and corporate governance characteristics, it is common to use some form of regression analysis. For example, a study might test for an association between the size of the board of directors and amounts of CRD. Third, it can be observed that studies of non-financial firms are more prevalent than studies of financial firms. This is likely to have arisen because of the difficulties inherent in analysing the risk disclosures of financial firms which are far more extensive and far more complex. In part, this is due to the nature of financial firms and in part due to their being subject to much more detailed and complex risk disclosure regulations. These regulations emanate from the Basel Committee on Banking Supervision Pillar 3 disclosure requirements. Therefore, it is understandable that some of these financial firm CRD studies choose not to examine the entire set of risk disclosures but instead look at only one sub-set of risk disclosures; for example, Barakat and Hussainey (2013) examine operational risk disclosures. Table 6.1 summarises key CRD studies for non-financial firms and Table 6.2 summarises key CRD studies for financial firms.

CRD practices and determinants: international experiences

USA and Canada

In the USA, an early study by Meier *et al.* (1995) examines the disclosure of political risks resulting from the 1990–1991 Gulf War. The study analyses annual reports of US companies operating in Kuwait before and during the war and the overall findings establish that there is a low level of political risk disclosure. Likewise, some studies explore the disclosure of market risks associated with the use of derivative financial instruments and/or analyse the impact of introducing new disclosure regulations, such as the Financial Reporting Release (FRR) 48, on the pattern and attributes of this type of disclosure and the volatility of interest rates, exchange rates, commodity prices, trading volumes and equity prices (Abdelghany, 2005; Rajgopal, 1999; Roulstone, 1999; Blankley *et al.* 2002; Linsmeier *et al.* 2002). These studies conclude that companies tend to disclose more information on market risks in response to the newly adopted disclosure requirements.

Recently, there have been studies that examine the impact of mandatory risk disclosure requirements on the amount of risk information disclosed in the risk factor section (1A) of the 10-K report and its relevance to investors and other users of information (Campbell *et al.* 2014; Kravet and Muslu, 2013; Mirakur, 2011). Companies are obliged under SEC disclosure requirements to provide quantitative and qualitative information on risks within the form 10-K, and the three studies find that the level of risk disclosure has improved following the introduction of the mandatory disclosure requirements. Campbell *et al.* (2014) conclude that risk disclosure helps investors assess company risk profile and predict stock prices as well as alleviating the information asymmetry problem by ensuring the availability of risk information to all interested parties. However, Kravet and Muslu (2013) argue that despite risk communication potentially reducing investors' uncertainty, companies are prone to provide boilerplate risk disclosures. Moreover, Mirakur (2011) reveals that a company's future performance cannot be measured based on the current level of CRD.

In the Canadian context, Lajili and Zeghal (2005) conduct a content analysis of the annual reports of 300 Canadian listed companies, finding that companies have disclosed an increasing amount of risk information in their annual reports. However, they still raise concerns about the quality of risk reporting and the lack of quantified risk information. As a consequence, they call for improving risk reporting so that the same risk information is made available to all shareholders and other stakeholders to overcome the information asymmetry problem.

UK

In the UK, there has been a greater amount of literature published on CRD practices and determinants. Most studies have focused on examining the nature and quantity of risk information as well as the factors influencing CRD within corporate reports and annual reports in particular (see, for example; Linsley and Shrives, 2006; Abraham and Cox, 2007; Elzahar and Hussainey, 2012; Elshandidy *et al.* 2013). Other longitudinal studies have been conducted to explore the changes in the volume and attributes of risk reporting over time considering the implementation of additional disclosure requirements (Hill and Short, 2009; Rajab and Handley-Schachler, 2009). Overall, the results show that there is a trend of increasing risk reporting by UK companies. The findings also show that the implementation of additional risk disclosure requirements have contributed to improving CRD practices. Moreover, the results find that company size, US dual listing and industry type are the most important factors in determining the volume of risk disclosure. Another common finding is that companies tend

Table 6.1 Summary of prior annual report-based risk disclosure studies: non-financial firms

Author(s)	*Year*	*Sample*			*Method*	*Theory(ies) utilised for hypothesis development (where applicable)*	*Summary of key findings/comments on paper (RD = risk disclosures)*
		Size	*Country(ies)*	*Period*			
Beretta and Bozzolan	2004a	85 listed firms	Italy	2001	Manual content analysis	Not applicable	Non-monetary RD significantly greater than monetary RD Past RD significantly greater than forward-looking RD Firm industry does not explain level of RD Constructs an index to attempt to measure RD quality (but this index is, ultimately, quantity-based)
Linsley and Shrives	2006	79 listed firms	UK	2000	Manual content analysis	Not applicable	Positive association between company size and RD No association between company risk level and RD Non-monetary RD significantly greater than monetary RD RD dominated by general statements of risk management policy
Abraham and Cox	2007	71 listed firms	UK	2002	Manual content analysis	Agency theory	Firm industry does not explain level of RD No association between RD and (i) number of executive directors, (ii) ownership by outside managed pensions plans Positive association between RD and (i) number of non-executive directors, (ii) ownership by life assurance funds, (iii) dual US listing Negative association between RD and ownership by in-house managed funds
Dobler, Lajili and Zeghal	2011	160 listed firms	USA, Canada, UK and Germany	2005	Manual content analysis	Not applicable	US firms provide greater RD Predominant RD characteristics are historic/non-time specific and qualitative Positive association between company size and RD Mixed evidence regarding any association between company risk level and RD

(*continued*)

Table 6.1 Continued

Author(s)	*Year*	*Sample*					
		Size	*Country(ies)*	*Period*	*Method*	*Theory(ies) utilised for hypothesis development (where applicable)*	*Summary of key findings/comments on paper (RD = risk disclosures)*
Lajili, Dobler and Zeghal	2012	30 listed manufacturing firms	USA	2006–2009	Manual content analysis	Not applicable	Predominant RD characteristics are forward-looking, bad news and qualitative RD unaffected by global financial crisis 2007–2008 Negative association between RD and (i) board size, (ii) board independence Positive association between RD and profitability
Miihkinen	2012	198 firm-year observations	Finland	2005–2006	Manual content analysis to derive RD quality indicators	Not applicable	The paper examines the effect of introducing an RD standard in Finland in 2006 Results suggest the introduction of the standard increased RD disclosure quality Firm size, profitability and having a listing on NYSE are also determinants of RD quality
Miihkinen	2013	386 firm-year observations	Finland	2006–2009	Manual content analysis to derive RD quality indicators	Not applicable	RD quality has negative effect upon (i.e. reduces) information asymmetry RD is more useful if provided by small firms, high tech firms and low analyst coverage firms
Elshandidy, Fraser and Hussainey	2013	1216 firm-year observations	UK	2005–2009	Computerised textual analysis using keywords	Disclosure theory including agency, signalling and regulatory theory	Firms with higher levels of systematic, financing and risk-adjusted risk provide greater voluntary RD Firms that are larger, have higher dividend yields, higher board independence, more effective audit environments provide greater RD High risk firms display greater sensitivity to risk levels leading to higher RD disclosure

Mokhtar and Mellett	2013	105 listed firms	Egypt	2007	Manual content analysis to derive RD index for voluntary/ mandatory RD	Agency theory	Predominant RD characteristics are backward-looking, good news and qualitative Positive association between RD and (i) barriers to entry (voluntary RD), (ii) board size, (iii) auditor type (mandatory RD) Negative association between RD and (i) ownership concentration (mandatory RD), (ii) role duality (mandatory RD) No association between RD and (i) firm size, (ii) industrial sector
Kravet and Muslu	2013	28110 firm-year observations	USA	1994–2007	Computerised textual analysis using keywords	Not applicable	Positive association between yearly changes in RD and stock return volatility, filing volume, trading volume changes, volatility forecast revisions Suggests RD increase risk perceptions of investors
Ntim, Lindop and Thomas	2013	50 listed companies	South Africa	2002–2011	Manual content analysis	Multi-theoretic approach adopting legitimacy, agency, stakeholder and resource dependency theory	Predominant RD characteristics are historic, good news, qualitative and non-financial Trend is for increasing RD over the period but the financial crisis period 2007–2008 is not significantly different to other periods Positive association between RD and (i) board size, (ii) board diversity, (iii) non-executive directorships Negative association between RD and (i) block ownership, (ii) institutional ownership
Campbell, Chen, Dhaliwal, Lu and Steele	2014	9076 firm-year observations	USA	2005–2008	Computerised textual analysis using keywords	Not applicable	Positive association between RD and firm risk as based on pre-disclosure measures Positive association between that part of RD which is unexpected and investor assessment of firm risk as based on market beta and stock return volatility

(*continued*)

Table 6.1 Continued

Author(s)	*Year*	*Sample*					
		Size	*Country(ies)*	*Period*	*Method*	*Theory(ies) utilised for hypothesis development (where applicable)*	*Summary of key findings/comments on paper (RD = risk disclosures)*
Elshandidy, Fraser and Hussainey	2015	3685 firm-year observations	Germany, UK and USA	2005–2010	Computerised textual analysis using keywords	Neo-institutional theory	Mandatory and voluntary RD vary significantly across the three countries Mandatory and voluntary RD significantly influenced by risk level, legal system and cultural values Firm and country characteristics have greater explanatory power for variations in mandatory RD than voluntary RD
Elshandidy and Neri	2015	1890 firm-year observations	UK and Italy	2005–2010	Computerised textual analysis using keywords		UK firms display higher levels of voluntary RD influenced by corporate governance factors of board size, non-executive directors, lower dividend yields and firm size Italian firms display higher levels of mandatory RD influenced by board size, non-executive directors, audit quality and firm size In UK context RD practices improve market liquidity In Italy voluntary RD practices improve market liquidity for strongly governed firms
Marzouk	2016	31 listed companies	Egypt	2011	Manual content analysis	Not applicable	Predominant RD characteristics are quantitative, forward-looking and good news Positive and significant relationship between company size and RD Positive but insignificant association between RD and (i) industry type, (ii) profitability, (iii) cross-listing Negative but insignificant association between RD and corporate reserves

Table 6.2 Summary of prior annual report-based risk disclosure studies: financial firms

Author(s)	*Year*	*Sample*					
		Size	*Country(ies)*	*Period*	*Method*	*Risk type(s) examined*	*Summary of key findings/comments on paper (RD = risk disclosures)*
Linsley, Shrives and Crumpton	2006	18 banks	UK and Canada	2001	Manual content analysis	All risk types	Predominant RD characteristics are forward-looking, generalised and qualitative No significant difference between UK and Canada RD Positive association between RD and bank size No association between RD and bank risk
Barakat and Hussainey	2013	85 banks	20 EU member countries	2008–2010	Manual content analysis to create RD index	Operational risk	Negative association between operational RD and (i) bank entry requirements, (ii) powers/independence of supervisor, (iii) proportion of voting rights held by largest shareholder Positive association between operational RD and number of audit committee meetings per year
Maffei, Aria, Fiondella, Spanò and Zagaria	2014	66 banks	Italy	2011	Manual content analysis	All risk types	Predominant RD characteristics are inter-temporal, neither good news nor bad news and quantitative
Al-Hadi, Hasan and Habib	2016	677 financial firm-year observations	The 6 countries of the Gulf Co-operation Council	2007–2011	Manual content analysis to create RD index	Market risk	Examining the connection between risk committee (RC) characteristics and market RD RC size and qualifications of RC members are positively associated with RD index RCs in mature firms significantly improve market RD

to provide more information on risks to shareholders over time (Abraham and Cox, 2007; Elzahar and Hussainey, 2012; Hill and Short, 2009; Linsley and Shrives, 2005a; Linsley and Shrives, 2006; Rajab and Handley-Schachler, 2009). Some have, however, argued that currently the risk disclosures provided are insufficient and too vague (Linsley and Shrives, 2005a; Linsley and Shrives, 2006). Likewise, they have highlighted the lack of quantified risk information and raised concerns about the relevance of risk information provided to shareholders and other stakeholders. Abraham *et al.* (2007) analyse the quality of narrative risk disclosure within the annual reports of UK listed companies in light of four criteria: formulaic, specificity, capability of measurement and evidence of measurement. They conclude that narrative risk disclosure made by UK companies in their annual reports is poor and further recommend that regulatory bodies act to stimulate companies to disclose higher quality risk information.

Abraham and Shrives (2014) propose a model to measure and enhance risk disclosure quality. The model they suggest is based upon ensuring the presence of a number of criteria in the risk information provided by companies. First, companies should disclose specific company-related information rather than general information that could apply to different companies. Second, companies need to revisit their disclosure to provide up-to-date risk information. Third, reporting material events that could have serious impacts on company performance in prior and subsequent annual reports is important. Their results in general reveal that companies provide poor quality and generalised risk information which is uninformative to annual report users. The findings also show that companies neglect reporting significant events in prior or subsequent annual reports. The study also sheds light on the need for more detailed and specific CRD requirements.

Elshandidy *et al.* (2013) examine the determinants of total, voluntary and compulsory narrative CRD by UK non-financial companies within their annual reports. They find that companies exposed to higher levels of risk provide more risk-related information in terms of total, voluntary and compulsory CRD. The findings also indicate that company size and a number of corporate governance characteristics are positively correlated with corporate total and voluntary risk disclosures.

Continental Europe

There is also growing empirical evidence on risk and risk management disclosure practices in different European countries. Berger and Gleißner (2006) analyse risk disclosure practices within the annual reports of a sample of 92 German non-financial listed companies over the period 2000–2005, examining the impact of the introduction of the German Accounting Standard (GAS 5) on the level and pattern of risk reporting. Their findings show an increase in the total number of risk disclosures under GAS 5, but with little improvement in the quality of risk disclosure.

In Italy, Beretta and Bozzolan (2004a; 2004b) argue that risk disclosure quality cannot be measured by reference to the quantity of risk information provided by companies. They suggest a framework to analyse and assess the quality of CRD whilst also investigating the effect of company size and industry type on the amount of risk information Italian listed companies reveal within annual reports. They find positive relationships between the level (quantity) of CRD and both company size and industry type. Other Italian studies include Neri (2010) and Greco (2012). Neri (2010) concludes that there has been an increased level of risk disclosure by companies and finds a positive association between the quantity of risk disclosure and company size. Greco (2012) finds that even with the introduction of mandatory risk disclosure regulations, risk disclosure level and practices have not changed and concludes that managers are reluctant to provide more information on risk. This is attributed to either management reluctance to provide commercially sensitive information that may affect the company's competitive position and overall performance or the desire of managers to avoid potential legal claims.

Vandemaele *et al.* (2009) find that, for Belgian listed firms, the volume of risk disclosure is significantly positively associated with company size and level of risk. Moreover, none of the aspects of corporate governance such as audit quality, the existence of risk committee or manager, CEO duality and board composition, is related to the amount of risk information provided.

Miihkinen (2012) explores the impact of applying a new national accounting standard on the quality of risk reporting by Finnish listed companies and examines the factors influencing CRD quality. The results demonstrate that the introduction of the accounting standard has improved both the quantity and quality of risk information disclosed. He finds that less profitable companies tend to disclose better quality risk information and that large firms and firms cross-listed in the USA provide more quantitative information on risks.

In Portugal, Oliveira *et al.* (2011) in their content analysis of 81 annual reports of Portuguese non-financial companies consider the implementation of IAS/IFRS and the European Union's Modernisation Directive in 2005 to examine their impact on the extent and quality of CRD. They find that the risk disclosures of the Portuguese companies are vague and conclude that neither the level nor the quality of risk disclosure was improved by the newly adopted disclosure regulations. In Spain, Cabedo and Tirado (2004) highlight the importance of reporting upon risks and the measurement of risks prior to disclosure and recommend that companies prepare a separate additional statement to report on risks.

Deumes (2008) examines Dutch listed companies and concludes that Dutch companies provide sufficient risk information in prospectuses that should help investors assess changes in stock prices. Meijer (2011) undertakes a study that covers the period 2005 to 2008 for the annual reports of Dutch listed companies, exploring the changes in the types of risk disclosed in the annual reports after the financial crisis. He uses content analysis to measure the quantity of risk disclosure, whilst a disclosure index is used to measure quality. The results reveal there has been an increase in both the quantity and quality of risk disclosures after the global financial crisis and the types of risk reported upon have also increased.

Australia

Exploring the introduction of the International Financial Reporting Standards (IFRS) in annual reports of Australian listed companies, Taylor *et al.* (2009) find that the level of financial risk disclosure has improved and this level is positively correlated with both corporate governance and corporate capital raising. On the other hand, they find a negative association between the risk disclosure attributes and cross-listing. Zhang *et al.* (2013) examine narrative risk disclosures made by a number of Australian listed companies and their relationship to institutional shareholders and the audit committee. The study finds that CRD is significantly positively associated with both transient-type institutional block shareholders (and not with dedicated-type institutional block shareholders) and audit committee independence (and not the financial expertise).

Asia

The research relating to Asia has principally focused on Japan and Malaysia. In relation to Japan, Mohobbot (2005) finds companies tend to voluntarily provide risk information within their annual reports, although they disclose more qualitative and backward-looking (historical) risk information. The empirical findings also reveal that company size is the key determinant of the level of CRD, whereas no relationships were found between the level of CRD and company level of risk, profitability and ownership structure. In another study, Kim and Fukukawa (2013) find a positive association between the level of risk disclosure and auditor size, and that companies that have been audited by the same auditor for a longer period of time disclose less risk information.

In the Malaysian context, Arshad and Ismail (2011), using survey data, find that the better the managers' understanding of risks and risk disclosure, the higher the level of risk disclosure reported to shareholders. Zadeh and Eskandari (2012) assess the degree of disclosure compliance by Malaysian listed firms with additional disclosure regulations and conclude that a vast majority of companies respond to the implementation of disclosure regulations by reporting more risk information.

Ismail *et al.* (2012) have investigated the usefulness of risk disclosure to companies by examining the effect of the quantity and quality of voluntary risk disclosure on the market value of the firm. They investigate risk reporting practices in the annual reports of Malaysian companies in two years, 2006 and 2009, considering new disclosure requirements issued in 2007 to further identify the impact of these regulations on the amount and quality of CRD. The empirical findings reveal that there has been little change in the quantity and quality of voluntary risk disclosure. They find a positive significant relationship between the amount of voluntary risk disclosure and a company's market value. However, a negative significant relationship is found between the quality of voluntary risk disclosure and the firm's market value. Amran *et al.* (2009) find that Malaysian companies disclose less risk information compared to the level of CRD by UK companies as indicated by Linsley and Shrives (2006). They further indicate that both industry type and company level of risk affect the amount of risk information in annual reports positively.

Africa and the Middle East

Recently, there has been increasing interest in examining CRD practices in Africa and the Middle East, with studies that use content analysis in respect of Iran, South Africa, Dubai, United Arab Emirates, Bahrain and Egypt. These studies show some similar findings with research that has been carried out in other parts of the world.

In a South African study, Ntim *et al.* (2013) investigate the nature of risk information disclosed by non-financial companies listed on the Johannesburg Stock Exchange (JSE), finding a positive association between the extent of CRD and board diversity, board size and independent non-executive directors. The study also shows that block ownership and institutional ownership are negatively related to the quantity of CRD, whereas dual board leadership structure is insignificantly correlated with the quantity of CRD.

In an Iranian study, Ramezani *et al.* (2013) examine the relationship between the disclosure of market risk information by Iranian listed companies and corporate characteristics. They determine that company size, financial leverage and co-variability earnings are significantly positively correlated with the level of market risk disclosure, whilst there is a significant negative relationship between the level of market risk disclosure and current ratio, dividend per share and profit growth.

In an attempt to contribute to narrowing the gap in risk disclosure literature in the Arab world, four empirical studies have been undertaken. In 2009, Hassan conducted a study to identify the determinants of CRD for companies listed on the Dubai Financial Market and Abu

Dubai Security Market. The study finds a significant relationship exists between the number of risk disclosures and both the firm level of risk and industry type. In a later study, Uddin and Hassan (2011) examine the effect of CRD within the annual reports of UAE listed companies on share price variances. It is assumed that the increased level of CRD should minimise share variances and hence reduce investors' potential losses and exposure to market risks. However, the finding is that enhanced risk disclosure cannot aid investors in predicting the changes in share prices, but it can assist them in building better investment portfolios to avoid potential risks and losses. Likewise, Mousa and Elamir (2013) have investigated risk-related information within the annual reports of companies listed on Bahrain Bourse (BHB). These companies in Bahrain provide little information on risks in annual reports. The major determinants of risk disclosure, in respect of both systematic and unsystematic risk, are company size, level of risk, firm listing, issuance of shares, profitability and percentage of free float.

Mokhtar and Mellett (2013) examine the level and attributes of CRD in the annual reports of Egyptian companies. Their findings show a low level of both mandatory and voluntary risk disclosures and that companies provide more information on financial than non-financial risks. In a recent study, Marzouk (2016) provides some new empirical evidence on the nature and determinants of CRD practices of Egyptian non-financial listed companies during the 2011 political (crisis) uprising in Egypt. The main findings reveal that companies provided more monetary, forward-looking and good risk disclosures. The results also demonstrate that the quantity of CRD is significantly positively related to firm size, whereas a positive but insignificant association was found between the amount of CRD and industry type, profitability and cross-listing respectively. Lastly, the amount of reserves was found to be negatively but insignificantly related to the amount of CRD.

It can also usefully be noted that broader cross-country studies (Dobler *et al.* 2011; Elshandidy *et al.* 2015; Linsley *et al.* 2006; Probohudono *et al.* 2013; Woods and Reber, 2003) generally reveal that there are no significant differences among companies across the different countries with regard to risk disclosure patterns and attributes. This may be because all the countries covered by the studies are highly regulated—such as the USA, UK, Germany and Canada—and generally in these countries there is a high level of compliance exhibited by companies as well as relatively high levels of enforcement by regulators and capital market authority. However, there are other influencing factors and motives for CRD that differ from one context to another considering country-specific characteristics. For example, Elshandidy *et al.* (2015) find that German companies disclose greater amounts of both voluntary and mandatory risk information than UK and US companies. They attribute these variances to the different regulatory frameworks and cultural contexts. Moreover, the results demonstrate that there is an increasing trend of CRD amongst companies across countries.

Conclusion and the issue of CRD quality

According to the Financial Accounting Standards Board (FASB) (2010), the ultimate purpose of corporate reporting is to enhance information users' decisions by providing useful information. This is of importance in the context of CRD discussions as it should also be the purpose of risk reporting that it satisfies this criteria of decision usefulness which, it may be argued, is the prime indicator of the quality of risk disclosures provided in an annual report.

However, assessing CRD quality is problematic. Many prior studies examine CRD by counting risk sentences or words. Beretta and Bozzolan (2004a) rightly argue that CRD quantity cannot be used as a proxy for quality. Information quality is not solely about how much a company discloses, but also about the 'informativeness' of disclosures to the users of information. This implies that characteristics of information quality such as accuracy, completeness, comparability and relevance are pertinent to assessing the quality of CRD.

It could be argued that some previous studies which have focused on examining the quantity of CRD have also addressed quality to some extent. However, none of these studies seem to have investigated the characteristics of good information using, for example, the criteria set by FASB in 2010 including relevance, materiality, faithful representation, comparability, verifiability, timeliness and understandability. The problem is that prior studies that seek to address CRD quality and/or usefulness apply the same research method (content analysis) used in the majority of previous CRD studies and the result is their assessment of CRD quality is ultimately resting on numbers of words or sentences. Quality of risk disclosure is a more comprehensive concept. FASB (2010) emphasises the great significance of the concept of 'usefulness' in corporate reporting stating that 'usefulness in making decisions is the objective of financial reporting' (p. 12). Therefore, risk disclosure should be deemed useful, and of good quality, if it meets the decision-making needs of the users of information.

From the discussion above, it is evident there is a growing interest in risk disclosure within the accounting literature. Previous studies have mainly focused on investigating the quantity and attributes of risk information, as well as examining the determinants (firm-specific and corporate governance characteristics) of CRD. On the whole, there seems relatively good agreement across previous studies that CRD lacks coherence, clarity and usefulness as companies tend to provide vague and generalised risk information that could apply to different companies in different industries. Prior literature also indicates that there is a lack of quantifiable and forward-looking risk information. Studies that have been conducted in highly regulated countries do find an increasing trend of CRD but still argue that risk information provided to investors and other stakeholders is insufficient.

Many of these prior studies use quantity as a proxy for quality of CRD and this highlights that little empirical work has addressed risk disclosure quality. A future avenue for risk disclosure research is therefore a more direct examination of CRD quality in annual report disclosures. This is likely to be difficult and may require re-thinking whether content analysis is an appropriate methodology to adopt for such studies. It is also implies that, in advance, there is a great need for work to be done that grapples with the concept of quality in the context of CRD and in a fundamental way. This is likely to require discussions that err towards the philosophical but would be invaluable in forming a base for future CRD quality-focused studies.

References

Abdelghany, K. (2005), 'Disclosure of Market Risk or Accounting Measures of Risk: An Empirical Study', *Managerial Auditing Journal*, 20(8), pp. 867–875.

Abraham, S. and P. Cox (2007), 'Analysing the Determinants of Narrative Risk Information in UK FTSE 100 Annual Reports', *The British Accounting Review*, 39, pp. 227–248.

Abraham, S., C. Marston and P. Darby (2012), *Risk Reporting: Clarity, Relevance and Location*. Edinburgh: Institute of Chartered Accountants of Scotland.

Abraham, S. and P. Shrives (2014), 'Improving the Relevance of Risk Factor Disclosure in Corporate Annual Reports', *The British Accounting Review*, 46, pp. 91–107.

Abraham, S., A. Solomon and J. Stevenson (2007), *A Ranking of Risk Disclosure in UK Annual Reports*. Working paper. Edinburgh, UK: Napier University.

Airmic (2013), Risk reporting. London: Airmic.

Al-Hadi, A., M. Hasan and A. Habib (2016), 'Risk Committee, Firm Life Cycle and Market Risk Disclosures', *Corporate Governance: An International Review*, 24(2), pp. 145–170.

Amran, A., A. Bin and B. Hassan (2009), 'Risk Reporting: An Exploratory Study on Risk Management Disclosure in Malaysian Annual Reports', *Managerial Auditing Journal*, 24(1), pp. 39–57.

Arshad, R. and F. Ismail (2011), 'Discretionary Risk Disclosure: A Management Perspective', *Asian Journal of Accounting and Governance*, 2, pp. 67–77.

Barakat, A., and K. Hussainey (2013), 'Bank Governance, Regulation, Supervision, and Risk Reporting: Evidence from Operational Risk Disclosures in European Banks, *International Review of Financial Analysis*, 30, pp. 254–273.

Beretta, S. and S. Bozzolan (2004a), 'A Framework for the Analysis of Firm Risk Communication', *The International Journal of Accounting*, 39, pp. 265–288.

Beretta, S. and S. Bozzolan (2004b), 'Reply to: Discussion of "A Framework for the Analysis of Firm Risk Communication"', *The International Journal of Accounting*, 39, pp. 303–305.

Berger, T. and W. Gleißner (2006), 'Risk Reporting and Risks Reported: A Study on German HDAX-Listed Companies 2000 to 2005'. Unpublished paper presented at the *5th International Conference on Money, Investment and Risk*. Risk Management Competence Europe. 1–3 November 2006, Nottingham.

Blankley, A., R. Lamb and R. Schroeder (2002), 'The Disclosure of Information on Market Risk: Evidence from the Dow 30', *Managerial Auditing Journal*, 17(8), pp. 438–451.

Cabedo, J. and J. Tirado (2004), 'The Disclosure of Risk in Financial Statements', *Accounting Forum*, 28, pp. 181–200.

Campbell, J., H. Chen, D. Dhaliwal, H. Lu and L. Steele (2014), 'The Information Content of Mandatory Risk Factor Disclosures in Corporate Filings', *Review of Accounting Studies*, 19, pp. 396–455.

Deumes, R. (2008), 'Corporate Risk Reporting: A Content Analysis of Narrative Risk Disclosures in Prospectuses', *Journal of Business Communication*, 45(2), pp. 120–157.

Dobler, M., K. Lajili and D. Zeghal (2011), 'Attributes of Corporate Risk Disclosure: An International Investigation in the Manufacturing Sector', *Journal of International Accounting Research*, 10(2), pp. 1–22.

Elshandidy, T., I. Fraser and K. Hussainey (2013), 'Aggregated, Voluntary, and Mandatory Risk Disclosure Incentives: Evidence from UK FTSE All-Share Companies', *International Review of Financial Analysis*, 30, pp. 320–333.

Elshandidy, T., I. Fraser and K. Hussainey (2015), 'What Drives Mandatory and Voluntary Risk Reporting Variations across Germany, UK and US?' *The British Accounting Review*, 47(6), pp. 376–394.

Elshandidy, T. and L. Neri (2015), 'Corporate Governance, Risk Disclosure Practices, and Market Liquidity: Comparative Evidence from the UK and Italy', *Corporate Governance: An International Review*. DOI:10.1111/corg.12095.

Elzahar, H. and K. Hussainey (2012), 'Determinants of Narrative Risk Disclosures in UK Interim Reports', *Journal of Risk Finance*, 13(2), pp. 133–147.

Financial Accounting Standards Board (FASB) (2010), *Conceptual Framework for Financial Reporting*. Connecticut: FASB.

Greco, G. (2012), 'The Management's Reaction to New Mandatory Risk Disclosure: A Longitudinal Study on Italian Listed Companies', *Corporate Communications: An International Journal*, 17(2), pp. 113–137.

Hassan, M. (2009), 'UAE Corporations-Specific Characteristics and Level Of Risk Disclosure', *Managerial Auditing Journal*, 24(7), pp. 668–687.

Hill, P. and H. Short (2009), 'Risk Disclosures on the Second Tier Markets of the London Stock Exchange', *Accounting and Finance*, 49, pp. 753–780.

Institute of Chartered Accountants in England and Wales (1997), *Financial Reporting of Risk – Proposals for a Statement of Business Risk.* London: ICAEW.

Institute of Chartered Accountants in England and Wales (1999), *No Surprises: The Case for Better Risk Reporting*. London: ICAEW.

Institute of Chartered Accountants in England and Wales (2002), *No Surprises: Working for Better Risk Reporting*. London: ICAEW.

Institute of Chartered Accountants in England and Wales (2011), *Reporting Business Risks: Meeting Expectations*. London: ICAEW.

Ismail, R., R. Arshad and S. Othman (2012), 'The Influence of Voluntary Risk Disclosure on Firms' Market Value'. Unpublished paper presented at the *3rd International Conference on Business and Economic Research (ICBER)*. 12–13 March. Bandung.

Kim, H. and H. Fukukawa (2013), 'How is an Auditor Involved with Corporate Business Risk Disclosure?' Unpublished paper presented at the *Dialogue on Audit Quality and Corporate Disclosures*, The American Accounting Association annual meeting and conference on teaching and learning in accounting. 3–7 August. California.

Kravet, T. and V. Muslu (2013), 'Textual Risk Disclosure and Investors' Risk Perceptions', *Review of Accounting Studies*, 18(4), pp. 1088–1122.

Lajili, K., M. Dobler and D. Zeghal (2012), 'An Empirical Investigation of Operational Risk Disclosures', *The International Journal of Management and Business*, 3(2), pp. 53–65.

Lajili, K. and D. Zeghal (2005), 'A Content Analysis of Risk Management disclosures in Canadian Annual Reports', *Canadian Journal of Administrative Sciences*, 22(2), pp. 125–142.

Linsley, P. and P. Shrives (2000), 'Risk Management and Reporting Risk in the UK', *Journal of Risk*, 3(1), pp. 115–129.

Linsley, P. and P. Shrives (2005a), 'Examining Risk Reporting in UK Public Companies', *Journal of Risk Finance*, 6(4), pp. 292–305.

Linsley, P. and P. Shrives (2005b), 'Transparency and Disclosure of Risk Information in the Banking Sector', *Journal of Financial Regulation and Compliance*, 13(3), pp. 205–214.

Linsley, P. and P. Shrives (2006), 'Risk Reporting: A Study of Risk Disclosures in the Annual Reports of UK Companies', *The British Accounting Review*, 38, pp. 387–404.

Linsley, P., P. Shrives and M. Crumpton (2006), 'Risk Disclosure: An Exploratory Study of UK and Canadian Banks', *Journal of Banking Regulation*, 7(3/4), pp. 268–282.

Linsmeier, T., D. Thornton, M. Venkatachalam and M. Welker (2002), 'The Effect of Mandated Market Risk Disclosures on Trading Volume Sensitivity to Interest Rate, Exchange Rate, and Commodity Price Movements', *The Accounting Review*, 77(2), pp. 343–377.

Maffei, M., M. Aria, C. Fiondella, R. Spanò and C. Zagaria (2014), '(Un)useful Risk Disclosure: Explanations from the Italian Banks', *Managerial Auditing Journal*, 29(7), pp. 621–648.

Marzouk, M. (2016), 'Risk Reporting During a Crisis: Evidence from the Egyptian Capital Market', *Journal of Applied Accounting Research*, 17(4), pp. 378–396.

Meier, H., S. Tomaszewski and R. Tobing (1995), 'Political Risk Assessment and Disclosure in Annual Financial Reports: The Case of the Persian Gulf War', *Journal of International Accounting Auditing and Taxation*, 4(1), pp. 49–68.

Meijer, M. (2011), Risk Disclosures in Annual Reports of Dutch Listed Companies During the Years 2005–2008. Unpublished Master's dissertation, University of Twente.

Miihkinen, A. (2012), 'What Drives Quality of Firm Risk Disclosure? The Impact of a National Disclosure Standard and Reporting Incentives under IFRS', *The International Journal of Accounting*, 47, pp. 437–468.

Miihkinen, A. (2013), 'The Usefulness of Firm Risk Disclosures under Different Firm Riskiness, Investor-Interest, and Market Conditions: New Evidence from Finland', *Advances in Accounting, Incorporating Advances in International Accounting*, 29, pp. 312–331.

Mirakur, Y. (2011), *Risk disclosure in SEC corporate filings*. [Online] UPenn. Available at: http://repository.upenn.edu/wharton_research_scholars/85/ [Accessed 15/07/2013].

Mohobbot, A. (2005), *Corporate Risk Reporting Practices in Annual Reports of Japanese Companies*. [Online] JAIAS. Available at: jaias.org/2005bulletin/p113Ali%20Md.Mohobbot.pdf [Accessed 20/07/2013].

Mokhtar, E. and H. Mellett (2013), 'Competition, Corporate Governance, Ownership Structure and Risk Reporting', *Managerial Auditing Journal*, 28(9), pp. 838–865.

Mousa, G. and E. Elamir (2013), 'Content Analysis of Corporate Risk Disclosures: The Case of Bahraini Capital Market', *Global Review of Accounting and Finance*, 4(1), pp. 1–27.

Neri, L. (2010), *The Informative Capacity of Risk Disclosure: Evidence from Italian Stock Market*. [Online] SSRN. Available at http://papers.ssrn.com/sol3/papers.cfm?abstract_id=1651504 [Accessed 25/11/2012].

Ntim, C., S. Lindop and D. Thomas (2013), 'Corporate Governance and Risk Reporting in South Africa: A Study of Corporate Risk Disclosures in the Pre- and Post-2007–2008 Global Financial Crisis Periods', *International Review of Financial Analysis*, 30, pp. 363–383.

Oliveira, J., L. Rodrigues and R. Craig (2011), 'Risk-related Disclosures by Non-finance Companies: Portuguese Practices and Disclosure Characteristics', *Managerial Auditing Journal*, 26(9), pp. 817–839.

Probohudono, A., G. Tower and R. Rusmin (2013), 'Diversity in Risk Communication', *Australian Accounting, Business and Finance Journal*, 7(1), pp. 43–58.

Rajab, B. and M. Handley-Schachler (2009), 'Corporate Risk Disclosure by UK Firms: Trends and Determinants', *World Review of Entrepreneurship, Management and Sustainable Development*, 5(3), pp. 224–243.

Rajgopal, S. (1999), 'Early Evidence on the Informativeness of the SEC's Market Risk Disclosures: The Case of Commodity Price Risk Exposure of Oil and Gas Producers', *The Accounting Review*, 74(3), pp. 251–280.

Ramezani, A., H. Ebrahimpour, M. Emamgholipour and M. Aghahosseini (2013), 'The Relationship Between Disclosure of Market Risk and Accounting Measures of Risk: Evidence from the Tehran Stock Exchange', *World of Sciences Journal*, 4, pp. 118–128.

Roulstone, D. (1999), 'Effect of SEC Financial Reporting Release No. 48 on Derivative and Market Risk Disclosures', *Accounting Horizons*, 13(4), pp. 343–363.

Solomon, J., A. Solomon and S. Norton (2000), 'A Conceptual Framework for Corporate Risk Disclosure Emerging from the Agenda for Corporate Governance Reform', *British Accounting Review*, 32, pp. 447–478.

Taylor, G., G. Tower and J. Neilson (2009), 'Corporate Communication of Financial Risk', *Accounting and Finance*, 50(2), pp. 417–446.

Uddin, M. and M. Hassan (2011), 'Corporate Risk Information in Annual Reports and Stock Price Behavior in the United Arab Emirates', *Academy of Accounting and Financial Studies Journal*, 15(1), pp. 459–476.

Vandemaele, S., P. Vergauwen and A. Michiels (2009), *Management Risk Reporting Practices and Their Determinants*. [Online]. Available at http://hdl.handle.net/1942/9392 [Accessed 22/12/2012].

Woods, M. and B. Reber (2003), A Comparison of UK and German Reporting Practice in Respect of Risk Disclosures Post GAS 5. *EAA 2003 Congress*. 2–4 April. Seville, Spain.

Zadeh, F. and A. Eskandari (2012), 'Looking Forward to Financial Risk Disclosure Practices by Malaysian Firms', *Australian Journal of Basic and Applied Sciences*, 6(8), pp. 208–214.

Zhang, J., D. Taylor, W. Qu and J. Oliver (2013), 'Corporate Risk Disclosures: Influence of Institutional Shareholders and Audit Committee', *Corporate Ownership and Control*, 10(4), pp. 341–353.

7

Risk in government outsourcing and risk-sharing

Rhetoric or reality?

Carolyn Cordery

Introduction

A key focus of the New Public Management (NPM) reforms in many countries (particularly the UK, Australia and New Zealand), was to increase the public sector's efficiency and effectiveness, making decision-makers accountable for achieving results (effectiveness), along with the need for frugality (efficiency) (Hood, 1995). Key to NPM is adopting private sector practices, privatisation and contracting-out (Broadbent *et al.* 2008).[1] Involving external parties presents risk-sharing opportunities. Nevertheless, where government maintains control, it must carefully monitor providers to maximise efficiency and effectiveness, limit misspending of public funds (financial risk), ensure service quality, and reduce reputational/political risks.

Government is known as being risk averse and focused on 'something going wrong' (Bhatta, 2003; Comptroller and Auditor General and National Audit Office, 2000; Gershon, 2004; Barrett, 2001). Although government employees are advised to strike a balance between monitoring and third-party autonomy (Controller and Auditor-General (CAG), 2006; Comptroller and Auditor General and National Audit Office, 2000; The Treasury, 2009), Maddock (2002) finds that they fear failure and limit contractors' effectiveness by close scrutiny, rather than allowing autonomy (due to agency theory implications: Schwartz, 2005; English, 2005).

NPM reforms saw governments privatising non-core services which could also minimise governments' residual risk. Following privatisation of prior government monopolies, governments often manage residual risk through regulation (e.g. New Zealand's electricity and telecommunications regulation).[2] Contracting for services and outcomes (outsourcing) differs from privatisation because the public sector retains control (specifying either the services or outcomes), actively managing and evaluating these services (Jensen & Stonecash, 2005). However, while outsourcing allows risk sharing, governments retain high residual risks when providers experience financial failure and fraud (Schmid, 2003; Schwartz, 2005) and fail to meet service standards in a 'race to the bottom' (Schmid, 2003). These damage governments' reputations (Padovani and Young, 2008).

This chapter analyses strategies, techniques and structures governments use to share and to manage or mitigate risk, and the relevant financial accounting. Drawing on predominantly Anglo-American literature and examples, it finds that, despite governments divesting services delivery through outsourcing, they are not entirely successful in sharing or reducing risk, due to multiple agents, incomplete contracts and complex motivational issues. The chapter focuses broadly on outsourcing risk relating to services and infrastructure, rather than other risks such as natural disasters.

Defining risk in public sector outsourcing

Whether public sector organisations outsource or deliver services themselves, they risk not meeting the stated objectives. Outsourcing should lead to risk-sharing, as well as opportunities (the 'up-side' of risk).[3] Yet, Sundakov and Yeabsley (1999) note that risk is pervasive and that public sector risk is more complex than private sector risk. Public servants must be accountable for public funds, and 'balance complex political, social and economic objectives' (Barrett 2000, p. 58).[4] Outsourcing is riskier where there is high citizen sensitivity, no competitive market, and high switching costs (Padovani and Young, 2008). Thus, quantitative, 'objective' private sector procurement practices utilising cost-benefit analyses are less applicable to social services containing qualitative and subjective aspects. Table 7.1 shows three risk types germane to this chapter.

First, public servants need to carefully establish goals, as ambiguity reduces successful risk-sharing and risk management (Woods, 2011). Secondly, they must identify risks, and analyse and evaluate them through analytical tools and other management techniques (Woods, 2011; Strategy Unit, 2002), then determine the appropriate risk treatment: avoidance, sharing or transfer (Fone and Young, 2000). Risk matrices are commonly used by the public sector to assess the potential impact of an adverse event and the potential likelihood of that event occurring (for example, Treasury Board of Canada Secretariat, 2001; Woods, 2011). Matrices not only depend on the situational risk appetite (Baccarini and Archer, 2001; Strategy Unit, 2002; CAG, 2008), but also lack precision, especially for qualitative assessments (Pickering and Cowley, 2010).

Non-shareable risk should be borne by the party best placed to manage it (CAG, 2006). Hence, financial and service risks are shared through insurance/pooling, and through carefully defining the outsourced services and the type of organisational provider required (CAG, 2008). The funding method chosen also shares risk.[5] For example, a study of the

Table 7.1 Types of outsourcing risks and examples

Type of outsourcing risk	*Examples*
Service delivery: provider fails to meet service standards. Risks arise from a challenging public service agenda, and risk transfers to the private sector.	Resource dependent providers manage financial instability through reducing beneficiary care levels (Schmid, 2003). Increased risk occurs when minimal market competition is accompanied by high switching costs (Farneti and Young, 2008).
Financial: risks of increasing costs/costs overruns, provider's financial failure, or fraud.	Holtfreter's (2008) US-based study found providers experiencing fraud had poor financial controls, management oversight and performance reporting.
Political/reputational: government's reputation may be damaged in public's eyes, making it hard to carry out its policies.	Schwartz's (2005) study reports local government providers exerting undue pressure on staff and elected officials, being uncooperative and refusing to service all of a target group, and expecting more resources.

United States' (US) health sector by Romzek and Johnston (2005) found that government's continuum of payment models affected providers' financial and service risks where service delivery costs exceeded government funding. Providers experienced the least risk when they were reimbursed for actual patient services delivered; and most risk when paid for the number of patients enrolled (capitation).[6] Erridge and Greer's (2002) study of a home energy project found greater risk-sharing if government also compensated providers for high start-up costs in limited-life projects.

While financial and service risks can be shared, transferring reputational risks to third parties is difficult, 'as the public rightly expects government to be accountable for services delivered on its behalf' (Strategy Unit, 2002, p. 13). Information-sharing is fundamental to risk-sharing, but is hampered by commercial sensitivity and privacy concerns, suggesting contracts must be transparent (Barrett, 2003; Cordery, 2012).

Effective risk management and monitoring requires tailored arrangements proportionate to the risks, funds involved and the service being outsourced (CAG, 2006; The Treasury, 2009). Padovani and Young (2008) prefer periodic progress reviews against the contract (focusing on collectively agreed outcomes), identifying necessary corrective actions required, and checking their effectiveness. Such monitoring seeks relevant information only (Fone and Young, 2000), recognising the benefits of obtaining information useful to both provider and purchaser. Audits are also useful. To minimise political risk, government agencies work in partnership, use peer networks, peer review and a consistent approach to training (Strategy Unit, 2002; Padovani and Young, 2008).[7]

Outsourcing strategies and techniques

Public sector outsourcing has a long history, although practices have changed dramatically since the NPM reforms. Yet, 'in the UK in 2008 roughly two-thirds of local public services were still provided in-house' (Bovaird, 2016, p. 3). This aligns to Bhattacharya *et al.*'s (2003) (private sector) argument, that entities should outsource only when they anticipate low risk.

This chapter considers the risks of specific types of outsourcing in two subsections: 'pay-for-services' and 'pay-for-success'. Pay-for-services compares a market approach and process-based contracting with a relational approach and performance-based contracting. Pay-for-success includes Public Private Partnerships and Social Impact Bonds. Each section focuses on the risks, risk-sharing, risk management, and the relevant financial accounting.

Reducing financial costs is a key reason to outsource. Jensen and Stonecash (2005) note that market-based outsourcing lowers government expenditure, whether the provider is from the private or public sector. Competitive markets reduce overpricing risks and reduce switching costs (Farneti and Young, 2008). Nevertheless, cost reductions often result in lower quality services being delivered than previously, with staff receiving low remuneration (Jensen and Stonecash, 2005). Reduced costs can therefore increase service and political risks due to citizen's sensitivity, which will require mitigation (Farneti and Young, 2008).

Pay-for-services

Public sector procurement contracts for social services and consultancy are not 'new' (Bovaird 2016), but NPM's specific focus on efficiency and effectiveness has spawned a burgeoning literature considering contracting issues, including risk (see Table 7.1). Accounting for pay-for-services contracts is uncontentious. The recently issued *Consultation Paper on the Recognition and Measurement of Social Benefits* by the International Public Sector Accounting Standards Board (IPSASB) (2015, p. 6) scopes out this 'reimbursement' expenditure, that is, 'cash payments made … to compensate a service provider … for all or part of the expenses incurred … [for] specific services'. Nevertheless, it indicates that standards for 'non-exchange expenditure'[8] require further development. Reimbursements are 'on-going expenses' in Government Finance Statistics (GFS), and International Financial Reporting Standards (IFRS).

The provider shares service delivery risks when specific services are outsourced. Managing financial and service risks, however, focuses primarily on governance. Considine and Lewis (2003; 1999) define four different approaches: procedural, corporate, market and network governance. They suggest public sector outsourcers will move from rules-based (procedural), through goal-driven (corporate) and cost-driven (market) arrangements to network governance—a flexible, relational approach. Nevertheless, many contracts mix these forms of governance, with market governance (competition) being an important tool in the NPM suite for risk-sharing and management. Accordingly, Schapper *et al.* (2006) dichotomise procurement risk management as a process-based approach (where funders focus on rules and micro-management), or a performance-based approach (where funders focus on co-production, partnership and building relationships) (Strategy Unit, 2002; HM Treasury, 2006; Controller and Auditor-General, 2008; Erridge and Greer, 2002).[9]

Process-based risk management approaches manage financial risk effectively when outputs are easily definable and measurable, are low value, low risk (Lavoie *et al.* 2010; Schapper *et al.* 2006) and have low citizen sensitivity. Yet, process-based approaches can be costly, fail to consider qualitative aspects of risk, and lack flexibility (Nowland-Foreman, 1997; Fone and Young, 2000). Focusing on processes and compliance, this approach diminishes learning and innovation, is adversarial, and ineffective in purchaser–provider conflicts (Scott, 1999; Nowland-Foreman, 1997; Lavoie *et al.* 2010; Bovaird, 2016).

Conversely, performance-based risk management approaches (or networked governance, as in Considine and Lewis, 1999; 2003) prioritise long-term relationships, seeking to respond to citizens' complex needs (Lavoie *et al.* 2010). These contracts are inherently riskier than short-term process-based contracts, and likely to occur in low-competition provider markets, bringing high switching costs and high citizen sensitivity (Schapper *et al.* 2006; Farneti and Young, 2008; Lavoie *et al.* 2010). Performance-based approaches remain interested in specific outputs, but have outcomes in mind. They may involve co-production where citizens and the state produce socially desirable outcomes, for example when communities co-design health programmes and promotion (Dunston *et al.* 2009; Ryan, 2012). Due to their involvement, citizens are likely to support these programmes.

However, performance-based approaches are riskier, requiring skills, knowledge and technologies not possessed by many public sector entities (Farneti and Young, 2008). Indeed, while transaction costs are lower, negotiating, relationship-building and monitoring costs are higher than for process-based contracting (Lavoie *et al.* 2010). Commissioning bulk services from a lead provider in a group increases economies of scale (Bovaird, 2016; Australian National Audit Office 2011). Nevertheless, it is also likely to engender higher service delivery risks, as government purchasers face high switching costs (Lavoie *et al.* 2010)

Practical steps to manage and monitor risks and build good purchaser–provider relationships, encourage trust, increase innovation and reduce costs include:

1 Transparently and fairly allocating public contracts (Organization of Economic Cooperation and Development (OECD), 2009);

2 Assessing strengths and weaknesses of risk management systems (Committee of Public Accounts, 2001; National Audit Office (NAO), 2004; The Treasury, 2009), noting complexities (CAG, 2006);
3 Recognising fear of failure, communicating and negotiating opportunities for innovation (Committee of Public Accounts, 2001; Strategy Unit, 2002);
4 Training public servants to identify, assess and manage risks (Committee of Public Accounts, 2001)[10] and practicing sound risk management principles (NAO, 2004);
5 "Passporting" or information-sharing between funders about providers,[11] recognising different departmental needs for monitoring and risk assessment (Pomeroy, 2007); and
6 Documenting and communicating accountability procedures clearly (e.g. audits) (Padovani and Young, 2008).

Cordery's (2012) New Zealand study found that factors driving the risk management approaches were: the public sector entity's operational structure (centralised versus decentralised), type of service (related to type of beneficiary), funder's leadership, central government advice, and provider interdependence. While interdependence drives a closer relationship and a performance-based approach (Cordery, 2012), the providers' prior behaviour, and negative media comments provide reasons to revert to process-based risk management. Better risk management occurs when government staff understand the provider, such as can occur with 'work shadow' schemes between the sectors.[12]

Farneti and Young (2008) find similar risk factors with Italian municipalities utilising process-based, competitively sourced outsourcing for simple services, due to low risk of citizen dissatisfaction (and thus reputational risk) and readily available alternative providers. Performance-based or networked approaches are used when social welfare services are interdependent (Farneti and Young, 2008).

Outsourcing models fail to differentiate between the provider's sector (for-profit or not-for-profit). Yet, increasingly, not-for-profit organisations contract with government (Forrer *et al.* 2010), providing services to those least able to pay who need government support. Some argue that not-for-profit providers are superior, as these organisations can better identify citizens' needs, are democratic (engage citizens) and mobilise volunteers and donations (Bode and Brandsen, 2014). In addition, the not-for-profit sector is known for its innovation,[13] for example by 'inventing' support schemes for elderly, sheltered housing, domiciliary care, and such like (Bode and Brandsen, 2014).

Nevertheless, outsourcing methods, in particular competitive contracting leading to marketisation of not-for-profit organisations (Furneaux and Ryan, 2014), 'erode one of their most distinguishing features' (Bode and Brandsen, 2014, p. 1060). Further, not-for-profit providers taking on government contracts may be ineffective in advocating for better policy and conditions for their beneficiaries or clients (Grey and Sedgwick, 2013). Not-for-profit organisations' cost-effectiveness remains hard to quantify, as voluntary and donated inputs are not valued (Bovaird 2014). Thus, for-profit sponsorships augment public sector funded outsourcing.[14]

Case study: Relationships Aotearoa

A case study highlights the range of risks faced in pay-for-services. Relationships Aotearoa (RA) provided counselling services for over 60 years, was a 'preferred partner' to the New Zealand Government, expanding to deliver government contracts. Its annual revenues averaged $8 million a year with a forecast loss of $1.5 million in the financial year ended 2015. RA's financial situation was 'exposed when government contract priorities and contracting practices changed and bids for further funding failed' (Vital Signs Consulting, 2015, p. 8). RA's contracts with four government departments comprised 73 per cent of its funding in the 2012–2013 year: Corrections (probation services), Ministry of Justice (MoJ) (ex-prisoners), Ministry of Social Development (MSD) (beneficiaries) and Child Youth and Family (CYF) (families) (Vital Signs Consulting, 2015). Corrections and MoJ paid NZ$165 per hour, while MSD and CYF paid NZ$95 per hour. RA lacked a costing system, but found (just before the liquidators were appointed) that NZ$95 per hour was unprofitable (PwC Advisory, 2015).

MSD and CYF processes to approve providers include an assessment under Business Viability and Programme Quality Standards. Approved providers are reviewed regularly and expected to act on recommendations. Assessors are a diverse group of professionals and receive regular training. Poorly performing providers are either suspended or their status revoked.[15]

RA's unsustainability was signalled in 2012. Its budget deficit was NZ$181,000; it lost key finance, information systems (IT) staff and replaced its chief executive in early 2013 (Vital Signs Consulting, 2015). RA's new chief executive discovered it had delivered unreported services totalling NZ$400,000 and requested reimbursement from its funders. Reductions in philanthropic funding also ensued, although RA continued to deliver services. The MSD, concerned about RA's sustainability and its own financial risks, provided RA with a Capability Investment Programme grant from September 2013 (Vital Signs Consulting, 2015). An MoJ review also supported organisational change (PwC Advisory, 2015).

RA reduced its expenditure by NZ$545,000 in 2013–2014, forecasting savings of NZ$1.243 million by 2015. Nevertheless, RA's poor IT integration meant unnecessary duplication of effort and poor reporting practices (Vital Signs Consulting, 2015). Poor records stymied RA's requests for extra funding, and unexpected costs arose. Although the MSD grant enabled RA to develop integrated IT systems and to enhance their governance and leadership, RA was placed in liquidation in June 2015 (PwC Advisory, 2015). Financial failure occurred despite agencies' regular reviews and RA's counselling skills.

The government's reputation suffered, as it was blamed by a public empathetic to RA. The media fuelled the fire, suggesting misuse of RA's client data, and inferring that potential replacement providers were 'stealing' RA's work. Relationships between RA and government were irrevocably broken,[16] at a time when the New Zealand Productivity Commission (2015) was pushing to improve social services delivery through 'joined-up' approaches and smarter purchasing from not-for-profit providers. Although risk assessment, monitoring and management had improved, RA's downfall led to a media storm which damaged the government's reputation.

Pay-for-success

Two main pay-for-success structures are now discussed: Public Private Partnerships (PPPs) and Social Impact Bonds (SIBs).

Public Private Partnerships: Governments entered into PPPs from around 1990 'to allocate the risks of infrastructure delivery more effectively than alternative contracting options' (Hellowell *et al.* 2015, p. 71).[17] PPPs differ widely operationally depending on the project, context and country (Broadbent *et al.* 2008; Grimsey and Lewis, 2005; Torres and Pina, 2001). Generally, PPPs involve a private sector contractor or consortium financing asset construction and government lease-back (Connolly *et al.* 2008). PPPs have three major aspects: a long term relationship, private sector deciding on optimal delivery, and risk-sharing between the public and private sectors (Forrer *et al.* 2010). Key risks in PPPs (additional to those listed in Table 7.1) include uncertain final costs in large infrastructure projects, technology of design and construction, and demand for future services (Jensen and Stonecash, 2005). These uncertain liabilities could accrue to government, therefore risk parameters differ markedly from pay-for-service outsourcing and traditional public infrastructure contracts. Thus, PPPs require carefully designed governance arrangements to effectively transfer risk and operational control 'while reserving the capacity for the public sector entity to protect public interest and enforce government policy objectives' (Barrett, 2003, p. 13).

A competitive bidding market is deemed to reduce the risk that a PPP contract will be over-priced (Cunha Marques and Berg, 2011). Yet, the 'market' tends to include only large firms (Andrews *et al.* 2015). Complex PPPs require network instruments (Van Gestel *et al.* 2012) or consortia of private sector contractors and public sector purchasers. These reduce risky information asymmetry (Andrews *et al.* 2015). Nevertheless, such arrangements can 'lead to the worst of both worlds' (Cunha Marques and Berg 2011, p. 1590) when there are weaker contractual controls and consumers bear consequences, rather than private and public sector entities. While Cunha Marques and Berg (2011) recommend an independent regulatory agency to ameliorate risks, Andrews *et al.* (2015) and Van Gestel *et al.* (2012) recommend contractually embedding mediation and developing intra-consortia trust.

Private sector bidders are expected to include their risk exposures within their PPP pricing.[18] Public sector risks reduce when private sector contractors bear cost overruns and 'optimism bias' (the risk that operating costs rise above forecasts) (Jensen and Stonecash, 2005; Coulson, 2008).[19] Demand risk (insufficient demand for the infrastructure) arises when PPP contracts pay private sector operators based on user numbers (Coulson, 2008). Early Spanish PPPs for toll roads suffered from low usage with contractors renegotiating pricing or hand-back dates with government (Acerete *et al.* 2009), while in the UK, private financing resulted in high user-tolls (Shaoul *et al.* 2011). These issues occur when governments transfer risks they cannot control.

Achieving optimal risk requires assessing which risks should be borne by the private sector and which government retains (Barrett, 2003). Connolly *et al.*'s (2008) Northern Irish case studies dichotomise risk allocation beliefs, comparing accrual-accounting standards to professional PPP advisors (see Table 7.2). Private sector PPP contractors 'often require high premiums to accept risk or may not be prepared to accept certain kinds of risk at all' (Boardman and Vining, 2012, p. 124), thus such marked divergences are sub-optimal.

Additionally, the public sector cannot shift all risk and, as noted by Forrer *et al.* (2010, p. 479):

> … must devise a plan to mitigate the impact on the public of an interruption of services as a result of any failure on the part of either party or problems attributable to forces beyond their control.

For example, in education, a contractor faces penalties if classrooms are unavailable, but pupils and staff are also delayed and disturbed (Connolly *et al.* 2008). Other PPP delays also affect the public (see, for example, Demirag and Khadaroo, 2008; Broadbent *et al.* 2008).

Despite some examples of successful risk mitigation (Carpintero and Siemiatycki, 2015), examples of financial and service failure overrun them (for example, English, 2005; Torres and Pina, 2001; Barrett, 2003). Post-contractual problems include unrealistic/unreasonable assumptions of risk transfer (English, 2005) and unsuitable incentives (or none) (Jensen and Stonecash, 2005). For example, the La Trobe Hospital (Australia) PPP was rescued by government when the cheapest contractor failed financially and was unable to deliver the contracted services (Barrett, 2003). High political risks attend failed PPPs, due to constituents' unmet expectations of new services, and/or wasted resources (English, 2005; Torres and Pina, 2001). Private contract negotiations also concern the public (Shaoul *et al.* 2011).

Table 7.2 Comparison of opinions on who bears the risk

Risks	*Project Advisors*	*Authors*
Demand risk	Purchase (insignificant)	Purchase (significant)
Residual value risk	Not relevant	Purchaser
Design risk	Operator	Purchaser or shared
Performance/availability risk	Operator	Purchaser
Potential changes in relevant costs	Operator	Operator
Obsolescence	Operator or shared	Not relevant

Source: Connolly *et al.* 2008, p. 960.

PPP monitoring is essential. Post-contractual problems include increased interest costs (Hellowell and Pollock, 2010), especially when increased credit risks raise the cost of capital. Governments also bear the costs and risks of public guarantee schemes developed to ensure PPPs' continuation (Hellowell and Vecchi, 2012; Shaoul *et al.* 2008). These include debt guarantees, subordinated debt schemes, repaying lenders (on refinancing), or providing debt capital, especially when usage is overstated (see Barrett's 2003 Eurostar UK study).[20] Government therefore reclaims unexpected risks and costs and the Canadian Council for Public Private Partnerships recommends these be recognised as contingent liabilities. Often, switching providers for better terms is not an option (Shaoul *et al.* 2008).[21]

Not only is risk valuation problematic (Cuthbert and Cuthbert, 2010), but also financial accounting asks who bears the risks and rewards of ownership and who controls the arrangement (Heald and Georgiou, 2011). Due to the relative costs of capital, to be cost effective, the risk transferred must be greater than in a finance lease (Barrett, 2003). Under lease accounting, the holder of both the risks and rewards (the PPP contractor) accounts for the underlying asset, future cash flows flowing from that holding, and any ensuing debt from bearing the risks and rewards of this asset (Heald and Georgiou, 2011; Mühlenkamp, 2014). On the contrary, the concept of control focuses on which entity controls the asset, considering the contract's form rather than its substance (Heald and Georgiou, 2011). The control concept was cited in IFRIC 12 *Service Concession Arrangements* (IFRS Interpretations Committee, 2006). Here the party reporting the asset (and any liabilities) is the party ultimately controlling the asset at the PPP's conclusion and the party who controls what services are delivered (Heald and Georgiou, 2011; Mühlenkamp, 2014). Government typically controls these factors. IPSAS 32 *Service Concession Arrangements: Grantor* also follows this ruling (IPSASB, 2011). On the contrary, the GFS utilises the risks and rewards approach asset (Mühlenkamp, 2014; Accounting Task Force of The Canadian Council for Public-Private Partnerships (CCPPP), 2008).

Under IFRSs and IPSASs, it is likely that PPPs would be 'on' governments' balance sheets, but 'off' balance sheet for their GFS reporting. Indeed, numerous authors perceive PPPs as merely accounting devices, structured favourably to record the infrastructure as the contractor's asset, and rented back to government under a service contract, rather than as a lease with ownership characteristics (Connolly *et al.* 2008; CCPPP, 2008).

Following the risks and rewards (leasing) argument, risk must be transferred from the public to private sector to keep the built infrastructure 'off' government's balance sheet (Connolly *et al.* 2008). Under the Eurostat rule, at least two of three risks (construction, demand, and availability) must be transferred to the private sector, if government is to avoid recognising PPPs in their financial statements (Cunha Marques and Berg, 2011). Although Cunha Marques and Berg (2011) find most European contracts protect the contractor against these risks, governments do not recognise them. CCPPP (2008) calls for more guidance, but note that payment mechanisms indicate the extent of risk transfer.

As an early driver for PPPs was improving governments' balance sheets (Torres and Pina, 2001; Coulson, 2008), governments prefer to believe the rhetoric that risk has been transferred. Yet, Heald and Georgiou (2011) analysed over 600 UK PPP schemes, finding merely 13 per cent of them are 'on' the relevant public sector entity's balance sheet (these represented 43 per cent of the contracts' total value). Information aggregation further obscures necessary detail (Shaoul *et al.* 2008; 2013), with diverse capitalisation of operations and maintenance costs and minimum lease payments, relevant discount rate choice, and timing of recognition (CCPPP 2008). Government can significantly underestimate liabilities, arguing that risks cannot be economically valued or are impractical to identify, assign and value (CCPPP 2008).

Social Impact Bonds: Government has begun outsourcing the risks relating to intransigent social problems to the private not-for-profit sector through Social Impact Bonds (SIBs). They evidence increased privatisation of social services and are similar to PPPs, with the contractor raising most of the project funding. Rather than paying for an infrastructure asset, governments pay for delivery on social outcomes, such as reducing recidivism. These outcomes are unlikely to produce future revenue generation (as a PPP often does). If the contractor meets its target, government will repay the agreed amount and social bond holders receive a return on their 'investment'. As with PPPs, transparency in specifying outcomes and selecting bids is essential. The most difficult SIB aspects are correctly estimating costs and evaluating the outcomes (von Glahn and Whistler, 2014).

World Bank output-based aid subsidies paid as lump sums to not-for-profit development agencies for outputs delivery provide early examples of this pay-for-success model (Tineo, 2007). Similar to PPPs, common risks for this model include construction (where built infrastructure is required), operational, and demand (due to estimates required on the number of beneficiaries). Directing output-based aid to infrastructure use reduces construction risk, as service providers are unlikely to create excess capacity; further, funders' service delivery risks are reduced when payments are linked to the service provider meeting performance targets outputs (International Development Association, 2009; Tineo, 2007). The service providers bear most risk when the intended beneficiaries fail to utilise the service because, unless they meet the key performance targets, they will not receive the aid payments. They must engage with their communities to do so (International Development Association, 2009).

The UK government has used SIBs (also called social bonds) for intransigent social problems since 2010. While SIBs are unsuitable for all forms of social provision, this nascent tool is becoming prevalent in the US, Canada, Australia and beyond (von Glahn and Whistler, 2014; Martin, 2014; Jeram and Wilkinson, 2015). Government contracts for specified outcomes, with the contractor utilising private operating capital while it works on achieving the outcomes over periods of up to eight years. If, within the contract term, their 'treatment group' achieves superior outcomes to a 'control group', the contractor receives the agreed amount, including a return to investors (von Glahn and Whistler, 2014). As stated, the benefits for government are low financial and service risks, with von Glahn and Whistler (2014) highlighting the public sector's incentives to pilot opportunities or scale existing programmes. Indeed, the risk reduction may free the public sector to fund preventative programmes (rather than merely being a safety net), and mitigate its risk averse attitudes. Nevertheless, Cooper *et al.* (2014) find risk aversion in public sector selection of SIB bids, which is likely to limit innovation—a core reason for these bonds.

Further, as not-for-profit organisations struggle to amass equity reserves, they will likely seek for-profit funders to provide operating capital. In addition to bond-holders' financial risks, government bears political risks. For example, New Zealand's media complained that investors would profit 'from our poorest people', perceiving that SIB investors would take funding normally directed at social needs. Cooper *et al.* (2014) note that SIB programme beneficiaries also bear risk when these fail, and are least able to do so.

Although the term 'bond' is used, the debt financing takes numerous forms (von Glahn and Whistler, 2014). SIBs have little or no security due to a lack of infrastructure. Nevertheless, the funding needs and risk levels mean only larger not-for-profit organisations bid for SIBs, and often need to sub-contract out to achieve the desired outcomes (Cooper *et al.* 2014).

The Peterborough Prison recidivism SIB in the UK narrowly missed its early outcome targets[22] but expected to meet the overall target of 7.5 per cent reduction in reoffending (von Glahn and Whistler, 2014; Martin, 2014). Martin (2014) notes that investors' returns could reach 13 per cent, although the SIB was cancelled due to measurement difficulties and high monitoring costs.[23] Due to the risk of such political decisions, Jerram and Wilkinson (2015) suggest that a derivative product (options) be developed to provide investors with the opportunity to match the risk profile with their risk appetite. Strong interest from philanthropists means grants could partially fund SIB projects (von Glahn and Whistler, 2014; Martin, 2014).

While governments' service risks are low under a SIB, Ross Philipson Consulting Ltd (2011) notes significant policy risks. Decisions on potentially successful programmes must also consider how the public will perceive government's stance on its most vulnerable citizens (Cooper *et al.* 2014). Further, financial risks are higher than the World Bank's output-based aid programmes suggest, due to difficulties in pricing outcomes values (Ross Philipson Consulting Ltd, 2011). Further, risks include defining correctly the control group's behaviour, and measuring the treatment group's outcomes (Cooper *et al.* 2014; Ross Philipson Consulting Ltd, 2011). Nevertheless, Innocenti (2015) reports on a successful US SIB, which delivered high-quality preschool education to vulnerable children. A 'picture vocabulary test' was administered to all pre-schoolers and the SIB provider showed that their programme led to higher educational achievements and dramatically reduced special education needs after preschool. Although SIBs were beneficial, Innocenti (2015) found many concerned about their negative aspects, including that private investors received a financial return from public funds.

As with PPPs, SIB contracts differ markedly. For government's accounting, SIBs are likely to be an executory contract—mutually unperformed until the due date. Yet, the IASB's (2015) Conceptual Framework Exposure Draft discusses the differences between executory contracts and lease contracts, asking whether the right to exchange resources (e.g. SIBs' outcomes for cash) results in an asset and liability (similar to an option) or whether, due to the inability to withdraw from a contract, an executory contract like a SIB means a liability only is recognised. Nevertheless, the rewards are received by a third party (the beneficiary of the SIB's activity), making it a non-exchange expense. In a similar way to the pay-for-services accounting under IPSASB (2015) discussed above, there appears to be no obligation for governments to recognise and measure SIBs, although a contingent liability may exist.

Discussion and conclusion

This chapter analysed how governments share and manage risk when they outsource, suggesting it is less successful than the rhetoric suggests. Efficiency and effectiveness are limited by risk averse public sector decision-making. Key risks include service and financial which engender political risk. Barrett (2003, p. 38) recommends a 'proactive and consistent stance to the scrutiny of contracts involving public funds'. Understanding risk management is important.

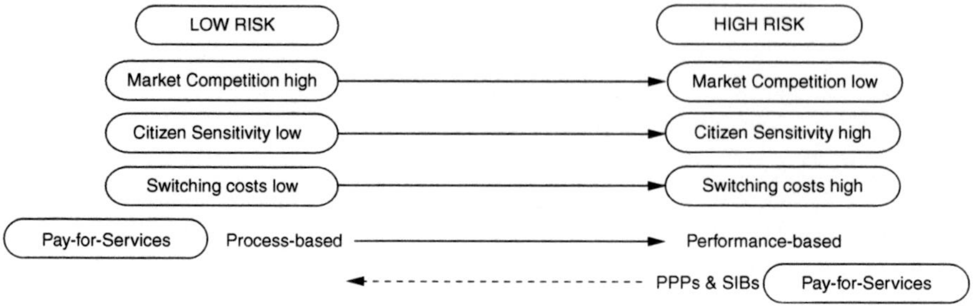

Figure 7.1 Factors in outsourcing that impact risk.

Key problems in public sector risk-sharing and risk management are ambiguous goals and measuring success. Uncertain measurement reduces success in recognising and sharing risks of failure. Subjective risk assessments are unsuited to risk matrices which are commonly used. How government funds (e.g. payment timing or interest rates) directly impacts risk-sharing. Managing risk requires information sharing, which is impaired by privacy issues, thus risk averse managers may monitor excessively, crippling contractors' innovation.

Drawing on Farneti and Young's (2008) risk factors, Figure 7.1 compares pay-for-services and pay-for success outsourcing. It shows that the best contexts for process-based pay-for-services contracts are high market competition, low switching costs and low citizen sensitivity. Conversely, as the context changes, pay-for-services outsourcing has lower transaction costs when it is performance-based and relational. Pay-for-success outsourcing (PPPs and SIBs) occurs in contexts of low market competition and high switching costs (due to their scale, complexity and long-term nature), but have citizen sensitivity. They are at the high risk end of Figure 7.1. Contracts must be carefully specified and managed to move these down the risk 'line'. Van Gestel *et al.* (2012) recommend relational arrangements (network instruments) for complex PPPs, similar to network governance in pay-for-services contracts.

This chapter has also considered relevant financial accounting issues—an area where change is expected as IPSASB reviews non-exchange expenditure, and the IASB reviews its Conceptual Framework.

The chapter finds that for-profit entities with investors seeking good returns bid for profitable, 'easy' PPP contracts. Riskier services are outsourced to not-for-profit entities through annual contracting and SIBs. While SIBs may mitigate government's service risks, it will likely retain financial risk through contracting with an under-resourced (not-for-profit) sector to deliver SIB outcomes with precarious funding. Nevertheless, the engagement of philanthropists provides further risk-sharing opportunities, but leaves government to manage reputational risks while it hopes for success.

Notes

1 Broadbent *et al.* (2008) suggest that this privatisation brought 'the rest of the world' in line with the US model of public service provision.
2 Nevertheless, governments have rescued privatised entities facing financial failure (for example, banks), as insurers of last resort.
3 Risk and uncertainty are often conflated (Froud 2003). Uncertainties are those things that really are unknown—such as how a natural disaster will affect a community or obsolescence of an innovation, as opposed to risk which is a danger that is actively confronted and assessed (Kenny 2000).
4 Barrett (2000) suggests that these goals include consideration of client satisfaction, the public interest, fair play, honesty, justice and equity.

5 A range of funding regimes are outlined by The Treasury (2009). These include fee-for-service, block payments, cost and volume, paying the cost of a particular input, a hybrid, or special payments for activities outside the normal scope of service. Contracts, letters of agreements and grants may operationalise these payments.
6 The UK Treasury (HM Treasury, 2006) also emphasises the need for government purchasers to agree on the timing of payments and make payments as agreed.
7 Due to goal ambiguity and the range of qualitative aspects of public sector risk, training is likely to include models such as the Neustadt–May (1986) Subjective Risk Model as further developed by Adams (1998). This model identifies individuals' psychological characters, enabling decision-makers to appreciate possible risk management solutions from the viewpoint of the multiple stakeholders involved.
8 Expenditure for which the public sector does not itself receive equal value.
9 Lavoie *et al.* (2010) use the terms 'classical' and 'relational' for this dichotomy in their study of indigenous health outsourcing in Canada, Australia and New Zealand.
10 The NAO (2004) and Erridge and Greer (2002) found poor training and a lack of staff incentives to work in partnership with other agencies.
11 Assessment of not-for-profit providers was trialled in the UK but validations were difficult due to a lack of trust between funders. Hence, the UK Government initially funded Guide Star UK as a neutral charity information site.
12 NCVO "A Day in the Life: A work shadow scheme for DCLG and voluntary and community organisations' staff" Downloaded from: http://www.ncvo-vol.org.uk/campaigningeffectiveness/projects/index.asp?id=14614.
13 However, innovation introduces 'unwelcome' calculated risks and potential failures (Cordery 2012).
14 For instance, low decile schools in New Zealand receive breakfasts from a cereal company (Sanitarium), a milk processor (Fonterra), volunteers and government funds (Ministry of Social Development, 2014)
15 The frequency of audit and review (between six-monthly and two-yearly) depends on the risk profile of the organisation, including the activities and levels of funding they receive, as well as the number of complaints and other anecdotal information that is quantified for the purposes of categorising the provider. Data on risk management collected for Cordery (2012).
16 Information from: 'Anne Tolley questions Relationship Aotearoa client numbers' downloaded from http://www.stuff.co.nz/national/politics/69470348/anne-tolley-questions-relationsip-aotearoa-client-numbers; '"Mischievous nonsense" from Relationships Aotearoa, says Government' downloaded from: http://www.stuff.co.nz/national/politics/69177842/Mischievous-nonsense-from-Relationships-Aotearoa-says-Government; 'Relationships—broken and building' downloaded from: http://community.scoop.co.nz/2015/05/relationships-broken-and-building/.
17 Connolly *et al.* (2008, p. 955) state that the UK's Conservative Government initially called PPPs 'Public Finance Initiatives' (PFIs), but the incoming New Labour Government 'expanded the policy of PFI and re-branded it under the umbrella of PPP'. The generic term PPP will be used here.
18 While the bid price should not depend on demand, governments often assume more risk is transferred than actually is, as the provider expects reimbursement from low usage (Boardman and Vining, 2012).
19 Forrer *et al.* (2010) detail specific risk factors which depend on the PPP contract.
20 The UK's PF2 approach responds to credit risk, limiting providers' gearing.
21 Shaoul *et al.* (2011) are concerned that transfer pricing allows for for-profit entities to realise excess profits even when the PPP contractor is a not-for-profit entity.
22 They achieved 8.4 per cent instead of 10 per cent. Downloaded from: http://www.thirdsector.co.uk/peterborough-prison-social-impact-bond-pilot-fails-hit-target-trigger-repayments/finance/article/1307031.
23 "Why the social impact bond at Peterborough prison is being halted" downloaded from: http://www.thirdsector.co.uk/why-social-impact-bond-peterborough-prison-halted/finance/article/1294813.

References

Accounting Task Force of The Canadian Council for Public-Private Partnerships (CCPPP) (2008), *Public Sector Accounting for Public-Private Partnership Transactions in Canada*. A Position Paper, Toronto, Canada.

Acerete, B., J. Shaoul and A. Stafford (2009), 'Taking Its Toll: The Private Financing of Roads in Spain', *Public Money and Management*, 29(1), pp. 19–26.
Adams, J. (1998), *Risk*, London: UCL Press.
Andrews, R., M. Esteve and T. Ysa (2015), 'Public–private Joint Ventures: Mixing Oil and Water?' *Public Money and Management*, 35(4), pp. 265–272.
Australian National Audit Office (2011), *Establishment and Use of Procurement Panels*, Canberra, ACT: ANAO.
Baccarini, D. and R. Archer (2001), 'The Risk Ranking of Projects: A Methodology', *International Journal of Project Management*, 19(3), pp. 139–145.
Barrett, M. (2001), 'A Stakeholder Approach to Responsiveness and Accountability in Non-Profit Organisations', *Social Policy Journal of New Zealand*, 17, pp. 36–51.
Barrett, P. (2000), 'Balancing Accountability and Efficiency in a More Competitive Public Sector Environment', *Australian Journal of Public Administration*, 59(3), pp. 58–71.
Barrett, P. (2003), 'Public Private Partnerships: Are There Gaps in Public Sector Accountability?' *2002 Australasian Council of Public Accounts Committees 7th Biennial Conference*, Melbourne, Australia.
Bhatta, G. (2003), 'Don't Just Do Something, Stand There! Revisiting the Issue of Risks in Innovation in the Public Sector', *The Innovation Journal*, 8(17), p. 15.
Bhattacharya, S., R.S. Behara and D.E. Gundersen (2003), 'Business Risk Perspectives on Information Systems Outsourcing', *International Journal of Accounting Information Systems*, 4(1), pp. 75–93.
Boardman, A.E. and A.R. Vining (2012), 'The Political Economy of Public-private Partnerships and Analysis of Their Social Value', *Annals of Public and Cooperative Economics*, 83(2), pp. 117–141.
Bode, I. and T. Brandsen (2014), 'State–third Sector Partnerships: A Short Overview of Key Issues in the Debate', *Public Management Review*, 16(8), pp. 1055–1066.
Bovaird, T. (2014), 'Efficiency in Third Sector Partnerships for Delivering Local Government Services: The Role of Economies of Scale, Scope and Learning', *Public Management Review*, 16(8), pp. 1067–1090.
Bovaird, T. (2016), 'The Ins and Outs of Outsourcing and Insourcing: What Have We Learnt from the Past 30 Years?, *Public Money and Management*, 36(1), pp. 67–74.
Broadbent, J., J. Gill and R. Laughlin (2008), 'Identifying and Controlling Risk: The Problem of Uncertainty in the Private Finance Initiative in the UK's National Health Service', *Critical Perspectives on Accounting*, 19(1), pp. 40–78.
Carpintero, S. and M. Siemiatycki (2015), 'PPP Projects in Local Infrastructure: Evidence from Schools in the Madrid Region, Spain', *Public Money and Management*, 35(6), pp. 439–446.
Committee of Public Accounts (2001), *Managing risk in government departments*, London: UK Commons.
Comptroller and Auditor General and National Audit Office (2000), *Supporting Innovation: Managing Risk in Government Departments*, London: National Audit Office.
Connolly, C., G. Martin and A. Wall (2008), 'Education, Education, Education: The Third Way and PFI', *Public Administration*, 86(4), pp. 987–1008.
Considine, M. and J.M. Lewis (1999), 'The Frontline Bureaucrat Level in the Age of Markets and Networks', *Public Administration Review*, 59(6), pp. 467–480.
Considine, M. and J.M. Lewis (2003), 'Bureaucracy, Network, or Enterprise? Comparing Models of Governance in Australia, Britain, the Netherlands and New Zealand', *Public Administration Review*, 63(2), pp. 131–140.
Controller and Auditor-General (CAG) (2006), *Principles to underpin management by public entities of funding to non-government organisations*, Wellington, New Zealand.
Controller and Auditor-General (2008), *Public sector purchases, grants, and gifts: Managing funding arrangements with external parties*, Wellington, New Zealand.
Cooper, C., C. Graham and D. Himick (2014), *Social Impact Bonds: Can Private Finance Rescue Public Programmes?* Available from http://criticalperspectivesonaccounting.com/wp-content/ uploads/2014/07/paper-cpa-204.pdf
Cordery, C.J. (2012), '"Procurement Approaches": Why Are There Differences Among Government Agencies in how They Contract for Services from Third- sector Organisations?' *Third Sector Review*, 18(3), pp. 75–97.
Coulson, A. (2008), 'Value for Money in PFI Proposals: A Commentary on the UK Treasury Guidelines for Public Sector Comparators', *Public Administration*, 86(2), pp. 483–498.
Cunha Marques, R. and S. Berg (2011), 'Public-private Partnership Contracts: A Tale of Two Cities with Different Contractual Arrangements', *Public Administration*, 89(4), pp. 1585–1603.

Cuthbert, M. and J. Cuthbert (2010), 'The Royal Infirmary of Edinburgh: A Case Study on the Workings of the Private Finance Initiative', *Public Money and Management*, 30(6), pp. 371–378.
Demirag, I. and I. Khadaroo (2008), 'Accountability and Value for Money in Private Finance Initiative Contracts', *Financial Accountability and Management*, 24(4), pp. 455–478.
Dunston, R. et al. (2009), 'Co-Production and Health System Reform: From Re-Imagining To Re-Making', *Australian Journal of Public Administration*, 68(1), pp. 39–52.
English, L. (2005), 'Using Public-private Partnerships to Achieve Value for Money in the Delivery of Healthcare in Australia', *International Journal of Public Policy*, 1(1/2), pp. 91–121.
Erridge, A. and J. Greer (2002), 'Partnerships and Public Procurement: Building Social Capital through Supply Relations', *Public Administration*, 80(3), pp. 502–522.
Farneti, F. and D.W. Young (2008), 'A Contingency Approach to Managing Outsourcing Risk in Municipalities', *Public Management Review*, 10(1), pp. 89–99.
Fone, M. and P.C. Young (2000), *Public Sector Risk Management*, London: Butterworth-Heinemann.
Forrer, J. et al. (2010), 'Public-private Partnerships and the Public Accountability Question', *Public Administration Review*, 70(3), pp. 475–484.
Froud, J. (2003). 'The Private Finance Initiative: Risk, Uncertainty and the State', *Accounting, Organizations and Society*, 28(6), pp. 567–589.
Furneaux, C. and N. Ryan (2014), 'Modelling NPO–Government Relations: Australian Case Studies', *Public Management Review*, 16(8), pp. 1113–1140.
Gershon, P. (2004), *Releasing Resources to the Front Line: Independent Review of Public Sector Efficiency*, Norwich: HM Treasury.
Grey, S. and C. Sedgwick (2013), 'The Contract State and Constrained Democracy: The Community and Voluntary Sector under Threat', *Policy Quarterly*, 9(3), pp. 3–10.
Grimsey, D. and M.K. Lewis (2005), 'Are Public Private Partnerships Value for Money? Evaluating Alternative Approaches and Comparing Academic and Practitioner Views', *Accounting Forum*, 29(4), pp. 345–378.
Heald, D. and G. Georgiou (2011), 'The Substance of Accounting for Public-Private Partnerships', *Financial Accountability and Management*, 27(May), pp. 217–247.
Hellowell, M. and A.M. Pollock (2010), 'Do PPPs in Social Infrastructure Enhance the Public Interest? Evidence from England's National Health Service.', *Australian Journal of Public Administration*, 69, pp. S23–S34.
Hellowell, M. and V. Vecchi (2012), 'An Evaluation of the Projected Returns to Investors on 10 PFI Projects Commissioned by the National Health Service', *Financial Accountability and Management*, 28(February), pp. 77–100.
Hellowell, M., V. Vecchi, and S. Caselli (2015), 'Return of the State? An Appraisal of Policies to Enhance Access to Credit for Infrastructure-based PPPs', *Public Money and Management*, 35(1), pp. 71–78.
HM Treasury (2006), *Improving Financial Relationships with the Third Sector: Guidance to Funders and Purchasers*, London: HM Treasury.
Holtfreter, K. (2008), 'Determinants of fraud losses in nonprofit organizations', *Nonprofit Management and Leadership*, 19(1), pp. 45–63.
Hood, C. (1995), 'The "New Public Management" in the 1980s: Variations on a Theme', *Accounting, Organizations and Society*, 20(2–3), pp. 93–109.
IFRS Interpretation Committee (2006), *IFRIC Interpretation 12 Service Concession Arrangements*, London: IASB.
Innocenti, M. (2015), 'Op-ed: Pay for Success model changes lives', *The Salt Lake Tribune*. 20 November 2015 downloaded from http://www.sltrib.com/opinion/3218435-155/op-ed-pay-for-success-model-changes
International Accounting Standards Board, 2015. *Conceptual Framework for Financial Reporting: Exposure Draft ED 2015/3*, IASB, London.
International Development Association (2009), *A Review of the Use of Output-Based Aid Approaches*. World Bank, Washington DC.
International Public Sector Accounting Standards Board (IPSASB) (2011), *IPSAS 32—Service Concession Arrangements: Grantor*, Toronto: IPSASB.
International Public Sector Accounting Standards Board (IPSASB) (2015), *Recognition and Measurement of Social Benefits Consultation Paper*, Toronto: IPSASB.
Jensen, P.H. and R.E. Stonecash (2005), 'Incentives and the Efficiency of Public Sector-outsourcing Contracts', *Journal of Economic Surveys*, 19(5), pp. 767–787.

Jeram, J. and B. Wilkinson, (2015), 'Investing for Success: Social Impact Bonds and the Future of Public Services', *The New Zealand Initiative*, (December), pp. 1–24.

Kenny, S. (2000), 'Third Sector Organisations and Risk', *Third Sector Review*, 6(1/2), pp. 71–87.

Lavoie, J., A. Boulton and J. Dwyer (2010), 'Analysing Contractual Environments: Lessons from Indigenous Health in Canada, Australia and New Zealand', *Public Administration*, 88(3), pp. 665–679.

Maddock, S. (2002), 'Making Modernisation Work: New Narratives, Change, Strategies and People Management in the Public Sector', *The International Journal of Public Sector Management*, 15(1), pp. 13–43.

Martin, M. (2014), 'The New Frontiers of Philanthropy in Global Perspective', in L.M. Salamon (ed.), *The New Frontiers of Philanthropy*. Oxford: Oxford University Press, pp. 604–635.

Ministry of Social Development (2014) 'Kick Start' 20 November ... Available from: https://www.msd.govt.nz/about-msd-and-our-work/newsroom/stories/2014/kickstart.html

Mühlenkamp, H. (2014), 'Public-Private Partnerships and Government Debt', *CESifo DICE Report*, 03/2014, pp. 24–30.

National Audit Office (NAO) (2004). Managing Risks to Improve Public Services, National Audit Office, London p.73.

Neustadt, R. and E. May (1986), *Thinking in Time*, New York: Free Press.

New Zealand Productivity Commission (2015), More effective social services, Wellington, New Zealand: The New Zealand Productivity Commission.

Nowland-Foreman, G. (1997), 'Can Voluntary Organisations Survive the Bear Hug of Government Funding under a Contracting Regime? A View from Aotearoa New Zealand', *Third Sector Review*, 3, pp. 5–39.

Organization of Economic Cooperation and Development (2009), *OECD Principles for Integrity in Public Procurement*, OECD, Paris, available at http://www.oecd.org/gov/ethics/48994520.pdf

Padovani, E. and D.W. Young (2008), 'Toward a Framework for Managing High-risk Government Outsourcing: Field Research in Three Italian Municipalities' *Journal of Public Procurement*, 8(2), pp. 215–247.

Pickering, A. and S. Cowley (2010), 'Risk Matrices: Implied Accuracy and False Assumptions', *Journal of Health and Safety Research & Practice*, 2(1), pp. 9–16.

Pomeroy, A. (2007), 'Changing the Culture of Contracting: Funding for Outcomes', *Social Policy Journal of New Zealand*, 31(July), pp. 158–169.

PwC Advisory (2015), *Relationships Aotearoa Report to the Board of Governance*, Pricewater houseCoopers, Wellington.

Romzek, B.S. and J.M. Johnston (2005), State Social Services Contracting: Exploring the Determinants of Effective Contract Aaccountability', *Public Administration Review*, 65(4), pp. 436–449.

Ross Philipson Consulting Ltd (2011), *The Potential for Social Impact Bonds in New Zealand: A Report Prepared for the Department of Internal Affairs*, Wellington, New Zealand: Ross Philipson Consulting Ltd

Ryan, B. (2012), 'Co-production: Option or Obligation? *Australian Journal of Public Administration*, 71(3), pp. 314–324.

Schapper, P.R., J.N. Veiga Malta and D.L. Gilbert (2006), 'An Analytical Framework for the Management and Reform of Public Procurement', *Journal of Public Procurement*, 6(1/2), pp. 1–26.

Schmid, H. (2003), 'Rethinking the Policy of Contracting out Social Services to Non-governmental Organizations', *Public Management Review*, 5(3), pp. 307–323.

Schwartz, R. (2005), 'The Contracting Quandary: Managing Local Authority-VNPO Relations', *Local Government Studies*, 31(1), pp. 69–83.

Scott, G. (1999), 'Managing Operational and Policy Risks at the Centre of Government', in A. Sundakov and J. Yeabsley (eds.), *Risk and the Institutions of Government*. Wellington: Institute of Policy Studies, Victoria University of Wellington, pp. 14–34.

Shaoul, J., Shepherd, A., Stafford, A. and Stapleton, P. (2013), 'Losing Control in Joint Ventures: The Case of Building Schools for the Future'. Available at: http://icas.org.uk/stafford/

Shaoul, J., A. Stafford and P. Stapleton (2008), 'The Cost of Using Private Finance to Build, Finance and Operate Hospitals', *Public Money and Management*, 28(2), pp. 101–108.

Shaoul, J., A. Stafford and P. Stapleton (2011), 'Private Finance: Bridging the Gap for the UK's Dartford and Skye Bridges?' *Public Money and Management*, 31(1), pp. 51–58.

Strategy Unit (2002), *Risk: Improving Government's Capability to Handle Risk and Uncertainty*, London: Strategy Unit.

Sundakov, A. and J. Yeabsley (1999), *Risk and the Institutions of Government*, Wellington: Institute of Policy Studies, Victoria University of Wellington.

The Treasury (2009), *Guidelines for Contracting with Non-Government Organisations for Services Sought by the Crown*, Wellington: The Treasury Kaitohutohu Kaupapa Rawa.

Tineo, L. (2007), 'Procurement Issues in Performance-Based Contracts: The World Bank Experience With Output-Based Aid Subsidies', *Journal of Public Procurement*, 7(1), pp. 62–83.

Torres, L. and V. Pina (2001), 'Public–Private Partnership and Private Finance Initiatives in the EU and Spanish Local Governments', *European Accounting Review*, 10(3), pp. 601–619.

Treasury Board of Canada Secretariat (2001), Integrated Risk Management Framework, Treasury Board of Canada Secretariat, Government of Canada, Ontario.

Van Gestel, K., J. Voets and K. Verhoest (2012), 'How Governance of Complex PPPs Affects Performance', *Public Administration Quarterly*, 36(2), pp. 140–188.

Vital Signs Consulting (2015), *Funders Year End Report Relationships Aotearoa Capability and Sustainability Programme to 31 December 2014*, Vital Signs Consulting, Wellington.

von Glahn, D. and C. Whistler (2014), 'Social-Impact Bonds/Pay-for-success Financing, in L.M. Salamon (ed.), *The New Frontiers of Philanthropy*, Oxford: Oxford University Press, pp. 424–456.

Woods, M. (2011), *Risk Management in Organizations: An Integrated Case Study Approach*, London: Routledge.

8

Case study: Carbon risk management in a regulatory context

The case of New Zealand

Binh Bui

Introduction

Risk management is a topic that receives significant attention from both academics and professionals, not least because of the increasing uncertainties and changes characterising today's business environment. Climate change and the proposed introduction of emissions trading scheme (ETS) in different countries around the world have added to the existing internal and external risks that businesses are exposed to in their operating environments. A number of scholars argue that organisational risk and uncertainty have an external control over organisations and determine organisational behaviour and performance (Hannan and Freeman, 1977; Aldrich, 1979; McKelvey, 1982). There is emerging literature that investigates how organisations respond to climate change issues (Jones and Levy, 2007; Weinhofer and Hoffmann, 2010; Jeswani *et al.* 2008). However, little empirical insight is available from a risk management perspective regarding the risks emerging from climate change and an ETS for specific industries and businesses, or the effectiveness of organisational responses. As firms' environments are increasingly driven by carbon-related risks, it is important to understand how these risks are managed to maintain organisational performance and achieve organisational objectives.

Using an enterprise risk management framework, this chapter reports a study aimed at examining and explaining the process used by organisations to identify and evaluate carbon-related risks and the changes that have been, or planned to be, undertaken to manage such risks. Towards this aim, the study has four main objectives, including first, to identify the carbon-related risks; second, to examine how organisations analyse and evaluate such risks; third, to understand how these risks are communicated and monitored; and fourth, to explore the plans organisations use to treat these risks.

To achieve these objectives, the risk perspective from the Risk Management Standard ISO (International Organization for Standardization) 31000:2009 (ISO, 2009) is employed to facilitate the assessment of risk and enable the explanation of organisational response to particular risks. The context and subject for investigation are 30 New Zealand organisations of varying sizes that operate in the public and private sectors. A field study approach is employed to guide the study, involving interview data and analysing them using both qualitative and quantitative approaches.

The findings suggest different approaches to carbon risk management (CRM). Organisations identify different operational and strategic risks associated with carbon issues. They can analyse carbon risks financially or non-financially, but are unlikely to put a threshold in evaluating the risks. Monitoring and reviewing of carbon risks are often undertaken monthly and integrated in routine performance review. However, the monitoring is often passive and relying on a third party. Diverse plans are established to treat the risks and carbon information is often disseminated widely within the organisation. However, CRM is relatively immature with development required to improve data accuracy. By applying a risk management perspective, this field study offers risk-based explanations for organisational response to carbon issues. The findings of this field study contribute to and extend prior literatures in risk management and carbon management.

The rest of the chapter is organised as follows. First, prior literature on risk and risk management is reviewed. This will be followed by a section that provides a background on NZ ETS in New Zealand and CRM. The methodology section will follow to outline the choice of subjects and methods for collecting and analysing data. Next, the findings are presented. Then the chapter is concluded with contributions and limitations.

Literature review

The concept of risk

Concepts of risk and risk management literature have been addressed in other chapters of the book. However, a review is provided here so that this case study can serve as a stand-alone chapter that can be used independently of the rest of the book.

Extensive research on risk has not been able to provide a widely acceptable definition of risk (Renn, 1998). Risk is conceptualised in accounting and finance as the probability or degree of loss. In Frank Knight's book, *Risk, Uncertainty and Profit* (1921), he defined risk as a state of not knowing what future events will happen, but having the ability to estimate the odds, while uncertainty was a state of not knowing the odds. However, the term has been used too commonly to represent decision situations which involve uncertainty as well as risk and where degree of uncertainty is subject to change and difficult to reliably estimate in advance (Ritchie and Brindley, 2007).

Recently, the definition of risk has been extended to capture additional exposures in the business environments. The International Federation of Accountants (IFAC) (1999, p. 4) defined risk as 'uncertain future events that could influence the achievement of the organisation's strategic, operational and financial objectives'. This definition also shifts risk from a negative concept to a positive interpretation, of which risk management can bring about enhancements in organisational performance. Accounting professions around the world have adopted similar definitions to IFAC's (1999) definition (IRM, 2002; Financial Reporting Council, 2003; Standards Australia and Standards New Zealand, 2004). Similarly, Risk Management Standard ISO 31000 (2009, p. 1)explicitly recognises risk as 'the effect of uncertainty on objectives' with the effect being the positive or negative deviation from the expected result. Risk is conceptualised in this chapter in accordance with this definition. This allows the coverage of both negative and positive risk to the achievement of organisational objectives.

Risk management

Many organisations have found that risk management has become a business requisite. According to the Institute of Risk Management (IRM, 2002, p. 2), risk management is a central part of any organisation's strategic management and defined as 'the process whereby organisations methodically address the risks attaching to their activities with the goal of achieving sustained benefit within each activity and across the portfolio of all activities'. Risk management focuses on identifying and treating these risks with an aim to add maximum value to the activities conducted by the organisation. Risk management is considered a process that should be conducted continuously and throughout an organisation's strategy and the implementation of that strategy. As such, it ensures effective achievement of strategy, increases chance of success and reduces probability of failure and uncertainty in the organisation's operating environments (IRM, 2002). Risk management is concerned with both negative and positive aspects of risk (ISO, 2009). Hence, managing risk is about identifying and responding to business opportunities as well as taking action to avoid or reduce the chance of things going wrong (ISO, 2009).

From the late 1990s and early 2000s, professionals and experts developed different risk management frameworks. The most widely known are enterprise risk management (ERM) frameworks. ERM assumes that organisations exist to provide value to stakeholders and hence management's role is to strike a balance between growth and return goals and related risks (Committee of Sponsoring Organizations of the Treadway Commission (COSO), 2004). ERM incorporates 'risks of achieving strategy, maintaining quality, achieving financial and non-financial performance targets and continual improvement' with an aim to maintain and achieve a competitive advantage (Collier, 2009,p. 10). Further, the integration of risk management in strategic planning enables the focus upon performance improvement, rather than mere compliance to corporate governance and risk guidelines and frameworks. An effective strategy will need to fulfil the dual need to reduce risks and increase returns, and ultimately, secure organisational performance and survival (Ritchie and Marshall, 1993). In addition to performance improvement, ERM enables improved accountability, better access to strategic information and planning, promotes operational efficiency and economy, facilitates better relationships with stakeholders, and enhances organisational reputation and personal well-being (ISO, 2009). New boundaries can also be created, limiting or enabling organisational activities and leading to organisational change (Bhimani, 2009; Mikes, 2009).

Overall, risk management is increasingly recognised by regulators, practitioners and academics alike as an integral part of the process of corporate governance, and an aid to the achievement of strategic objectives (Alkaraan and Northcott, 2006; Northcott and Alkaraan, 2007; Woods, 2009). The spread and rise of risk management has been seen as a social phenomenon, 'the risk management of everything' (Power, 2004, p. 59). However, little is known about how risk management works in practice (Mikes, 2009). Specifically, insight is lacking regarding how organisations identify and evaluate risks, how they formulate controls and strategies to treat the risks, and how such risks are monitored and reviewed. This study aims to provide some empirical evidence for this issue, using the risk management framework recommended in risk management standard ISO 31000:2009. This framework is briefly explained next.

Risk management framework

The risk management framework recommended by ISO (2009) and reproduced elsewhere (such as AS/NZS ISO 31000:2009) includes the following steps: establish the context, assess risk, treat risk, communicate and consult, and monitor and review.

Establishing the context: the organisation has to consider both external and internal context when managing risk. External context includes the external stakeholders and environment and any external factors that may influence organisational objectives. Internal context includes internal stakeholders, governance approach, contractual relationships, capabilities, standards and cultures.

Risk assessment is comprised of three activities: risk identification, risk analysis, and risk evaluation. Risk identification is a process used to find, recognise and describe the risks affecting organisational objectives. Risk analysis helps understand the nature, source, consequence (the level of impact of the risk on organisational performance), and probability of risk (the likelihood of the event/incident happening that give rise to the risk). Risk evaluation compares risk analysis with predefined risk criteria so as to decide whether certain risk is acceptable or not.

Risk treatment is used to modify the risk. Organisations have the option of implementing one or several treatment plans for each risk. When a plan is implemented it becomes a control or modifies existing controls. The treatment plans can help avoid, reduce the likelihood or consequence of a risk, share the risk with external organisations or retain the risk through an internal absorption strategy. For positive risks (opportunities) organisations can also seek the risks or increase the probability or consequence.

Communication and consultation are the dialogue between the organisation and its stakeholders to share and receive information regarding the management of risk. This communication enables the organisation to make decisions regarding different aspects of risk management such as risk tolerance level, and risk treatment plans.

Monitoring requires the supervision and regular check and observation of risk. It helps determine the current status of the risks and assess whether the expected performance is being achieved. Differently, review is required of risk management plans, policy, risks, risk criteria, risk treatment, controls and residual risks. These reviews help determine whether these aspects of risk management are adequate or suitable.

Making risk quantitative and procedural through a risk management framework increases the capacity for risk to be managerially actionable (Bhimani, 2009). Hence, following this framework, understanding can be gained regarding which extent organisations operationalise risk management and affect the level of risk to which they are exposed.

New Zealand ETS and carbon risk management

The New Zealand Government recognises that New Zealand needs to do its share to help the world deal with the challenge presented by climate change (New Zealand Government, 2007b). On 19 December 2002, the New Zealand Government ratified the Kyoto Protocol (MfE, 2009). A carbon tax plan was proposed in April 2002 but was cancelled following a review. In October 2007, the Labour-led Government announced its new package of climate change policies, including an Emissions Trading System (NZ ETS) and supporting sustainability initiatives. The ETS was legislated in September 2008. Accordingly, the NZ ETS would be implemented on a nation-wide level, including all sectors and all gases (New Zealand Government, 2007a).

In 2008 the National Party won the election and became the new government. Consequently, the ETS was reviewed and has been revised several times since. Under the Moderated ETS Bill (2009) organisations with an ETS obligation (known as 'ETS participants') will be given transitional assistance measures, including 2-for-1 obligation and price safety, for the period from 2008 to 2012. The 2-for-1 obligation means that organisations only have to surrender 1 carbon credit for every two tonnes of carbon emissions. Price safety means the organisations have the option of paying NZ$25 per credit directly to the government instead of surrendering the carbon credits. A number of further changes were enacted in 2013, among which is the extension of transitional measures beyond 2012. Additionally, in August 2009, the government announced a mid-term emissions reduction target of 10 per cent to 20 per cent below 1990 levels by 2020, contingent on the actions of other developed and developing countries. In July 2015 a provisional post-2020 target of 30 per cent below 2005 emissions level has also been adopted (MfE, 2014)

A number of prior studies examine corporate response to an ETS and climate change issues. For example, Kolk and Pinkse (2005) research 136 Global 500 companies and find a number of strategies, including internal innovation, external compensation, and cooperation with supply chain partners or beyond their supply chain (e.g. non-government organisations (NGOs) or government organisations). Jones and Levy (2007) suggest that firms pursue different response strategies to climate change and the comprehensiveness of these responses depends on organisational exposure to climate risks, their sectoral location, organisational capabilities, and top management preferences. Further, some emphasise internal innovation aimed at carbon reduction while others focus on carbon trading. Similarly, Weinhofer and Hoffmann (2010) report that electricity generators use three types of climate change strategies, namely carbon compensation (e.g. participating in the ETS and generating carbon offsets), carbon reduction (i.e. internal innovation to lower carbon footprint of products and production), and carbon independence (designing carbon-free production and products). These strategies are often combined, and differ according to region, company size, and emission levels. These studies overall suggest that climate change responses vary according to certain organisational factors and, particularly, emissions levels and associated risks. However, no prior study has explicitly employed a risk management framework to investigate how organisations manage climate change risks, especially under a regulatory context such as an ETS. The next section highlights the methods used by this study to examine organisations' CRM practices.

Methodology

Research subjects

To enable us to understand CRM in variety of settings, a field study approach is adopted. This approach has the advantage over a case study approach, which only explains organisational response in a particular setting (Arjaliès and Mundy, 2013; Mikes, 2009; Kraus and Lind, 2010). It is also a preferred approach over surveys, as prior studies do not provide established research instruments and variables regarding CRM. Through interviews, understanding is gained at a more in-depth level of the process with which organisations identify and manage carbon-related risks. Further, a field study enables data collection over a number of organisations, and hence can yield a more complete picture of the risk management practice in a given industry or country at a particular point in time. Therefore, the insights gained can also be compared with past or future research that are conducted in different settings (Engels, 2009).

Organisations that satisfy a number of criteria are chosen, including having an obligation under the ETS, and/or are relatively energy-intensive, and/or are environmentally responsible as demonstrated in publicly available information such as annual reports or newspapers. Additionally, organisations that do not satisfy these criteria are also contacted in order to gain a balanced sample that include firms that are likely to pay either significant or little attention to climate change issues. Overall, 30 organisations agree to participate in the research with 12 being participants under the ETS and 18 not having an ETS obligation.

Thirty-eight interviews are conducted with 39 interviewees from these 30 organisations. The interviewees are managers who have the highest responsibility for carbon management within each organisation. These can be a senior manager—such as the chief financial officer (CFO) or the chief executive officer (CEO)—risk manager, environmental manager, or operations manager, or the purchasing manager. The interviews lasted from 1 hour to 2 hours.

Analytical methods

This study relies on both qualitative and quantitative methods in data collection and analysis. Thematic coding and analytical tools are used to code and analyse the interview data. Thematic analysis gives the flexibility that can potentially yield 'rich and detailed, yet complex, accounts of data' (Braun and Clarke, 2006, p. 78). Consistent with the risk management framework in Figure 8.1 and the key issues emerging from data analysis, the data are coded into the following themes:

- Risk communication and consultation
- Risk identification
- Risk monitoring and review
- Risk analysis
- Risk evaluation
- Risk treatment plans

The step of 'establishing the context' is omitted as this chapter refers to the only context common to all the organisations: the regulatory environment under the ETS and the risks associated with this regulation.

Within each theme different approaches are identified, and then the percentages are calculated to understand the distribution of approaches across the sample. For example, within risk review, how many and what percentage of organisations review carbon performance monthly, quarterly and annually, are identified. Additionally, scoring is done for the approach used by each organisation on different scales from 0 to 5, so as to assess the responsiveness with which the risk management takes place. A higher score denotes a more complex and resource-demanding approach to risk management. The scores are then added across the themes in order to gain an aggregate score representing the comprehensiveness of an organisation's CRM process. The presence of all the elements represents the effectiveness of enterprise risk management (COSO, 2004). The scoring methodology is provided in Table 8.1.

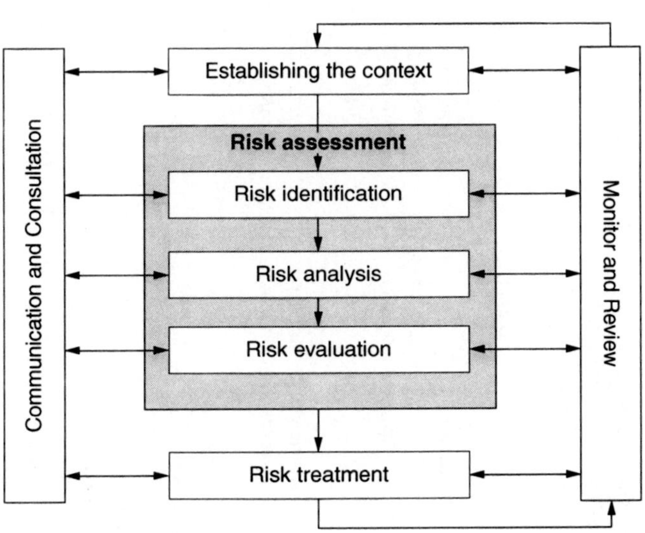

Figure 8.1 Risk management framework (adapted from ISO, 2009).

Table 8.1 Scoring methodology

Score	*0*	*1*	*2*	*3*	*4*	*5*
Risk consultation	No communication	between environmental manager/ accounting and operations	between environmental manager + operations + some top management	dedicated group	extensive top management involvement	disseminated throughout org + dedicated team
Carbon price monitoring	no monitoring	passive (third party) monitoring	actively daily monitoring	actively monthly monitoring		
Emissions monitoring	no monitoring	annual supplier invoices	monthly supplier invoices or operations report	onsite continuous monitors	onsite monitors + supplier invoices	
Carbon performance review	no review	annual review	quarterly review	monthly review		
Risk identification	no risk	1 risk/opportunity	2 risks/opportunities	3 risks/ opportunities	4 risks/ opportunities	5 risks/opportunities
Risk analysis	no analysis	carbon footprint only	convert to carbon cost and loss/gain	multiple years risk assessment		
Risk evaluation	no threshold or separation	some threshold of tolerable risk				
Cost from suppliers	no plan	internalise carbon in fuel price	monitor and manage overcharge	self-manage and give credits to suppliers		
Price management	no plans	buy at market price	forward purchase			
Capital investment	no integration in modelling	carbon integrated in modelling				
Energy efficiency	no plan	some initiatives	extensive initiatives			
Cost pass-on		cost pass-on	no cost pass-on[1]			
Carbon offset	no offsets	buy external offsets	self-generate offsets			
Customer education	no education	educating customers on carbon				

Findings

Risk communication and consultation

For effective management of climate change risks, it is important that climate change issues are widely discussed and communicated within the organisation. Overall, most organisations communicate carbon issues widely (Figure 8.2). A combined 42 per cent of the firms either involve top management extensively in the monitoring and review of climate change risks, or disseminate and discuss climate change information throughout the organisation. In addition, 10 per cent communicate these issues within a dedicated group, which often includes a member of the top management team, the environmental manager, an operations manager and a carbon accountant. The senior manager provides oversight and leadership to the group. The environmental manager collects carbon information from operations and calculates total carbon emissions levels, which accounting converts into carbon liability and costs, and reports to relevant parties. Operations monitor and manage actual carbon levels. Sometimes the team includes a procurement officer who buys carbon credits for voluntary offsetting or meeting ETS surrendering obligation. Overall, over half (52 per cent) of the organisations disseminate carbon information to different levels of management, suggesting the high importance of climate change issues. For the remaining half, consultations about climate change issues only take place among a few managers, either between environmental manager and accountant with operations (24 per cent) or between environmental manager and accountant and a senior manager (10 per cent), while 14 per cent of the organisations do not undertake any form of carbon-related consultation.

Identifying climate change risks

This identification of carbon risks and their impacts on the organisation normally takes place at the senior level, but also can involve consultation with lower levels of management and external stakeholders, through an interactive system, especially when the risks are seen as having strategic implications and uncertainty (Simons, 1995). Risk identification is one of the most important elements of effective carbon management (Tang and Luo, 2014). Risk understanding, especially through an interactive system, enables organisations to anticipate the unexpected and uncertainty associated with climate change policy and formulate appropriate strategies and processes (Arjaliès and Mundy, 2013).

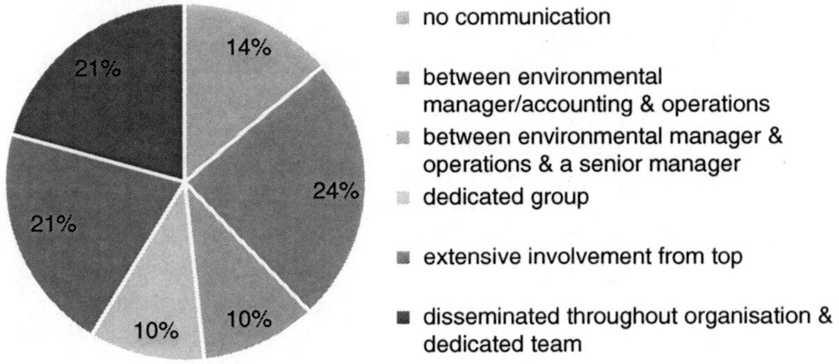

Figure 8.2 Communication and consultation of climate change risks.

The risks identified are both strategic and operational in nature (Figure 8.3). Strategic and competitive risks are the most common risks (recognised by 48 per cent), suggesting that many firms consider that climate change issues affect the sustainability of their business model or market competitiveness. This is followed by compliance risks (41 per cent) related to the measurement, reporting, auditing of carbon data and surrendering of carbon credits. Compliance risks are understandably one of the foremost concerns for many, due to their obligation under the ETS. An equal number of the organisations are concerned about either price exposure, energy efficiency, or carbon footprint/accountability (34 per cent). Price exposure relates to the fluctuations of carbon prices, leading to buying carbon credits at the wrong time or of the wrong amount, resulting in excessive carbon costs. Energy efficiency relates to the efficiency of energy usage in organisational operations and facilities, such as buildings, machines, staff travel, paper consumption and waste. Low energy efficiency leads directly to high energy costs and high carbon levels, which in turn lead to high carbon costs. Further, organisations are also concerned that high carbon footprint reflects low corporate social responsibility and hence they try to manage carbon levels to demonstrate accountability. Only 14 per cent recognise a risk of supplier overcharge regarding carbon costs. Many interviewees are surprised to learn of the possibility that their company might have been overcharged by suppliers. It is a common practice in some industries that suppliers charge a nominal rate for carbon (e.g. NZ$25) while the actual market price is very low (around NZ$5 per credit). This suggests the low understanding and knowledge of the workings of the carbon markets by most firms. Finally, a small number of firms identified the risks associated with carbon offset loss (e.g. forest fire), billing (accurate billing or separation of carbon costs from other costs), and regulatory risks. Some interviewees suggest that firms are comforted by low market prices and hence ETS-related regulatory changes are not perceived to pose a serious threat.

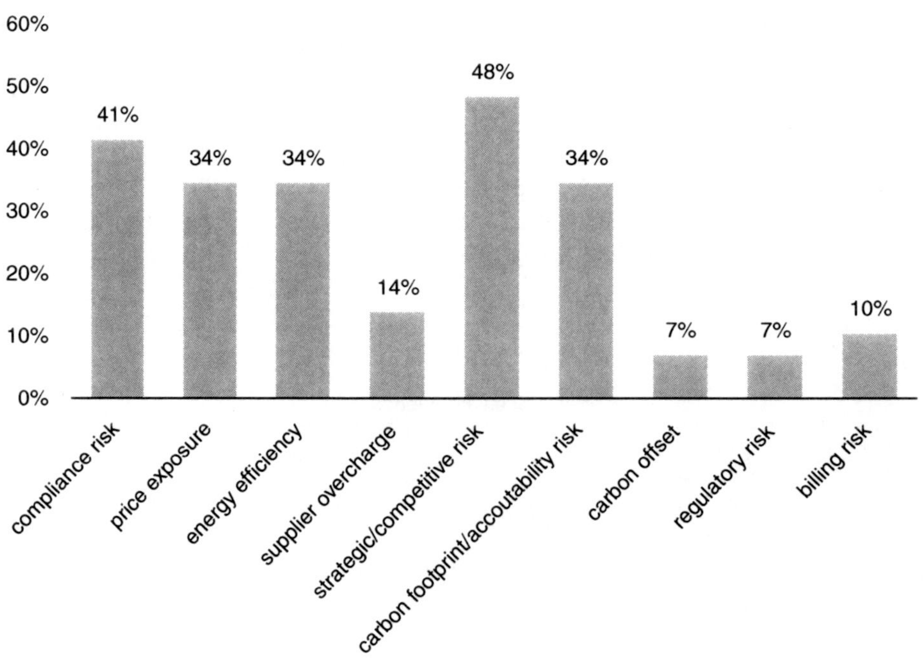

Figure 8.3 Climate change risks identified.

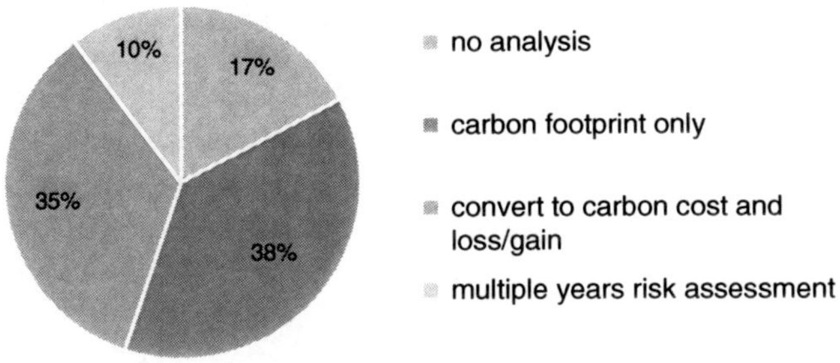

Figure 8.4 Risk analysis.

Risk analysis

In analysing climate change risks, organisations have the choice of considering the physical or monetary component of the risks. Approximately an equal number of organisations either analyse only the carbon footprint (38 per cent) or convert it into carbon cost and loss/gain (35 per cent) (Figure 8.4). In calculating carbon footprint, organisations often rely on supplier invoices or operational records to gain information on energy use and carbon-related activities, and then multiply by an appropriate emissions factor. Some firms that use onsite monitors can directly measure and test emissions levels, and so they only have to aggregate emissions levels from different sites to get total organisational carbon footprint. Firms that are highly energy intensive and those with an ETS obligation also convert carbon footprint into carbon cost or liability using the prevailing market carbon prices. A small group (10 per cent) also undertake multiple-year risk assessment that involves analysing carbon footprint or cost over the long term. This reflects a forward-looking, future-oriented approach to risk management, as opposed to the short-term, past-oriented carbon calculation. However, apart from direct carbon costs, the organisations do not calculate possible gains or losses from such risks as competitive advantage/disadvantage, supplier overcharge, and energy (in)efficiency. This suggests a relatively narrow scope of carbon risk analysis.

Risk evaluation

Most organisations do not differentiate between different levels of risk in their risk evaluation (Figure 8.5). Seventy-two per cent do not distinguish between tolerable versus non-tolerable risks or establish a threshold for doing so. However, without a quantitative threshold, organisations implicitly put a qualitative judgement on the 'major' risks. For example, many consider energy costs to be the biggest costs, which drive a high level of carbon emissions. Hence, carbon costs associated with energy costs are seen as the risk that deserves the most managerial attention. However, the fact that many do not put a quantitative value on other risks such as supplier overcharge or competitive disadvantage, or attempt to evaluate them using a definite threshold, suggests a narrow scope of CRM.

Twenty-eight per cent of the organisations establish a threshold in evaluating carbon risks. For example, C7 has the policy of 'not wanting to be in a net liability position', and hence always buys more or enough carbon credits to cover for the estimated emissions levels. These organisations undertake forward purchase to manage the risk of carbon price fluctuations. The threshold varies, suggesting different risk tolerance levels, with some choosing to buy forward 25 per cent of the obligation balance, or as small as 10 per cent of the annual emissions. The organisations consider risks presented by the remaining emissions as tolerable and hence accept exposure to the market.

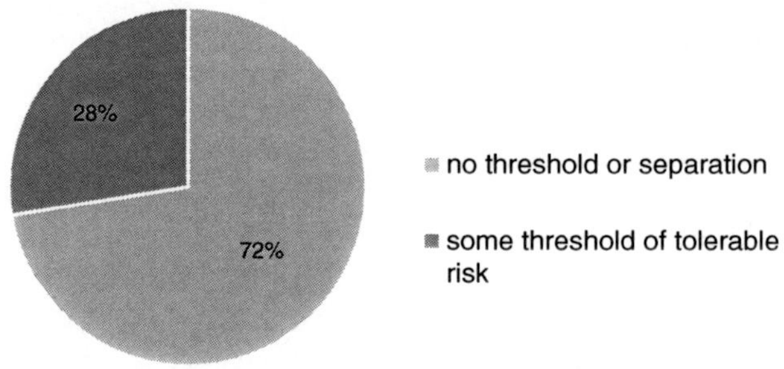

Figure 8.5 Risk evaluation.

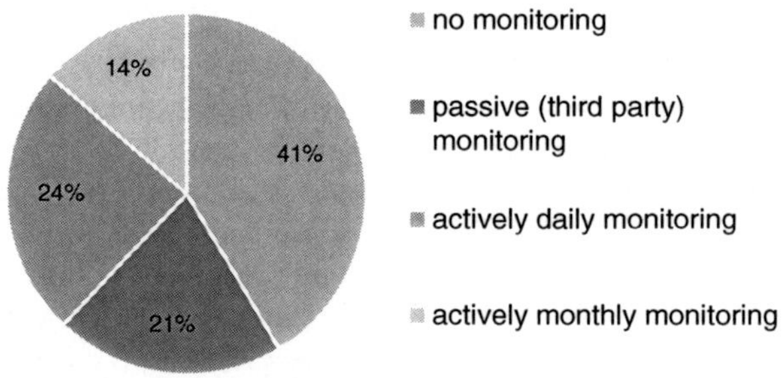

Figure 8.6 Carbon price monitoring system.

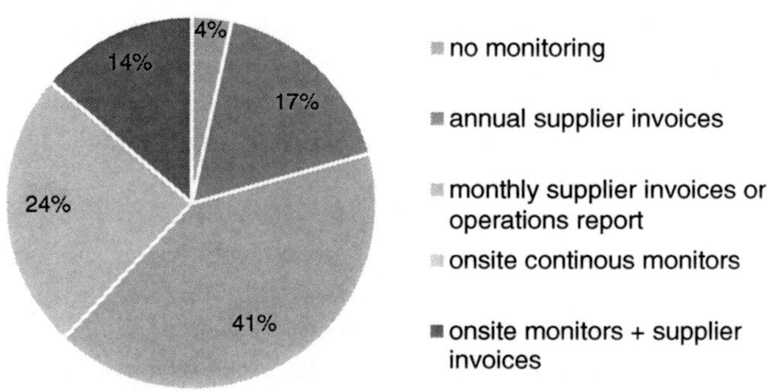

Figure 8.7 Emissions monitoring system.

Monitoring risks: carbon price and emissions levels

To enable effective risk management, organisations need to monitor carbon prices and/or emissions levels. As price exposure is identified as one of the major risks, monitoring price fluctuations is understandably a key activity for many firms. However, 41 per cent do not undertake any monitoring (Figure 8.6). Of the 59 per cent that pay attention to fluctuations in carbon prices, 21 per cent only monitor passively, through a report from a third party. Despite receiving this report, organisations do not analyse the information or act on it. In contrast, 38 per cent undertake active monitoring, either monthly (14 per cent) or daily (24 per cent). This is compatible with the 34 per cent of the firms that consider price exposure as a key climate change risk.

In contrast to price monitoring, 96 per cent of the organisations undertake some form of emissions monitoring (Figure 8.7). The most common type of monitoring is through monthly supplier invoices or operations reports. Seventeen per cent also use supplier invoices, but only on an annual basis. They ask suppliers to provide a breakdown of the emissions associated with the energy purchase in the supplier invoices. Operations report is provided by operational functions, detailing the level of emissions by fuel type and plant. However, a monthly operations report or annual supplier invoices are not very accurate and do not provide timely information for decision making. In contrast, 24 per cent employ onsite continuous monitors, which deliver a high level of data accuracy and high frequency of information provision. A small number of organisations (14 per cent) combine onsite monitors (providing information on energy consumption) and supplier invoices (providing information on energy purchase), enabling verification of energy use and emissions levels, hence providing the highest level of data accuracy.

Treat carbon-related risks

Data analysis suggests that there are different approaches adopted by companies to treat climate change risks (Figure 8.8). The most common approaches are: having a formal carbon management strategy (66 per cent), internal energy efficiency (62 per cent), followed by participation in policy processes (50 per cent), voluntary data verification/audit (45 per cent), carbon price management (41 per cent), and capital investment (41 per cent).

Two-thirds of the interviewed organisations have a formal carbon management and/or sustainability strategy. A carbon management strategy demonstrates organisational awareness and commitment to managing carbon-related risks. The development of a formal strategy requires financial and personnel investments to assess risks and opportunities, then discussion at board and managerial level to formalise the strategy. Strategy implementation in turn requires resource allocation to specific operational and strategic initiatives.

As opposed to capital investment, energy efficiency initiatives require less resource investment and commitment, representing ‘low-hanging fruit’ that most organisations can utilise. Hence, internal energy efficiency is unsurprisingly a popular approach to managing emissions.

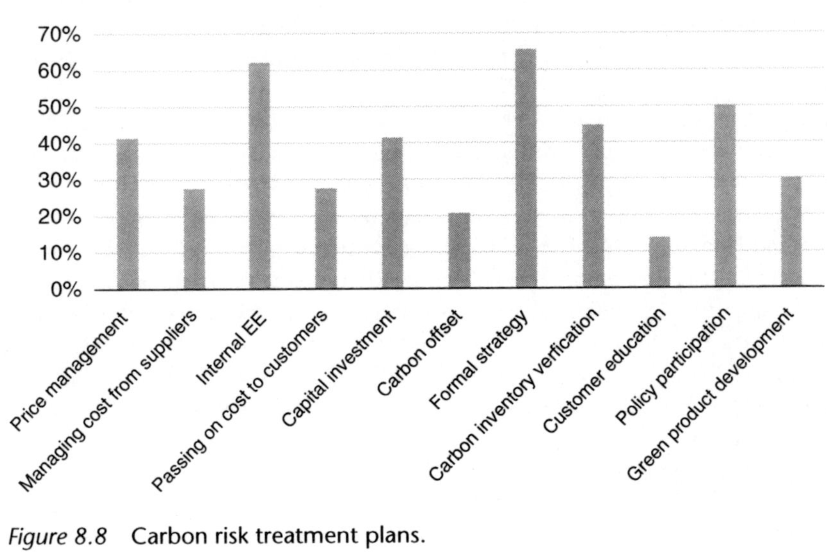

Figure 8.8 Carbon risk treatment plans.

Energy efficiency through initiatives such as managing fuel and energy consumption of machines and buildings, waste management, recycling and staff travel streamlining lower the level of direct and indirect emissions arising from organisational operations. Furthermore, energy efficiency reduces the amount of energy use, hence indirectly reducing the amount of carbon cost passed on from electricity and fuel suppliers. This is consistent with Kolk and Pinkse (2004) who also find that most organisations choose internally oriented measures that aim at improving energy efficiency as a key climate change response.

Fifty per cent of the organisations participate in ETS policy processes through submissions to various consultations associated with ETS reviews. By participating in the ETS policy development process, organisations can negotiate and influence the source of the risks—the government and its climate change policy (Bonardi and Keim, 2005). Firms participate in policy processes to maintain or gain a competitive advantage and hurt their rivals (Mahon, 1989; Hillman and Hitt, 1999). Thermal-based generators or highly energy intensive manufacturers participate in this process to delay or prevent the ETS introduction so as to avoid emissions liabilities and costs. Others argue for government assistance mechanisms to reduce carbon costs or liability (affecting risk consequence). Some who have a low emissions level positively seek the opportunity by supporting full carbon pricing, which will provide them a cost advantage over more emissions-intensive competitors. Cho *et al.* (2006) suggest that firms with lower environmental performance spend more in political activities so as to manage public policy pressures. The findings suggest that political participation is not limited to those with higher emissions levels, but is a common policy across organisations with diverse interests.

Voluntary data audit or verification is undertaken by 45 per cent of the organisations. Data verification increases data integrity and quality, hence reducing the risk of wrong decisions based on emissions data. Furthermore, some organisations keep track of their emissions inventory and have it verified by external auditors or verifiers. External verification increases information quality and the credibility of emissions reporting, thereby demonstrating carbon management responsibility and promoting a green image for the organisation.

Forty-one per cent of the organisations actively manages risks associated with carbon price fluctuations. They do so by undertaking forward purchases, at fixed prices, for varying proportions of their total carbon liability (from 10 to 50 per cent). This reduces the probability of being exposed to price fluctuations. Three organisations also manage risk consequence by relying on external organisations to conduct the purchases. They believe that external organisations are specialised in carbon trading and hence have the expertise to optimise the cost of carbon purchases.

Capital investments is undertaken by 41 per cent of the organisations. This approach manages risk at source as it avoids the use of high carbon-intensive machinery and facilities and prevents emissions risks from occurring in the first place (Hunt and Auster, 1990; Gupta, 1995; Eiadat *et al.* 2008). Access to long-term investment capital ensures effective environmental innovation (Irwin and Hooper, 1992). Hence, it can be considered as one of the most proactive approaches to managing carbon-related risks. Electricity generators increase or switch to renewable generation and development, while manufacturers adopt high energy-efficient equipment to minimise emissions. Five organisations also invest in research and development of carbon mitigating technologies, by themselves or in conjunction with industry partners (Kolk and Pinkse, 2004). This helps reduce the loss from failure as well as share the return from successful development.

In contrast to risk avoidance, proactive organisations can actively seek activities that can enhance or create positive risks which in turn can be turned into a competitive advantage and economic gains (Roarty, 1997; Irwin and Hooper, 1992). Thirty per cent of organisations research and develop low-emissions products to cater to increasing societal and customer carbon-focused pressures and achieve a market advantage. For example, C29 develops paint with low emissions and toxic level. C6 reduces energy use and buys offsets so that their beer product become carbon-neutral. C21 researches hybrid and electric cars. Such 'product-greening' innovation strengthens and increases consumer pressures for greener products from other firms, thereby effectively creating additional (competitive) risks for their competitors.

Twenty-eight per cent of the organisations directly buy the carbon credits and surrender those to the suppliers to meet the obligation associated with their energy purchase. By doing so, they avoid the risk of being overcharged for carbon costs. Some manage the risk consequence by still absorbing the carbon costs as part of fuel charge but supplement this with negotiation and monitoring of suppliers, and requesting a breakdown of fuel and carbon charge from suppliers.

On the other hand, 28 per cent of the firms pass on carbon costs to their customers. This helps share carbon costs and hence reduce organisational exposure to carbon costs or fluctuations of carbon prices. However, some firms choose not to pass on such costs, as they believe doing so will impair their market competitiveness.

Some activities are less common and are only undertaken by the most proactive firms. Six firms (21 per cent) purchase offsets for their carbon emissions. This enables them to capture the opportunity of rising societal carbon-focused expectations and helps create a green image for the organisation. Additionally, three companies generate their own offset through renewable or forestry projects, thereby reducing their exposure to the carbon market in meeting ETS surrendering obligation.

The very different plans and strategies undertaken are consistent with findings of Jones and Levy (2007) who studied North American firms. They suggest that the multi-dimensionality of corporate response to climate change is due to the weak carbon regime, uncertainty associated with market and technologies, and the complex nature of possible responses. Hence, firms focus more on management processes and political participation rather than major capital investment aimed at carbon reduction. In contrast, this study found that firms focus both on political participation and carbon trading (price management) as well as internally oriented measures such as energy efficiency. This ensures that the firms can affect the source of the risks (ETS policy) as well as the consequence of the risk through making organisational change to enable carbon reduction. This is possibly due to the enforceable and relatively more certain nature of NZ ETS. Similar to Weinhofer and Hoffmann (2010), this study found evidence regarding carbon compensation, internal innovation and carbon independence. Additionally, this study also identified cost pass-on, carbon offset, managing cost from suppliers, and customer education as corporate responses. This shows the complexity in the corporate responses to climate change.

Carbon performance review

Besides monitoring, it is important that carbon management plans are regularly reviewed to ensure smooth implementation of such plans and effective management of carbon-related risks. The reviews occur most commonly through monthly management meetings (49 per cent of the organisations) (Figure 8.9). For example, a manager from C11 explained: 'so we have a monthly community and environment meeting where CEO attends, most of the top management attend ... we review a programme of work that's in place in both around community and environment ... . Um, it gets a lot of focus, a lot of attention'. These reviews are often attended by operational managers, the CFO, and environmental manager because they are responsible for different aspects of the carbon management plan. The form of review varies. Carbon issues

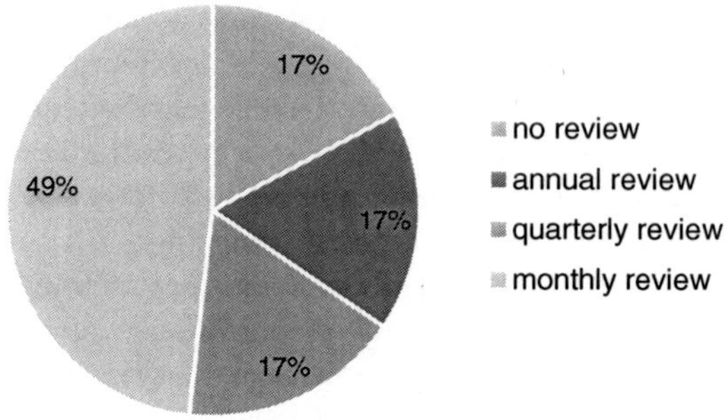

Figure 8.9 Carbon performance review.

can be included in an exposure report that also includes information on market trends, interest rates and other types of exposure. Alternatively, carbon performance is integrated in the energy report in which emissions levels (or intensity levels) are reported as a supplementary indicator of energy efficiency. Some firms that consider carbon issues to be more important employ a dedicated carbon report. Once the performance is reviewed, the feedback is provided to relevant managers, such as operational managers to tighten processes around emission control, or procurement managers around managing carbon purchase costs.

An equal number of firms (17 per cent) either undertake an annual, quarterly or no review at all. This suggests that half of the organisations do not consider carbon risks to be highly important, and hence—though they may have risk treatment plans in place—they do not review the performance of such plans frequently. However, many integrate the carbon review process as part of the annual routine performance review process that also covers budgeting and strategic planning. This suggests that carbon issues are integrated in business-as-usual, rather than particular risks that receive special attention.

The comprehensiveness of CRM

To understand the differences between organisations in their CRM systems, the above aspects of the risk management are scored, from 1 to 5, as outlined in Table 8.1. These scores are then added up for each organisation to reach the total score of risk management. Accordingly, three groups of organisations fitting into three models of CRM can be distinguished (Figure 8.10).

The first group with the lowest score of under 10 are six organisations that are smaller in size, have no ETS obligation and are less energy-intensive than the remaining organisations. Therefore, they do not identify many carbon-related risks, establish appropriate treatment plans, or communicate carbon risks widely within the organisation. This is called 'Minimal CRM', whereby organisations have very limited understanding of carbon exposure and do not have an active monitoring system or review of carbon management plans.

The second group contains twelve organisations with a score from 10 to less than 18. Though these organisations do not have an ETS obligation, they are energy-intensive. Therefore, they do not monitor carbon prices actively or have plans to manage price exposure. However, they monitor emissions levels and undertake energy efficiency or capital investment to reduce energy and carbon-related costs. They also do not tend to have analysed the risk financially or established a threshold to distinguish different levels of risks, only considering carbon footprint as a by-product of energy consumption rather than a direct risk to focus managerial attention. This is termed 'physically-focused CRM', whereby organisations use physical measures of carbon risks and focus on improving energy efficiency among a limited group of managers.

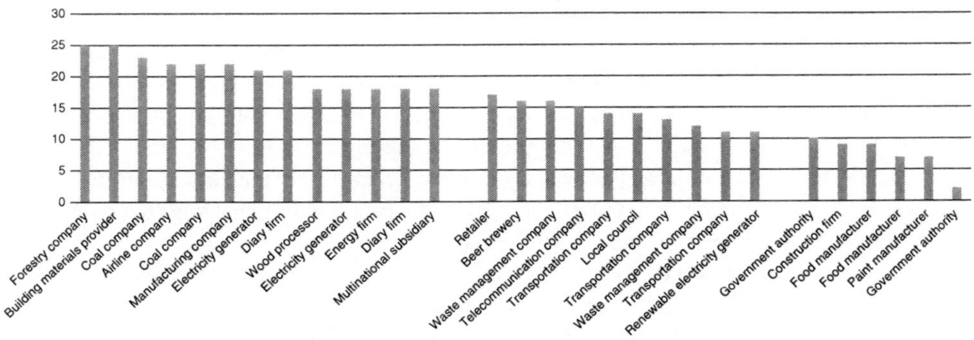

Figure 8.10 Comprehensiveness of carbon risk management.

The third group contains eleven organisations that have a score of over 18. Nine of these organisations have an ETS obligation, are big in size, and are highly energy-intensive. They identify a variety of carbon-related risks through wide consultation with both internal and external stakeholders, convert carbon footprint into carbon liability or costs, and in some cases, also form thresholds to evaluate the risks. Different risk treatment plans are established, including energy efficiency, capital investment, cost pass-on, managing supplier overcharge and price exposure. Furthermore, they monitor both carbon prices and emissions levels actively, and review carbon performance regularly. The two organisations that do not have an ETS obligation but still fall into this group are subsidiaries of multinationals that are considered leaders in climate change issues. Hence, their CRM systems inherit the characteristics of the parent company and are very comprehensive. This model of risk management is called 'comprehensive CRM', involving both physical and financial measures of carbon risks, multiple risk treatment plans, and active monitoring and review, as well as wide risk communication with internal and external stakeholders.

The findings support prior contingency-based risk management research. Woods (2009) suggests that there are differences across organisations in their risk management structure due to specific contingencies including central government policies, information and communication technology, and organisational size. Similarly, Mikes (2009) points to the different risk management mixes that correspond to the organisational contexts. Weinhofer and Hoffmann (2010) note that climate change strategies differ according to region, company size and emission levels. Additional to size and emission levels, this field study highlights additional contingencies: energy/carbon intensity, ETS obligation, and parent company risk management policy.

Conclusion

The field study examined 30 New Zealand organisations to understand their approaches to managing carbon-related risks. A risk management framework is employed to analyse how organisations identify, evaluate, treat, review and communicate carbon risks.

The findings suggest that many organisations either involve top management in their risk discussion or disseminate carbon information throughout the organisation. The risks identified are mostly strategic and competitive in nature, suggesting that the organisations consider carbon issues to have a long-term effect. Compliance risks are also a common concern, as half of the organisations have an ETS compliance obligation. However, considering that the ETS had been in operation for four years at the time of data collection, the concern regarding the accuracy of data collection and reporting suggests low maturity of the carbon measurement and monitoring system. Additionally, the organisations can either analyse only carbon footprint or convert it into carbon cost or loss/gain. However, rather than using onsite continous emissions monitors, the organisations tend to rely on proxy measures such as supplier invoices or operational records. This approach to data collection may affect data integrity, explaining why compliance risk is a major concern. Further, the scope of risk identification and evaluation is narrow, with most only focusing on direct carbon costs rather than associated risks such as competitive disadvantage or supplier overcharge. Only a few organisations set an explicit threshold in evaluating and managing carbon-related risks.

Most organisations undertake some form of emissions monitoring but commonly through supplier invoices or operational records. Additionally, many monitor fluctuations of carbon markets passively through a third party report. Furthermore, the review of carbon performance or carbon management plans is often undertaken monthly, in alignment with routine operational review. This suggests that carbon risks are not considered highly strategic and their monitoring is superficial. However, carbon management is integrated in the business-as-usual and routine activities of most organisations.

To manage carbon risks, establishing a formal carbon management strategy is the most common response. This seems contrary to the passive carbon risk monitoring at the operational level. This suggests that while top management is committed to addressing carbon risks through setting a formal policy, implementing this policy at lower levels has been problematic. Deeper analysis of interview data reveals that operations often consider carbon management to be unimportant or inconducive to their daily activities. Further, in terms of individual treatment plans, organisations choose less resource-demanding activities such as internal energy efficiency, and making submissions to the ETS policy. Treatment plans that require more internal efforts and commitment such as capital investments, or carbon offset generation, is relatively less common. The organisations undertake a variety of plans to manage the different carbon risks recognised, which go beyond carbon compensation, internal innovation or carbon independence suggested in prior research. The findings reveal the complexity and multi-dimensionality in organisational response to climate change.

The findings also support a contingency relationship between CRM and organisational context. Three models of CRM are identified: minimal CRM, physically-focused CRM, and comprehensive CRM. The key contingencies affecting which model is adopted by an organisation are: size, energy/carbon intensity, ETS obligation, and parent company risk management policy. Accordingly, firms that are bigger, more energy intensive, have ETS obligations or have a parent company that has a formal carbon management policy tend to have a more comprehensive CRM system.

This field study makes two contributions to the literature. By using a risk management framework, it highlights organisational practices in identifying, evaluating, treating, monitoring and reviewing carbon-related risks. As climate change can bring risks and opportunities, understanding the significance of these risks and opportunities and how organisations address them is important for both academics and practitioners. The study suggests that even in a regulatory context, organisations have not developed a mature CRM system even though they have integrated carbon management as part of the business-as-usual. However, a variety of plans emerge to deal with carbon risks, which suggests that dealing with carbon risks requires coordination and commitment throughout the organisation. Further, using a risk management framework suggests that New Zealand organisations have undertaken most steps to deal with carbon risks, that is: risk identification, analysis, evaluation, treatment, monitoring and review. The findings also reveal the different approaches to identify, analyse and treat carbon risks, and hence will be useful for practioners and managers in guiding their organisations through carbon management.

As this field study is conducted in a single country and at a specific time, the findings may not be generalisable to other settings. Future research should compare the insights gained from New Zealand's regulatory context to other countries or regulatory contexts, such as the EU ETS. Further, investigating a voluntary context where there is no government policy or regulation can reveal whether organisations exhibit a different level of responsiveness regarding carbon risk management in the absence of regulation.

Note

1 Firms that do not pass on the costs have to internalise the costs and reduce them through emissions control, as opposed to those that pass on the costs and do not emphasise internal reduction efforts.

References

Alkaraan, F. and D. Northcott (2006), 'Capital Investment Decision-making: A Role for Strategic Management Accounting?' *British Accounting Review*, 38, pp. 149–173.

Arjaliès, D.-L. and J. Mundy (2013), 'The Use of Management Control Systems to Manage CSR Strategy: A Levers of Control Perspective', *Management Accounting Research*, 24, pp. 284–300.

Bhimani, A. (2009), 'Risk Management, Corporate Governance and Management Accounting: Emerging Interdependencies', *Management Accounting Research*, 20, pp. 2–5.

Bonardi, J.P. and G.D. Keim (2005), 'Corporate Political Strategies for Widely Salient Issues', *The Academy of Management Review*, 30, pp. 555–576.

Braun, V. and V. Clarke (2006), 'Using Thematic Analysis in Psychology', *Qualitative Research in Psychology*, 3, pp. 77–101.

Cho, C.H., D.M. Patten, and R.W. Roberts (2006), 'Corporate Political Strategy: An Examination of the Relation between Political Expenditures, Environmental Performance, and Environmental Disclosure', *Journal of Business Ethics*, 67, pp. 139–154.

Collier, P.M. (2009), *Fundamentals of Risk Management for Accountants and Managers: Tools and Techniques*, London: Butterworth-Heinemann.

Committee of Sponsoring Organizations of the Treadway Commission (COSO) (2004), *Enterprise Risk Management: Integrated Framework*, New York: COSO.

Eiadat, Y., A. Kelly, F. Roche and H. Eyadat (2008), 'Green and Competitive? An Empirical Test of the Mediating Role of Environmental Innovation Strategy', *Journal of World Business*, 43, pp. 131–145.

Engels, A. (2009), 'The European Emissions Trading Scheme: An Exploratory Study of How Companies Learn to Account for Carbon', *Accounting, Organizations and Society*, 34, pp. 488–498.

Financial Reporting Council (2003), Combined Code on Corporate Governance. *FRC PN 152*, UK: Financial Reporting Council.

Gupta, M.C. (1995), 'Environmental Management and Its Impact on the Operations Function', *International Journal of Operations & Production Management*, 15, pp. 34–51.

Hillman, A.J. and M. Hitt (1999), 'Corporate Political Strategy Formulation: A Model of Approach, Participation and Strategy Decisions', *Academy of Management Review*, 24, pp. 825–842.

Hunt, C.B. and E.R. Auster (1990), 'Proactive Environmental Management: Avoiding the Toxic Trap', *Sloan Management Review*, 31, pp. 7–18.

IFAC (1999), *Enhancing Shareholder Wealth by Better Managing Business Risk*, New York: International Federation of Accountants, Financial and Management Accounting Committee.

IRM (Institute of Risk Management). 2002. Risk Management Standard. London: Institute of Risk Management.

International Organization for Standardization (ISO) (2009), *ISO 31000:2009: Risk management – Principles and guidelines*, Geneva: ISO.

Irwin, A. and P. Hooper (1992), 'Clean Technology, Successful Innovation and the Greening of Industry: A Case-study Analysis', *Business Strategy and the Environment*, 1, pp. 1–11.

Jeswani, H.K., W. Wehrmeyer and Y. Mulugetta (2008), 'How Warm is the Corporate Response to Climate Change? Evidence from Pakistan and the UK', *Business Strategy and the Environment*, 17, pp. 46–60.

Jones, C.A. and D.L. Levy (2007), 'North American business strategies towards climate change', *European Management Journal*, 25, pp. 428–440.

Knight, F. (1921), *Risk, Uncertainty and Profit*, New York: A.M. Kelley.

Kolk, A. and J. Pinkse (2004), 'Market Strategies for Climate Change', *European Management Journal*, 22, pp. 304–314.

Kolk, A. and J. Pinkse (2005), 'Business Responses to Climate Change: Identifying Emergent Strategies', *California Management Review*, 47, pp. 6–20.

Kraus, K. and J. Lind (2010), 'The Impact of the Corporate Balanced Scorecard on Corporate Control: A Research Note', *Management Accounting Research*, 21, pp. 265–277.

McKelvey, B., (1982), *Organizational Systematics*. Berkeley: University of California Press.

Mahon, J.F. (1989), 'Corporate political strategy', *Business in the Contemporary World*, 2, pp. 50–62.

MfE (2009), *Projects to Reduce Emissions (PRE)*. Available from: http://www.mfe.govt.nz/climate-change/reducing-greenhouse-gas-emissions/former-government-initiatives [Accessed 1/08/2009].

MfE (2014), *New Zealand's Emissions Reduction Targets*, Wellington: Ministry for the Environment.

Mikes, A. (2009), 'Risk Management and Calculative Cultures', *Management Accounting Research*, 20, pp. 18–40.

New Zealand Government (2007a), *A Framework for New Zealand Emissions Trading Scheme*, Wellington: Ministry for the Environment and The Treasury.

New Zealand Government (2007b), *New Zealand Climate Change Solutions: An Overview*, Wellington: Ministry for the Environment and The Treasury.

Northcott, D. and F. Alkaraan (2007), 'Strategic Investment Appraisal', in T. Hopper, D. Northcott and R. Scapens (eds), *Issues in Management Accounting*, 3rd edn., Essex, England: Pearson Education, pp. 199–221.

Power, M. (2004), 'The Risk Management of Everything', *The Journal of Risk Finance*, 5, pp. 58–65.

Renn, O. (1998), 'Three Decades of Risk Research: Accomplishments and Challenges', *Journal of Risk Research*, 1, pp. 49–71.

Ritchie, B. and C. Brindley (2007), 'Supply Chain Risk Management and Performance', *International Journal of Operations & Production Management*, 27, pp. 303–322.

Ritchie, B. and D. Marshall (1993), *Business Risk Management*, London: Chapman & Hall.

Roarty, M. (1997), 'Greening Business in a Market Economy', *European Business Review*, 97, pp. 244–245.

Simons, R. (1995), *Levers of Control: How Managers Use Innovative Control Systems to Drive Strategic Renewal*, Boston: Harvard Business School Press.

Standards Australia and Standards New Zealand (2004), *Risk Management AS/NZS 4360: 2004*, Standards Association of Australia.

Tang, Q. and L. Luo (2014), 'Carbon Management Systems and Carbon Mitigation', *Australian Accounting Review*, 24, pp. 84–98.

Weinhofer, G. and V.H. Hoffmann (2010), 'Mitigating Climate Change: How Do Corporate Strategies Differ?' *Business Strategy and the Environment*, 19, pp. 77–89.

Woods, M. (2009), 'A Contingency Theory Perspective on the Risk Management Control System within Birmingham City Council', *Management Accounting Research*, 20, pp. 69–81.

Part III
Management accounting and risk

9

Supporting decision-making under uncertainty

The management accountant as risk manager

Gillian Lees

Introduction

This chapter focuses on the way in which an effective management accounting function makes an important contribution to risk management by improving decision-making and thus helping organisations to succeed in achieving their objectives. It starts by considering why decision-making is now more challenging and important than in the past as well as the role that management accounting plays in decision-making. It then explores the key principles on which an effective management accounting function should be built and applies these specifically to the practice of risk management. It explains the importance of integrating risk management into the normal course of business and how, as a consequence, good risk management is good management accounting.

The chapter provides a number of examples to show how management accounting practice is developing in terms of achieving this integrated approach. It also explores an emerging area of development in which an organisation's business model is used as a framework for deepening the risk assessment process.

Finally, to provide further insights and examples, the chapter explores how good risk management principles should be applied to both a key management process, the innovation process and an emerging megatrend risk: the impact of a more dispersed, open workforce.

The chapter concludes by emphasising the need to apply sound management accounting principles to risk management practice, particularly:

- to ensure that risk is managed as an integral part of managing the organisation as a whole;
- to understand and respond to changes in the external environment and the organisation's specific circumstances in order to build long-term resilience and success.

The overall aim of the chapter is to set out the direction of travel in terms of emerging risk management practice. Through the medium of case studies and examples, the chapter aims to provide readers with a range of ideas to stimulate their thinking as to what good practice might look like in their own organisations and how they might develop it further.

Improving decision-making: the imperative

To be confident of success, organisation need to make better-quality decisions to create and preserve value in the short, medium and long terms. However, a number of megatrends are coming together to make this more challenging. Globalisation, disruptive technology, connectivity and digitisation are creating a significantly accelerated rate of change and complexity, as evidenced by the exponential growth in information. For example, Google's Eric Schmidt has claimed that society now creates as much new information every two days as it did from the dawn of civilisation until 2003 (Siegler, 2010). It has been estimated that by 2020, the volume of all data ever produced could reach more than 40,000 exabytes (Dobbs *et al.*, 2015)[1]—an increase of nearly 300-fold since 2005. This is accompanied by accelerating rates of adoption of communications technologies. While the printing press took hundreds of years to reach a mass audience, social networks took a mere handful (Sammartino, 2014, p. 85). It is little surprise that these megatrends have been described as 'no ordinary disruption' (Dobbs *et al.*, 2015).

For organisation, these developments are making quality decision-making more important and more difficult. For example, revenue streams can disappear almost overnight, as in the case of some markets where SMS text messaging has been largely superseded by WhatsApp and other new mobile messaging apps. Not only have decisions become more complex, their consequences take less time to make an impact, and rapid acceleration has made the timing of decisions more important. Organisations no longer have the luxury of being able to delay long-term decisions until they have resolved all the uncertainties involved (Bhimani and Bromwich, 2010).

Furthermore, an abundance of information, rather than being liberating, can actually be debilitating for an organisation. It can lead to decision paralysis or hasty action. Against this complex background, organisation need to be able to identify whether and what decisions need to be taken and then attempt to achieve the best possible outcome in the circumstances. Conventionally, more information has tended to mean less uncertainty, but this relationship is changing because although information-processing capabilities have improved, much of the increased volume of data is unstructured and complex—for example, social media posts and voice recordings.

In this context, it may not be surprising that there is greater awareness and concern in relation to risk. For example, a recent survey of over 1,300 executives around the world (Beasley *et al.*, 2015) found that 60 per cent agreed that they faced a wide array of complex and increasing issues, and 38 per cent had faced a significant operational surprise over the previous five years. However, 35 per cent or fewer had formal enterprise-wide risk management (ERM) in place, and only about a quarter described their organisation's risk maturity as mature or robust. Moreover, 40 per cent or fewer were satisfied with the reporting of information about top risk exposures to senior management, and less than half (42 per cent) discussed risk information generated by the ERM process during board discussions of the organisation's strategic plan.

Organisational success in this uncertain environment requires a much stronger and more robust methodology for making decisions than ever before to ensure that risks are managed effectively. An effective management accounting function is essential to this.

The role of management accounting

Management accounting can be defined as 'the sourcing, analysis, communication and use of decision-relevant financial and non-financial information to generate and preserve value for organisations' (CGMA, 2014c).

Good management accounting improves decision-making because it extracts value from information. It places the best available evidence and forecasted information at the centre of the decision-making process to provide more objective insight on which to base judgements and reach conclusions.

Being forward-looking and outward-looking, management accounting brings structured solutions to unstructured problems. It provides the decision-relevant data, rigorous analysis and informed judgement required to make better decisions and to communicate them with impact. Where uncertainty is high, management accounting provides forecasts, which can be based on an extensive range of information.

Effective management accounting should be based on robust principles to guide practice. These are articulated in the following section.

The Global Management Accounting Principles

The Global Management Accounting Principles were developed by the Chartered Institute of Management Accountants (CIMA) and the American Institute of Certified Public Accountants (AICPA) to help organisation build effective management accounting functions. The principles describe the fundamental values, qualities, norms and features to which the management accountant should aspire. As shown in Figure 9.1, four overarching principles are key to achieving this.

Communication provides insight that is influential

The objective of the Communication Principle is to drive better decisions about strategy and its execution at all levels. Management accounting begins and ends with conversations. It improves decision-making by communicating insightful information at all stages of the decision-making process. Good communication of critical information allows management accounting to cut across silos and facilitates integrated thinking. The consequences of actions in one area of the business on another area can be better understood, accepted or repaired. This is particularly crucial in embedding effective ERM, where risks are often interconnected and risk responses need to be coordinated. Risk information needs to flow freely throughout

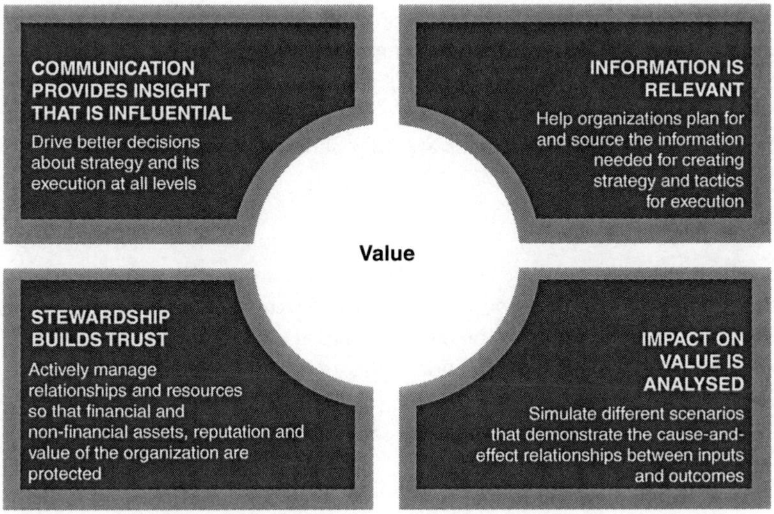

Figure 9.1 The Global Management Accounting Principles – detailed.

the organisation to dismantle what has been termed the 'risk management glass ceiling' (Tomorrow's Good Governance Forum, 2013, p. 7). This ceiling is caused by a lack of integration between managers, who are focused mostly on operational risks, and board members and senior executives, who are mostly focused on strategy. What can seem like a reasonable decision at the operational level—for example, a cost-saving initiative—may have adverse strategic and reputational consequences for the organisation. A possible solution to this gap between strategic and operational risks is to use the business model as a means of framing the risk management process. This is considered in the section 'Using the business model to achieve integrated risk management' below.

The Communication Principle also emphasises the need to engage with decision-makers to understand their requirements and to ensure that the most relevant information can be sourced and analysed so that all recommendations are useful to the decision-maker. Again, the importance of this in supporting managers throughout the organisation to manage risk is significant. The combination of the manager's functional expertise with the management accountant's decision support ensures that the right risk questions are asked. For example, the management accountant can help to break down complexity and provide transparency about how conclusions are reached. The management accountant influences effective and information-based decision-making by ensuring that the right people have the right information at the right time so that they are better placed to take decisions that will drive long-term value creation.

A key element of this principle is that communication is tailored to users of the information, to the decision under discussion and to different decision styles. The management accountant must understand the level of the audience's risk and financial knowledge so that information can be presented in a way that the audience can relate to and understand. This requires both a high degree of technical knowledge and the so-called 'softer' influencing and communication skills. A good example of this is provided by a management accountant who was the risk director of a major media organisation and found himself working with very creative music and media experts, none of whom had much time for conventional management terms such as 'strategy' and 'risk'. His response was to present risk information in a visual way, using bright colours and cartoon pictures, as well as exploiting clever use of language: for example, the risk assessment process (RAP) was recast as 'rapping'. This approach helped to break down what could have been an insurmountable barrier but without losing the required robustness and timeliness. This is an example of impactful and influential communication based on a willingness to listen to users' needs, which in turn facilitates better decisions. In a highly digitised, technological environment, the ability to facilitate a greater degree of collaboration between different experts is increasingly important to ensure that risks are fully understood and managed.

Information is relevant

The objective of the Information Principle is to help organisations plan for and source the information needed to support effective decision-making. After following the Communication Principle, the decision at hand and the needs of the decision-maker are known and understood. The Information Principle focuses on the identification, collection, validation, preparation and storage of information.

It requires achieving an appropriate balance between each of the following:

- past, present and future-related information;
- internal and external information;
- financial and non-financial information.

The information must be relevant to the decision being taken, and it must be the best available. Where it is necessary to present incomplete or unverified data, it should be flagged as such so that decision-makers can take a view on the level of confidence they wish to have in the data. This is a significant issue in risk management when making assessments about likelihood and impact of specific risk events, for example, or when generating possible future scenarios that might play out to help with identifying key risks. It is also important to generate information on actual risk events, including near misses as well as the impact of any corrective action taken to address weaknesses.

A key source of relevant information for effective risk management is the external environment. In addition to conventional monitoring—such as PESTEL analysis, which identifies changes to the organisation's political, economic, social, technological, environmental and legal conditions—it is now also important to monitor information on reputation, such as sentiment ratings, feedback on external websites and social media discussions. These can provide a valuable source of insight: for example, a hotel chain may learn about problems at a particular site much more quickly. Such cases reinforce the need for the management accountant to draw together information from both internal and external sources to derive effective key risk indicators and actionable insights.

With their skills in translating analytical insights from data into commercial impact, management accountants have the opportunity to deliver value, including through the enhancement of risk management by data. Financial professionals are becoming increasingly aware of some of these new opportunities arising from data. When they were asked where they felt their organisation could benefit most from improved data quality and analysis, monitoring external risks featured in the top five answers (CGMA, 2013a).

However, given the broad sweep of possibilities, organisations need to relate the data to the questions that need answering. Once relevant information has been prepared across all aspects of the risk management cycle, it can be used to model and analyse value generation within the context of the organisation's strategic objectives.

Impact on value is analysed through scenario analysis and models

The objective of the Impact on Value Principle is to simulate different scenarios that demonstrate the cause-and-effect relationships between inputs and outcomes.

The focus of this principle is the interaction between management accounting and the business model. By modelling the impact of opportunities and risks, the effect on strategic outcomes is quantified, and the likelihood that a given outcome will generate, preserve or destroy value is assessed. The section 'Using the business model to achieve integrated risk management' explores this in more detail below.

Management accounting uses relevant information as defined by the Information Principle to develop scenario models that are proportionate to the decision being made. Some scenario models will be relatively simple, while others will require a greater level of sophistication and consider a wide range of complex factors, including the external environment in which the organisation operates.

Scenario analysis brings rigour to the evaluation of information. By running scenario models to evaluate the likelihood and impact of particular risks and opportunities, organisations can determine appropriate responses that preserve or create value. They can also understand the trade-offs to be made between different risk responses and ensure that the organisation allocates its scarce resources effectively to prioritise the risks and opportunities that have the greatest impact on desired outcomes.

A good example of how analytics and modelling tools can enhance risk management relates to supply chain risk. The supply chain can be modelled with vulnerabilities identified at various points, and organisations can quantify the impact of, for instance, a supplier's facility being out of commission for a given period. Such models and analysis can help organisations prioritise their risk management responses to target the most vulnerable parts of the supply chain. One study has shown that the most significant exposures can lie in unlikely places: for example, application of modelling techniques to companies such as the Ford Motor Company showed little correlation between the annual spend on procurement at a specific site and the impact that the site's disruption would have on company performance. This meant that risks associated with low-cost commodity suppliers were often overlooked (Simchi-Levi *et al.*, 2014). Another example is that of the UK-based bank RBS, which has invested in data analytics and data warehousing to assess risk across its business customers' supply chains (*Twentyman*, 2014). By combining internal data generated from transactions and payments processed by the bank with external information, RBS is able to use predictive analytics to provide its corporate customers with insight into supply chain risk by mapping interdependencies between companies.

Stewardship builds trust

Whereas the three previous principles apply to the discipline of management accounting, the Stewardship Principle applies to the individual behaviours of the management accountant—thus, in effect, bringing the principles to life. The objective of the principle is for the management accountant to actively manage relationships and resources so that the financial and non-financial assets, reputation and value of the organisation are protected. It requires the management accountant to behave with independence and objectivity, and to constructively challenge any decision that does not align with corporate values. This can require a certain degree of courage at times; perhaps more importantly, however, it requires a prevailing organisational environment, or culture, that encourages debate, challenge and open discussion at all levels to ensure learning from mistakes takes priority over the question, 'Whose fault was it?'

The management accountant needs to balance the needs of different stakeholders involved in the decision-making process with the needs of those affected by the resulting decision. It requires the management accountant to take a broad macro view of the overall risk agenda: for example, by incorporating the impact of megatrends such as climate change, resource scarcity and population growth on the organisation's long-term resilience while understanding the need to build trust and an ethical reputation in order to preserve society's 'licence to operate'.

Application of management accounting principles to risk management

As shown in Figure 9.2, the management accounting function encompasses a range of key activities or practice areas, such as financial strategy, external reporting, investment appraisal and risk management.

In terms of required competencies, the management accountant is expected to apply accounting and finance skills in the context of the business to influence the decisions, actions and behaviours of others, in this way playing a leadership role within the organisation (CGMA, 2014b). This means the management accountant needs a combination of both technical and people skills, together with a strong understanding of the business.

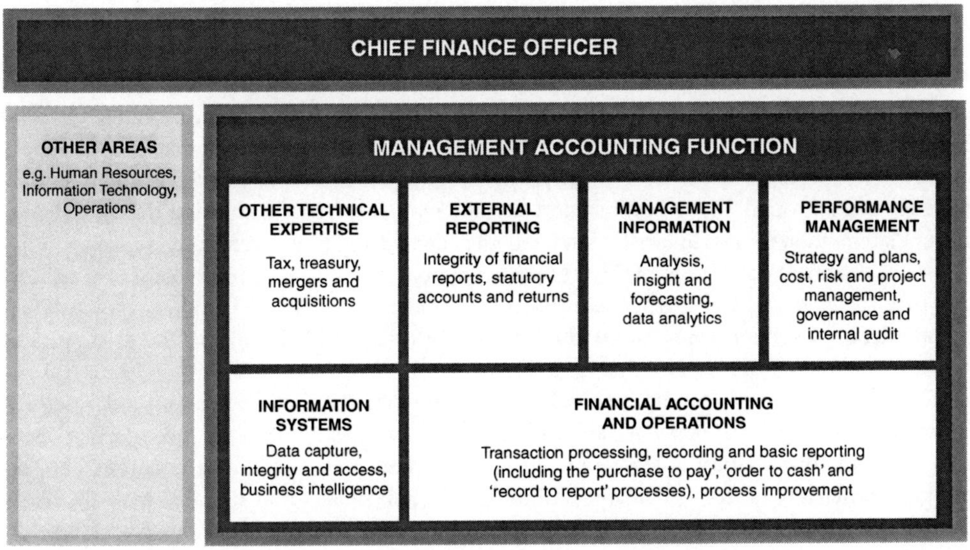

Figure 9.2 The key activities of a management accounting function.

Effective management accounting is therefore built on competent people applying management accounting principles to robust practices—in this case, risk management practices. The management accountant contributes to risk management practice by:

- identifying risks and advising on appropriate responses that are relevant and proportionate to the size of risk, the organisation and its environment;
- embedding risk management within their thinking and considering it alongside planning and performance;
- supporting non-finance colleagues to assess the likelihood and impact of all risks and to determine appropriate risk responses.

This reflects a shift in thinking about risk management, from an emphasis on compliance and prevention towards the integration of risk management into the organisation's day-to-day management processes as a tool to support good decision-making and the achievement of the organisation's strategic objectives. 'The nature of the risk landscape is such that being able to identify and "manage" all the risks to an organisation is no longer possible' (Tomorrow's Good Governance Forum, 2015, p. 16), so risk management practice needs to focus increasingly on building resilience and value creation. This is particularly important given that it is strategic rather than compliance risks that tend to have the greatest impact: for example, research by CEB has established that strategic risk accounted for 86 per cent of losses in market value over the past decade, whereas legal and compliance risks accounted for just 3 per cent and financial reporting risks for 2 per cent (*Harvard Business Review*, 2015).

The importance of risk management to good decision-making that creates and preserves long-term value makes it an integral part of good management accounting. In turn, the application of management accounting principles is helping to create new and innovative responses to risk management, largely thanks to the drawing together of financial and non-financial considerations, a thorough understanding of the business at the strategic and operational levels, and both a future and a historical orientation. These factors, combined with the independence and objectivity underpinning professional management accountants' training, make them natural risk managers.

A key role for the management accountant is to embed risk management considerations into the decision-making process—often to the point that risk management becomes virtually invisible, because it is so implicit in everything that the organisation does that it is no longer identifiable as separate steps (IFAC, 2015). This requires organisations to ensure a high level of risk awareness throughout the organisation so that employees become the first line of defence. It is not uncommon to hear that risk management is considered to be everybody's responsibility within an organisation: for example, 'risk management is the responsibility of every IBMer' (*Harvard Business Review*, 2015), with risk managers helping front-line employees with training and decision-support tools. Similarly, Unilever has described risk management as 'part of everyone's job, every day' (IFAC, 2015, p. 7).

Because many employees automatically think about how issues will help or hinder them in achieving their objectives, they are already managing risk implicitly; as a consequence, there is some degree of integration. However, 'the approach adopted may not be coherent, consistent, comprehensive or communicated effectively, which means that its outcomes are likely to be unreliable' (IFAC, 2015, p. 7). To address this, some organisations, such as Unilever, are looking to embed risk management in the normal course of business so that it is no longer managed as a separate standalone activity but is performed in a considered, structured, controlled and effective way.

Emerging best practice

Examples of the explicit approach to risk management integration and emerging best practice are becoming increasingly apparent.[2] One such case is that of the US insurance and financial services company MassMutual (CGMA, 2014a), which aligned its strategy, planning and risk processes for improved governance and performance. To achieve this, it developed and operationalised its strategic planning framework. This supported a culture of knowledge sharing, transparency and communication to help the organisation become more strategically agile and aligned.

Risk management and the decision-making process

Although MassMutual emerged from the 2008–2009 financial crisis stronger than many of its peers and competitors, the experience convinced the new CEO and the board of directors that more formal governance around strategy and risk was needed, including greater alignment between the financial plan and the strategic planning process. The company focused on better connecting the company's business units, ERM, corporate control functions, executive leadership and board. While it had an effective strategic planning framework, it needed a better ability to evaluate business intelligence and assess the potential impact of strategic opportunities and risks.

In order to do this, the company developed what it calls a Pinwheel framework, so named because it aligns two separate planning and performance cycles—one at CEO and executive leadership level and the other at subsidiary and business unit level—requiring the continual collaborative exchange of information between business units and the corporate executive leadership team and between executive leadership and the board of directors. The key in the development of the framework was the partnering of the Strategy and Corporate Development team with the ERM team, which enabled the formalisation of strategic risk management.

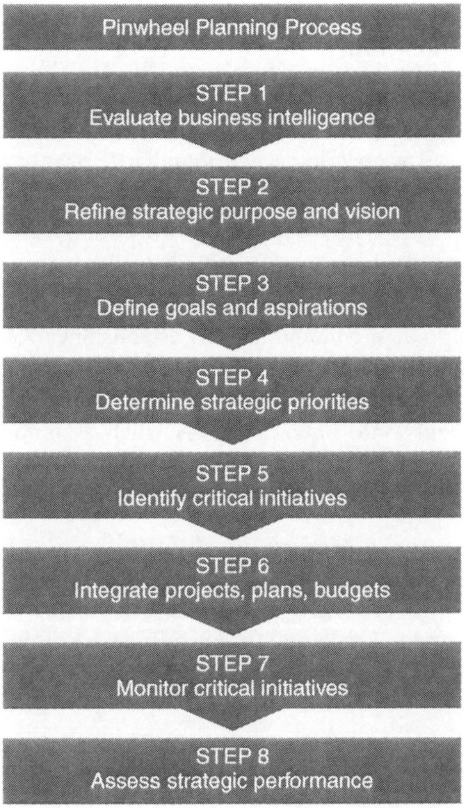

Figure 9.3 The Pinwheel Planning Process.

Use of the eight steps of the Pinwheel Planning Process shown in Figure 9.3 enabled MassMutual to expand business by launching a successful new line of stable value investment funds, exceeding the $4 billion sales target by 50 per cent. It is notable how risk is fully embedded at all the relevant parts of the process.

This is an outline of the concerns an organisation might address at each stage of the Pinwheel Planning Process.

Steps 1–3

Evaluate business intelligence, refine strategic purpose and vision, and define goals and aspirations—what are the threats and opportunities that could transform or disrupt our competitive advantages?

Step 4

Develop strategic priorities—potential threats to achieving aspirational goals and objectives are identified and evaluated. Underlying assumptions are challenged, and scenarios are created to evaluate the potential impact of alternative developments and outcomes. Key questions to ask are:

- What are the best opportunities to defend or create competitive advantages that drive innovation and growth?

- What are the risks and projected returns?
- Are we balancing short-term and long-term interests?

Step 5

Identify critical initiatives—what strategic as well as operational and compliance risks are associated with these initiatives?

Step 6

Integrate projects, operating plans and budgets. Important considerations here are the identification of key risk indicators that need to be monitored and the establishment of sound ERM practices across the company to address operating risk.

It is at this step of the process that the partnership between the finance function, the ERM function and the CFO comes strongly into play, as this is when assumptions, underlying plans and projections are tested by developing scenarios to determine the potential impact of significant deviations in key variables—both controllable and uncontrollable.

Step 7

Monitor critical initiatives, including the managing of risks and the overall impact of the new product on the organisation.

Step 8

Assess strategic performance, including both conformance and performance risks.

The key to the framework is connectivity—of risk and performance; of strategy and operations; of group and individual business units or subsidiaries; and of internal and external factors. This integration helps to incorporate risk at all stages of the decision-making process, enabling a more rapid and resilient response as well as greater confidence in seizing new business opportunities and embarking on major new programmes.

Another example of emerging best practice is the application of foresight during the risk incubation period (Lauder and Baker, 2014)—the point from which a plan has been agreed up to the point of no return. This ensures that organisations consider what can jeopardise their plan well before the crisis point hits. A useful stimulus to ensure foresight thinking is a risk governance framework of seven questions, developed and applied by a practising management accountant. The questions aim to provoke deep debate and provide the impetus for improved risk management:

1. Who cares about what?
   Executives are likely to have different views on most issues, resulting in lack of agreement on priorities. The frequent sharing of differences may change opinions, or at least result in greater openness and help to ensure that everyone is pulling in the same direction. Having a debate that promotes greater alignment may prompt actions that can mitigate or prevent adverse events.
2. Are we ready to launch?
   This question prompts an evaluation of whether the right structures, resources and capabilities are in place for success.

3 Has there been an unconscious drift from accepted practices?
Has this occurred to the point at which operational practices are no longer fit for purpose? Product mis-selling or recalls could be warning signs here.
4 Are our structures and processes preventing crucial data from getting to the people who need it?
5 Are our assumptions valid?
Every considered decision involves a number of tacit and explicit assumptions. These need to be reviewed regularly, given the ever-changing context.
6 Do we have dysfunctional momentum?
Organisations have a natural momentum and may need to consciously change direction to avoid trouble. The classic examples here are where organisations are reluctant to cannibalise their existing businesses, as occurred when Kodak invented the digital camera in the 1970s and more recently with retailers that failed to embrace online retailing effectively.
7 Are we creating unintended consequences?
This question prompts lateral thinking. It is a challenging question, one where looking at the business model as a whole may help with identifying such adverse consequences. This is explored in the following section.

There is a significant body of knowledge around risk management, with global frameworks, standards and guidance available. However, what the above examples show is that if effective integration is to be achieved, organisations need to tailor risk management to their own specific circumstances. In simple terms, no organisation would dream of developing its strategy and operating model 'off the shelf', so this principle should apply equally to its approach to risk management. This is consistent with the overall orientation of the management accountant, who is trained to adopt a principles-based approach to applying a broad range of tools and techniques to meet the specific needs of an organisation.

Using the business model to achieve integrated risk management

As we have seen, the Global Management Accounting Principles emphasise the importance of an integrated approach to risk management and the need to model the impact of risks and opportunities on value.

One emerging approach being developed by Airmic[3] and CIMA is to use the business model as a means of framing the risk management conversation, particularly at board and executive management level, when there is a perceived need for improvement (McKinsey, 2013).

As set out in *The International <IR> Framework* (IIRC (International Integrated Reporting Council), 2013), the business model is defined as the organisation's 'system of transforming inputs, through its business activities, into outputs and outcomes that aims to fulfil the organisation's strategic purposes and create value over the short, medium and long term'.

A thorough understanding of the business model within the context of the external environment provides a comprehensive basis for risk and opportunity assessment.

The inputs and outputs of the business model are expressed in terms of what *The International <IR> Framework* calls the 'six capitals', meaning the organisation's key resources and relationships: financial, manufactured, intellectual, human, natural, and social and relationship. This ensures a broad, integrated view of value creation that takes intangibles as well as externalities into consideration.

How does risk assessment using the business model differ from traditional approaches? The latter tend to be based on a risk register that identifies a series of possible risk events. The benefit of using the business model as the basis for risk assessment is to ensure that risks are viewed in an integrated way over the short, medium and long terms at the strategic, tactical and operational levels. The aim is to help decision-makers gain a better understanding of the connectivity between risks as well as cause and effect so that they have more oversight over the organisation's principal risks. For example, understanding the quality of key inputs such as people or relationships may help decision-makers to assess whether the organisation is setting up potential problems for the future such as product mis-selling, poor customer or patient care and industrial accidents, all of which have caused major problems for a number of organisations in recent years.

The business model approach uses the four components of the value creation process—inputs, activities, outputs and outcomes—as a basis for identifying risk.

This systematic process of identification creates the basis for an integrated risk analysis and evaluation, which informs how the risks need to be managed.

Figure 9.4 shows that risks need to be identified for each component of the value creation process. For example, in relation to inputs, each of the six capitals needs to be considered in terms of cost, availability and quality. The outcome of this process is a systematic identification of all the risks related to inputs, business activities, outputs and outcomes. Figure 9.4 also shows the key considerations relating to each category.

It is important to integrate these key considerations so that they can be analysed and used to create a risk narrative. For example, an organisation may identify as a risk that it is not able to access talent with the required skills in sufficient numbers to deliver its services effectively (risk to an input). It can track this risk through the value creation process by connecting it to the risk of process failure (risk to business activity), resulting in poor service delivery (risk to output) and ultimately damaged reputation (risk to outcome). This process therefore also provides a way of embedding reputational risk considerations into decision-making. The process can help to flush out risks that may have been missed using an events-based approach, and it also enables risks arising from the different capitals to be integrated: for example, poorly

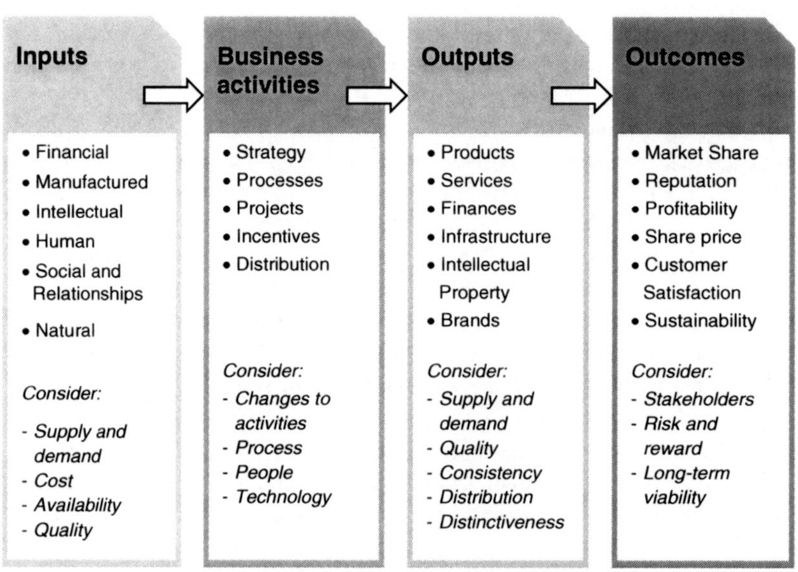

Figure 9.4 Managing risk through the business model.

trained people combined with inadequate equipment may result in poor customer experience and at worst a serious accident.

This process of integration enables a richer risk assessment by:

- helping to identify recurring or particularly strong risk themes, such as safety;
- developing a more comprehensive understanding of causes, effects and consequences, leading to more complete risk responses. For example, an organisation may address the risks of poor service delivery by investing in employee training, which may prevent short-term problems. However, in the long term, it may be necessary to address the talent issue at a deeper level by collaborating with education providers, automating processes and outsourcing activities.

Based on this risk analysis, the organisation can determine risk responses over different time-scales and at three levels:

- strategic;
- tactical;
- operational.

Based on the above analysis, what would be the components of an impactful internal risk report designed to support decision-makers in gaining an effective overview of the organisation's resilience to risk? It is envisaged that the report would have three core components to support the risk conversation, as follows:

1 A report on the risk management process, including the risk context
   a How can we set the context and tone from the top?
   b Is the risk management process effective?
   c Do we have reasonable assurance that we are identifying and discussing the principal risks?
2 A report on the recurring and dominant risk themes or 'stories'—for example, safety or talent
   a Would we expect these to be dominant themes for our organisation?
   b Are there other dominant themes we should reasonably expect to see? What are we missing?
   c Are the risk responses consistent with our risk appetite and risk culture?
   d Is our organisational culture giving rise to these risks? Are we getting people to do the right thing?
3 A report on key business model risks. Each principal risk is supported by a strong narrative that maps causes and consequences, integrating all the aspects of the business model framework and proposing appropriate responses at the strategic, tactical and operational levels.
   a In view of these risks, is our business model fundamentally sustainable?
   b Are we comfortable that we are not risking catastrophic loss?
   c What metrics do we need to monitor these risks?
   d Is our business model giving rise to additional risks?

What decision-makers receive is integrated and focused risk information that is underpinned by the logic of the organisation's business model and how it creates value. This should help decision-makers spend time on the risks that have the greatest potential for damage. By using the value creation process as the basis for risk identification, decision-makers also avoid the trap—the risk management glass ceiling referred to earlier—of focusing only on strategic risks and missing operational disasters that cause reputational damage. As we have seen, risks identified through this process need to be considered on every level—strategic, tactical and operational.

This approach is experimental, but at its heart is the notion of viewing risk through a number of different lenses—going beyond the traditional events-based approach—and achieving a better integration of risk management into decision-making. It is built on the idea of improving risk identification by identifying risk from different perspectives rather than relying on a one-dimensional approach. Organisations may find it useful to identify other angles or lenses through which they could view their business: for example, through the eyes of all their key stakeholders.

Risk management and the innovation process

It seems clear that best practice in risk management is moving towards integration into key processes within the organisation, such as the strategic planning process. This section applies this principle to a specific organisational process that is growing in importance—the innovation process.

With the fast pace of technological change, the way organisations innovate is increasingly crucial to their survival and renewal. The threat of obsolescence is more pressing than ever before, and organisations such as Amazon and Apple have managed to disrupt whole industries. The biggest risk of all, it seems, is failure to innovate, so organisations have to find effective ways of future-proofing their businesses while managing the risks of doing so.

A model for embedding risk management into the innovation life cycle is shown in Figure 9.5.

A key element of this model is the creation of an environment that ensures that good ideas are identified, encouraged, financed and delivered effectively to market. The management accountant has an important role to play in ensuring that ideas are challenged and refined to create a stronger business case. The trade-offs and risks associating with betting finite resources on unproven ideas need to be considered properly, but without killing off an idea prematurely. This can be a hard balance to strike, but one approach is to ring-fence ideas in some way. For example, early-stage proposals may need to be allowed to fully form before formal evaluation processes are applied. Organisations can earmark dedicated budgets for innovation that are subject to different performance criteria than those used in the operational business, and use systematic processes for innovation.

It is also important to adopt a portfolio approach to innovation so that risk management is used as a strategic tool to manage trade-offs of risk and reward. This ensures that minor or incremental innovations, which are generally low-risk, balance the major innovations that are risky but have the potential to transform business growth.

It can be instructive to map out the innovation pipeline in its entirety that indicates the overall likely distribution of innovation risk and reward. However, perhaps the most difficult risk that needs to be factored in is the intangible risk of not innovating. Assessing this risk may require judgement as well as analytics and is most difficult in the case of disruptive innovation, which may cannibalise an existing business. This reinforces the importance of an integrated approach in which risk management is firmly embedded within strategic decision-making. Without this anchor it is very challenging to assess such risk, but doing so is important to ensure the long-term sustainability of a business.

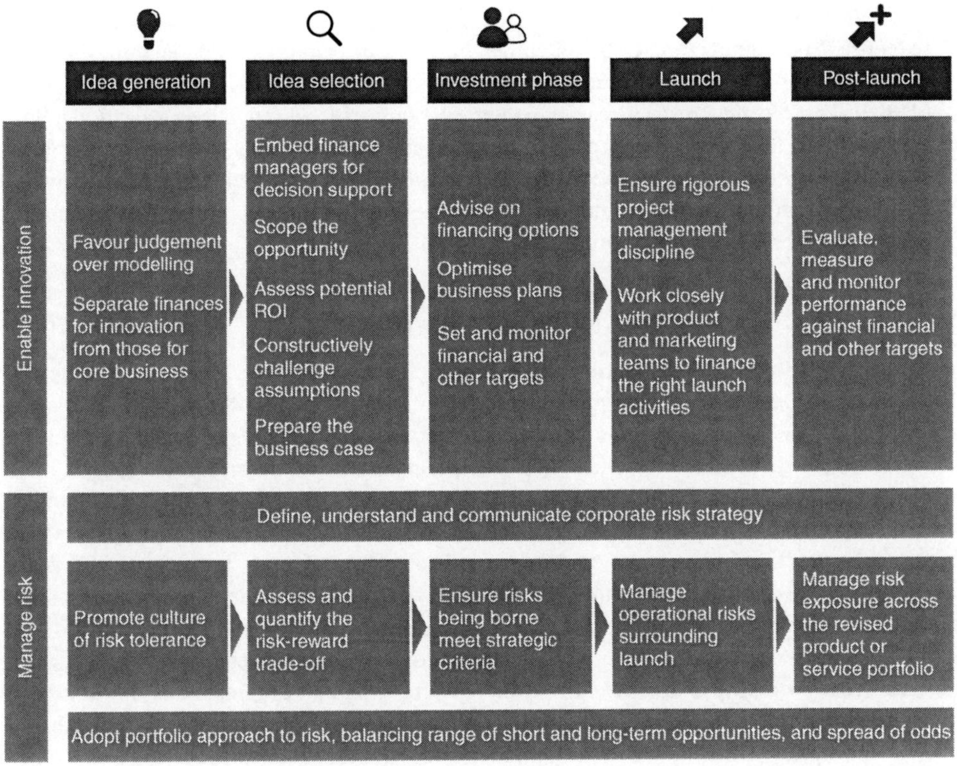

Figure 9.5 A model for embedding risk management into the innovation life cycle (CGMA, 2013b).

The management accountant performs an invaluable co-piloting role in the innovation process by bringing together financial and non-financial resources while ensuring the effective management of risk. A key responsibility is to support the process while ensuring robustness and implementing appropriate controls at different stages of the process.

Making sense of the changing external environment

An essential element of risk management is effective monitoring of the external environment, and tools such as PESTEL analysis are useful in supporting this. However, organisations face a number of challenges in making sense of the external environment:

- They must prioritise the most important trends to focus on, as they should focus on the most relevant trends for their market situation. For example, in the case of the consumer goods industry, demographic trends are a powerful and predictable yet often underused source of insightful information.
- They must apply this knowledge about external trends within the specific context of the business to strategy and risk management. For example, based on its analysis of demographic data, a travel organisation might conclude that an ageing population may prompt it to revise its offering and to overhaul its assessment of risk.

- They must detect significant trends that go under the radar but require an appropriate response. Such trends tend to be outcomes of a cluster of bigger shifts and are therefore difficult to spot through conventional techniques such as PESTEL analysis. An example of such a trend is the emergence of the open workforce, discussed in the case study below. It is useful to take a broad approach to monitoring external trends by studying scenarios such as those developed by the World Economic Forum's *Global Risks Report*, which builds on its annual analysis of major risks by constructing three comprehensive scenarios each year (World Economic Forum, 2015).

Case study: the risks of managing the open workforce

The converging forces of globalisation and technological change have given rise to a powerful new force in business: a phenomenon referred to as the open workforce. In addition to employed staff, the open workforce comprises external talent including outsourced service providers, suppliers, contractors, consultants, temporary staff, interns and freelancers.

To a greater or lesser extent, organisations have always drawn on a mixture of talent. However, research has indicated that organisations are now using external talent for mission-critical goals on a significant scale, and this is expected to accelerate in the next few years. For example, in a recent research study (CGMA, 2014d), more than one in four senior leaders reported that external talent made up over half of their organisation's total workforce, and over one-third planned to increase their use of such talent over the next 5 years.

However, what was also apparent from the research was that organisations did not really appreciate the dramatic implications of these changes for their organisations, so they had not made the appropriate adjustments to performance and risk management processes and to decision-making and organisational structures. At best, high-performing organisations were struggling to do so. Organisations need to understand how to extract the almost limitless potential of a workforce that can now encompass a diverse range of talent, skills, knowledge and experience, yet at the same time they must ensure that an appropriate degree of oversight is maintained as the team becomes more disparate and dynamic.

A particular role for the management accountant in this context is to understand the changing nature of risks that arise from the open workforce, as the research indicated overall weaknesses in this area. Although organisations indicated concerns over information leaks, whether because of cybersecurity issues or intellectual property theft, there appeared to be little awareness of the potential reputational risks that arise when vital tasks are performed by people and partner organisations that do not necessarily share the organisation's values or quality standards. It also appeared that attention needed to be paid to the decision-making process itself, which was becoming more risky and challenging due to difficulties in:

- ensuring consistent, quality decision-making at all levels of the organisation;
- creating the right incentives to secure and retain talent, both internal and external;
- ensuring good collaboration across in-house and external talent;
- ensuring the internal and external workforces were aligned to clearly defined goals and a shared vision.

A useful list of risks arising from the open workforce is as follows:

- information and data security breaches;
- disclosure of competitively sensitive information;

- fraud and corruption;
- weakening of loyalty and engagement across the workforce;
- potential brand or reputational damage;
- loss or theft of intellectual property;
- inadequate training and development;
- hollowing out of in-house capabilities;
- loss of oversight and control;
- project failure;
- cultural mismatches and communication difficulties;
- less timely decision-making.

These risks arising from the open workforce can be applied within the context of the business model approach set out above. To help with risk identification, it might be useful to apply a risk approach that has been developed in relation to strategic alliances and categorise risks as performance risks—for example, the failure to deliver a product or service of the right quality—and relational risks: for example, the loss of intellectual property (Das and Teng, 2001).

Conclusion

Decision-making has become more challenging in our increasingly fast-changing and complex business environment. This external environment demands a broader approach to risk management—one that is integrated into the achievement of strategic objectives and day-to-day management processes of the organisation as a whole. Applying sound principles of management accounting can support effective risk management, but it is important for organisations to apply these principles to their own specific circumstances so that they can create and preserve long-term value and resilience.

With its focus on value creation and preservation, the use of the business model as a framework for risk assessment could help to support this broader approach and represents an interesting avenue for further research. The key challenge is to develop a practical framework that enables a comprehensive risk assessment without unnecessary complexity and that also fully integrates risk management into strategy and performance management. Such a framework needs to be based on a widely accepted and workable understanding of the business model, so establishing this is an important first step in ensuring that organisations can identify and manage the risks that have the greatest potential to destroy value over the short, medium and long terms.

Notes

1 One exabyte is the equivalent of more than 4,000 times the information stored in the US Library of Congress (Dobbs *et al.* 2015, p. 39).
2 The International Federation of Accountants (IFAC 2015) sets out a useful framework.
3 Airmic is the UK association for risk managers and insurance buyers. See: https://www.airmic.com.

References

Beasley, M.S., B.C. Branson and B.V. Hancock (2015), *Global State of Enterprise Risk Oversight 2nd Edition: Analysis of the Challenges and Opportunities for Improvement*, London: Chartered Global Management Accountant. Available from: http://www.cgma.org/Resources/Reports/DownloadableDocuments/2015-06-13-The-global-state-of-enterprise-risk-oversight-report.pdf [Accessed: 27/08/2015].

Bhimani, A. and M. Bromwich (2010), *Management Accounting: Retrospect and Prospect*, Oxford: CIMA Publishing.
CGMA (2013a), *From Insight to Impact: Unlocking Opportunities in Big Data*, London: CGMA. Available from: http://www.cgma.org/Resources/Reports/Pages/insight-to-impact-big-data.aspx [Accessed: 27/08/2015].
CGMA (2013b), *Managing Innovation: Harnessing the Power of Finance*, London: CGMA.
CGMA (2014a), CGMA Case Study: Aligning Strategy, Planning and Risk Processes at MassMutual, London: CGMA.
CGMA (2014b), *CGMA Competency Framework*, London: CGMA. Available from: http://www.cgma.org/Resources/Tools/DownloadableDocuments/competency-framework-complete.pdf [Accessed: 21/09/2015].
CGMA (2014c), *Global Management Accounting Principles*, London: CGMA. Available from: http://www.cgma.org/Resources/Reports/DownloadableDocuments/global-management-accounting-principles.pdf [Accessed: 27/08/2015].
CGMA (2014d), *New Ways of Working: Managing the Open Workforce*, London: CGMA.
Das, T.K. and B.-S. Teng (2001), 'Trust, Control and Risk in Strategic Alliances: An Integrated Framework', *Organization Studies*, 22(2), pp. 251–283.
Dobbs, R., J. Manyika and J. Woetzel (2015), *No Ordinary Disruption*, New York: PublicAffairs.
Harvard Business Review (2015), 'Strategy: How to Live with Risks (Idea Watch)', July–August, pp. 20–21.
IFAC (2015), *From Bolt-On to Built-In: Managing Risk as an Integral Part of Managing an Organization*, New York: International Federation of Accountants.
IIRC (2013), *The International <IR> Framework*, London: International Integrated Reporting Council. Available from: http://integratedreporting.org/wp-content/uploads/2015/03/13-12-08-THE-INTERNATIONAL-IR-FRAMEWORK-2-1.pdf [Accessed: 27/08/2015].
Lauder, M. and M. Baker (2014), 'How Applying Foresight during the Risk Incubation Period Can Improve Risk Management', *Financial Management*, December, pp. 59–60.
McKinsey (2013), 'Improving Board Governance: McKinsey Global Survey Results'. Available from: http://www.mckinsey.com/insights/strategy/improving_board_governance_mckinsey_global_survey_results [Accessed: 8/09/2015].
Sammartino, S. (2014), *The Great Fragmentation and Why the Future of Business Is Small*, Milton: John Wiley & Sons Australia.
Siegler, M.G. (2010), 'Eric Schmidt: Every 2 Days We Create as Much Information as We Did up to 2003', *TechCrunch*. Available from: http://techcrunch.com/2010/08/04/schmidt-data [Accessed: 27/08/2015].
Simchi-Levi, D., W. Schmidt and Y. Wei (2014), 'From Superstorms to Factory Fires: Managing Unpredictable Supply-Chain Disruptions', *Harvard Business Review*, January–February, pp. 96–101.
Tomorrow's Good Governance Forum (2013), *Tomorrow's Corporate Governance: The Boardroom and Risk*, London: Tomorrow's Company. Available from: http://www.cimaglobal.com/Thought-leadership/Research-topics/Governance/The-boardroom-and-risk [Accessed: 21/09/2015].
Tomorrow's Good Governance Forum (2015), Tomorrow's Risk Leadership: Delivering Risk Resilience and Business Performance, London: Tomorrow's Company. Available from: http://www.cimaglobal.com/Documents/Thought_leadership_docs/Enterprise_governance/Tomorrows-Risk-leadership.pdfx [Accessed: 27/08/2015].
Twentyman, J. (2014), 'Royal Bank of Scotland Sees Opportunities in Assessing Supply Chain Risk', *Financial Times*, 26 March. Available from: https://www.ft.com/content/964bb2be-adb5-11e3-9ddc-00144feab7de [Accessed: 05/01/2017].
World Economic Forum (2015), *Global Risks Report*, Davos: World Economic Forum.

10

Risk and performance management

Two sides of the same coin?

Tommaso Palermo

Performance management

Since the late 1980s, organisations have been engaged in rethinking their control systems. As stated by Eccles (1991, p. 131), 'new strategies and competitive realities demand new measurement systems'. Growing criticism has been levelled against traditional measurement frameworks, which have been deemed to be past-oriented and unable to satisfactorily reflect how performances are affected by changing business environments (Johnson and Kaplan, 1987). The way in which management control issues (e.g. how to ensure the achievement of organisational objectives) are addressed has changed with changes in the context in which organisations operate (Otley, 2003). Several examples can be given: the shift from vertical integration to outsourcing, process re-engineering and value chain management; the use of non-financial performance measures to complement financial controls; the growing relevance of corporate governance and external control to ensure alignment between the interests of senior managers and business owners; and budgeting and planning problems as the uncertainty in some business environments increases.

Each of these themes can be related to one or more new management techniques. The escalating emphasis on business processes, particularly under the banner of business process re-engineering (BPR) (Hammer and Champy, 1993), draws attention to process-focused instruments such as activity-based costing (ABC) and activity-based management (ABM) (Friedman and Lyne, 1995). Strategic management accounting (SMA) draws attention to the analysis of data about business context and competition to monitor the alignment between internal operations and customer requirements (Bromwich and Bhimani, 1989). The use of non-financial measures is linked to the rise in importance of the balanced scorecard (BSC) (Kaplan and Norton, 1992, 1996, 2001). The focus on ensuring that senior managers act in the interests of shareholders led, especially in the United States, to performance measures such as Stern Stewart's Economic Value Added (EVA). The decline of traditional budgeting processes under conditions of increased uncertainty stimulated the Beyond Budgeting movement (Hope and Fraser, 2003) and discussion of other ways to incorporate uncertainty and non-controllable factors in budgeting processes (Van der Stede and Palermo, 2011; Becker *et al.* 2016).

As stated by Otley (2008, p. 230), 'there has been more management accounting innovation over the past two decades than in the previous fifty years'. This innovation supports the view that managers may well be responsible for some elements of strategy, management control and operational controls. As a consequence, management control research has started to pay greater attention to neglected elements of strategy and operations.[1] This shift of focus has been categorised under the general banner of performance management (Otley, 1999, 2001, 2003, 2008; Ferreira and Otley, 2009; Broadbent and Laughlin, 2009). The use of the term 'performance management' stresses that management accounting is only one of the ways in which it is possible to design and use information for organisational control. Performance management provides 'an umbrella under which we can study the more formal processes that organisations use in attempting to implement their strategic intent' (Otley, 2001, p. 250). The category of performance management underscores key characteristics of innovative management control techniques that flourished in the 1990s: the focus on the achievement of corporate strategy; the organisation-wide scope, with emphasis on organisational interdependencies and operational responsibilities of line managers; and the attention dedicated to detecting weak signals from the environment and providing a more timely and long-term view of the business. In short, the term 'performance management' emphasises enterprise-wide control systems that look beyond the ex-post measurement of performance and provide a future-oriented view of the business.

The framework developed by Otley (1999) and subsequently refined by Ferreira and Otley (2009) provides more details about the elements that characterise performance management. Ferreira and Otley state clearly that they do not try to develop a 'well-articulated theory' but rather aim to identify key issues that are relevant to many different organisations. The focus of the framework and its extensions, as claimed by the authors, is 'to provide a descriptive tool that may be used to amass evidence upon which further analysis can be based' (Ferreira and Otley, 2009, p. 266). The authors view performance management as a set of evolving formal and informal mechanisms, processes, systems and networks, which can be used by organisations for different aims: first, conveying the key objectives elicited by management; second, assisting strategic processes and ongoing management through analysis, planning, measurement and rewarding; and third, supporting and facilitating organisational learning and change.

This framework and its extensions have already been discussed, as noted by Scapens (2009). Drawing on a longitudinal case study, Collier (2005) focuses on the interaction between formal, systems-based controls and social controls. Specifically, the author shows the marginalisation of traditional management accounting and non-financial performance measurement techniques in a multinational packaging equipment supplier, whilst recognising the importance of belief and boundary systems. Broadbent and Laughlin (2009) expand the analysis of contextual and cultural factors, which are relatively underexplored in Ferreira and Otley's (2009) framework. The authors argue that a range of contextual factors underpin different specifications of performance management. As a result, a performance management system can be positioned in a continuum, with functional systems directed to specific outcomes on the one end and more participatory systems, where objectives and indicators are discursively agreed, on the other.

To summarise, the literature reviewed in this section suggests that performance management is essentially concerned with defining, controlling and managing the achievement of expected outcomes as well as the means used to achieve these results. The focus is placed at the organisational rather than individual level in order to understand the functioning of enterprise-wide control systems that go beyond the ex-post measurement of performance and financial outcomes.

Risk management

Risk calculation and quantification is not new in for-profit companies (Gallagher, 1956). It was initially associated with the insurance-buying function, and later with specific processes such as labour safety and information systems security (Meulbroek, 2002; Power, 2007). The 1990s, however, witnessed a major shift in risk management practice. The concept of risk became more broadly defined to include a wide set of events that could affect the achievement of corporate objectives: corporate reputation, regulatory compliance, operational activities and strategic decisions (DeLoach, 2004; Nocco and Stulz, 2006; Power, 2007; Woods, 2007). Risk management is today viewed from a broader perspective (Spira and Page, 2003; Holt, 2004; Woods, 2007). It focuses upon achieving control over corporate strategy (Dickinson, 2001; DeLoach, 2004; CIMA (Chartered Institute of Management Accountants), 2005; Nocco and Stulz, 2006; Woods, 2007); it aims to include all potential threats and opportunities (Beasley *et al.* 2006); it emphasises an integrated approach, improving senior managers' ability to oversee the risks portfolio (Sobel and Reding, 2004); it is cascaded down throughout the whole organisation via line management (Beasley *et al.* 2006; Woods, 2007).

In recent years, we have also witnessed a change in risk measurement. On the one hand, since the early 1990s risk has been studied, analysed and calculated as volatility in financial returns, based on mathematical mean-variance analysis (Power, 2007). As a result, different risk measures have been developed and have rapidly became a common measurement framework for financial (and, more recently, non-financial) institutions. Risk measures such as value at risk (VaR), originally calculated for internal risk reporting purposes in financial institutions, have started to become diffused among for-profit companies for both internal and external risk reporting purposes (Jorion, 1997; Woods *et al.* 2004). On the other hand, the practice literature discusses key risk indicators (KRIs) (Davies and Haubenstock, 2002; Lam, 2006; Scandizzo, 2005; Beasley *et al.* 2010). A KRI is defined as a measure that can be used to monitor either the level of risk in an organisation or the quality of controls around that risk. Different categories of KRIs can be devised. For example, Davies and Haubenstock (2002) distinguish between loss measures (e.g. actual out-of-pocket costs), process measures (e.g. quality of operations) and internal and external environmental measures (e.g. policy limits).

In the last decade, professional organisations have played a major role in defining the core elements of the new risk management. These efforts span different disciplines and professionals: risk managers (e.g. the Institute of Risk Management (IRM)), management accountants (e.g. CIMA and the Institute of Chartered Accountants in England and Wales (ICAEW)), internal auditors (e.g. the Institute of Internal Auditors (IIA)), consultancy firms (e.g. Deloitte, 2015; EY, 2015; PwC, 2009) and insurance managers (e.g. Airmic). *Enterprise Risk Management: Integrated Framework*, published in 2004 by the Committee of Sponsoring Organizations of the Treadway Commission (COSO, 2004), has been elaborated with the support of different accounting and auditing professional associations (Hayne and Free, 2014).

The practice documents in this growing body of the literature share similar concerns about value creation and the achievement of corporate objectives. In general, risk management is conceived as a process related to the risks that might affect an entity's objectives (COSO, 2004). As stated by CIMA (2005, p. 53), risk management is the 'process of understanding and managing the risks that the entity is inevitably subject to in attempting to achieve its corporate objectives'. The practice documents also provide frameworks that exemplify the different steps of the risk management process. Figure 10.1 provides an illustration of the framework proposed by IRM. This is an illustrative example of the main components of a typical new risk management process.

The overall process (IRM, 2002, pp. 5–11) is divided into four main steps: risk analysis and evaluation, risk reporting, risk treatment and risk monitoring. Risk analysis aims at

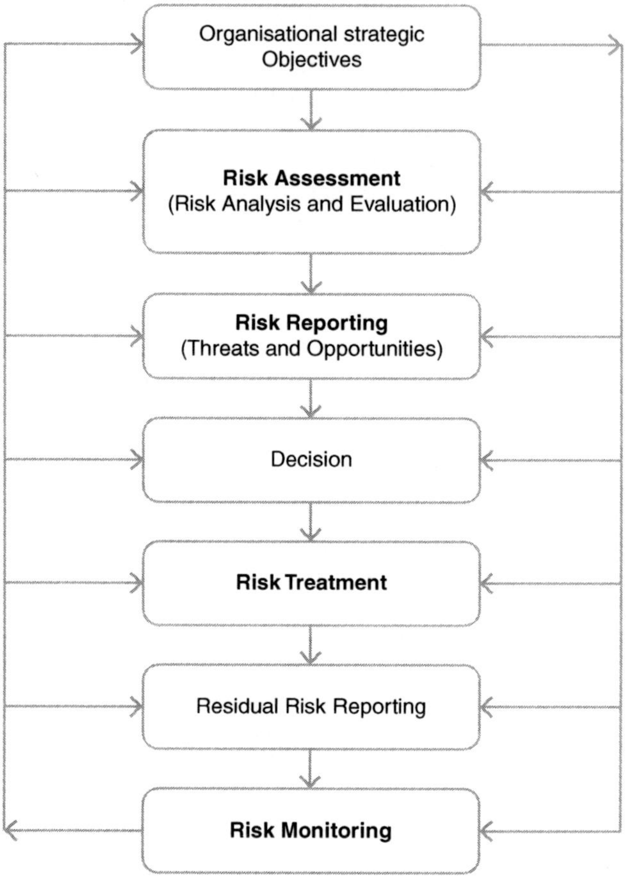

Figure 10.1 Risk management process (adapted from IRM, 2002, p. 4).

identifying, describing and estimating risks; risk evaluation is used to make decisions about the significance of risks to the organisation and whether each specific risk should be accepted or treated. Risk reporting is concerned with the communication at different organisational levels (e.g. board, business unit, individual and external stakeholder levels) of information about the risk management process. Risk treatment is the process of selecting and implementing measures to address risks (e.g. risk transfer and risk avoidance). Finally, the monitoring process should provide assurance that there are appropriate controls in place and procedures are understood and followed.

Several instruments can become part of the risk management process outlined in Figure10.1: risk maps and registers, SWOT and PESTLE analyses, statistical modelling, one-to-one interviews and workshops, and risk committees. As expressed by some scholars (Holt, 2004; Power, 2007; Miller *et al.* 2008), these form the more-or-less standardised set of risk practices expected to be found in any organisation. As Holt (2004, p. 254) states:

> Most risk management begins in the drafting of a risk register—a matrix of risk types or families, probabilities and impacts focused at distinct levels: division; organisation; sector; domestic economy; global economy. Its compilation can be approached either from a board level or from an operational level, or a combination of both. … The matrix is used

> to determine gross risks (the probability of an event occurring coupled to the extent of its impact), from which important or targeted risks can be identified. Those of greatest potential in terms of exposure and opportunity can be quantified using statistical models. Once identified, these can be managed through either mitigation strategies ... or avoidance strategies ... specific to each risk.

To summarise, risk management shifted in the 1990s towards a growing concern with value proposition and the achievement of corporate objectives. Risk management is viewed as a central part of an organisation's strategic management: a process that ensures that organisations address the risks linked to their activities with the goal of achieving sustained performance across different business areas.

Risk and performance management

It is possible to identify four different streams of the literature that address the relationship between risk and performance management. The following sections describe these streams, their contributions to our understanding of the relationship between risk and performance, and their limitations.

The levers of control framework

The first stream of research relates to the work of Robert Simons (1991, 1995). Simons studied the design and functioning of organisational controls with a ten-year-long research programme that culminated in the 1995 book *Levers of Control: How Managers Use Innovative Control Systems to Drive Strategic Renewal*. The author identifies four distinct uses of control systems. Diagnostic systems monitor critical performance variables and lead to corrective actions following a deviation from standard. Interactive systems are formal controls that managers use to become regularly involved in the decision activities of subordinates, and they become the basis for continual exchange between top managers and lower levels of management as well as among organisational members. Belief systems communicate core values of an organisation; they use culture, norms and values to drive action. Finally, boundary systems inhibit managers' ability to undertake inappropriate activities.

Simons's work on the levers of control contributes to risk management from the viewpoint of management control research (Otley, 2010). Boundary systems, in particular, are represented as 'the risks to be avoided in organisations' (Simons, 1995, p. 85). Practically, boundaries are represented by standards of ethical conduct (e.g. codes of business conduct that prohibit improper activities) and by strategic systems ensuring that people avoid opportunities that could diminish the business's competitive positions. As put by Simons (1995, p. 86):

> A large computer company, for example, uses its strategic planning process to segregate its product and market opportunities into what managers call green space and red space. Green space is the acceptable domain for new initiatives. Red space represents the products and markets in which senior managers have decided they do not want to pursue new opportunities, although the organisation could compete in those products and markets given its competencies.

In subsequent work, Simons (1999) explicitly states that his research on the levers of control can be framed as addressing risk management issues: 'The levers, simply stated, are the mechanisms managers can adjust to control risk as a company pursues its strategy' (p. 92). An important implication is that mechanisms of integration between risk and performance management need not entail an examination of formal risk management systems. The way in which performance management instruments (or, drawing on Simons's work, levers of control) are used helps to uncover different risk management dimensions. The case of Johnson & Johnson, a leading company in the healthcare sector, is frequently recounted by Simons (1999, p. 94) as an example:

> Johnson & Johnson provides an illustration of a company that uses an effective risk-controlling device. Its managers use their profit-planning and long-range-planning system in a highly interactive way to continually assess opportunities and threats. As they constantly revise projections, managers are forced to confront three questions: What has changed? Why? And, what are we going to do about it? Through such an interactive process, Johnson & Johnson's managers have successfully navigated the shoals of the changing health care industry and have managed to stay, year after year, on the shortlist of America's most admired companies.

Simons' work has been extensively investigated in the last decade (see, for example, Bisbee and Otley, 2004; Widener, 2007; Tessier and Otley, 2012). However, the idea that different uses of management control systems can lead to risk management has not been explored so far, with limited exceptions (CIMA, 2010). This is not to say that risk is a marginal element in research on the levers of control framework. Widener (2007), for instance, suggests that two types of strategic elements—strategic uncertainties and strategic risk—drive the importance and role of control systems. But risk is considered as an antecedent to different uses of management control systems, rather than a focus of management through the levers of control.

To summarise, Simons addresses risk management issues in his work on the levers of control. An important implication is that one does not need to examine formal risk management systems to study the relationship between risk and performance management. The way in which management control processes and instruments (i.e. the levers of controls) are used can be indicative of ways to manage risk and performance in an integrated way.

Enterprise-wide risk management

A second stream of the literature (e.g. Mikes, 2009, 2011; Woods, 2009; Arena *et al.* 2010; CIMA, 2010; Tekathen and Dechow, 2013; Palermo, 2014) offers a perspective diametrically opposed to Simons's work. Instead of looking at the potentially important role to be played by management control systems for risk management, they draw attention to new formal risk management systems for management control. These studies focus their attention primarily on enterprise-wide risk management (ERM), which represents an emergent theme in the literature with implications for research in strategy, accounting and governance (Bhimani, 2009; Soin and Collier, 2013).

Research on ERM focuses on different contexts (e.g. the public and private sectors) and uses different theoretical perspectives (e.g. contingency theory and institutional theory). For example, Woods (2009) adopts a contingency-based theoretical frame to study risk management in a public sector organisation. The author explores risk management as a dimension of corporate governance and suggests that, even though basic structures of risk management are common across large organisations, specific contingencies can shape risk management control systems. Mikes (2009), based on a field study of two financial institutions, argues that organisations might exhibit distinct calculative styles underpinning different risk management mixes. In so doing, Mikes's work extends the boundaries of contingency-based concepts of control practices. Arena *et al.* (2010) investigate organisational variations of ERM through a longitudinal multiple case study based on three companies operating in non-financial sectors. The study highlights how ERM in practice reveals distinct trajectories within the three organisations as it encounters different logics, experts and rationalities. This includes the hybridisation of risk and control practice, as exemplified by the claim of the rise of a 'new hybrid ERM/budget style' (Arena *et al.* 2010, p. 14) in one of the organisations. Tekathen and Dechow (2013) examine the design and use of COSO-ERM in a German top-tier corporation. The company's manifestation of COSO-ERM includes tools that mobilise people in unexpected ways. For instance, the authors shed light on an information system that supports the aggregation and reporting of risk information. Based on the type of entrance for single risks, the system automatically aggregates risks based on pre-defined risk categories and the organisational structure of the company. However, not all fields are mandatory, leading to ambiguity about what counts as a risk and uncertainty about the resulting aggregated risks. Finally, Palermo (2014) explores the adoption of a formal organisation-wide risk management framework in a public sector organisation. Drawing on new institutional theory, the study reveals how the use of the new framework depends on risk managers' relational skills, knowledge of business activities and prior professional experience.

Despite differences in approaches, theories and context, there are two common themes in these studies. First, the authors tried to gain a sense of how risk management was working in concrete organisational settings, and examine how the operation of enterprise-wide risk controls affect performance management. Although these studies are primarily devoted to a management accounting audience, there are few references to traditional accounting issues such as the use of risk-adjusted returns for capital allocation. The researchers have instead focused on the processes, systems and controls around risk management. An important implication of this literature is that risk 'has broken out of the finance function' (CIMA, 2010, p. 11). Second, all these studies call for further investigation of the relationship between risk and performance management. The core message is that, when studying the dynamics of ERM, researchers need to consider the interactions between risk and other management control and information systems (Mikes, 2009; Arena *et al.* 2010). For instance, the study by Mikes (2009, p. 23) suggests that 'the interface between accounting and risk controls is riddled with possibilities and tensions'.

To summarise, management accounting research is starting to pay increasing attention to the analysis of the transformative role of ERM processes on management control activities. It is recognised that this topic could constitute a fertile ground for future research.

Risk and control

A third stream of the literature examines the development of risk management and governance processes, with a particular focus on organisations operating in the UK since the publication of policy documents such as the Turnbull Report and its adoption in the Combined Code on Corporate Governance (Collier and Berry, 2002; Collier *et al.* 2007; Woods *et al.* 2008; Collier, 2008). A related theme is the exploration of the role of management accountants in risk management processes (Collier *et al.* 2007; Collier and Berry, 2008).

The main findings have been summarised in a book entitled *Risk and Management Accounting: Best Practice Guidelines for Enterprise-Wide Internal Control Procedures* (Collier *et al.* 2007). This research provides insights into the relationship between risk, management accounting and corporate governance. First, risk management in the sample of organisations studied was observed to arise from institutional and internal processes rather than a greater perceived riskiness of the environment in which organisations operate. Second, the researchers found that heuristic methods of risk management, especially subjective judgement based on experience, were used much more than procedural and systems-based approaches. This contrasts with the 'unspoken assumption' (Corvellec, 2009, p. 286) in much risk management research that risk management is best associated with formal processes and instruments. Third, management accountants, contrary to professional claims (e.g. Pollara, 2008), had a marginal role in relation to risk management in the majority of organisations.

This body of the academic literature raises questions about the relative pre-eminence of processes to manage risks over management controls and performance management processes. For instance, drawing on Simons's work, Collier (2008) argues that a risk-based approach to control is consistent with the deployment of boundary and belief systems and an interactive use of controls. For instance, boundary systems determine the risks facing an organisation; belief systems are supported by the definition of expectations around organisational risk appetite and risk culture (on the role of risk culture, see Power *et al.* 2013). It is shown that it is possible to find forms of risk-based approaches to control (e.g. the Just in Time environment described by Collier and Berry, 2002), where existing controls are specifically related to the assessment of business risks.

To summarise, this stream of research has important implications for research on the relationship between risk and performance management. It shows that risk management does not necessarily originate from a riskier world (economic and strategic calculation) but rather from institutional and internal processes; that managers prefer to use heuristic methods rather than formal risk management calculations; and that management accountants play a marginal role in risk management. Overall, a risk-based approach to control could be a way of leveraging existing management controls and performance management processes as a driver for integrated risk and performance management.

The practice view

A growing body of the practice literature examines models and mechanisms that link risk and performance management (e.g. Scholey, 2006; Beasley *et al.* 2006; Woods, 2007; Van der Stede, 2009; Van der Stede and Palermo, 2011). The underlying theme is that risk and performance could and should be linked to each other because they present complementarities that can be leveraged to achieve higher organisational performance. Common expressions are that risk and performance are 'two sides of the same coin' (e.g. Van der Stede, 2009) or that risk and performance 'go hand in hand' (e.g. Scholey, 2006).

The issue has been addressed conceptually with the notion of 'enterprise governance' (Van der Stede, 2009). Enterprise governance is a conceptual framework that puts reliable scrutiny and sustainable performance under one umbrella, addressing how organisations can align both items in the short and long terms. The idea is to reverse the perverse tendencies—under-scrutiny in periods of good fortune and over-scrutiny in periods of declining demand—that cause performance and risk management to become misaligned. Practice articles also describe new instruments that can be used to balance organisational attention between risk and performance issues. The case of 'risk scorecards' can be pointed out. A number of contributions (IMA (Institute of Management Accountants), 2006; Calandro and Lane, 2006; Scholey, 2006; Beasley *et al.* 2006; Woods, 2007) describe how the structure of the BSC can be used to complement key performance measures with a set of key risk indicators. Risk scorecards can provide a single point of access to critical risk and performance information that resides in disparate data sources. They may, therefore, represent the one instrument that raises the level of managers' risk awareness, providing an integrated framework for risk and performance measurement and reporting.

Risk scorecards also provide a bridge between practice and academic literature. It is recognised that the management of risk has not strongly featured in the literature on the BSC[2] (Kaplan and Norton, 1992, 1996, 2001). However, it is also argued that the BSC framework could provide a valid infrastructure to manage strategy risks (Kaplan, 2009; Kaplan *et al.* 2009). A risk scorecard can be devised based on an entity's strategy map. The risk scorecard first identifies for each strategic objective the primary risk events that would prevent the objective from being achieved; it then presents for each risk event a selection of metrics to be used as early warning indicators of when the risk event might be occurring. A rising trend in risk metrics, or even a single observation above a pre-set control limit, generates a management alert requiring immediate attention.

To summarise, bearing in mind that professional literature offers a consultative approach to the problem at stake, practice contributions provide insights into ways of integrating risk and performance. In general, a strong emphasis is placed on the use of existing performance management infrastructures as a platform for new risk and performance management integrated instruments.

Discussion and conclusions

Academic research and practice literature shows that risk and performance management are converging towards a common set of characteristics. Risk management shows a growing concern with value propositions, performance and achievement of corporate objectives. Performance management looks beyond the ex-post measurement of performance to the management of performance that provides a future-oriented view of the business. On this basis, risk and performance management can be seen as 'two sides of the same coin'.

This chapter has reviewed and synthesised four streams of the literature, different in their focus and audience, that help to delineate what being 'two sides of the same coin' may mean in practice. Bearing in mind the risk of oversimplification, Table 10.1 provides a synthetic overview of the literature reviewed. First, it is possible to make a distinction based on the starting point of investigation. On the one hand, there are studies that use performance management as a primary focus of investigation; they provide insights into how it is possible to leverage performance management processes for risk management. On the other hand, there are studies that focus attention on risk management; research here builds on the analysis of risk management processes or risk-based controls to investigate how they may affect and complement performance management.

Second, it is possible to differentiate the four streams of the literature according to their focus on new or existing processes and procedures. On the one hand, there is research that investigates how new instruments and processes can contribute to enhance knowledge on the relation between risk and performance management (e.g. risk scorecards on the performance side and ERM on the risk side). On the other hand, there are contributions that show how different uses of existing risk and performance management processes can become a source for integrated risk and performance management. Research here does not look specifically to the presence of new tools; rather, it investigates how different uses of existing tools can have an effect on the way in which risk and performance are managed as 'two sides of the same coin'.

Table 10.1 Overview of research on risk and performance management

		Starting point of investigation	
		Performance	*Risk*
Focus on the presence of new formal processes	Low	**Levers of control** (mid 1990s): uses of management control systems for effective risk management	**Risk-based control** (late 2000s): a risk-based approach to management control helps to leverage existing risk controls and mental models as a driver for performance management
	High	**Practice literature** (mid 2000s): risk and performance management can be integrated via new risk and performance management infrastructures	**Enterprise-wide risk management** (late 2000s): new processes such as ERM processes shape existing management control systems

By providing an overview of the different streams of research, Table 10.1 sheds light on two elements for further reflection. First, we enter into a recent field of research. Most of the contributions have been made within the last decade. Even the levers of control framework, which has been extensively investigated since the mid-1990s, has never been explicitly tested in relation to the ability of different control systems to help organisations to manage risks (Collier, 2008; Otley, 2010). Second, the different research streams suggest contrasting views on how the problem of managing risk and performance as 'two sides of the same coin' can be addressed. For example, does linking risk and performance management require (or benefit from) the formalisation of new instruments and processes? Or can organisations simply leverage existing processes and tools? Is risk management relatively pre-eminent over performance management, or vice versa? Further work could be beneficial to enhance knowledge of the ways in which risk and performance management processes and instruments can be related. Moreover, further work may help to confirm or challenge the argument presented in this chapter that risk management and performance management are converging towards a common ground.

Notes

1 Seminal work by Anthony (1965) separated out the activities of 'management control' from the wider activities of 'strategic planning' and the more detailed and technically diverse activities of 'operational control'.
2 The sole exception is the discussion of risk management as an internal process in the 2001 book *Strategy Maps* (Kaplan and Norton, 2001, pp. 73–77).

References

Anthony, R. (1965), *Planning and Control Systems: A Framework for Analysis*, Boston: Harvard Business School Press.

Arena, M., M. Arnaboldi and G. Azzone (2010), 'The Organizational Dynamics of Enterprise Risk Management', *Accounting, Organizations and Society*, 35, pp. 659–675.

Beasley, M., A. Chen, K. Nunez and L. Wright (2006), 'Working Hand in Hand: Balanced Scorecard and Enterprise Risk Management', *Strategic Finance*, March, pp. 49–55.

Beasley, M.S., B.C. Branson and B.V. Hancock (2010), *Developing Key Risk Indicators to Strengthen Enterprise Risk Management*, COSO, pp. 1–12.

Becker, S.D., M.D. Mahlendorf, U. Schäffer and M. Thaten (2016), 'Budgeting in Times of Economic Crisis', *Contemporary Accounting Research*, 33(4), pp. 1489–1517.

Bhimani, A. (2009), 'Risk Management, Corporate Governance and Management Accounting: Emerging Interdependencies', *Management Accounting Research*, 20, pp. 2–5.

Bisbee, J. and D. Otley (2004), 'The Effects of the Interactive Use of Management Control Systems on Product Innovation', *Accounting, Organizations and Society*, 29, pp. 709–737.

Broadbent, J. and R. Laughlin (2009), 'Performance Management Systems: A Conceptual Model', *Management Accounting Research*, 20, pp. 283–295.

Bromwich, M. and A. Bhimani (1989), 'Management Accounting: Evolution Not Revolution', *Management Accounting*, 67(9), pp. 5–6.

Calandro, J. and S. Lane (2006), 'Insights from the Balanced Scorecard: An Introduction to the Enterprise Risk Scorecard', *Measuring Business Excellence*, 10, pp. 31–40.

CIMA (Chartered Institute of Management Accountants) (2005), *Official Terminology*, Oxford: CIMA Publishing.

CIMA (Chartered Institute of Management Accountants) (2010),'Reporting and Managing Risk: A Look at Current Practice at Tesco, RBS, Local and Central Government', *Research Executive Summary Series*, 6(8), pp. 1–13.

Collier, P. (2005), 'Entrepreneurial Cognition and the Construction of a Relevant Accounting', *Management Accounting Research*, 16, pp. 321–339.

Collier, P. (2008), 'Risk-Based Control or Control-Based Risk?' *2nd European Risk Research Conference*. Milan, 11–12 September 2008.

Collier, P. and P. Berry (2002), 'Risk in the Process of Budgeting', *Management Accounting Research*, 13, pp. 273–297.

Collier, P. and P. Berry (2008), 'The Role of the Management Accountant in Risk Management', in M. Woods, P. Kajüter, and P. Linsley (eds.), *International Risk Management*, London: CIMA Publishing.

Collier, P., A. Berry and G. Burke (2007), *Risk and Management Accounting: Best Practices and Guidelines for Enterprise-wide Internal Control Procedures*, London: CIMA Publishing.

Corvellec, H. (2009), 'The Practice of Risk Management: Silence Is Not Absence', *Risk Management*, 11, pp. 285–304.

COSO (2004), *Enterprise Risk Management: Integrated Framework*, New York: COSO.

Davies, J. and M. Haubenstock (2002), 'Building Effective Indicators to Monitor Operational Risk', *RMA Journal*, May, pp. 40–43.

DeLoach, J. (2004), 'The New Risk Imperative: An Enterprise-Wide Approach', *Handbook of Business Strategy*, 5(1), pp. 29–34.

Deloitte (2015), Enterprise Risk Management: A 'Risk-Intelligent' Approach, available at www2.deloitte.com/uk/en/pages/risk/articles/enterprise-risk-management.html

Dickinson, G. (2001), 'Enterprise Risk Management: Its Origins and Conceptual Foundation', *The Geneva Papers on Risk and Insurance*, 26(3), pp. 360–366.

Eccles, R.G. (1991), 'The Performance Measurement Manifesto', *Harvard Business Review*, January–February, pp. 131–137.

EY (2015), Enterprise Risk Management: An Integrated Approach towards Effective and Sustainable Risk Management, available at http://www.ey.com/Publication/vwLUAssets/EY-enterprise-risk-management/$FILE/EY-enterprise-risk-management.pdf

Ferreira, A. and D. Otley (2009), 'The Design and Use of Performance Management Systems: An Extended Framework for Analysis', *Management Accounting Research*, 20, pp. 263–282.

Friedman, A. and S. Lyne (1995), *Activity-Based Techniques: The Real Life Consequences*, London: CIMA Publishing.

Gallagher, R.B. (1956), 'Risk Management: New Phase of Cost Control', *Harvard Business Review*, 34(5), pp. 75–82.

Hammer, M. and J. Champy (1993), 'Reengineering the Corporation: A Manifesto for Business Revolution', *Business Horizons*, 36, pp. 90–91.

Hayne, C. and C. Free (2014), 'Hybridized Professional Groups and Institutional Work: COSO and the Rise of Enterprise Risk Management', *Accounting, Organizations and Society*, 39(5), pp. 309–330.

Holt, R. (2004), 'Risk Management: The Talking Cure', *Organization*, 11, pp. 251–270.

Hope, J. and R. Fraser (2003), 'Who needs budgets?' *Harvard Business Review*, 81(2), pp. 108–127.

IMA (2006), *Enterprise Risk Management: Frameworks, Elements, and Integration*, IMA.

IRM (2002), *A Risk Management Standard*, London: IRM.

Johnson, H.T. and R. Kaplan (1987), *Relevance Lost: The Rise and Fall of Management Accounting*, Boston: Harvard Business School Press.

Jorion, P. (1997), *Value at Risk*, Chicago: Irwin.
Kaplan, R. (2009), 'Risk Management and the Strategy Execution System', *Balanced Scorecard Report*, 11, November–December, pp. 1–6.
Kaplan, R. and D. Norton (1992), 'The Balanced Scorecard: Measures That Drive Performance', *Harvard Business Review*, 70(1) pp. 71–79.
Kaplan, R. and D. Norton (1996), *The Balanced Scorecard: Translating Strategy into Action*, Boston: Harvard Business School Press.
Kaplan, R. and D. Norton (2001), *The Strategy-Focused Organization*, Boston: Harvard Business School Press.
Kaplan, R., A. Mikes, R. Simons, P. Tufano and M. Hofmann (2009), 'Managing Risk in the New World', *Harvard Business Review*, October, pp. 1–8.
Lam, J. (2006), *Emerging Best Practices in Developing Key Risk Indicators* and *ERM Reporting*, James Lam & Associates.
Meulbroek, L. (2002), 'The Promise and Challenge of Integrated Risk Management', *Risk Management and Insurance Review*, 5(1), pp. 55–66.
Mikes, A. (2009), 'Risk Management and Calculative Cultures', *Management Accounting Research*, 20(1), pp. 18–42.
Mikes, A. (2011), 'From Counting Risk to Making Risk Count: Boundary-Work in Risk Management'. *Accounting, Organizations and Society*, 36(4–5), pp. 226–245.
Miller, P., L. Kurunmäki and T. O'Leary (2008), 'Accounting, Hybrids and the Management of Risk', *Accounting, Organization and Society*, 33, pp. 942–967.
Nocco, B.W. and R.M. Stulz (2006), 'Enterprise Risk Management: Theory and Practice', *Journal of Applied Corporate Finance*, 18, pp. 8–20.
Otley, D. (1999), 'Performance Management: A Framework for Management Control Systems Research', *Management Accounting Research*, 10, pp. 363–382.
Otley, D. (2001), 'Extending the Boundaries of Management Accounting Research', *British Accounting Review*, 33, pp. 243–261.
Otley, D. (2003), 'Management Control and Performance Management: Whence and Whither?' *British Accounting Review*, 35, pp. 309–326.
Otley, D. (2008), 'Did Kaplan and Johnson Get It Right?' *Accounting, Auditing & Accountability Journal*, 2, pp. 229–239.
Otley, D. (2010), 'Plenary Address to MCA Conference', University of Greenwich, September.
Palermo, T. (2014), 'Accountability and Expertise in Public Sector Risk Management: A Case Study', *Financial Accountability & Management*, 30(3), pp. 322–341.
Pollara, J. (2008), 'FGRC: Seize the Opportunity', *Strategic Finance*, May, pp. 58–59.
Power, M. (2007), *Organized Uncertainty: Designing a World of Risk Management*, Oxford: Oxford University Press.
Power, M.K., S. Ashby and T. Palermo (2013), *Risk Culture in Financial Organisations: A Research Report*, London: Centre for Analysis of Risk and Regulation (CARR). Available from: www.lse.ac.uk/researchAndExpertise/units/CARR/pdf/Final-Risk-Culture-Report.pdf.
PwC (PriceWaterhouseCoopers) (2009), *Seizing Opportunity: Linking Risk and Performance*. Available from: https://www.pwc.com/us/en/risk-performance/assets/pwc-risk-performance-2009.pdf.
Scandizzo, S. (2005), 'Risk Mapping and Key Risk Indicators in Operational Risk Management', *Economic Notes*, 34, pp. 231–256.
Scapens, R. (2009), 'Frameworks for Performance Management and Control Systems Research', *Management Accounting Research*, 20(4), p. 262.
Scholey, C. (2006), 'Risk and the Balanced Scorecard', *CMA Management*, 32, pp. 32–35.
Simons, R. (1991), 'Strategic Orientation and Top Management Attention to Control Systems', *Strategic Management Journal*, 12, pp. 49–62.
Simons, R. (1995), Control in an Age of Empowerment, *Harvard Business Review*, March–April, pp. 80–88.
Simons, R. (1999), 'How Risky Is Your Company', *Harvard Business Review*, 71, pp. 85–94.
Sobel, P.J. and K.F. Reding (2004), 'Aligning Corporate Governance with Enterprise Risk Management', *Management Accounting Quarterly*, Winter, pp. 29–37.
Soin, K. and P. Collier (2013), 'Risk and Risk Management in Management Accounting and Control', *Management Accounting Research*, 24(2), pp. 82–87.

Spira, L.F. and M. Page (2003), 'Risk Management: The Reinvention of Internal Control and the Changing Role of Internal Audit', *Accounting, Auditing & Accountability Journal*, 16, pp. 640–661.
Tekathen, M. and N. Dechow (2013), 'Enterprise Risk Management and Continuous Re-alignment in the Pursuit of Accountability: A German Case', *Management Accounting Research*, 24(2), pp. 100–121.
Tessier, S., and Otley, D. (2012), 'A Conceptual Development of Simons' Levers of Control Framework', *Management Accounting Research*, 23(3), pp. 171–185.
Van der Stede, W.A. (2009), 'Enterprise Governance', *Financial Management*, February, pp. 38–40.
Van der Stede, W.A. and T. Palermo (2011), 'Scenario Budgeting: Integrating Risk and Performance', *Finance & Management*, January, pp. 11–13.
Widener, S.K. (2007), 'An Empirical Analysis of the Levers of Control Framework', *Accounting, Organizations and Society*, 32(7–8), pp. 757–788.
Woods, M. (2007), 'All in the Performance', *Excellence in Leadership*, 2, pp. 32–35.
Woods, M. (2009), 'A Contingency Theory Perspective on the Risk Management Control System within Birmingham City Council', *Management Accounting Research*, 20, pp. 69–81.
Woods, M., K. Dowd and C.G. Humphrey (2004), 'Credibility at Risk? The Accounting Profession, Risk Reporting and the Rise of VaR', CRIS Discussion Paper Series.

11

Incorporating risk considerations into planning and control systems

The influence of risk management value creation objectives

Christopher D. Ittner and Thomas Keusch

Introduction

Formal, top-down planning and control lies at the heart of enterprise-wide risk management (ERM). ERM frameworks developed by the Committee of Sponsoring Organizations of the Treadway Commission (COSO, 2004), the International Organization for Standardization (ISO, 2009) and others present structured risk management processes that begin by linking ERM activities to organizational strategies and objectives through the establishment of accountabilities and incentives for risk management. The processes continue through the identification, assessment and categorization of all types of risks across the enterprise, and the use of risk information to optimize risk responses (i.e. avoid, mitigate, share, transfer or accept). Finally, ongoing risk monitoring and reporting ensures that decisions fall within the enterprise's chosen risk appetite (the amount of risk exposure the firm is willing to accept to achieve its objectives) and risk tolerances (the acceptable variation in outcomes related to each risk) and that emerging risks are not overlooked. By applying these steps in a consistent, integrated fashion across functions and decision contexts, enterprises are said to be in a position to effectively identify, manage and respond to material risks of all kinds.

Contingency theory suggests that the extent to which an enterprise adopts these practices should be a function of cost–benefit tradeoffs that vary with the organization's strategic and environmental context (e.g. Gordon *et al.*, 2009; Woods, 2009). Although prior research provides evidence on some of the contextual factors associated with the adoption or maturity of ERM processes, the vast majority of large-sample studies examine aggregate measures of overall ERM use rather than the adoption of individual risk-focused planning and control practices. Similarly, most research on the performance implications of ERM focuses on measures of overall ERM adoption or maturity, overlooking the possibility that some risk-focused planning and control practices have greater effects on enterprise decision-making and performance than others.[1]

More importantly, research examining the determinants and performance implications of ERM has not investigated enterprises' strategies for creating value through risk management. Risk management value creation objectives can include mitigating downside risks or their effects within a given budget; minimizing the total cost of risk by trading off investments in risk control and the costs of risk failures; and using an organization's greater understanding of both the upsides and downsides of risk to create value by optimizing the entity's risk–return tradeoffs. Practitioner-oriented publications contend that the benefits from different risk-focused planning and control practices vary with specific risk management value creation objectives pursued by the enterprise, with greater integration of risk considerations into the organization's performance management practices becoming more beneficial as the focus shifts from compliance and mitigation to increasing stakeholder value through the consideration of both the upsides and downsides of risk (EY, 2013; KPMG, 2009; McKinsey, 2014; Wallis, 2012).

In this chapter, we explore the influence of risk management value creation objectives on planning and control systems using survey data from a broad international sample of listed, private and non-profit entities. The detailed survey responses allow us to provide evidence on the adoption of a wide variety of risk-focused planning and control practices in order to examine how these practices vary with risk management objectives and other contingency factors, and to investigate whether enterprises that make greater use of these practices are more likely to have changed strategic direction as a result of new information or understanding concerning a major risk. In addition, we extend prior large-sample ERM studies by examining the performance implications of risk-focused planning and control practices and risk management objectives using survey-based and publicly-reported proxies for enterprise risk-taking and value.

ERM and risk-focused planning and control systems

Risk management traditionally has operated within functional silos, with a strong focus on regulatory compliance and loss mitigation through financial instruments such as derivatives and insurance. ERM differs from traditional risk management by taking a more integrated, holistic approach that first, considers the potential impact of all types of risks across the enterprise's processes, functions and stakeholders; second, incorporates a strategic perspective that assesses both upside risk (opportunities) and downside risk (potential losses or damage) in the context of strategic objectives; and third, makes risk considerations part of the organizational fabric by embedding them in all decision-making.

The ERM literature contends that risk considerations must be incorporated into the organization's planning and control systems if ERM is to become an integral component of performance management. According to ERM advocates, formal accountability and incentives for risk management processes and outcomes must be established to set the appropriate 'tone at the top' and encourage and reward the identification and management of risk-related opportunities and challenges. The use of quantitative techniques for assessing risks and risk interdependencies relative to the organization's risk appetite and tolerances can then be applied to measure the likelihood and impact of each potential risk event and risk response (Mun, 2010; Curtis and Carey, 2012).

Incorporating risk assessment results into financial and strategic planning processes ensures that ERM becomes an established component of operational and strategic decision-making (Aberdeen, 2012; Deloitte, 2012). Risk-based budgeting supports resource allocations that are consistent with the desired risk–return profile and within the organization's financial capacity to bear the desired risks (Alviniussen and Jankensgard, 2009). Incorporating risk assessments into capital budgeting ensures that interactions between risks that are shared across multiple business units, projects and time periods are considered, and it promotes improved coordination of capital requirements, cash-flow potentials and risk exposures (Froot and Stein, 1998; Ai *et al.*, 2012). Including risk assessment results in the strategic planning process allows an organization to evaluate whether one strategic initiative introduces risks that conflict with the goals of another and enables it to consider whether the combined risks of the various strategic choices fall within the organization's risk appetite and collectively support its strategic objectives (Beasley and Frigo, 2010).

Performance measurement and monitoring complete the ERM feedback loop. At the board-of-directors level, frequent reporting of key and emerging risks, risk management activities and risk outcomes provides the information needed to fulfill the board's risk oversight responsibilities. Management-level identification and reporting of key risk indicators and goals can foster greater accountability; facilitate effective implementation of risk management processes and activities; promote the evaluation of the contribution being made by risk management and the appropriateness of the control mechanisms that have been selected; and enhance the monitoring of emerging risks.

Existing evidence

Although risk-focused planning and control practices are argued to be essential elements of ERM in both for-profit and not-for-profit organizations, surveys indicate that their adoption is relatively limited (AFP (Assocation for Financial Professionals), 2014; Milliman, 2014; PwC, 2015). One potential explanation for the limited adoption is that these practices, on average, are not beneficial. Difficulties in defining a firm's risk appetite and tolerances, limitations in quantitative risk assessment and forecasting practices, and the inability to anticipate infrequent or extreme events can limit the effectiveness of risk-focused planning and control practices (Taleb, 2007; Danielsson, 2008; Power, 2009; Mikes, 2009). Incorporating risk considerations into planning and control systems may also hinder performance if they provide managers with a false sense of security or cause overconfidence in tenuous assumptions and forecasts (Kahneman and Lovallo, 1993; Durand, 2003).

Even if some or all of the suggested risk-focused planning and control practices are not appropriate in every circumstance, their use may still be beneficial in certain settings. Empirical studies have identified a number of contingency factors that are significantly associated with the adoption or maturity of ERM processes, including organizational size and complexity, ownership and governance structures, industry, and country (Gatzert and Martin, 2015). In addition, the risk management literature suggests that the value creation objectives that organizations set for their ERM processes have a strong influence on the potential benefits from specific risk-focused planning and control practices. Field research finds that organizations adopt a variety of risk management value creation strategies (Shenkir *et al.,* 2010). Some focus on improving compliance and avoiding or minimizing losses. Others take a broader perspective on the value of downside risk reduction by evaluating the total cost of risk (TCOR). TCOR represents the aggregate cost of managing risks, including the costs of risk management controls, retained losses, external insurance costs and external risk management costs. By focusing on measuring and reducing the total cost of risk ownership, organizations attempt to identify internal inconsistencies in risk management practices; highlight areas where too many resources are dedicated to certain risks relative to others (allowing the organization to reallocate its risk management budget); pinpoint inefficiencies in the risk management process (generating direct cost savings); and determine where additional investments in risk management can increase value by reducing overall insurance premiums, risk control costs, administrative costs and self-retained losses over time.

Surveys indicate that a smaller set of organizations take a more strategic approach to value creation that considers both the upsides and downsides of risk. These enterprises seek to align their risk appetites and tolerances with organizational strategy by identifying events that could have an adverse effect on the achievement of strategic goals as well as by identifying strategic but risky opportunities that, if undertaken, can facilitate the achievement of organizational goals. By accepting and managing risk, these enterprises seek to increase stakeholder value by limiting some risks and exploiting others.

Practitioner-oriented ERM publications contend that the required level and sophistication of risk-focused planning and control practices increase as organizations move from cost-focused compliance objectives to more strategic objectives that consider both the upsides and downsides of risk (EY, 2013; KPMG, 2009; McKinsey & Company, 2014; Wallis, 2012). However, evidence on the influence of risk management objectives on planning and control systems is limited. Although field research has begun to investigate the roles of budgeting (Arena and Arnaboldi, 2013), performance measurement (Woods, 2007) and quantitative risk assessment (Mikes, 2009) in ERM, large-sample empirical studies have primarily focused on the determinants or performance implications of aggregate measures of ERM use or maturity, shedding little light on individual risk-focused planning and control practices.[2] Moreover, none of these studies examine how differences in risk management value creation objectives affect the use or performance implications of risk-focused planning and control practices. We investigate these issues in this chapter.

The use of risk-focused planning and control practices

We conduct our analyses using data from Aon's Risk Maturity Index (RMI) survey. Aon, a leading provider of insurance brokerage, risk management and human resource services, designed the RMI as a self-assessment tool for organizations to evaluate and benchmark their ERM capabilities.[3] The online survey was developed in collaboration with academics and industry risk experts, and it covers the major elements of the COSO (2004) ERM framework. Respondents are high-level risk management and C-suite executives who are actively involved in their firms' risk management activities.[4] Potential participants must contact Aon prior to receiving authorization to complete the survey in order to confirm they have the requisite knowledge of the firm's risk management practices to accurately answer the questions. Participants are informed that their responses will be used by Aon and for academic research purposes.

We examine data from RMI surveys taken between 2011 and 2013. Our sample contains 313 listed firms, 250 private firms and 123 not-for-profit organizations; 10.8 per cent are government-affiliated. Table 11.1 lists the respondents' countries and industries. Slightly more than half (54.8%) are headquartered in North America, 27.4 per cent in Europe, 12.3 per cent in Asia Pacific and 5.5 per cent in other regions. A wide variety of industries are represented, with no sector comprising more than 12 per cent of the sample.

Risk management value creation objectives

The survey asked respondents to indicate executive management's objectives for creating value through risk management, from the following list (with multiple responses allowed): preventing negatives within a set budget; minimizing the total cost of risk; and identifying opportunities where the organization is the natural owner of a risk, enabling return generation from more risk-taking. Across the entire sample, 70.7 per cent listed preventing negatives within a set budget, 68.9 per cent listed minimizing the total cost of risk, and 39.2 per cent listed generating returns from greater risk-taking. Of the 44 per cent of respondents who identified only one objective, the most frequent was preventing negatives within a set budget (45.4%) followed by minimizing the total cost of risk (36.8%). One-third provided two responses, of which only 25.6 per cent listed return generation from risk-taking. Less than a

Table 11.1 Sample

Survey respondents by industry

	Frequency	*Per cent*
Business Equipment	24	3.51
Chemicals	40	5.86
Construction	37	5.42
Education	39	5.71
Energy	42	6.15
Healthcare	61	8.93
Logistics	17	2.49
Manufacturing	74	10.83
Financial Institutions	78	11.42
Non-Durables	35	5.12
Other	117	17.13
Professional Services	12	1.76
Shops	55	8.05
Telecommunication	16	2.34
Utilities	36	5.27
Total	683	100

Survey respondents by geographic region

	Frequency	*Per cent*
Asia-Pacific	84	12.3
Central America and Caribbean	5	0.73
Europe	187	27.38
Middle East and Africa	9	1.32
North America	374	54.76
South America	24	3.51
Total	683	100

quarter (22.9%) indicated that executive management views all three as mechanisms for value creation through risk management. The only significant difference across ownership types is a greater proportion of listed firms that emphasize return generation from greater risk-taking, relative to the proportions of not-for-profit, private and government-affiliated organizations providing this response.

Risk-focused planning and control practices

We examine the incorporation of risk considerations into four major components of planning and control systems: accountability and incentives, risk assessment, planning and budgeting, and performance measurement and reporting. In addition, we investigate the extent to which the respondents' planning and control systems take into consideration both the potential cost-reduction benefits of eliminating, mitigating or sharing downside risks and the potential upside benefits of improved risk management. The survey contains information on multiple risk management practices within each of these broad categories; the specific questions and their response frequencies are provided in the appendix.

Accountability and incentives

The sample exhibits wide variation in the extent to which the organizations have adopted the formal planning and control practices advocated in the risk management literature. With respect to risk-focused accountability and incentives, the vast majority of respondents state that executive-level risk ownership and accountability have been developed, but these responsibilities are frequently informally understood or assumed (56.7%) rather than being formally documented in job descriptions (33.2%). Organizational leaders communicate expectations for the execution of risk management activities by their teams to some extent, although these expectations are typically communicated on an inconsistent or ad hoc basis for selected risks rather than regularly and consistently for key risks.

The incorporation of risk management activities into performance evaluations and incentive structures is informal or inconsistent in most organizations. Only 13.7 per cent of the organizations formally incorporate risk management results in their executive- and management-level incentive structures. In 36.3 per cent, execution of risk ownership responsibilities is rarely or never incorporated into performance reviews. A further 45.9 per cent incorporate execution of risk ownership responsibilities inconsistently or informally, with performance reviews in only 17.8 per cent of organizations formally and consistently addressing these responsibilities. Similarly, 18.4 per cent of respondents rarely or never incorporate continuing development of the risk management framework into the risk management leader's performance reviews. An additional 45.8 per cent do so informally or only with reference to selected risk management activities, and just 36.2 per cent formally and consistently evaluate framework development with measurement of progress. Although surveys indicate that many organizations worldwide now evaluate their board members' performance (due in part to regulatory requirements or pressure from governance advocates to do so), just 30 per cent of our sample incorporate the execution of risk management roles and responsibilities into board-member performance evaluations.

Risk assessment

Despite the importance the risk management literature places on defining the organization's risk appetite and risk tolerances, executive management in more than a third of the organizations in our sample have not established risk appetite statements for their organizations or risk tolerances for key risks. Risk appetite is formally defined and documented in only 19.2 per cent of the enterprises, with the same percentage developing risk tolerances for all key risks.

Risk assessment scales are not used in 17.1 per cent of the organizations' risk management exercises and, when used, are primarily qualitative in nature (44.2%). The majority of respondents (63.6%) have developed their risk assessment criteria to align with management's risk tolerance perceptions rather than with quantified risk appetite and risk tolerance statements, and 16.9 per cent have not developed any risk assessment criteria at all. Respondents tend to consistently identify and document the drivers or causes of their key risks. However, identifying interdependencies *between* risks is far less common, with just 13.3 per cent formally leveraging common risk driver information to identify correlations and assess risk profiles.

Planning and budgeting

Given the inconsistent or informal application of risk assessment practices in many of the respondents' organizations, it is not surprising that similarly uneven practices characterise their risk-based planning and budgeting activities. Explicit and consistent reference to quantified risk appetites and tolerances when making significant project or investment decisions occurs in fewer than a quarter of the entities. Formally applying the concepts of risk appetite and tolerance to strategy development is even less frequent (13.6%).

The application of risk assessment results in planning and budgeting is also inconsistent. Risk profiles, which capture the number, types and potential effects of threats facing the enterprise, are typically developed for units or functions informally or through management gut-feel (59%) or not at all (16.3%). Only 35 per cent of respondents state that risk identification exercises during the strategic planning process are used to develop an emerging risk profile, and more than a third (38.5%) rarely or never explicitly reference risk assessments or analysis plans in their budgeting and resource allocation processes. Similarly, only 13.3 per cent consistently evaluate project risk profiles against the organization's overall risk profile when making significant capital investment decisions. The evaluation of risk management expenditures for effectiveness (i.e. cost savings vs exposure reduction) is rarely or never included in the budget allocation processes of 42.1 per cent of the organizations, and just 23.6 per cent explicitly set different risk-based return expectations for different business units and incorporate the different expectations in budget and resource allocation decisions.

Performance measurement and reporting

The risk-based performance measurement and reporting practices of our sample vary along several dimensions, including their content, frequency and level of quantification. They also fall into two statistically distinct reporting levels: executive/management and board of directors. With respect to executive- and management-level reporting, the majority of the organizations report risk management information on a routine basis, though the focus is more likely to be reactive (40.5%) than proactive (20%). At the executive level, the risk information is primarily qualitative in 22.4 per cent of the entities, primarily qualitative with inclusion of selected quantitative measures in 52.8 per cent, and primarily quantitative with supporting qualitative information in 39.5 per cent. Risk metrics and indicators for key risks are identified and tracked consistently in roughly 40 per cent of the units, with 55.2 per cent tracking risk management activity implementation and completion and 33.4 per cent tracking the resources used to implement and complete these activities. Quantitative thresholds and tolerances have not been established in 27.1 per cent of the sample, have been established inconsistently or on an ad hoc basis in 43.4 per cent, and have been established consistently for key risks in only 29.4 per cent.

The full board of directors, as well as board committees with risk oversight responsibilities, receive risk reports at least annually in more than three-quarters of the entities. Board reporting on the organizations' risk profiles most commonly includes key risks and risk management activities (86.6%), with more quantitative information on risk performance metrics and trends (39.4%) and risk tolerances and thresholds (37.5%) least common.

Incorporating risk upside considerations into planning and control systems

Two questions in the survey address the extent to which planning and control systems incorporate not only the concept of downside risk but also the potential value creation upside from risk-taking and risk management that is embodied in many ERM frameworks. The potential upside of risk is rarely or never acknowledged in the enterprise-level risk assessment approaches and tools employed by 25.2 per cent of the respondents, occasionally with a primary focus on downside in 54.5 per cent, and consistently (where applicable) in 20.3 per cent.

Similarly, communication from executives and management does not incorporate the concept of risk upside in 23.6 per cent of the organizations, inconsistently incorporates both upside and downside risk potential in 52.8 per cent, and consistently incorporates the concepts of upside and downside risks in just 23.6 per cent.

Determinants of risk-focused planning and control practices

So, what explains the large variations in our sample's incorporation of risk considerations into planning and control systems? And to what extent are these differences related to executive management's risk management value creation objectives? In particular, do organizations that consider the upside value creation potential from risk management activities as well as the risk elimination, mitigation and sharing benefits adopt more extensive and consistent risk-focused planning and control systems than those that only concentrate on minimizing the downside?

We begin addressing these questions by examining the determinants of the planning and control system components discussed above. We construct separate overall measures for the incorporation of risk considerations into accountability and incentives, risk assessment, planning and budgeting, management performance measurement and reporting, and board-level reporting, as well as a variable capturing the incorporation of risk upside considerations in management communications and risk assessments. Each construct represents the first principal component factor score for the questions related to that planning and control component. All of the questions associated with a given construct load on a single factor (with all loadings exceeding 0.4). The composite reliability for each of the constructs, as measured using Cronbach's alpha, exceeds 0.73, supporting the variables' statistical reliability.

In addition to examining the relation between these constructs and indicators for the three risk management value creation objectives, our analyses include several other potential risk management determinants identified in prior studies. These include organizational size (the log of revenues); the number of geographic regions in which the entity operates (a proxy for organizational complexity); ownership (listed, private or non-profit, with private firms the omitted category); and indicators for government affiliation, industry and regional location of the entity's headquarters. Studies also indicate that board-of-directors involvement in risk oversight influences risk management practices. Following Ittner and Keusch (2015), we proxy for board involvement using the location of risk oversight responsibilities within the board (no formal assignment of responsibilities, committee-level assignment only, overall board-level assignment only, and responsibilities assigned to both the overall board and one or more individual committees, with no formal assignment of board oversight responsibilities the omitted category). Year fixed effects are included in all of our models to control for the year the survey was completed, and standard errors are clustered by country to account for the error terms being correlated within nations.

The determinant model results are presented in Table 11.2. The evidence suggests that risk management value creation objectives are significant drivers of risk-focused planning and control practices. When executive management sees risk management as creating value by preventing negatives within budget, the extent and consistency of risk-based accountability and incentives are significantly *lower*, as is the incorporation of upside risk considerations in management communications and risk assessments. However, board risk reporting is significantly greater, consistent with survey evidence that many boards' risk oversight priorities are improving compliance and reducing downside risks (Grant Thorton, 2015). In contrast, when organizations seek to create value by minimizing the total cost of risk (even if it requires additional investment), risk considerations play a *greater* role in each of the planning and control

Table 11.2 Determinants of risk-focused planning and control practices

	Accountability/ incentives	*Planning/ budgeting*	*Risk assessment*	*Performance measurement*	*Board reporting*	*Include upside risk potential*
Board oversight: committee	13.225***	8.195***	17.894***	17.422***	24.780***	11.623***
Board oversight: board only	20.765***	12.338***	20.322***	22.868***	30.906***	11.146***
Board oversight: board & committee	22.434***	15.920***	22.991***	22.553***	36.512***	13.377***
Prevent negatives within budget	−3.542*	−3.399	−1.390	−0.967	2.141*	−5.586**
Minimize total cost of risk	8.869***	7.079***	5.244***	9.719***	5.036***	4.278**
Create value through risk taking	15.749***	18.543***	14.041***	17.481***	12.348***	28.301***
Ln(firm size)	1.231***	0.831*	1.084***	1.701***	1.443***	1.655**
Non-profit	0.895	1.975	−2.551	1.596	1.887	−0.512
Government affiliation	−0.153	−2.034	4.861**	1.841	1.366	−1.830
Listed	−0.143	−3.861**	−2.861*	−3.173**	−4.309**	−3.464**
# Geographic regions	0.236	0.459*	0.133	0.079	−0.424	0.217
Business equipment	3.302	5.617	5.373	4.256	3.440	8.969*
Chemicals	4.319	0.538	3.082	4.141	0.406	−0.127
Construction	9.869**	7.060**	4.760*	7.076	−1.299	8.813**
Education	−6.549***	−4.009	−4.942**	−3.381*	−10.721***	4.097
Energy	7.952**	8.002***	7.054**	4.270	1.601	−1.238
Healthcare	1.430	−2.586	−0.563	2.347	−2.534	5.945
Logistics	1.643	2.492	0.743	−1.377	−4.183	−4.817
Manufacturing	6.982*	5.358	4.869	6.427*	−2.962	2.745
Financial industry	5.880***	2.806	6.740***	4.767***	8.569*	5.575
Non-durables	−3.547	−2.200	−6.646	−6.204*	−4.202	−1.464
Professional services	−2.033	7.791	−2.357	−0.135	4.609	1.501
Shops	4.446*	5.049	2.642	6.570***	1.595	5.877*
Telecommunication	−5.654	−9.533	−4.344	0.617	−1.296	−7.515
Utilities	2.252	5.152	4.159	−0.790	4.117	0.522
Europe	1.655	2.860**	4.895**	−1.288	0.235	−0.778
South America	−3.678	−3.550*	−1.634	−9.691***	−6.674***	−6.584***
Asia-Pacific	6.244***	2.102	9.454***	2.950	6.878***	−1.882
Central America and Caribbean	−0.981	3.609	0.826	−3.374	−5.759	6.940
Middle East and Africa	−7.713	−1.648	0.563	−4.897	−7.618	6.683
Year fixed effects	Yes	Yes	Yes	Yes	Yes	Yes
Observations	683	683	683	683	683	683
R-squared	36.90%	29.00%	33.10%	37.50%	40.50%	31.20%

Ordinary Least Squares regressions examining the determinants of risk-focused planning and control practices. Test statistics based on standard errors clustered by country. ***, ** and * denote statistical significance at the 0.01, 0.05 and 0.1 levels respectively (two-tailed).

practices. The incorporation of risk considerations into planning and control systems increases even further when senior executives believe that the identification of opportunities to generate returns from greater risk-taking is a mechanism for value creation through risk management. Not only are the coefficients on the greater risk-taking variable positive and highly significant, they are significantly larger than the coefficients on the indicators for preventing negatives within budget and minimizing the total cost of risk. These results are consistent with the way in which the incorporation of risk into planning and control systems increases when organizations take a broader view of the potential benefits from risk management activities.

Consistent with prior studies, larger organizations tend to implement more sophisticated risk management practices. However, our geographic diversity variable is only significantly associated with the incorporation of risk into budgeting and planning practices. Listed firms exhibit lower risk-focused planning and control than private firms. This includes less emphasis on the upside potential of risk in management communications and risk assessments *after* controlling for differences in risk management value creation objectives across the organizations. The lower risk focus in listed firms' planning and control practices may reflect these entities' belief that their shareholders can minimize risks on their own through diversified shareholdings (Modigliani and Miller 1958). The reduced emphasis on risk upside in listed firms' communications and risk assessments is also consistent with these organizations' need to focus on minimizing downside risks due to more stringent regulatory compliance requirements (e.g. the internal control requirements of the United States's Sarbanes-Oxley regulation and its equivalents in other countries). The practices of not-for-profit organizations are not significantly different than those of private firms. Government-affiliated organizations report more sophisticated and consistent risk assessment practices, but they are not significantly different on the other planning and control dimensions.

The greatest industry differences are increased emphasis on risk considerations in the construction and energy sectors (both of which face significant operational and market risks) and financial institutions (which are subject to numerous risk-related regulatory requirements), and lower emphasis in the education sector. Relative to North American organizations (the omitted category), European respondents report greater focus on risk in budgeting and planning and more sophisticated and consistent risk assessment. Organizations headquartered in the Asia-Pacific region also report stronger risk assessment, along with greater risk-focused accountability, incentives and board reporting. In contrast, South American entities report lower risk-focused performance measurement and reporting, board reporting, and communication and assessment of upside risk potential.

Influence on strategic decision-making

One of the primary tenets of the ERM literature is the need to integrate risk management into strategic planning and decision-making. Yet surveys indicate that the level of interaction between risk management and strategic planning is often limited (Deloitte, 2013), with only 20 per cent of the firms surveyed by Marsh and RIMS (2014) believing that risk management has a significant impact on their setting of business strategy. We provide further evidence on the relation between risk-focused planning and control practices and strategic decision-making by asking the following survey question: 'In the last 2 years, has your organisation shifted the focus of its strategic plan or changed strategic direction as a result of new information or understanding concerning a major risk?' Of the 686 organizations in our sample, 26.4 per cent responded affirmatively. We estimate linear probability models with the dependent variable coded one if the respondent answered yes to this question and zero otherwise. Independent variables are the individual planning and control constructs and the other predictor variables included in our earlier tests. We examine each of the planning and control system constructs separately to avoid problems with multicollinearity.[5] The exception is the upside risk potential construct, which is included together with the other planning and control system variables in some of our tests.

If organizations change their plans and decisions based on improved information from their planning and control systems regarding key risks, their drivers and their potential impacts, we would expect the planning and control constructs to be positively associated with the strategic change indicator. The results in Table 11.3 generally support this prediction. When we

Table 11.3 Risk-focused planning and control practices and strategic change

Panel A					
Accountability	0.001				
Budgeting/planning		0.003***			
Risk assessment			0.001		
Performance measurement				0.001**	
Board reporting					0.001*
Ln(firm size)	0.02	0.018	0.022*	0.02	0.02
Non-profit	0.065	0.061	0.069	0.064	0.061
Government affiliation	−0.064	−0.051	−0.066	−0.063	−0.063
Listed	−0.003	0.002	0.001	0	−0.003
# geographic regions	0.006	0.004	0.006	0.006	0.006
Region fixed effects	Yes	Yes	Yes	Yes	Yes
Industry fixed effects	Yes	Yes	Yes	Yes	Yes
Year fixed effects	Yes	Yes	Yes	Yes	Yes
Observations	683	683	683	683	683
R-squared	3.70%	5.20%	3.50%	3.80%	3.90%
Panel B					
Accountability	0.001				
Budgeting/planning		0.002**			
Risk assessment			−0.001		
Performance measurement				0	
Board reporting					0.001
Include upside risk potential	0.002***	0.001*	0.002***	0.002***	0.002***
Ln(firm size)	0.017	0.017	0.018	0.018	0.017
Non-profit	0.066	0.062	0.067	0.067	0.064
Government affiliation	−0.054	−0.05	−0.051	−0.055	−0.055
Listed	−0.003	0.001	0.002	0	−0.002
# geographic regions	0.005	0.004	0.006	0.005	0.005
Region fixed effects	Yes	Yes	Yes	Yes	Yes
Industry fixed effects	Yes	Yes	Yes	Yes	Yes
Year fixed effects	Yes	Yes	Yes	Yes	Yes
Observations	683	683	683	683	683
R-squared	0.047	5.40%	4.70%	4.60%	4.70%

Linear Probability Models predicting the incidence of changes in corporate strategy as a result of new information or understanding concerning a major risk. Test statistics based on standard errors clustered by country. ***, ** and * denote statistical significance at the 0.01, 0.05 and 0.1 levels respectively (two-tailed).

estimate the models without controlling for the extent to which the upside potential of risk is incorporated into management communications and risk assessments, all the coefficients on the planning and control constructs are positive, with budgeting and planning, performance measurement and reporting, and board reporting statistically significant. We find no association between our risk assessment construct and strategic change, implying that more consistent and sophisticated risk assessment activities have little impact on strategic change when their results are not incorporated into resource allocation and strategic planning processes.

We next include the upside potential construct in the models to examine whether this key difference in risk management objectives influences strategic planning and decision-making. The upside risk potential construct has a highly significant positive relation with strategic change, with the positive coefficient on the budgeting and planning construct remaining significant. However, the two reporting variables become insignificant. This loss of significance suggests that it was not greater risk reporting that led to strategic change in these organizations, but rather greater consideration of the upside potential of risk (which tends to be higher in organizations with more extensive risk reporting). Overall, the evidence in Table 11.3 indicates that greater risk accountability and reporting and more consistent and sophisticated risk assessments, in themselves, did not lead our sample to change their strategic plans or directions based on new risk information. Instead, greater consideration of risks when carrying out planning activities and greater focus on the upside potential of risk-taking appear to have driven strategic change in these enterprises.

Performance implications of risk-focused planning and control

The ultimate question is whether incorporating risk considerations into planning and control systems influences organizational performance. As discussed earlier, the answer to this question is not self-evident, with many observers arguing that the formal, top-down process in ERM frameworks may be counterproductive. Moreover, existing studies on the performance implications of risk management practices provide relatively little evidence on the association between specific risk-focused planning and control practices and organizational outcomes, and no evidence on the influence of risk upside considerations on these outcomes. Our remaining tests attempt to shed light on these issues.

One difficulty that arises when studying the performance implications of risk management practices is specifying the results variable. An extreme outcome from poor risk management is the occurrence of a major risk event that threatens the ongoing viability of the organization. The survey asked respondents whether their organization had experienced a risk-related event in the past two years that had the potential to threaten its viability. Over a quarter responded affirmatively, including 23.5 per cent of not-for-profit organizations, 25.3 per cent of government-affiliated entities, 25.6 per cent of listed firms and 28.8 per cent of private firms.

We examine the relations between responses to this question and our planning and control constructs in Table 11.4. Greater risk-related performance measurement and reporting has a significant negative association with the probability of experiencing a viability-threatening risk event. This result suggests that more routine, consistent and quantitative measurement and reporting can allow entities to anticipate and respond more effectively to serious risk events. The coefficients on the variable capturing the consideration of upside risk potential are negative (but generally insignificant) in all of the models, providing no evidence that greater emphasis on the potential benefits from greater risk-taking increased the respondents' exposure to extreme risk events. The other planning and control system attributes are not

Table 11.4 Risk-focused planning and control practices and the incidence of major risk events

Accountability	0.000				
Budgeting/planning		0.001			
Risk assessment			–0.001		
Performance measurement				–0.001**	
Board reporting					–0.001
Include upside risk potential	–0.001	–0.001**	–0.000	–0.000	–0.000
Ln(firm size)	–0.008	–0.008	–0.007	–0.006	–0.007
Non-profit	–0.003	–0.006	–0.003	0.003	0.002
Government affiliation	–0.046	–0.044	–0.044	–0.044	–0.045
Listed	–0.006	–0.005	–0.005	–0.004	–0.003
#geographic regions	0.006	0.005	0.006	0.006*	0.006
Region fixed effects	Yes	Yes	Yes	Yes	Yes
Industry fixed effects	Yes	Yes	Yes	Yes	Yes
Year fixed effects	Yes	Yes	Yes	Yes	Yes
Observations	683	683	683	683	683
R-squared	3.90%	4.20%	4.00%	4.40%	4.10%

Linear Probability Models predicting the incidence of a major risk event in the prior two years that threatened the organization's viability. Test statistics based on standard errors clustered by country. ***, ** and * denote statistical significance at the 0.01, 0.05 and 0.1 levels respectively (two-tailed).

significantly associated with the probability that the organization experienced a risk event that threatened its viability.

The results in Table 11.4 provide only a partial picture of the performance implications of risk-focused planning and control practices. Notwithstanding the recent spate of financial crises, natural disasters and security breaches, 'black swan' or 'tail' risk events that threaten an organization's viability are rare. As a result, they are difficult to plan for or manage, since the organization may never have experienced them in the past (Taleb, 2007). Furthermore, even an organization with poor risk management may not experience a black swan or tail risk event in a given period due to the rarity of these occurrences. Examining these rare risk events also ignores efforts to reduce less extreme ongoing risks or their costs, or to increase value through more informed risk-taking that does not threaten organizational viability.

We provide evidence on these other potential benefits using stock market and financial information for the listed firms in our sample. Focusing on listed firms has two advantages. First, a common objective of listed firms is maintaining or increasing shareholder value, whereas the objectives of non-listed firms can be quite diverse, making it difficult to identify risk-taking or value creation measures that apply across the entire sample. Second, the publicly available stock market and financial data provides standard, objective measures that are not influenced by limitations such as common respondent biases or lack of comparability that are frequently encountered using self-reported or subjective outcome measures.

We first examine the relations between the various planning and control practices and stock price volatility. The ERM literature argues that one of the primary benefits of effective risk-focused planning and control practices is reduced uncertainty and volatility (e.g. Meulbroek, 2002; Nocco and Stulz, 2006). We proxy for firm volatility using the standard deviation of daily stock returns for the 292 firms with available data, computed over the year *following* the survey response. This measure of aggregate firm risk has been used by Ellul and Yerramilli (2013) and others.

We also investigate the practices' value creation implications using Tobin's *Q*, calculated for the year following survey completion. Tobin's *Q* is the ratio of the market value of a firm's assets divided by the assets' replacement value, with larger *Q* ratios signifying greater value creation. Like prior risk management studies (e.g. Hoyt and Liebenberg, 2011; McShane *et al.*, 2011; Farrell and Gallagher, 2015), we proxy for Tobin's *Q* in the 312 listed firms with available data using the formula (Book Value of Debt + Market Value of Common Equity) / (Book Value of Debt + Book Value of Common Equity).

Stock price volatility tests

The volatility results in Table 11.5 indicate that each of the planning and control constructs has a significantly negative relation with stock price volatility when we do not control for the extent to which the upside potential of risk is incorporated into management communications and risk assessments. However, when we take into account the extent to which the upside potential of risk is considered, the only planning and control construct that remains significant is risk assessment. Greater consideration of upside risk potential, on the other hand, is negative and significant in each of the models. The negative relation between more consistent and sophisticated risk assessment and stock price volatility supports claims in the risk-based planning and control literature that these practices can improve understanding of current and emerging risks and help identify risks that fall outside of established tolerances, thereby allowing organizations to avoid or reduce risks that fall outside of acceptable limits (Mun, 2010; Curtis and Carey, 2012). Like the strategic change analyses, the insignificant results for the other planning and control constructs (after including the upside risk potential variable) suggest that it is the consideration of both the upside and downside of risk-taking in risk assessments and communications, rather than the mere adoption of more sophisticated risk-focused planning and control, that fosters greater risk reduction.

To provide further evidence on the influence of risk management value creation objectives on risk-taking, we re-estimate the volatility models after including separate indicator variables for first, preventing negatives within a set budget; second, minimizing the total cost of risk; and third, enabling return generation from more informed risk-taking. We also include interactions between these indicators and the individual planning and control constructs to test whether the planning and control practices' effects on volatility are contingent on the firms' risk management objectives.

The results (which are not reported in the tables) again suggest that companies that consider both the upside and downside of risk in decision-making achieve lower volatility. The value creation through risk-taking *main effect* is negative and significant, indicating that firms pursuing this objective have lower stock return volatility, independent of the firms' risk-focused planning and control practices. In addition, the *interaction* between risk assessment and the value creation through risk-taking indicator is also negative and significant. One implication of the latter result is that more sophisticated risk assessments that formally incorporate statements of risk appetite and risk tolerance are more quantitative, and they are also more focused on risk drivers and interdependencies have allowed organizations to reduce the volatility in existing operations while simultaneously searching for new opportunities to increase value through additional, more informed risk-taking.

Interestingly, the interaction between the accountability and incentives construct and the value creation through risk-taking indicator is *positive* and significant, while the coefficient on the accountability main effect is *negative*. Further examination of this estimated interaction indicates that greater risk-focused accountability and incentives are associated with lower

Table 11.5 Risk-focused planning and control practices and stock return volatility

Accountability	–0.002**	0.000								
Budgeting/planning			–0.004***	–0.002						
Risk assessment					–0.006***	–0.004**				
Performance measurement							–0.003***	–0.001		
Board reporting									–0.004***	–0.002
Include upside risk potential		–0.005**		–0.004*		–0.003*		–0.004**		–0.004**
Ln(firm size)	–0.101***	–0.093***	–0.097***	–0.092***	–0.092***	–0.088***	–0.095***	–0.091***	–0.097***	–0.091***
Government affiliation	–0.046	–0.101	–0.015	–0.073	–0.026	–0.060	–0.036	–0.086	–0.058	–0.088
# geographic regions	–0.026	–0.028	–0.025	–0.027	–0.029	–0.029	–0.028	–0.028	–0.027	–0.027
Region fixed effects	Yes	Yes	Yes	Yes	Yes	Yes	Yes	Yes	Yes	Yes
Industry fixed effects	Yes	Yes	Yes	Yes	Yes	Yes	Yes	Yes	Yes	Yes
Year fixed effects	Yes	Yes	Yes	Yes	Yes	Yes	Yes	Yes	Yes	Yes
Observations	292	292	292	292	292	292	292	292	292	292
R-squared	32.00%	33.50%	32.70%	33.60%	33.40%	34.00%	32.30%	33.50%	32.50%	33.70%

Ordinary Least Squares regressions predicting future stock return volatility. Coefficient estimates are multiplied by 100 for ease of exposition. Test statistics based on standard errors clustered by country but not tabulated. ***, ** and * denote statistical significance at the 0.01, 0.05 and 0.1 levels respectively (two-tailed).

volatility in firms that do not view upside risk as a value creation objective. Conversely, those viewing additional risk-taking as a potential value-enhancing objective while concurrently establishing greater accountability and incentives for risk management exhibit higher volatility, consistent with these firms taking on more risk in pursuit of higher returns.

Firm value tests

We extend the analyses to examine firm valuation implications in Table 11.6. The dependent variable in these tests is Tobin's Q, with a higher Q ratio indicating that the firm has created greater value from its available assets. Each of the planning and control constructs is positively and significantly associated with firm value in the year following survey completion. When we control for the extent to which the upside potential of risk is incorporated into management communications and risk assessments, the upside potential variable is significantly positive while the coefficients on the other planning and control constructs remain significantly associated with Tobin's Q. This evidence suggests that the individual risk-focused planning and control practices can have a beneficial effect on firm value, even though the influence of some of these practices on stock price volatility is insignificant.

In untabulated tests that include indicator variables for the three value creation objectives along with their interactions with the planning and control constructs, we find highly significant and positive main effects of return generation from more informed risk-taking on Tobin's Q. Interactions between this objective and the accountability and incentives, performance measurement and board-reporting constructs are also positive and significant, indicating that the valuation benefits from these risk-focused planning and control practices are greater when executives view the identification of opportunities to generate returns from greater risk-taking as one mechanism for creating value through risk management. In contrast, neither preventing negatives within a set budget nor minimizing the total cost of risk has a significant main or interactive effect on firm value. Although these insignificant relations provide no evidence that focusing on minimizing downside risks increases firm valuation, they do suggest that ERM is not leading risk-averse executives to pass up risky but valuable investment opportunities or reduce firm risk-taking to a level that is too conservative from a diversified shareholder's point of view.

Conclusions

Our results highlight the important influence that risk management value creation objectives can have on the use and benefits from risk-focused planning and control practices. Organizations that primarily focus on minimizing risks within budget or reducing the total cost of risks tend to make less use of these practices, have higher stock price volatility and achieve lower firm value than those that have taken greater steps to holistically consider both the upsides and downsides of risk. Our results also suggest that some risk-focused planning and control practices have greater effects on risk reduction efforts than others, although all practices are associated with firm value.

Like all large-sample studies, our analyses focus on central tendencies and incorporate only a small number of the potential factors that can influence ERM practices or their performance implications. Future research can extend our analyses to examine whether the implications of different risk management objectives vary across organizational, strategic and regulatory settings. Increasing our understanding of the contextual factors that influence the costs and benefits of specific ERM practices can help refine and improve this rapidly evolving and increasingly important management process.

Table 11.6 Risk-focused planning and control practices and firm valuation

Accountability	0.010**	0.006**								
Budgeting/planning			0.010**	0.006**						
Risk assessment					0.010**	0.006*				
Performance Measurement							0.012***	0.009***		
Board reporting									0.012***	0.009***
Include risk upside potential		0.007*		0.006*		0.007**		0.006*		0.007*
Ln(firm size)	–0.149*	–0.166*	–0.152*	–0.166**	–0.159**	–0.171**	–0.174**	–0.183**	–0.161*	–0.178**
Government affiliation	–0.629	–0.541	–0.654	–0.552	–0.598	–0.520	–0.637	–0.568	–0.554	–0.502
# geographic regions	0.103***	0.106***	0.103***	0.107***	0.111***	0.111***	0.109***	0.110***	0.106***	0.108***
Region fixed effects	Yes	Yes	Yes	Yes	Yes	Yes	Yes	Yes	Yes	Yes
Industry fixed effects	Yes	Yes	Yes	Yes	Yes	Yes	Yes	Yes	Yes	Yes
Year fixed effects	Yes	Yes	Yes	Yes	Yes	Yes	Yes	Yes	Yes	Yes
Observations	312	312	312	312	312	312	312	312	312	312
R-squared	14.30%	15.30%	14.30%	15.20%	14.10%	15.30%	15.30%	16.00%	15.00%	16.20%

Ordinary Least Squares regressions predicting Tobin's Q. Test statistics computed using standard errors clustered by country. ***, ** and * denote statistical significance at the 0.01, 0.05 and 0.1 levels respectively (two-tailed).

Appendix

Accountability and incentives

Executive-level risk ownership and accountability is: Limited or not yet developed (10.1%); Informally understood or assumed (56.7%); Formally documented in job descriptions and responsibilities (33.2%)

Leaders in the organisation have communicated expectations for execution of risk management activities by their teams: In rare cases or not at all (14.1%); Inconsistently or on an ad-hoc basis for selected risks (58.3%); Regularly and consistently for key risks (27.6%)

Executive- and management-level incentive structures are tied to risk management results: Rarely or never (48.1%); Informally or in certain areas of the organisation only (38.2%); Formally incorporated into incentive structures (13.7%)

Performance reviews incorporate execution of risk ownership responsibilities:

Rarely or never (36.3%); Yes, inconsistently or informally (45.9%); Yes, consistently (17.8%)

Continuing development of the risk management framework is incorporated into the risk management leader's performance reviews: Rarely or never (18.4%); Informally or with reference to selected risk management activities (45.8%); Formally and consistently over time with measurement of progress (36.2%)

Execution of risk management roles and responsibilities is incorporated into Board members' evaluations: No (70%); Yes (30%).

Risk assessment

Executive-management has established a statement of risk appetite for the organisation: No (39.9%); Yes, risk appetite has been informally discussed and understood (44.2%); Yes, risk appetite has been formally defined and documented (19.2%)

Executive-management has established statements of risk tolerance (i.e., acceptable levels of performance variability) for key risks: No, risk tolerance statements have not yet been developed (36.6%); Yes, for some key risks (44.2%); Yes, for key risks (19.2%)

Risk assessment criteria are developed to align with: Risk assessment criteria are not developed (16.9%); Management perceptions of risk tolerance (63.6%); A quantified risk appetite and statements of risk tolerance (19.5%)

Risk assessment scales at the organisational level are: Not used in risk management exercises (17.1%); Primarily qualitative criteria (i.e., High, Medium, Low) (44.2%); Developed with both qualitative and quantitative criteria (38.8%)

Risk drivers (causes of risks) are identified/documented: Rarely or never (6.4%); Inconsistently or on an ad-hoc basis for selected risks (42.4%); Consistently for key risks (51.2%)

The organisation leverages common risk driver information to identify correlation/relationships between risks: Analysis of correlation is not conducted (30.9%); Informally in management discussions and perceptions of risk (55.8%); Formally, and has documented the need for its consideration in risk assessment processes (13.3%).

Budgeting/planning

Executive management applies concepts of risk appetite/tolerance to strategy development: Rarely or never (26.8%); On an ad-hoc basis (59.6%); Through formal process (13.6%)

How does information from the risk management process inform strategic planning processes? Not included (16.8%); Informally incorporated (57.6%); Formally incorporated and integrated (25.7%)

Risk identification exercises during the strategic planning process are used to develop an emerging risk profile: Risk identification is not conducted during strategic planning (28%); No (37%); Yes (35%)

Significant project or investment decisions are made with explicit reference to quantified risk appetite and tolerance: Rarely or never (34.4%); Inconsistently (41.5%); Consistently (24.1%)

The organisation's budget/resource allocation processes explicitly reference and incorporate results of established risk assessment and analysis plans: Rarely or never (38.5%); Inconsistently or on an ad-hoc basis (42.3%); Consistently through a defined process (16.8%)

The organisation's budget/resource allocation process includes evaluation of risk management spend for effectiveness, i.e. cost-savings vs. exposure reduction: Rarely or never (42.1%); Inconsistently or on an ad-hoc basis (42.3%); Consistently through a defined process (15.6%)

Does the organisation have an understanding of the risk profiles for individual units/functions? No (16.3%); Informally or through management gut-feel (59%); Supported by formal quantitative analysis (24.6%)

Are different risk-based return expectations set for different business units and functions? No (34.7%); Yes, but not explicitly considered in budget decisions (41.7%); Yes, and incorporated into budget decisions and resource allocation decisions (23.6%)

In making significant capital investment decisions, the project risk profile is evaluated against/compared with the organisation's overall risk profile: Rarely or never (30.9%); Inconsistently or informally (55.8%); Consistently as part of a defined process (13.3%).

Performance measurement/reporting

Risk management information is typically communicated to the organisation:

Rarely/never (7%); On an ad-hoc basis or only in reaction to an event (32.5%); On a routine basis, though focus may still be reactive (40.5%); On a routine basis with a proactive focus (20%)

Evidence/information cited in risk management reports at executive levels of the organisation is: Primarily qualitative (22.4%); Primarily qualitative with inclusion of selected quantitative measures (52.8%); Primarily quantitative with supporting qualitative information (24.8%)

Risk metrics and indicators are identified and tracked at the enterprise level: Rarely or never (20.3%); Inconsistently or on an ad-hoc basis (43.4%); Consistently for key risks (39.5%)

Risk metrics and indicators for risk management activity implementation and completion are tracked at the enterprise level (55.2%)

Risk metrics and indicators for resources used to implement and complete risk management activities are tracked at the enterprise level (33.4%)

Quantitative thresholds and tolerances have been established: No (27.1%);

Inconsistently or on an ad-hoc basis (43.4%); Consistently for key risks (29.4%).

Board reporting

The full Board receives risk reports: Infrequently or not on a predefined schedule (22.4%); At least annually (31.9%); At least twice yearly (19.2%); Quarterly or more frequently (26.4%)

Board Committees (with risk management oversight responsibilities) receive risk reports: Infrequently or not on a predefined schedule (20.7%); At least annually (20.8%); At least twice yearly (20.4%); Quarterly or more frequently (38%)

Board reporting on the organisation's risk profile includes: Key risks and associated risk management activities (86.6%); Risk drivers and underlying causes (53.1%); Risk ownership responsibilities and accountabilities (65.5%); Risk management action plans and outcomes (64%); Risk tolerances and thresholds/limits (37.5%); Risk performance metrics/trends (39.4%); Information on emerging risks (56.3%).

Including risk-taking upside considerations in planning and control systems

Potential upside of risk is acknowledged in enterprise-level risk assessment approaches and tools: Rarely or never (25.2%); Occasionally, focus is typically on downside (54.5%); Consistently (where applicable) (20.3%)

Communication from executives/management: Does not incorporate the concept of the upside of risk (23.6%); Inconsistently incorporates concepts of upside and downside risk (52.8%); Consistently incorporates the concepts of upside and downside of risk (23.6%).

Notes

1 See Gatzert and Martin (2015) for a review of large-sample empirical studies on the determinants and performance implications of ERM.
2 Exceptions include performance studies by Cassar and Gerakos (2013), Farrell and Gallagher (2014) and Paape and Speklé (2012). Each of these studies finds that some risk-focused planning and control practices are positively associated with performance, while others are not. The authors do not examine the determinants of these practices or the influence of value creation objectives.
3 The authors have received no compensation or funding from Aon.
4 Risk management directors or managers represent the largest concentration of respondents (48.6%), followed by chief risk officers (14.1%), Chief financial officers (10.7%), treasurers or vice presidents of finance (6.6%), chief executive officers (4.8%), internal audit heads (3.5%) and general counsels or corporate secretaries (3.2%), with other positions comprising the remainder.
5 Correlations between the planning and control constructs range from 0.45 to 0.76 (median = 0.59). The smallest correlation is between board reporting and budgeting/planning, and the largest is between accountability/incentives and performance measurement/reporting.

References

Aberdeen (2012), *Financial Planning, Budgeting and Forecasting: Leveraging Risk-Adjusted Strategies to Enable Accuracy*, Boston: Aberdeen Group.

Ai, J., P. Brockett, W. Cooper and L. Golden (2012), 'Enterprise Risk Management through Strategic Allocation of Capital', *Journal of Risk and Insurance*, 79(1), pp. 29–55.

Alviniussen, A. and H. Jankensgard (2009), 'Enterprise Risk Budgeting: Bringing Risk Management into the Financial Planning Process', *Journal of Applied Finance*, 18, pp. 178–192.

AFP (2014), *AFP Risk Survey*, Bethesda, MD: AFP.

Arena, M. and M. Arnaboldi (2013), 'Risk and Budget in an Uncertain World', *International Journal of Business Performance Management*, 14(2), pp. 166–180.

Beasley, M. and M. Frigo (2010), 'ERM and Its Role in Strategic Planning and Strategy Execution', in *Enterprise Risk Management*, J. Fraser and B. Simkins (eds.), Hoboken, NJ: John Wiley & Sons, pp. 31–50.

Cassar, G. and J. Gerakos (2013), *Does Risk Management Work?* Chicago Booth research paper no. 13–13. Available from: http://ssrn.com/abstract = 1722250.

COSO (2004), *Enterprise Risk Management: Integrated Framework*, New York: COSO.
Curtis, P. and M. Carey (2012), *Risk Assessment in Practice*, New York: COSO.
Danielsson, J. (2008), 'Blame the Models', *Journal of Financial Stability*, 4, pp. 321–328.
Deloitte (2012), *Risk-Adjusted Forecasting and Planning: Navigating the 'New Normal' of Increased Volatility*, London: Deloitte.
Deloitte (2013), 'Risk-Adjusted Forecasting: More Certainty for Planning', *CFO Journal*, http://deloitte.wsj.com/cfo/2013/10/03/risk-adjusted-forecasting-more-certainty-for-planning.
Durand, R. (2003), 'Predicting a Firm's Forecasting Ability: The Roles of Organizational Illusion of Control and Organizational Attention', *Strategic Management Journal*, 24, pp. 821–838.
Ellul, A. and V. Yerramilli (2013), 'Stronger Risk Controls, Lower Risk: Evidence from U.S. Bank Holding Companies', *Journal of Finance*, 68(5), pp. 1757–1803.
EY (2013), *Turning Risk into Results: How Leading Companies Use Risk Management to Fuel Better Performance*, London: EYGN.
Farrell, M. and R. Gallagher (2015), 'The Valuation Implications of Enterprise Risk Management Maturity', *Journal of Risk and Insurance*, 82(3), pp. 625–657.
Froot, K. and J. Stein (1998), 'Risk Management, Capital Budgeting, and Capital Structure Policy for Financial Institutions: An Integrated Approach', *Journal of Financial Economics*, 47, pp. 55–82.
Gatzert, N. and M. Martin (2015), 'Determinants and Value of Enterprise Risk Management: Empirical Evidence from the Literature', *Risk Management and Insurance Review*, 18(1), pp. 29–53.
Gordon, L., M. Loeb and C. Tseng (2009), 'Enterprise Risk Management and Firm Performance: A Contingency Perspective', *Journal of Accounting and Public Policy*, 28, pp. 301–327.
Grant Thorton (2015), '2015 Governance, Risk and Compliance Survey'. Available from: https://www.grantthornton.com/~/media/content-page-files/advisory/pdfs/2015/BAS-AC-survey-foldover-150925FIN.ashx.
Hoyt, R. and A. Liebenberg (2011), 'The Value of Enterprise Risk Management', *Journal of Risk and Insurance*, 78, pp. 795–822.
ISO (2009), *Risk Management: Principles and Guidelines*, ISO 31000:2009, Geneva: ISO.
Ittner, C. and T. Keusch (2015), 'The Influence of Board of Directors' Risk Oversight on Risk Management Maturity and Firm Risk-Taking', working paper, University of Pennsylvania and Erasmus University.
Kahneman, D. and D. Lovallo (1993), 'Timid Choices and Bold Forecasts: A Cognitive Perspective on Risk Taking', *Management Science*, 39, pp. 17–31.
KPMG (2009), *Placing a Value on Enterprise Risk Management*, New York: KPMG. Available from: https://www.kpmg.com/PT/pt/IssuesAndInsights/Documents/erm22432PHL.pdf.
Marsh and RIMS (2014), *Excellence in Risk Management Survey XI*, New York: Marsh and RIMS.
McKinsey & Company (2014), *From Compliance to Value Creation: The Journey to Effective Enterprise Risk Management for Insurers*, New York: McKinsey & Company.
Mcshane, M.K., A. Nair and E. Rustambekov (2011), 'Does Enterprise Risk Management Increase Firm Value?' *Journal of Accounting, Auditing & Finance*, 26, pp. 641–658.
Meulbroek, L. (2002), 'A Senior Manager's Guide to Integrated Risk Management', *Journal of Applied Corporate Finance*, 14(4), pp. 56–70.
Mikes, A. (2009), 'Risk Management and Calculative Cultures', *Management Accounting Research*, 20(1), pp. 18–40.
Milliman (2014), *Creating Value through Enterprise Risk Management*, Chicago, IL: Milliman Risk Institute.
Modigliani, F. and M. Miller (1958), 'The Cost of Capital, Corporation Finance and the Theory of Investment', *American Economic Review*, pp. 261–297.
Mun, J. (2010), *Modeling Risk: Applying Monte Carlo Simulation, Strategic Real Options, Stochastic Forecasting, and Portfolio Optimization*, Hoboken, NJ: John Wiley & Sons.
Nocco, B. and R. Stulz (2006), 'Enterprise Risk Management: Theory And Practice', *Journal of Applied Corporate Finance*, 18, pp. 8–20.
Paape, L. and R. Speklé (2012), 'The Adoption and Design of Enterprise Risk Management Practices: An Empirical Study', *European Accounting Review*, 21(3), pp. 533–564.
Power, M. (2009), 'The Risk Management of Nothing', *Accounting, Organizations and Society*, 34, pp. 849–855.
PwC (2015), *Risk in Review: Decoding Uncertainty, Delivering Value*, New York: PwC.

Shenkir, W.G., T.L Barton and P.L. Walker (2010), 'Enterprise Risk Management: Lessons from the Field', in J. Fraser and B.J. Simkins (eds.), *Enterprise Risk Management*, Hoboken, NJ: John Wiley & Sons, pp. 441–463.

Taleb, N. (2007), *The Black Swan: The Impact of the Highly Improbable*, New York: Random House.

Wallis, P. (2012), 'Risk Management: Achieving the Value Proposition', *Government Finance Review*, February, pp. 36–42.

Woods, M. (2008), 'Linking Risk Management to Strategic Controls: A Case Study of Tesco Plc', *International Journal of Risk Assessment & Management*, 7(8), pp. 1074–1088.

Woods. M. (2009), 'A Contingency Theory Perspective on the Risk Management Control System within Birmingham City Council', *Management Accounting Review*, 20, pp. 69–81.

12
Risk reporting to the board of directors

Regine Slagmulder

Introduction

Over the past few years, risk management and risk oversight have received increased attention in the corporate world, powered by calls for legislative and regulatory action to mitigate the effect of the 2008 economic crisis. Recent business failures have often been attributed to boards of directors not being properly informed about the risks facing their organizations, the consequences of which may range from reputational damage to serious financial setback and even bankruptcy. The regulations that emerged from the global financial crisis have triggered a wave of change in risk oversight over the past decade, especially in the financial sector, including higher standards for risk reporting. For example, the US Securities and Exchange Commission (SEC) mandated that a publicly traded company's annual proxy statements include a description of the board's role in risk oversight. In a similar vein, the Dodd–Frank Wall Street Reform and Consumer Protection Act requires large publicly traded financial firms to have a separate board risk committee composed of independent directors, while the EU Commission has established various directives to increase companies' transparency with respect to their risks and risk management policies.[1] Regulations for financial institutions have been formulated by the Basel Committee on Banking Supervision (2014),[2] the European Banking Authority (2011),[3] the Financial Stability Board (2013)[4] and the OECD (2014),[5] with a particular emphasis on risk governance. The topic is also widely discussed amongst practitioners and professional organizations in other industries. For example, a recent international survey reported that improving the quality and quantity of risk-related information flowing to the board and coordinating risk oversight responsibilities among the board's committees should be the board's primary focus in order to keep pace with the changing risk environment (KPMG, 2016). The Chartered Institute of Management Accountants (CIMA, 2010) published a discussion paper that identified board strategic oversight, board performance and effective risk management as key research themes.

The board's ability to oversee how a company monitors and manages risk has broad relevance and impacts a wide range of stakeholders, including investors, employees and the community at large. Several responsibilities are placed upon the board in terms of risk oversight, from monitoring strategic business risks and establishing the right level of risk appetite to ensuring that executive compensation schemes do not lead to excessive risk-taking. The fiduciary duties of boards require that directors collect all relevant information and make reasonable decisions in the corporation's best interest. A key question for boards is thus how to ensure they are apprised of the most significant risks for the organization in order to adequately carry out their supervisory role. Despite widespread regulatory and practitioner interest, the topic of risk reporting to the board remains barely touched upon in the academic literature. Even though prior research has extensively covered topics related to the design of reporting systems for managerial use on the one hand and the determinants of board effectiveness on the other hand, few studies to date combine the two research areas.

Accounting scholars have extensively published on corporate governance-related topics, mostly from an external reporting perspective. Much less attention has been devoted to internal reporting related to how boards of directors receive and use information to carry out their duties. This is surprising because seminal studies have cited lack of adequate information as one of the main factors that hinders the work of boards (Lorsch and MacIver, 1989; Lorsch, 2012). Given the increased responsibilities placed on the board, both through legislation and codes of conduct, it seems likely that board members need more and better information to perform their duties. A field study by Johanson (2008) confirms that the availability of accurate and relevant information is viewed as an integral part of efficient governance by the board of directors.

The main objective of risk reporting is that information flows quickly and without distortion through the organization—from those in the business to top management to the board. The necessity for the board to receive proper risk information is linked to the information asymmetry problem that is central to agency theory. The board of directors provides strategic oversight of management and business operations, but only in a part-time capacity. This creates a potential agency problem, as directors are dependent on executive knowledge and judgement and on the quality and volume of the information that the CEO makes available to them for evaluating the company's performance (Adams and Ferreira, 2007; Lorsch and MacIver, 1989; Hendry and Kiel, 2004). Any information provided to board members has necessarily been filtered by management to avoid information overload. According to agency theory, the asymmetrical distribution of information allows CEOs to act opportunistically. If gaps or biases influence the reporting process, it can quickly create hazards and missed strategic opportunities. Most directors and management acknowledge that risk analysis is typically presented to the board as pre-packaged corporate information, designed to present opportunities that executives wish to pursue in the best possible light. The provision of appropriate risk information for board decisions is, therefore, largely dependent on executive integrity (Nowak and McCabe, 2003). To overcome the information asymmetry problem and to protect shareholders' interests, the quality and timeliness of managerial reporting, including risk reporting, to the board of directors is critically important.

Whereas financial institutions and energy companies have had a long history of developing the risk oversight capabilities of their directors, an increasing number of boards in other sectors are also becoming more attentive to risk oversight matters. While most boards have taken on the challenge of upgrading their risk oversight capabilities in response to stricter regulations, we observe significant diversity in actual risk oversight and risk reporting practices across companies. The purpose of this chapter is to shed light on the matter and offer a number of suggestions for further research. To get a better understanding of the practice of reporting risks to boards of directors, we conducted case study research in five European companies from different industries that had extensive experience with risk management.

Board risk oversight and risk reporting

Risk oversight is defined as the board's supervision of the risk management framework and processes being used in the company. It does not include risk management itself, which is the responsibility of the company's management team. The role of the board in the risk oversight process is defined as 'ensuring that management has identified and brought the major risks faced by the enterprise to the board's attention and has plans to deal with such risks', as well as having its 'own mechanisms for analysing and monitoring risk and risk policy' (Ingley and Van der Walt, 2008).

There is a growing acknowledgement of the need for boards to fully understand the risk exposure and risk profile of their organization, and this is increasingly being incorporated into corporate governance guidelines and reporting requirements in most jurisdictions. A review of the corporate governance literature shows a significant emphasis on risk oversight since the collapse of Enron in 2002. The focus of the largely prescriptive early literature is on formal governance characteristics, such as the role of audit and compliance in the governance process. More recently, scholars have investigated the impact of firm and board characteristics on the implementation of risk management arrangements (Kleffner *et al.*, 2003; Beasley *et al.*, 2005; Desender, 2011; Paape and Speklé, 2012; Baxter *et al.*, 2013). Despite this increased attention, there are relatively few empirical studies investigating risk governance and risk oversight practices at board level, which might be a potentially fruitful area of research.

Essential elements of board risk oversight include formal governance mechanisms to oversee the risk management system, such as risk reports submitted to the board on a regular basis; an organizational structure to support risk management; and a culture of risk awareness throughout the firm (Lundqvist, 2015). In this chapter, we will first briefly discuss the formal structure and roles and the risk reporting mechanisms at board level before summarizing some of our own case study findings.

Structure and roles

The bulk of the risk oversight work at board level, such as reviewing risk reports and conducting meetings with management to generate insights, is typically allocated to audit committees and risk committees. It is important that the committee responsible for the process takes a forward-looking, business-oriented approach instead of a 'checklist' approach to risk oversight. Prior research on the role of board committees in relationship to risk management claims that risk management is beyond the scope and capabilities of the audit committee given the narrow focus of this committee on financial reporting and related compliance risks (Brown *et al.*, 2009). A separate risk committee at board level has been observed in regulated industries, such as financial services, healthcare, pharmaceuticals and utilities (Bates and Leclerc, 2009). Survey results indicate that the majority of boards in public companies with a stand-alone risk committee rate themselves as highly effective or effective in handling risk, while boards that delegate risk to the audit committee rate themselves as less effective (NACD, 2008). However, regardless of the activities of specific committees, the full board remains responsible for overseeing risk-taking by the company (Larcker and Tayan, 2011). The identification of company-level strategic risks, regular updates of the corporate risk register and a review of the internal risk analysis processes and outcomes allow the board to gain deeper insights into the risks taken by the management and should not be delegated entirely to risk or audit committees (Long, 2007).

With respect to the organizational functions involved in internal risk reporting, previous studies point at the internal audit function and the chief risk officer (CRO). Goodwin-Stewart and Kent (2006) clarify the role of internal audit as complementary to other risk management mechanisms installed in a company (i.e. separate risk functions). Sarens and De Beelde (2006) suggest that the internal auditor might provide advice on risks to the board and play a key role in monitoring the company's risk profile. Furthermore, they find that companies with integrated risk management are inclined to use internal audit for risk management purposes. In contrast, professional publications seem to oppose this point of view, emphasizing that internal auditors should not be involved in some of the core risk management activities and should limit their role to independent assurance; as a result, the auditor's role in championing risk management is likely to reduce as an organization's risk maturity increases (IIARF (Institute of Internal Auditors Research Foundation), 2011; FERMA-ECIIA (Federation of European Risk Management Associations and European Confederation of Institutes of Internal Auditing), 2014; Gupta and Leech, 2014). Empirical research on this topic could shed further light on how this tension is dealt with in practice.

Besides the audit function, the extant research acknowledges risk reporting as one of the key responsibilities of a dedicated CRO. The literature suggests that the CRO should report directly to the board of directors (Garnier, 2009; Mongiardino and Plath, 2010). Direct reporting not only reduces the information asymmetry problem but also prevents the unwitting or deliberate distortion of risk information by the senior management. Practitioner surveys, however, have shown that it is an infrequent practice for the risk function to report directly to the board (EIU, 2010). Berg and Westgaard (2011) also failed to find support for this in their study of Norwegian risk reporting practices.

Whereas several authors have studied the factors influencing enterprise-wide risk management (ERM) implementation and ERM quality (Beasley *et al.*, 2005; Desender, 2011; Paape and Speklé, 2012; Baxter *et al.*, 2013; Gatzert and Martin, 2015), to our knowledge there are only a few studies that zoom in specifically on the determinants of board risk oversight structures and roles. Empirical evidence suggests that the level of risk governance is related to the size of the firm, leverage and dividend payments, and the CEO's influence on the board (Lundqvist, 2015). Yatim (2010) finds an association between the existence of a risk management committee and strong board structures based on the structural characteristics usually associated with board efficiency, such as higher proportions of non-executive directors, board expertise and CEO duality. However, this research does not explore whether having a risk management committee enables the board to enhance their risk oversight. The formal allocation of board risk oversight roles and responsibilities (to the board as a whole rather than to certain board committees) has been identified as a major determinant of the board practices used for monitoring the organization's key risks, risk management strategies and risk profile (Ittner and Keusch, 2015).

An extensive body of literature examines the effect of corporate governance characteristics, such as board size and board independence, on company performance, especially in the context of financial institutions. For example, several studies find that shareholder-friendly boards can negatively affect banks' performance by encouraging risk-taking (Aebi *et al.*, 2012; Iqbal *et al.*, 2015). Much of the existing research on the governance–performance link provides mixed results, however. In contrast with the extensive corporate governance literature, only a few studies focus on the specific effect of risk governance on performance and risk-taking. Risk-related governance mechanisms have been found to positively affect performance. For example, banks in which the CRO reports to the board of directors performed significantly better during the credit crisis than banks in which the CRO reports to the CEO (Aebi *et al.* 2012). In the same vein, a strong and independent risk management function leads to a reduction of banks' risk exposure (Ellul and Yerramilli, 2013). In addition to further exploring these effects in other sectors, the relationship between board characteristics and risk governance practices, including reporting lines, on the one hand and the effect on performance and risk-taking on the other hand offers interesting opportunities for further research.

Risk reporting to the board

Risk reporting is a statutory requirement for listed companies in Europe, so legislators are concerned with mandatory risk disclosure. The research literature on risk reporting also focuses predominantly on external as opposed to internal risk reporting (Linsley and Shrives, 2006; Deumes and Knechel, 2008; Oliveira *et al.*, 2011). Empirical research on internal risk reporting, especially to the highest corporate levels, is scarce although academic studies have stressed the need for the board to be informed by a risk management system that provides early warning signals (Dulewicz *et al.*, 1995; Mackay and Sweeting, 2000). Directors who have access to high-quality information, especially in situations where significant uncertainty and risk are involved, are in a better position to make decisions, leading to superior performance. Whereas the availability of accurate and relevant information is viewed as an integral part of the effective functioning of the board of directors (Johanson, 2008), this aspect remains largely unexplored in the academic research literature. A notable exception is a study of how risk is reported to the board and how the observations accord with best practice in Norwegian financial institutions and power companies (Berg and Westgaard, 2012). This research concluded that risk reporting to the board of directors is primarily compliance-driven as opposed to being rooted in strategy.

This chapter considers risk information as a subset of management accounting information. Management accounting systems have long been accepted as one of the central sources of information in an organization, providing information that is used for various internal purposes, from managerial decision-making to organizational learning (Hopwood, 1972). Empirical studies have characterized management accounting systems in terms of four information characteristics: scope, integration, aggregation and timeliness (Chenhall and Morris, 1986). Scope refers to how the information system extends in time (future/historical), space (external/internal) and focus (financial/non-financial). Timeliness relates to the frequency and speed of reporting. Aggregation pertains to the way data is aggregated in time periods, in functional areas and in connection with analytical or decision models. Finally, integration relates to the provision of information that reflects the interaction and coordination between different functions in the organization. These four dimensions have been used in other studies to describe the level of sophistication of reporting systems (Gul, 1991; Bouwens and Abernethy, 2000) and their impact on organizational effectiveness (Abernethy and Guthrie, 1994). Reporting systems with a low level of sophistication contain ad hoc and delayed reporting of information that is purely financial, internally focused and historical rather than future-oriented, and where the information flow is highly siloed with no aggregation of information across functional areas. In contrast, mature reporting systems have a high average level in all the four dimensions defined by Chenhall and Morris (1986), providing information that is broad in scope (containing both financial and strategic information), both internally and externally oriented, and with a historical and future time horizon. In addition, the reporting is frequent, has a short time lag, is integrated both with performance reporting and across different organisational functions, and ensures enterprise-wide involvement (Bouwens and

Abernethy, 2000). A similar categorization could be meaningfully applied to the context of risk reporting to the board. For example, one of the ways in which companies may gain an advantage over their competitors is through broader scope and more timely access to information about risk events and their consequences, allowing them to craft a superior response to the situation, whereas a risk reporting system that is split up into functional silos may result in a fragmented and uncoordinated approach to risk-related problems.

Case study findings

In order to get a better understanding of practices for reporting risk to the board of directors in non-financial companies, we conducted field interviews with board members and senior risk officers from different industries in five European companies. The companies selected for this study are multinational companies that have been operating a risk management system for at least five years; generate stable profit levels; use one of the Big Four consultancies as their external auditor; and guaranteed us access to company data and key informants. Our analysis is primarily intended to be exploratory and descriptive. The case studies provide evidence of a number of similarities but also significant variation in the companies' risk reporting practices, both in terms of the information content and the structure of board risk oversight. In the absence of specific guidelines or regulations, companies appear to define their own ways of tackling the issue. The establishment of formal risk reporting in all of the companies in our sample dates back to the early 2000s, before the financial crisis of 2008. While the crisis was not the primary trigger for companies' risk management efforts, there was clear evidence that it created greater risk awareness and caused companies to further enhance their risk oversight practices.

All the companies studied have established formal mechanisms for risk reporting to the board of directors. Partly, this is a compliance-driven result, as reporting on risks is an obligatory requirement for publicly quoted companies according to corporate governance legislation in Europe. However, from our observations, we also conclude that first, risk is mostly integrated into performance reporting to the board, and second, formal reporting is not the only input boards of directors receive on risk-related matters. Board members tend to be actively engaged in risk discussions, perform their own risk assessment exercises and actively search for information outside formal risk reports. This proactive information seeking behaviour is intended to reduce information asymmetry, as expressed by one board member:

> By gathering new information, board members do not have to rely solely on the information that is provided and controlled by the management. This way we hope to minimize hazardous blind spots and avoid missing critical pieces of information that may act as early warning signals of a deeper crisis.

We observed that risk reporting to the board comes in two forms (see Figure 12.1). One approach is to leave operational risks as the responsibility of the management, enabling risk reporting to the board to focus solely on strategic issues and global risks that might affect the strategy of the company. Another approach is a mostly bottom-up exercise that focuses more on operational risks and aggregates those risks up the corporate hierarchy to determine the top 10 or 20 risks that are ultimately reported to the board. In addition to the day-to-day risk management at the business unit, country or regional level, there is also a clear reporting line up to the board on the risks identified. Thus, management is responsible for handling their own

Design Parameters in Risk Reporting to the Board

- Board-level strategic risks versus bottom-up aggregation
- Separate function responsible for risk reporting
- Harmonising risk reporting across functions
- Major risks included in board-level strategic dialogues
- Integration of risk and performance reporting
- Board readiness to deal with disruptive risks remains a challenge
- Deep-dive board meetings to maintain strategic focus on risk
- Limited formalisation of risk appetite at board level
- Tone at the top helps create the right risk culture

Figure 12.1 Summary of case study observations.

operational risks, while the board receives high-level information mostly on risks directly linked with strategic questions. In most cases, the risks reported to the board are limited to the top risks that are truly global in the context of the company.

In all cases, there is a separate function in the company who has been assigned the task of assisting the management with risk assessment, and who ultimately aggregates all the information for subsequent reporting to the board. In the publicly listed companies in our sample, the reporting is done directly to the audit committee of the board. An internal auditor is involved in risk management in two cases, assisted or not by the head of risk and insurance who consolidates the information. On the board side, it is the audit committee that is most frequently in charge of the risk management. In our case studies, we found that risk management in general and risk reporting in particular could be fairly mature even in the absence of a CRO. Contrary to the conclusions from previous research (Beasley *et al.*, 2005; Mongiardino and Plath, 2010), we did not observe that the appointment of a CRO signalled greater commitment to risk management in a company.

In large organizations faced with various complex risks, functional specialization into distinct areas of risk enables better focus. However, this silo-based approach may result in a fragmented and uncoordinated approach to risk-related problems due to insufficient information-sharing, inconsistent methods for dealing with risk, duplication of efforts and lack of a comprehensive view on the totality of risks that the company is facing. The companies in our case study address these silo problems by standardizing risk reporting practices and by establishing a common language for risk management. This leads to a better understanding and management of risk interactions. It also improves access to and comfort with risk specialists across the organization.

The board members in our sample generally seem to be very aware of the importance of considering risks in their decisions and in performance evaluation. As one board member mentioned:

> Talking about risk for me is not something new; it has always been a part of the ongoing management control in the company. What was previously done in a more implicit manner has simply received greater attention and has been subjected to increased formalisation.

In some companies, an update on risks and trends was included in the yearly overview of the control environment, investments and key performance indicators (providing links with different risks). In others, integrated reports were sent to the board on the company's aggregate exposure on both the asset and liability sides, to the financial markets reflecting the 'big risk questions'. In one company, strategic site reviews were produced containing information on such issues as resources, utilization, health and safety, community, number of complaints, staffing and risks gathered per site, and these were reported in a consolidated way. Board members perform their own risk assessment with respect to strategic risks when they discuss new strategic initiatives. Such board risk assessments are often not formalized, but they are part of the regular discussions on long-term strategy and potential uncertainties related to that strategy. We also found that it is common practice for management to identify and report risks to the board as part of merger and acquisition (M&A) proposals, business development plans and strategic reviews. Such strategic risk reporting typically comes in addition to the specialized reporting that focuses specifically on the top (operational) risks.

In most companies, we observed that risks are explicitly viewed not only in a negative light (i.e. as a threat) but also from a positive perspective (i.e. as value-creating opportunities). The reporting on risks is thus closely intertwined with reporting on potential opportunities, in this sense providing a close integration between risk and performance (see Figure 12.2). Because such integrated reporting puts risk information in the context of other types of information on performance, strategy and operations, it adds to a more in-depth understanding of how the business is doing. In contrast, separate risk reporting zooms in specifically on the risk aspects of the business and has the propensity to be more compliance-driven. Our respondents emphasized that specialized risk reporting may lead the company into a 'compliance trap', with the whole risk management turning into a 'box-ticking exercise'.

The rapid pace of change and unanticipated disruptions in today's global marketplace trigger a seemingly endless series of risks that can erode or even destroy an organization's business model. The board members in our sample all agreed that they face a tremendous challenge in

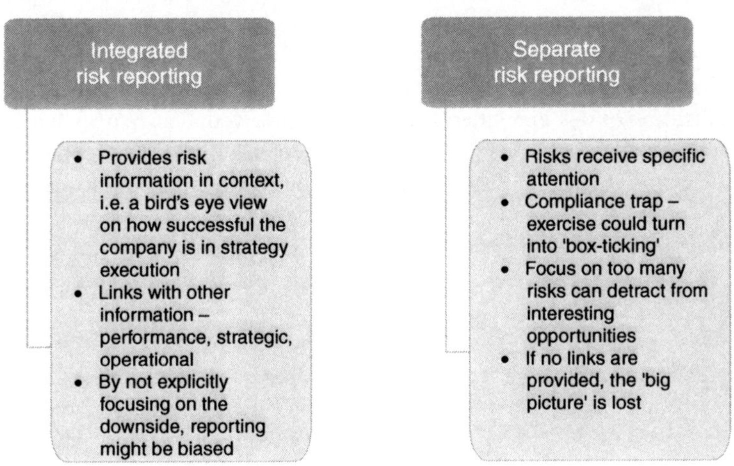

Figure 12.2 Integration of risk and performance reporting.

overseeing all the regulatory, technological, competitive, reputational, human resources-related and other risks that may affect—both positively and negatively—the organization's strategic success. Paradoxically, the increased strategic importance of risk seems to reduce the relevance of the classic risk management function and processes within companies. The goal of risk management is traditionally to protect the company against knowable and measurable risks that may arise during the normal course of business. Such loss prevention programmes are typically not designed to address strategic risks that may be disruptive to a company's value proposition or business model and are generally difficult to foresee and mitigate. In addition, ownership of such risk exposures within the company is often not clear. The question for boards is whether they are prepared to recognize and act upon the presence of existential threats to the company. In addition, strategic risks usually have a flip side in that they often provide the opportunity to achieve significant growth and differentiation if accounted for in an effective and timely manner.

The challenge of keeping the board's risk discussions at a strategic level is dependent on the type of information directors receive from management. Often, companies' risk programmes and management attention—and therefore, reports to the board—are predominantly focused on quantitative or quantifiable risks (based on financial and operational data) as opposed to the less easily defined qualitative types of risks that extend beyond familiar ground. Because it is largely shaped by the standard information provided by management, such as the classic heat maps, the boardroom risk dialogue has the tendency to digress away from strategic risks toward more routine operational, compliance and financial reporting risks. To help counteract this tendency, the boards of several companies in our sample conduct an annual off-site or 'deep dive' meeting dedicated to understanding the broad range of strategic uncertainties and challenging the underlying assumptions of strategic moves, the range of possible outcomes and the associated risks and payoffs.

In order to contextualize our research findings, we also investigated whether companies had a defined risk appetite and how these were approved. Some practitioner reports suggest that defining a company's risk appetite is a crucial first step, claiming that 'designing risk management without defining your risk appetite is like designing a bridge without knowing which river it needs to span' (EY, 2010). However, whereas risk management procedures are in place in all companies we studied, the formal definition of risk appetite remains a fairly rare practice. In fact, our field study demonstrated a continuum in terms of board-level definition and approval of risk appetite, ranging from no definition at all to some attempts at formal definitions by the board of directors—with most companies being at the lower end of the spectrum. In general, we observed that in those companies that favoured a more integrated view of risk, the attitude towards formalization of risk appetite remained fairly reserved. One reason quoted for this is that the companies prefer to stay flexible and adjust their risk appetite based on the particular project or strategic initiative at hand, and as a consequence want to avoid too much *ex ante* formalization.

All the interviewees in our sample also emphasized that the so-called 'tone at the top' is very important to enhance the information flow between executives and non-executives. As one board member noted:

> Board risk oversight is not only about the reports; it is about the processes and the culture. If the culture does not support management's reporting of unfavourable issues or risks to the board, these issues may not be reported at all. This allows situations to escalate and become worse.

The board is instrumental in creating a risk culture at all levels in the firm that encourages open communication and constructive challenging of assumptions.

Opportunities for future research

One of the key reasons frequently cited for why boards failed to adequately manage risk during the 2008 financial crisis is that board members did not have access to relevant information on the risks incurred. The reality is that risk is an inevitable part of the performance of any business, regardless of whether it is managed formally or ignored altogether. Despite the fact that risks are prevalent in today's interconnected world, our research finds significant variation in companies' risk reporting practices, both in terms of information content and risk oversight structure. Our field observations suggest that risk reporting in companies can be put on a continuum, from limited historical reporting at one end of the spectrum to elaborate, broad-scope reporting on the other. While the initial motivation to set up risk reporting is often to comply with regulation, risk oversight is increasingly owned by the board and embedded in the business rather than perceived as an overlay process effected by support staff. Boards view risk oversight as an item on the strategic agenda, explicitly considering risk in any major decision that they evaluate—not just as an afterthought whenever risk oversight appears on the compliance agenda.

Much of the academic research on boards of directors draws on agency theory and examines the antecedents and consequences of different board structures, including factors such as board size and composition (Daily *et al.*, 2003; Pye and Pettigrew, 2005). While the large body of empirical studies on the link between board characteristics and performance has added to our understanding of corporate governance issues, there is a growing sentiment that further research is needed that investigates the intervening processes and behaviours that boards engage in to carry out their duties. In particular, limited attention has been given to date to the strategic information processes at board level, and more specifically to the content and use of risk-related reporting at the level of the board of directors. However, we believe that besides the formal structure and information characteristics of risk reporting, process plays an important part in board risk oversight.

Research on actual board processes can help improve our understanding of board behaviour and open the 'black box' of what happens inside the boardroom (Huse, 2005; Van Ees *et al.*, 2009). Empirical research on board processes is scarce, however, due to the fact that data collection on board processes is very difficult because of restricted access (Pye and Pettigrew, 2005). Nonetheless, such a process perspective is important, from both a theoretical and an empirical perspective, especially in the context of risk reporting. Our field study highlighted further examination of the determinants and implications of risk reporting to the board as a potential avenue for a process study (see Figure 12.3). We advocate for in-depth research that uses qualitative techniques to uncover the processes and behaviours that influence boards' ability to effectively carry out their risk oversight duties.

Figure 12.3 Directions for future research.

Board involvement as antecedent of risk reporting

Cross-case analysis enabled us to discover some of the reasons behind the observed differences in risk reporting practices in our field study. One factor identified as potentially influencing the way risk reporting is organized is board involvement in the strategy process. Board involvement is defined as 'the overall level of participation of board members in making non-routine, organization-wide resource allocation decisions that affect the long-term performance of an organization' (Judge and Zeithaml, 1992). The extent of board involvement in a company's strategic decisions is a widely debated topic in the management literature (Pugliese *et al.*, 2009; Zattoni and Pugliese, 2012), which links it to different types of boards (Nadler *et al.*, 2006; Golden and Zajac, 2001). The literature distinguishes between two broad schools of thought. The first one—passive—considers the board as a 'rubber stamp' with no real influence on the strategy process, while the second—active—views the board as an independent body that contributes to shaping the strategic direction of the company (Golden and Zajac, 2001; Hendry and Kiel, 2004). Ingley and Van der Walt (2008) assert that the role of the board with regard to corporate strategy can be placed on the 'continuum, with a traditional perception of the role of the board as approving, monitoring and reviewing strategy at one end, to a leadership role of active involvement in establishing goals, values and setting direction at the other end' (Ingley and Van der Walt, 2008).

The preliminary findings from our exploratory field research indicate that in companies where board strategic involvement is high, more formal structures for risk reporting to the board are put in place, and the content of risk reporting to the board is quite sophisticated. This aligns with the conclusions from earlier field research that the extent to which directors are able to gather information plays a critical role in determining the board's level of strategic involvement (McNulty and Pettigrew, 1999). In addition, as boards move beyond their role of providing basic legitimacy, directors will no longer be satisfied with general financial statements but will require more detailed reviews (Boulton, 1978). As the board takes up a 'directing' role and the time horizon becomes more future-oriented, 'board discussions become progressively related to choices between alternative directions, strategies and investments' (Boulton, 1978). Such choices, in their turn, imply the availability of the necessary information. Based on these claims, we expect that a high level of board involvement in the company's strategy process may lead to different risk information requirements than low involvement. Given the importance of considering risks in making strategic decisions (Buchanan and O'Connell, 2006), investigating how risk reporting content and structures are related to board involvement in strategy constitutes an interesting research direction.

The impact of risk reporting on board-level decisions

A second research question worth investigating is whether the anticipated benefits of high-quality risk reporting are indeed realized. To measure impact, empirical research in the risk management domain frequently uses the effect on company financial performance, such as accounting returns or stock price performance (Gordon *et al.*, 2009; Baxter *et al.*, 2013; Hoyt and Liebenberg, 2011). A comparable approach is used to study whether and how management accounting innovations have an impact on the performance of a company. For example, the adoption and use of activity-based costing has been associated with increased financial performance because superior costing information leads to improved decision-making under appropriate enabling conditions (Cagwin and Bouwman, 2002; Narayanan and Sarkar, 2002). Similarly, researchers have studied the impact of the balanced scorecard on a variety of performance-related items (Davis and Albright, 2004; De Geuser *et al.*, 2009). These empirical studies, however, do not provide an in-depth process perspective on how exactly the impact on performance is achieved.

The main objective of an information system is to provide information that supports the decision-making process (Johanson, 2008). The usefulness of this information is conditional upon its ability to relate to what people do (Mintzberg, 1973). In a board context, information can be considered useful for the board to the extent that the information supports board-level strategic decisions about the long-term direction of the firm; the scope of firm's activities; the matching of these activities to the firm's environment and resource capabilities; the allocation of major resources within the firm; and consideration of the expectations and values of the firm's stakeholders (Langfield-Smith, 1997). Risk information deserves special attention given its importance in strategic decision-making (Buchanan and O'Connell, 2006). However, the exact relationship between information received by the board and subsequent strategic decisions remains unclear. As a matter of fact, the type of information supplied to the board might determine what information is used as well as the functions that board members can and will perform (Johanson, 2008). This means that information in general, and risk information in particular, that is reported to the board might actually determine what decisions the board is able to make. The relationship between content and use of information by the board is therefore 'assumingly bi-directional and complex' (Johanson, 2008).

One potential area for further research is thus to examine the (perceived) usefulness of the risk information that boards receive and the impact of that information on subsequent strategic decisions. As mentioned above, risk reporting to the board is only part of the board risk oversight construct. Not only the information content but also the underlying structures for risk reporting to the board are expected to influence the decision-making process at board level. The findings from our exploratory field research hint at a positive effect derived from both the establishment of certain board-level committees and the enhancement of risk reporting to the board on strategic decisions taken by the board. Future studies could examine in depth how boards employ the risk information they receive and gather in an effort to effectively carry out their risk oversight duties.

Conclusion

Much of the discussion around board effectiveness stresses the importance of timely and balanced reporting by management and the need for board members to keep themselves apprised of the business and its risks (Ingley and Van der Walt, 2008). Even though reporting of a sufficient quantity of broad-scope information is acknowledged to play a crucial role in the context of boards (Lorsch, 2012; Nadler *et al.*, 2006), academic research on this topic is rather scarce (Johanson, 2008). Academic studies in corporate governance mainly examine the determinants and performance effects of structural characteristics of boards but do not focus on boards as receivers and users of information. In particular, there is limited research on how boards of directors use information from management accounting systems (Crombie and Geekie, 2010), despite claims that management accounting, corporate governance and risk management are 'increasingly and inextricably interdependent' (Bhimani, 2009).

This chapter pays particular attention to risk information given its importance in strategic decision-making. We advocate for an integrated analysis of board risk reporting that considers both the risk governance structures and information characteristics as predictors of the board's ability to effectively oversee risk. Based on our exploratory field research, we conclude that board-level risk committees and formal risk reporting lines are necessary but insufficient arrangements for boards to carry out their risk oversight responsibilities. Rather, effective risk oversight requires boards of directors to be actively engaged with the strategy of the business. By studying the relationship between the content and use of board-level risk information on the one hand and influencing factors such as board strategic involvement and risk outcomes on the other hand, we can gain deeper insight into the processes by which boards carry out their risk management responsibilities—a topic that remains poorly understood.

Notes

1 The EC Directive 2003/51/EC (Modernization Directive) requires a description of the main risks and uncertainties that the entity faces. The EC Directive 2001/65/EC (Fair Value Directive) requires disclosures about the entity's financial risk management objectives and policies as well as the entity's exposure to price risk, credit risk, liquidity risk and cash flow risk. The EC Directive 2004/109/EC (Transparency Directive) states that the half-yearly financial report must comprise an interim management report, including the description of the main risks and uncertainties for the remaining six months of the financial year. Finally, EC Directives 2014/56/EU and 2006/43/EC, art. 41 (Statutory Audit) assign clear duties to the board and the audit committee to monitor the effectiveness of the company's risk management and control systems.
2 Basel Committee on Banking Supervision, 2014. Corporate governance principles for banks.
3 European Banking Authority, 2011. EBA Guidelines on Internal Governance.
4 Financial Stability Board (FSB), 2013. Thematic Review on Risk Governance.
5 OECD, 2014. Risk Management and Corporate Governance, OECD Publishing.

References

Abernethy, M. and C. Guthrie (1994), 'An Empirical Assessment of the "Fit" between Strategy and Management Information System Design', *Accounting & Finance*, 34(2), pp. 49–66.

Adams, R. and D. Ferreira (2007), 'A Theory of Friendly Boards', *Journal of Finance*, 62(1), pp. 217–250.

Aebi, V., G. Sabato and M. Schmid (2012), 'Risk Management, Corporate Governance, and Bank Performance in the Financial Crisis', *Journal of Banking & Finance*, 36, pp. 3213–3226.

Bates II, E.and R. Leclerc (2009), 'Boards of Directors and Risk Committees', *Corporate Governance Advisor*, 17(6), pp. 15–17.

Baxter, R., J. Bedard, R. Hoitash and A. Yezegel (2013), 'Enterprise Risk Management Program Quality: Determinants, Value Relevance, and the Financial Crisis', *Contemporary Accounting Research*, 30, pp. 1264–1295.

Beasley, M., R. Clune and D. Hermanson (2005), 'Enterprise Risk Management: An Empirical Analysis of Factors Associated with the Extent of Implementation', *Journal of Accounting and Public Policy*, 24, pp. 521–531.

Berg, T. and S. Westgaard (2012), 'Risk Reporting to the Board of Directors: Comparison of Norwegian Power Companies and Banks', *Journal of Energy Markets*, 5(3), pp. 45–63.

Bhimani, A. (2009), 'Risk Management, Corporate Governance and Management Accounting', *Management Accounting Research*, 20(1), pp. 2–5.

Boulton, W. (1978), 'The Evolving Board: A Look at the Board's Changing Roles and Information Needs', *Academy of Management Review*, 3, pp. 827–836.

Bouwens, J. and M. Abernethy (2000), 'The Consequences of Customization on Management Accounting System Design', *Accounting, Organizations and Society*, 25, pp. 221–241.

Brown, I., A. Steen and J. Foreman (2009), 'Risk Management in Corporate Governance: A Review and Proposal', *Corporate Governance: An International Review*, 17(5), pp. 546–558.

Buchanan, L. and A. O'Connell (2006), 'A Brief History of Decision Making', *Harvard Business Review*, 84(1), pp. 32–41.

Cagwin, D. and M. Bouwman (2002), 'The Association between Activity-Based Costing and Improvement in Financial Performance', *Management Accounting Research*, 13(1), pp. 1–39.

Chenhall, R. and D. Morris (1986), 'The Impact of Structure, Environment, and Interdependence on the Perceived Usefulness of Management Accounting Systems', *Accounting Review*, 61(1), pp. 16–35.

CIMA (2010), 'Enterprise Governance: Restoring Boardroom Leadership', discussion paper, London: CIMA.

Crombie, N. and T. Geekie (2010), *The Levers of Control in the Boardroom.* Available from: http://hdl.handle.net/10092/4707.
Daily, C., D. Dalton and A. Cannella (2003), 'Corporate Governance: Decades of Dialogue and Data', *Academy of Management Review*, 28(3), pp. 371–382.
Davis, S. and T. Albright (2004), 'An Investigation of the Effect of Balanced Scorecard Implementation on Financial Performance', *Management Accounting Research*, 15(2), pp. 135–153.
De Geuser, F., S. Mooraj and D. Oynon (2009), 'Does the Balanced Scorecard Add Value? Empirical Evidence on Its Effect on Performance', *European Accounting Review*, 18(1), pp. 93–122.
Desender, K. (2011), 'On the Determinants of Enterprise Risk Management Implementation', in *Enterprise IT Governance, Business Value and Performance Measurement*, N. Si Shi and G. Silvius (eds.), IGI Global.
Deumes, R. and W. Knechel (2008), 'Economic Incentives for Voluntary Reporting on Internal Risk Management and Control Systems', *Auditing: A Journal of Practice & Theory*, 27(1), pp. 35–66.
Dulewicz, V., K. MacMillan and P. Herbert (1995), 'Appraising and Developing Boards and Their Effectiveness', *Journal of General Management*, 20(3), pp. 1–19.
Economist Intelligence Unit (EIU) (2010), *Fall Guys: Risk Management in the Front Line*, EIU.
Ellul, A. and V. Yerramilli (2013), 'Stronger Risk Controls, Lower Risk: Evidence from U.S. Bank Holding Companies', *Journal of Finance*, 68(5), pp. 1757–1803.
EY (2010), 'Risk Appetite: The Strategic Balancing Act', white paper.
FERMA-ECIIA (2014), 'Audit and Risk Committees: News from EU Legislation an Best Practices', white paper.
Garnier, M. (2009), 'Black Holes in Risk Governance', *Journal of Risk Management in Financial Institutions*, 2, pp. 116–120.
Gatzert, N. and M. Martin (2015), 'Determinants and Value of Enterprise Risk Management: Empirical Evidence from the Literature', *Risk Management and Insurance Review*, 18(1), pp. 29–53.
Golden, B. and E. Zajac (2001), 'When Will Boards Influence Strategy? Inclination x Power = Strategic Change', *Strategic Management Journal*, 22, pp. 1087–1111.
Goodwin-Stewart, J. and P. Kent (2006), 'The Use of Internal Audit by Australian Companies', *Managerial Auditing Journal*, 21(1), pp. 81–101.
Gordon, L.A., M. Loeb and C. Tseng (2009), 'Enterprise Risk Management and Firm Performance: A Contingency Perspective', *Journal of Accounting and Public Policy*, 28, pp. 301–327.
Gul, F. (1991), 'The Effects of Management Accounting Systems and Environmental Uncertainty on Small Business Managers' Performance', *Accounting and Business Research*, 22(85), pp. 57–61.
Gupta, P. and T. Leech (2014), *Risk Oversight: Evolving Expectations for Boards*, New York: The Conference Board.
Hendry, K. and G. Kiel (2004), 'The Role of the Board in Firm Strategy: Integrating Agency and Organisational Control Perspectives', *Corporate Governance, An International Review*, 12(4), pp. 500–520.
Hopwood, A. (1972), 'An Empirical Study of the Role of Accounting Data in Performance Evaluation', *Journal of Accounting Research*, 10, pp. 156–182.
Hoyt, R.E. and A. Liebenberg (2011), 'The Value of Enterprise Risk Management', *Journal of Risk and Insurance*, 78(4), pp. 795–822.
Huse, M. (2005), 'Accountability and Creating Accountability: A Framework for Exploring Behavioral Perspectives of Corporate Governance', *British Journal of Management*, 16, pp. 65–79.
Iqbal, J., S. Strobl and S. Vahamaa (2015), 'Corporate Governance and the Systemic Risk of Financial Institutions', *Journal of Economics & Business*, 82, pp. 42–61.
Ingley, C. and N. Van Der Walt (2008), 'Risk Management and Board Effectiveness', *International Studies of Management and Organization*, 38(3), pp. 43–70.
IIARF (2011), 'Internal Auditing's Role in Risk Management', white paper.
Ittner, C. and T. Keusch (2015), 'The Influence of Board of Directors' Risk Oversight on Risk Management Maturity and Firm Risk-Taking', working paper.
Johanson, D. (2008), 'Corporate Governance and Board Accounts: Exploring a Neglected Interface Between Boards of Directors and Management', *Journal of Management and Governance*, 12(4), pp. 343–380.
Judge, W. and C. Zeithaml (1992), 'Institutional and Strategic Choice Perspectives on Board Involvement in the Strategic Decision Process', *Academy of Management Journal*, 35, pp. 766–794.
Kleffner, A., R. Lee and B. McGannon (2003), 'The Effect of Corporate Governance on the Use of Risk Management: Evidence from Canada', *Risk Management and Insurance Review*, 6(1), pp. 53–73.

Langfield-Smith, K. (1997), 'Management Control Systems and Strategy: A Critical Review', *Accounting, Organizations and Society*, 22(2), pp. 207–232.

Larcker, D. and B. Tayan (2011), *Corporate Governance Matters*, Upper Saddle River: Pearson Education.

Linsley, P. and P. Shrives (2006), 'Risk Reporting: A Study of Risk Disclosures in the Annual Reports of UK Companies', *British Accounting Review*, 38(4), pp. 387–404.

Long, T. (2007), 'The Evolution of FTSE 250 Boards of Directors: Key Factors Influencing Board Performance and Effectiveness', *Journal of General Management*, 32(3), pp. 45–60.

Lorsch, J. (2012), *The Future of Boards*, Boston: Harvard Business Review Press.

Lorsch, J. and E. MacIver (1989), *Pawns and Potentates: The Reality of America's Corporate Boards*, Boston: Harvard Business School Press.

Lundqvist, S. (2015), 'Why Firms Implement Risk Governance: Stepping beyond Traditional Risk Management to Enterprise Risk Management', *Journal of Accounting and Public Policy*, 34, pp. 441–466.

Mackay, I. and R. Sweeting (2000), 'Perspectives on Integrated Business Risk Management (BRM) and the Implications for Corporate Governance', *Corporate Governance: An International Review*, 8(4), pp. 367–374.

McNulty, T. and A. Pettigrew (1999), 'Strategists on the Board', *Organization Studies*, 20(1), pp. 47–74.

Mintzberg, H. (1973), *The Nature of Managerial Work*, New York: Harper & Row.

Mongiardino, A. and C. Plath (2010), 'Risk Governance at Large Banks: Have Any Lessons Been Learned?' *Journal of Risk Management in Financial Institutions*, 3(2), pp. 116–123.

Nadler, D., B. Behan and M. Nadler (2006), *Building Better Boards*, San Francisco: Jossey-Bass.

Narayanan, V.G. and R. Sarkar (2002), 'The Impact of Activity-Based Costing on Managerial Decisions at Insteel Industries: A Field Study', *Journal of Economics and Management Strategy*, 11(2), pp. 257–288.

NACD (National Association of Corporate Directors), (2008). *NACD Public Company Survey*. Available from: www.nacdonline.org.

Nowak, M. and M. McCabe (2003), 'Information Costs and the Role of the Independent Corporate Director', *Corporate Governance: An International Review*, 11(4), pp. 300–307.

Oliveira, J., L. Rodrigues and R. Craig (2011), 'Risk-Related Disclosures by Non-Finance Companies', *Managerial Auditing Journal*, 26(9), pp. 817–839.

Paape, L. and R. Speklé (2012), 'The Adoption and Design of Enterprise Risk Management Practices: An Empirical Study', *European Accounting Review*, 21(3), pp. 533–564.

Pugliese, A., P. Bezemer, A. Zattoni, M. Huse, F. Van den Bosch and H. Volberda (2009), 'Boards of Directors' Contribution to Strategy: A Literature Review and Research Agenda', *Corporate Governance: An International Review*, 17(3), pp. 292–306.

Pye, A. and A. Pettigrew (2005), 'Studying Board Context, Processes and Dynamics: Some Challenges for the Future', *British Journal of Management*, 16, pp. 27–38.

Sarens, G. and I. Debeelde (2006), 'Internal Auditors' Perception about their Role in Risk Management: A Comparison between US and Belgian Companies,' *Managerial Auditing Journal*, Vol. 21, No. 1, pp. 63–80.

Van Ees, H., J. Gabrielsson and M. Huse (2009), 'Toward a Behavioral Theory of Boards and Corporate Governance', *Corporate Governance: An International Review*, 17(3), pp. 307–319.

Yatim, P. (2010), 'Board Structures and the Establishment of a Risk Management Committee by Malaysian Listed Firms,' *Journal of Management and Governance*, Vol. 14, 17–36.

Zattoni, A. and A. Pugliese (2012), 'Boards' Contribution to Strategy and Innovation', in T. Clarke and D. Branson (eds.), *The SAGE Handbook of Corporate Governance*, London: Sage, pp. 217–232.

13

Supply chain quality risk

A food industry perspective

Ying Kei Tse and Minhao Zhang

Introduction

Consumer goods manufacturing is now a global business. Raw materials are sourced from different countries, and the manufacturing process is globalized. The increasingly complex supply chain exposes the limitations of ensuring product quality for practitioners. Recently, consumers have become increasingly concerned about a series of product harm scandals and begun to doubt the ability of industries and governments to ensure production safety and supply chain quality (Trienekens and Zuurbier, 2008; Marucheck *et al.*, 2011). A wide range of products, from consumer products (e.g. toys and automobiles) to food and drug products, are suffering a quality risk from the supply chain (Bogdanich, 2015; Roth *et al.*, 2008; Yang *et al.*, 2009; Berman and Swani, 2010). Because it can cause great damage to a company's reputation, a product harm scandal is potentially extremely costly to firms (Van Heerde *et al.*, 2007). Therefore, to preserve the company's reputation and sustain financial performance, tackling supply chain risk—in particular, quality risk—should be at the top of management's agenda.

Compared with other products, food products are more sensitive for the public, because they directly affect personal health and daily life. The horsemeat scandal that occurred in the United Kingdom in 2013 has raised public awareness of food fraud issues in the global supply chain. This scandal has put the spotlight on the complexity of our food supply chain. The problem was first discovered in January 2013, when horsemeat was found in frozen burgers on sale in the UK and the Republic of Ireland; the follow-up investigation identified similar adulteration in processed beef products and ready meals across the European Union (BBC, 2013). The UK Food Standards Agency (FSA) and food firms started large-scale DNA testing of meat products in the market. Although the test results showed that less than 1 per cent of products contained horsemeat,[1] the scandal had a great impact on consumers. According to consumer behaviour research conducted by the FSA in February 2013, around half (49%) of respondents stated that they intended to buy less processed meat and fewer ready meals as a result of the horsemeat incidents. Another report from the FSA in August 2013 indicated that 48 per cent of respondents believed that food manufacturers and their supply chain partners were ultimately responsible for the horsemeat contamination issue.[2]

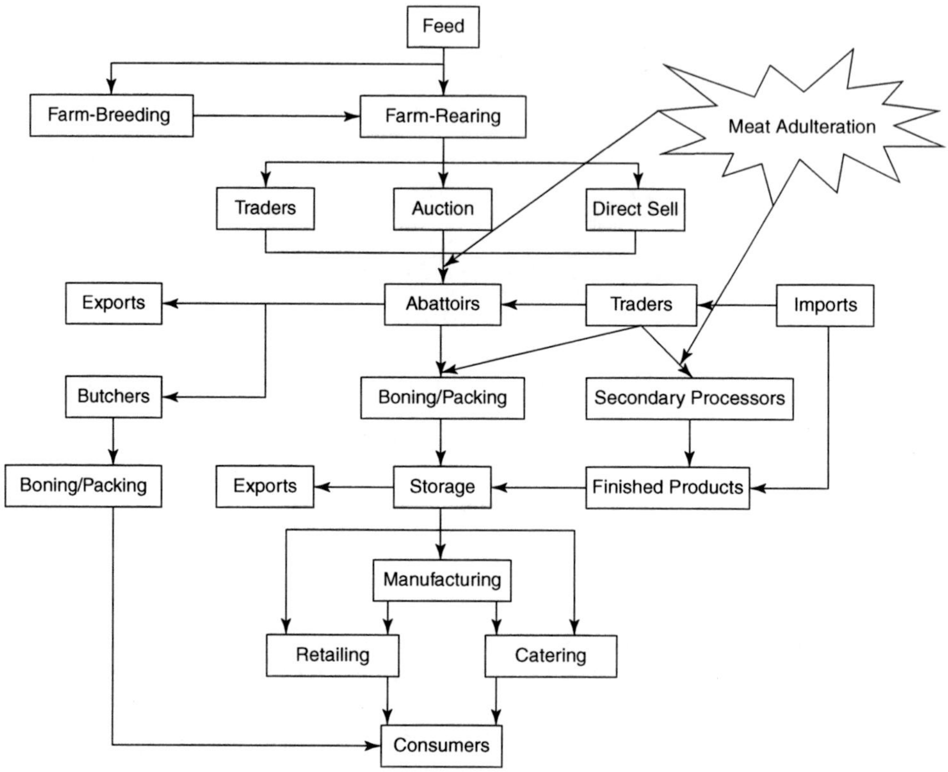

Figure 13.1 The complex meat supply chain (developed from MAFF (Ministry of Agriculture, Fisheries and Food), 1999; Safefood, 2008; Lindgreen and Hingley, 2003).

The horsemeat scandal revealed that quality risks in the upstream supply chain (as illustrated in Figure 13.1) can trigger a knock-on effect in society and create enormous implications for consumer confidence, brand identity and regulatory issues. Given the complex meat supply-chain network illustrated in Figure 13.1, it is difficult for practitioners and government to identify the supply chain risk. Therefore, it is important that practitioners and policymakers gain a better understanding of the nature of the food fraud problem—that is, quality risk in the food supply chain—which has become much more complex as a result of globalization. Furthermore, if practitioners and policymakers are to put in place appropriate response strategies to restore customer confidence, it is crucial that they understand the risk perception of consumers.

In this research, to assist better decision-making for practitioners and policymakers, we investigate how consumers perceive quality risk in the food supply chain. However, simply capturing the consumer's opinions is not sufficient to view the whole picture of the supply chain quality risk issue. To holistically understand the quality risk in the food chain, we also explore the attitudes of experts (food industry managers), including risk perception and trust towards the industry. Moreover, we are interested in how consumers differ from practitioners in responding to the news of horsemeat scandal, including in relation to the actions of information-seeking and risk avoidance.

In order to understand how consumers and practitioners perceived risk in the horsemeat contamination product recall, we adopt Slovic *et al.*'s (1985) psychometric model. We test the psychometric paradigm model using data collected from 279 consumers and 140 food industry managers of beef products to explore their risk perceptions and decisions. Slovic *et al.*'s approach is a useful tool to analyse and predict consumers' responses to various risks by identifying their similarities and differences (Feng *et al.*, 2010), and it has been widely adopted in risk and applied psychology literature (McDaniels *et al.*, 1995; Savadori *et al.*, 2004; Feng *et al.*, 2010). It is particularly useful to examine a risk that is newly arisen, such as the horsemeat scandal, and compare it with the existing risks along with a number of perception dimensions. Through comparing the risk perceptions of experts and laypeople, practitioners and policymakers will be able to understand the nature of new risks and potentially help the public to perceive risks in a more accurate manner (Feng *et al.*, 2010).

The remainder of this paper is organized as follows: first, we provide a literature review and examine the nature of supply chain quality risk; second, we describe the psychometric model analysis of a number of product recall cases in the food industry; third, we examine the response actions of consumers and practitioners; fourth, we provide a comprehensive action plan for practitioners; and finally, we present our conclusions.

Food fraud and supply chain quality risk

The horsemeat scandal can be defined as a kind of food fraud. According to the definition of the European Union law enforcement agency (Europol[3]) and the International Criminal Police Organization (Interpol[4]), food fraud is 'the deliberate placing on the market, for financial gain, foods which are falsely described or otherwise intended to deceive the consumer' (Elliot, 2013). Elliot (2013) claims that the horsemeat incident is a 'food crime' in that it involves complex, widespread and organized national and international activities rather than a few random acts by 'rogues' within the food industry.

In recent years, there has been an increase in food fraud incidents, and these have triggered high-profile product recalls or withdrawals that have seriously impacted on food firms, government agencies and consumers. Such fraud can be found in both raw ingredients and finished products and can affect a range of food items, including dairy products, meat products, olive oil, spices, tea and coffee. Food fraud becomes a supply chain quality integrity issue and impacts on every party in the supply chain. The increasing occurrence of the problem may be due to the magnitude of global sourcing and the complexity of the supply network; one result of this is that visibility and traceability in the supply chain tend to be weakened (Christopher and Peck, 2004; Roth *et al.*, 2008). In this research, we investigate the horsemeat scandal from a supply chain perspective rather than a criminological perspective. We claim that the food fraud in the horsemeat scandal is a quality risk in the food supply chain. Therefore, we have modified the definition of supply chain quality risk in our previous study (Tse and Tan, 2011), and we offer the following proposition:

> Inherent food fraud caused by adulteration/substitution/misleading labelling/false statements in the ingredients/finished product in any of the supply chain members triggers a cascading effect that spreads through a multi-tier supply chain.

Risk perception dimensions

In this study, we adopt Slovic *et al.*'s (1985) psychometric model to examine consumers' perception of quality risk in the horsemeat scandal. We also use a modified version of Feng's (2010) risk perception dimensions in lead-painted toys and tainted pet food as the measurement items of quality risk perception. The seven risk perception dimensions selected are controllability, dread, severity of consequences, voluntariness, knowledge of risk by those exposed to it, immediacy of effect, and risk newness. These risk perception dimensions reflect the risk characteristics in different areas, such as risk from technology (Fischhoff *et al.*, 1975), automobile safety defects (Slovic *et al.*, 1985), biotechnology (Savadori *et al.*, 2004), lead-painted toys and tainted pet food (Feng *et al.*, 2010). Each risk perception dimension is measured by a 7-point Likert scale. The measurement items are listed in Table 13.1.

We have chosen a number of recent food harm scandals in order to make comparisons with the horsemeat scandal—specifically, the melamine milk (2008), dioxin pork (2008), phthalate-plasticizer drink (2011) and carcinogenic cola (2013) scandals. The Irish dioxin pork scandal (2008) is chosen as one of the cases as it is also a quality risk issue related to meat products. The melamine milk and phthalate-plasticizer drink scandals are included because, as in the horsemeat incident, the food fraud happened in the upstream supply chain. The phthalate-plasticizer drink and carcinogenic cola incidents were food harm incidents that happened outside the UK; therefore, we can compare how UK consumers perceive food scandals that do not affect their home country. The carcinogenic cola scandal was not a supply chain quality risk incident since the carcinogenic substance (4-methylimidazole) was created during the production process, and it was not a food fraud that was inherent in the supply network. Therefore, we can analyse how consumers perceive a food harm scandal differently to a food fraud. In addition, we include a non-food product harm scandal, the flaming laptop incident (2006), which was caused by defective parts from the upstream supply chain partners. The purpose of adding this scenario to the analysis is that it can provide a comparison between food and

Table 13.1 Dimensions of psychometric paradigm

Scale	*Description*	*Scale end points*	
		Low	*High*
Controllability	Please rate to what extent you can, by personal skill or diligence, avoid taking the food fraud product, if exposed to the risk.	Controllable	Uncontrollable
Dread	Please rate to what extent this is a risk that you have learned to live with and can think about reasonably calmly, or one that you have great dread of—on the level of a gut reaction.	Not dread	Dread
Severity of consequences	Please rate how likely it is that the consequence will be fatal when the risk is realized in the form of a mishap or illness.	Consequences not fatal	Consequences fatal
Voluntariness	Please rate to what extent this risk is faced voluntarily.	Voluntarily	Involuntarily
Knowledge of risk by those exposed to it	Please rate to what extent the risks are known precisely by the consumer who faces those risks.	Known precisely	Not known
Immediacy of effect	Please rate to what extent the risk to health/safety is immediate, or whether sickness is likely to occur at some later time.	Effect immediate	Effect delayed
Newness	Please rate to what extent this risk is old and familiar or new and novel.	Old	New

Table 13.2 Selected case scenarios in psychometric risk perception model

Case	*Description*	*Year*	*Quality risk type*
Horsemeat	Processed beef products contained undeclared horsemeat. This food fraud happened in the upstream supply chain and was organized crime. Although horsemeat is not harmful to health, it is considered a taboo food in many countries. Public complaints were due to the fact that claims made on labels did not match the content of food products.	2013	Species substitution
Melamine milk	Dairy suppliers in the upstream supply chain used melamine[5] to inflate the protein level in order to cheat the test measuring nitrogen content. The tainted cans formed crystals that could cause kidney stones and kidney failure. The scandal triggered a large-scale product recall of dairy products, including chocolate.	2008	Ingredient adulteration
Dioxin pork	In order to reduce costs, animal feed manufacturers used electronic transformer oil instead of cooking oil to produce pork feed. The contaminated animal feeds were supplied to several farms across Ireland. As a result, a large number of products, including sausages, pizza and ready meals containing pork, were contaminated by dioxin and recalled from the market.	2008	Ingredient substitution
Phthalate-plasticizer drink	The plasticizer di-2-ethylhexyl phthalate (DEHP) was used by drinks manufacturers to replace palm oil as a clouding agent. This chemical agent can cause developmental problems in children as it affects hormones, and it can also lead to cancer.	2011	Ingredient substitution
Carcinogenic cola	4-methylimidazole (4-MEI), found in different types of caramel-coloured drinks, may cause cancer. The chemical can form as a trace impurity during the manufacturing of certain types of caramel colouring that are used to colour cola-type beverages and other foods.	2013	N/A
Flaming laptop	A massive product recall of laptop batteries occurred due to the risk of overheating and explosion. Apple, Dell, Toshiba and HP recalled the overheating batteries, which were purchased from Sony.	2006–2007	N/A

non-food supply chain quality risks. Table 13.2 shows the details of each case scenario and its classified type of quality risk.

Data and methods

Data collection

A merged contact list containing the contact information of 2405 target respondents in the UK was used in this research. A research assistant was employed to administer the collection of data. Initial emails were sent, followed by reminders after a week. Of the 2,405 entries on the mailing list, 1,140 had valid email addresses. After sending out 2,405 surveys, 315 responses were received. This represented a 13 per cent response rate, which was considered to be acceptable and consistent with other survey-based research. After removing inappropriate titles and deleting surveys with missing data, a total of 279 usable responses were analysed.

Data analysis

Risk perception matrix

The mean ratings on the risk dimensions for the six scenarios are shown in Table 13.3. The horsemeat scandal has the highest mean rating on the dimension of newness (mean = 4.57). Moreover, the respondents perceive the horsemeat scandal as the most involuntary (mean = 4.32), the most unknown (mean = 4.20) and the most delayed (mean = 4.25). This might be explained by the extensive media coverage of the horsemeat scandal and by the FSA continuing to announce the latest inspection results of the product.

In contrast, the flaming laptop scandal has the lowest mean rating in terms of immediacy (mean = 3.26). Among the food fraud cases, the melamine milk incident has the lowest mean rating in controllability (mean = 3.48). Thus, consumers perceive melamine milk as the most controllable risk among the scenarios. However, melamine milk is also rated as the most dreaded risk, while the second most dreaded risk is phthalate-plasticizer drink. Interestingly, both cases are related to food fraud in which 'plastic' was added to the products.

The intercorrelations among the mean ratings of the seven risk characteristics are shown in Table 13.4. Most of the risk perception dimensions are highly associated with one another. The exceptions are controllability and dread (r = –0.10); controllability and fatal (r = –0.04); controllability and newness (r = 0.05); and fatal and immediacy (r = 0.08). The result shows that controllability is the characteristic with the lowest correlation with other risk perceptions.

We conducted a principal component factor analysis using varimax rotation to explore the key risk factors underlying the seven risk characteristics. This is worthwhile due to the high intercorrelation of the seven dimensions. The factor loadings of the seven dimensions onto the three grouped factors are shown in Table 13.5. The accumulation of variance percentage is 68 per cent, which is an acceptable variance (>60%) in factor analysis. According to the literature, each risk factor is named by the dominant item in the factor. Therefore, we refer to Factor 1 as 'fatal risk', Factor 2 as 'newness risk' and Factor 3 as 'controllability risk' (Feng *et al.*, 2010; Slovic *et al.*, 1985). Furthermore, we employ the procedures proposed by Slovic *et al.*, (1985) to calculate the integrated factor scores for each risk perception dimension by identifying the weighting of scale proportion and then summing all across the scale. The integrated

Table 13.3 Mean rating for seven characteristics

	Controllability 1 = controlled	*Dread 1 = not dread*	*Fatal 1 = not fatal*	*Voluntariness 1 = voluntary*	*Knowledge by those exposed to risk 1 = precisely*	*Immediacy 1 = immediate*	*Newness 1 = old*
Horsemeat	3.681	4.272	3.878	4.315	4.201	4.254	4.570
Melamine milk	3.482	3.882	3.914	3.860	3.878	4.136	3.599
Dioxin pork	3.755	4.416	4.179	4.197	4.079	4.183	3.871
Phthalate-plasticizer drink	3.477	4.495	4.222	4.294	3.996	4.065	4.050
Carcinogenic cola	3.642	4.229	4.097	4.179	4.011	4.050	3.935
Flaming laptop	3.530	3.946	4.161	4.079	3.681	3.258	3.444

Table 13.4 Intercorrelations of the seven rating scales

Scale	*Controllability*	*Dread*	*Fatal*	*Voluntariness*	*Knowledge by those exposed*	*Immediacy*	*Newness*
		5	*3*	*6*	*6*	*5*	*5*
Controllability 1 = controlled	–	–0.102	–0.043	–0.130*	–0.213**	0.199**	–0.051
Dread 1 = not dread	–	–	0.547**	0.385**	0.310**	0.206**	0.180**
Fatal 1 = not fatal	–	–	–	0.495**	0.350**	0.076	0.164**
Voluntariness 1 = voluntary	–	–	–	–	0.210**	0.259**	0.121*
Knowledge by those exposed 1 = precisely	–	–	–	–	–	0.190**	0.420**
Immediacy 1 = immediate	–	–	–	–	–	–	0.208**
Newness 1 = old	–	–	–	–	–	–	–

*Remarks: *p < 0.05; **p < 0.01*

Table 13.5 Factor loadings across seven risk characteristics

Scale	*Controllability*	*Dread*	*Fatal*	*Voluntariness*	*Knowledge by those exposed*	*Immediacy*	*Newness*	*% of variance*
Factor 1 Fatal risk	0.124	0.766	0.834	0.779	0.293	0.210	0.016	34.965
Factor 2 Newness risk	0.241	0.182	0.112	0.053	0.767	0.336	0.849	17.298
Factor 3 Controllability risk	0.810	0.021	0.041	0.068	0.133	0.721	0.109	15.972
Communality	0.73	0.621	0.711	0.614	0.692	0.677	0.732	–

Remarks: Varimax rotation

Table 13.6 Integrated index of risk factors

	Factor 1: fatal risk	*Factor 2: newness risk*	*Factor 3: uncontrollable risk*
Horsemeat	4.14	4.28	4.02
Melamine milk	3.88	3.78	3.79
Dioxin pork	4.22	4.02	3.98
Phthalate-plasticizer drink	4.25	4.02	3.83
Carcinogenic cola	4.12	3.98	3.87
Flaming laptop	3.95	3.58	3.47

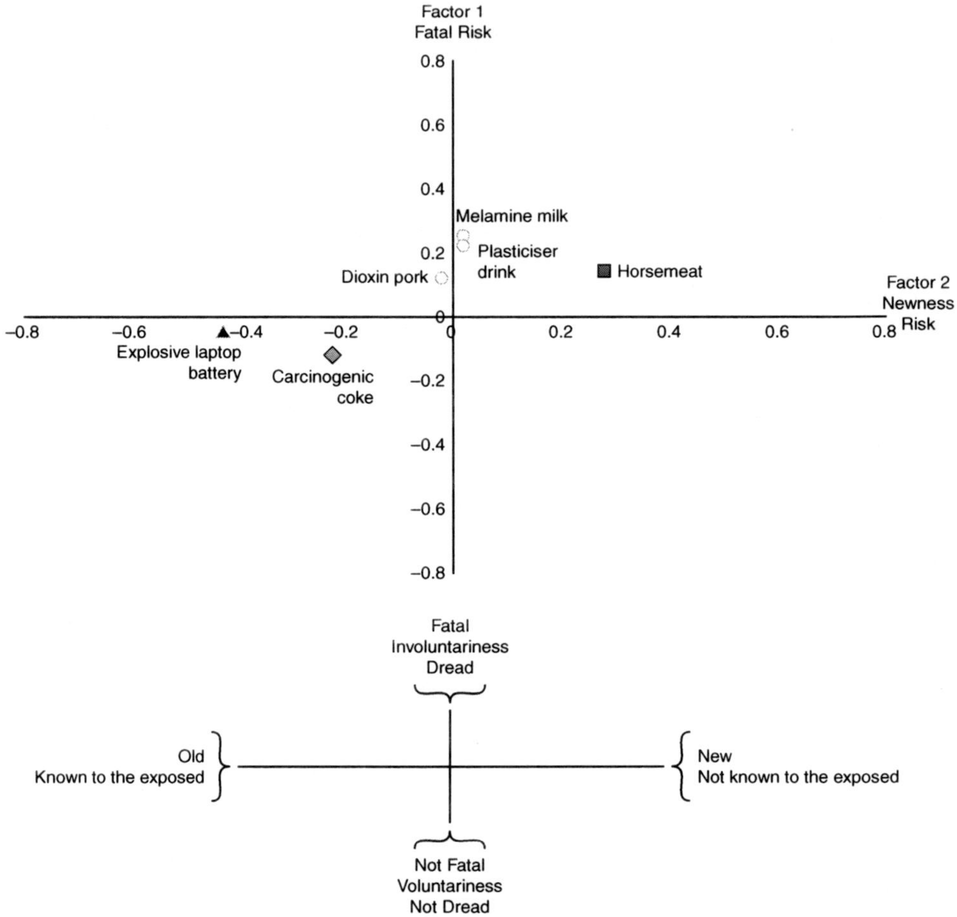

Figure 13.2 Fatal–newness risk perception map.

scores of the three risk factors are shown in Table 13.6. In addition, the risk factor scores are recoded from 1 to 7 scale into –3 to 3 scale in order to better illustrate the risk. We illustrate three risk perception maps to show the risk perception position in two factor dimensions: a fatal–newness risk perception map (Figure 13.2); a fatal–uncontrollable risk perception map (Figure 13.3); and a newness–uncontrollable risk perception map (Figure 13.4).

In Figure 13.2, we find that the phthalate-plasticizer drink, melamine milk and horsemeat incidents are in the upper-right quadrant. This indicates that respondents perceive these incidents as fatal risks, which can potentially have extremely severe consequences. The phthalate-plasticizer drink and melamine milk scandals occurred in the Asia-Pacific region and the United States respectively and are not well-known food fraud cases for UK consumers, which may explain why these two cases are located in a relatively neutral position on the scale of newness dimension. The horsemeat incident is viewed as a less fatal case than the phthalate-plasticizer drink and melamine milk cases. One possible explanation is that the horsemeat scandal was a kind of species adulteration, and horsemeat seems more likely to be safe to consume compared with the two cases in which 'plastics' were added to the food product. As shown in Figure 13.2, the Irish dioxin pork incident has a similar fatal level to the horsemeat

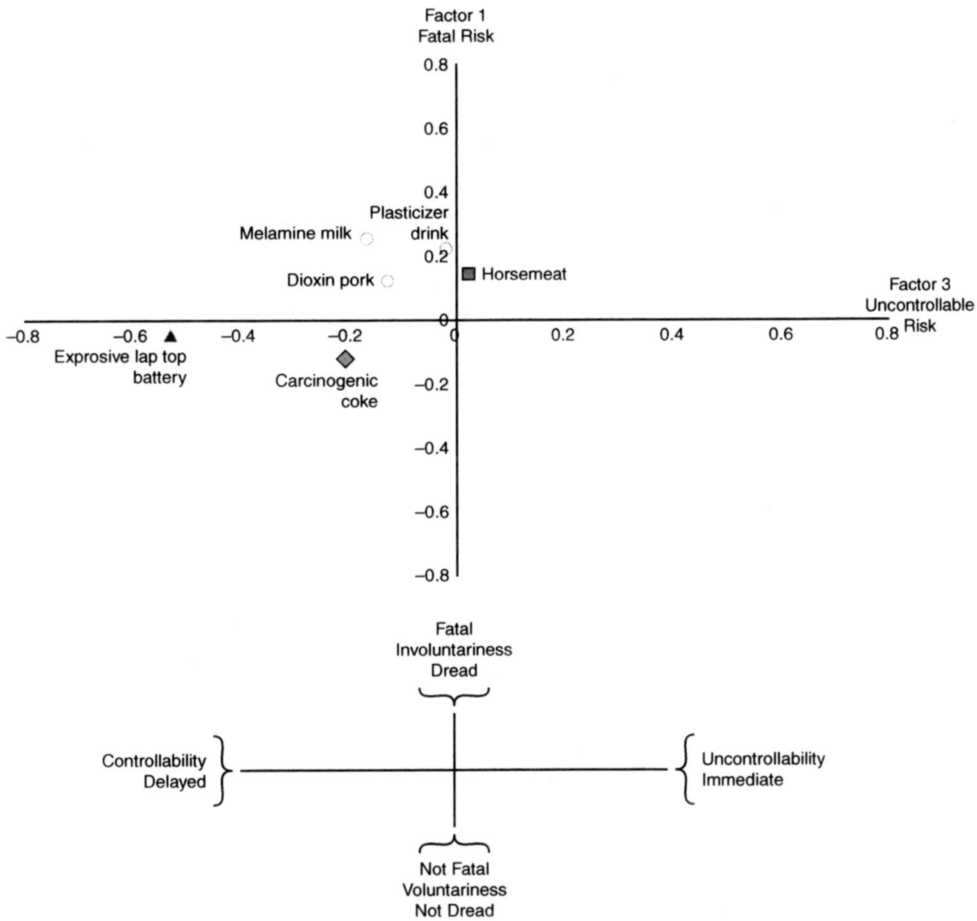

Figure 13.3 Fatal–uncontrollable risk perception map.

incident. This is an interesting finding since dioxin pork was another food risk, which happened at the bottom of the supply chain where pig feed was contaminated due to an ingredient substitution. It is quite surprising that the dioxin pork case has a similar fatal level to the horsemeat case, as dioxin is a well-known carcinogenic substance.

Figure 13.2 that horsemeat is the newest risk among all the cases. One possible explanation is that this is the first incident of adulteration in which horsemeat has been used in the processing of beef. Also, UK customers do not eat horsemeat, and it is viewed as taboo in British culture. Most importantly, consumers did not expect the food to contain ingredients that were not listed on the label. Mislabelling is a relatively new issue, and it seriously impacts on customer confidence. Additional questions in our survey provide further support for our argument. Answers to questions related to trust in food labelling and information sufficiency show a relatively low mean rating in the trust in labelling (mean rating = 3.03) and information sufficiency for safety justification (mean rating = 2.90).

In Figures 13.3 and 13.4, the horsemeat scandal is the only case located in the upper-right quadrant. This indicates that horsemeat is the most uncontrollable risk, but it is only slightly over the neutral point. It is also consistent with the findings of the additional question about

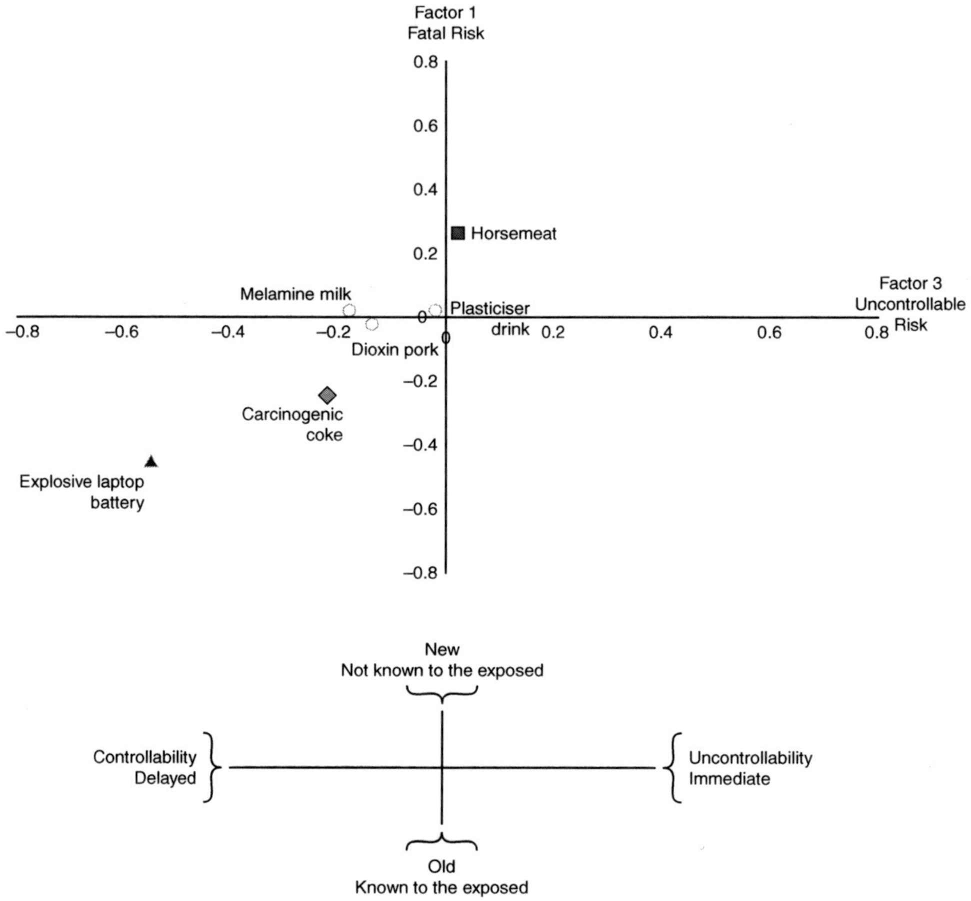

Figure 13.4 Newness–uncontrollable risk perception map.

supply chain food safety, where respondents show only slight concern regarding supply chain food safety issue (mean rating = 4.57). Compared with consumers, practitioners are less concerned about food safety, with an average value of 2.72. Practitioners tend to have more trust than consumers in the quality of food or their source material, with an average value of 3.93 on the question of trust in the product information (such as ingredients) provided by suppliers.

In addition, the carcinogenic cola incident is located in the lower left quadrant in all three risk perception maps. The carcinogenic cola incident is not judged as a supply chain quality risk since it is just a normal food safety incident caused by the manufacturer (Pepsi) and not a risk from a long supply chain. Surprisingly, respondents perceive the flaming laptop battery as a controllable and relatively old risk.

The issue of risks related to food products is an extremely sensitive one for the public. Managers in the food industry can represent the expert opinions in risk communication with the public. In order to compare the risk perception of consumers towards the food-related risk incidents, including the dioxin pork, melamine milk and horsemeat cases, with those of experts, we used the same measurement scale (seven dimensions of the psychometric paradigm) to test the data from managers of food industry. As shown in Table 13.7, the average level of consumer risk perception (mean = 4.167) is higher than the corresponding figure for

Table 13.7 Comparison in characteristics of risk perception in food-related risks

	Controllability 1 = controlled; 7 = uncontrollable	*Dread 1 = not dread; 7 = dread*	*Fatal 1 = not fatal; 7 = fatal*	*Voluntariness 1 = voluntary; 7 = involuntary*	*Knowledge by those exposed to risk 1 = know precisely 7 = unknown*	*Immediacy 1 = immediate; 7 = delay*	*Newness 1 = old; 7 = new*	*Overall average*
Consumers	3.681	4.272	3.878	4.315	4.201	4.254	4.57	4.167
Managers	3.366	4.444	3.811	4.146	3.933	3.348	4.034	3.869

Table 13.8 Respondents' potential actions in response to the recall of horsemeat products

Multiple choices	*Percentage*
You can choose more than one option. What would you do with any ready meals in your home that were suspected of containing horsemeat, when you heard that some meals had been contaminated? Check all that apply.	
• Talk with friends about their experience with the horsemeat issue	**68.1%**
• Read/listen to news coverage	**65.2%**
• Throw away all ready meals from this company	**49.1%**
• Check websites for more information	**33.7%**

managers (mean = 3.869). This might be because managers have more knowledge (i.e. they know more precisely about the risk) than the consumers, as indicated in the scores of 'knowledge by those exposed to risk'. Moreover, in comparison with consumers, managers perceive the food-related risks as an older and more controllable risk. Interestingly, in terms of the emotional factor, managers feel worse than consumers about the horsemeat scandal (i.e. they have a higher score in the dimension of dread).

Results on actions taken by consumers

Consumers' actions in response to the horsemeat scandal were also investigated. We have adopted Feng's (2010) product recall consumer response action list, and the result is shown in Table 13.8. The survey asked respondents to select as many responses as applicable from a list of actions they might have taken after hearing about the possible contamination of ready meals by horsemeat. The top three response actions were 'talk with friends about their experience with the horsemeat issue', 'read/listen to news coverage' and 'throw away all ready meals from this company'. The response action 'check websites for more information' received a rating of 33.7 per cent and is ranked fourth. This is an interesting finding, as Feng *et al.*'s (2010) research on similar product recall cases (tainted pet food and lead-painted toys) shows this to be the top-ranked action when consumers face a product recall.

In short, the result suggests that consumers prefer to discuss the horsemeat scandal with friends or seek official information from government and news media before taking any further actions. Half the respondents preferred to exercise caution by disposing of the suspected contaminated items. In addition, a few participants took alternative actions, such as 'eat it', and 'feed the dog'.

Results on actions taken by practitioners

In addition to those of consumers, the insights of managers are also critical. In risk communication of product quality problems, practitioners not only collect risk information from experts (such as government agencies), but also disseminate that information to the public. Like government agencies and research labs, it is important for practitioners to evaluate their risk information, for example by checking the suspected source materials and revisiting test reports. Generally, the response actions of practitioners are diverse. Based on the aim of each action, this study categories two main types: external consultancy and instant response of quality assurance.

The consulting actions are more interactive, involving not only seeking information but also communicating with experts to assess the risk. As reported in Table 13.9, half of the practitioners surveyed (50%) prefer to seek expert advice from government agencies such as the FSA and the Food and Environment Research Agency (FERA). These agencies, particularly the FSA, take a leadership role in food safety and food authenticity (Elliot, 2013, 2014). They have expert groups, such as the newly established Food Crime Unit, to undertake the investigation of food fraud or food crime.

The proportions of practitioners seeking expert advice from consulting firms and research labs are the same, at 31.73 per cent for each. Consulting firms can customize their services to suit the specific challenges their clients are facing; for example, in order to assist with tackling food fraud, they might provide food companies with reviews of manufacturing processes, quality systems and standards and help to develop protocols and procedures. Other than consulting firms, practitioners also seek help from scientific laboratories. Professional testing methods play an important role in identifying potential issues. Indeed, according to Elliot (2014), 'food fraud is often undetectable except by scientific analysis'. For instance, the horsemeat incident was first identified by the Food Safety Authority of Ireland (FSAI) through DNA testing.

After receiving news of food fraud, in addition to information-seeking, practitioners might also adopt some direct risk avoidance actions. In our survey (see Table 13.10), checking the suspected problematic supplier ranked top among managers' response actions (50%). Of practitioners, 30.77 per cent would identify the potential risks by revisiting previous quality and testing reports. In addition, more than a quarter of practitioners would reassess the

Table 13.9 Consulting

Consulting actions	*Percentage*
1. Seek expert advice from government agencies e.g. FSA, The Food and Environment Research Agency (FERA)	50.00%
2. Seek expert advice from consultants	31.73%
3. Seek expert advice from a research lab	31.73%

Table 13.10 Instant response of practitioners

Instant response actions	*Percentage*
1. Check whether the firm has sourced from a supplier suspected of having the same food fraud problem	50.00%
2. Revisit previous quality/testing reports	30.77%
3. Re-test the ingredient information of the source material as shown on the label	28.85%
4. Re-check the ingredient information of the finished goods as shown on the label	28.85%

ingredient information given on the labels of the source material (28.85%) and the finished goods (28.85%). In order to avoid potential risks, 26.92 per cent of practitioners would conduct extra tests (e.g. DNA tests) as a temporary measure to improve quality assurance.

Facing potential food fraud problems, practitioners tend to choose moderate actions (e.g. checking suppliers suspected of having the food fraud problem or revisiting previous quality reports), which might not be costly and do not affect stakeholders directly. They will adopt substantive actions only after they have ensured the accuracy of the risk information and identified the potential risk. This is because some response actions (e.g. holding back a shipment to customers or employing third-party inspections) might themselves be harmful to a company's reputation and consumer trust.

Managerial implications and recommendations

As an important contribution, we offer a practical set of actions that practitioners could begin to adapt and apply within the UK market in response to food fraud incidents such as the horsemeat scandal. According to risk information seeking and processing (RISP) theory, identifying the valuable source of risk information is useful to guide people to seek help in managing risks (Hovick *et al.*, 2011). Our findings show that information disseminated by governments is most helpful to managers. For instance, more than half of practitioners would consult the FSA after hearing news of a horsemeat scandal. We also identify what quality assurance actions would be adopted by practitioners during a food fraud incident. The results show that 'checking the suspected supply materials' is the top quality-assurance action adopted by managers.

The challenges of managing food fraud

The issue of inefficient food safety standards is discussed in the most recent report by Elliot (2014), where he suggests the establishment of a 'food crime unit' to focus on the issues of food fraud and food crime in the UK market. From an industry perspective, we suggest that practitioners should be proactive rather than reactive in managing the risks of food fraud. Redesigning the supply chain strategy might point the way to reducing risk.

The food supply chain is currently too complex to ensure food authenticity. The horsemeat incident has revealed that a food supply chain can involve more than six companies in five countries. A complex supply chain can impede traceability and visibility. Getting close to suppliers and building long-term relationships with them would contribute to preventing food fraud. Shortening the food chain can clarify the supply network, thus improving traceability and visibility. Furthermore, stable partnerships can enhance trust among supply chain members.

The vertical integration business model is well known in the food industry and has been adopted by some leading retailers, such as Morrison and Waitrose. For example, Morrison has acquired many of its upstream suppliers, such as farms and food processing companies. As stated by one of our respondents, 'the vertical integration helped us during the crisis; it gave us confidence, although we still had to demonstrate its efficacy through testing'. Vertical cooperation and integration should be part of the toolbox to improve visibility and trust in the food supply chain (Theuvsen, 2004; Bowman *et al.*, 2013). Food chain integration can come with formal or informal guidelines on procedures, thus standardizing the behaviour of business partners and enforcing obligatory and voluntary communication. In addition, food chain integration has positive effects on organizational barriers because it reduces the requirement for process interdependencies in supply chains (Frentrup and Theuvsen, 2006).

Prioritize the needs of consumers and enhance communication

One food fraud case could badly damage the reputation of a company and could even destroy public trust in the food industry. Practitioners should prioritize customer needs, which means putting food safety and food crime prevention before all other objectives (Elliot, 2014). The first step for practitioners is to provide sufficient information on the label, supported by a tracing system. For example, on pre-packed beef packaging, manufacturers should be required to provide the following traceability information: slaughterhouse license number, cutting plant license number, and 'origin place' confirming where the animal was born, reared and slaughtered. Ensuring a friendly communication channel with consumers is also important. Efficient risk communication should be a two-way process (START, 2012). Our findings show that the top response action of consumers facing the horsemeat scandal was to talk with friends about their experience. Therefore, we encourage practitioners to consider approaches to disseminating relevant information about food fraud to the community, for example through social media (such as Facebook groups or Twitter feeds). In that way, consumers could transfer accurate knowledge about the food fraud incident, such as product use, disposal and repurchase decisions, during discussion with friends.

Proactive communication with the government

Information and support from government has always been at the top of practitioners' checklist when facing food fraud issues. In order to identify the potential issues, an incentive mechanism should be established to encourage knowledge exchange among business partners within the supply chain. Importantly, the government—in particular, the FSA—should be responsible not only for disseminating the information but also for gathering the information. However, the information channel between the government and practitioners is not efficient. Our research reveals that practitioners believe information or knowledge travels in only one direction, from the FSA to practitioners (3.59 average value on a 1–5 Likert scale). There is no doubt that practitioners expect more government support for securing food integrity.

From the perspective of government, Elliot's (2014) suggestion to establish an 'FSA intelligence hub' is timely. This intelligence hub could take the lead in the collection, analysis and distribution of information and intelligence from a wide range of sources (such as local authorities, police, EU counterparts and industry). This report suggests that practitioners should also have a central role to play in offering intelligence to the government on the managing or identification of food fraud. The risk information should be transferred proactively, rather than passively, from government to the industry.

A comprehensive action plan

In the battle with food fraud, practitioners are on the front line. In order to protect and ensure food integrity, they should make an immediate, sustained shift from a defensive to a proactive stance in their leadership on this crucial issue. The recommendations set out above should not be adopted in isolation. Practitioners should develop a comprehensive plan that goes beyond their organizations to include all supply chain members, government and consumers (see Figure 13.5).

Conclusion

In this research, we have analysed the nature of quality risk in the supply chain. This research can potentially help practitioners and policymakers to gain a better understanding of the

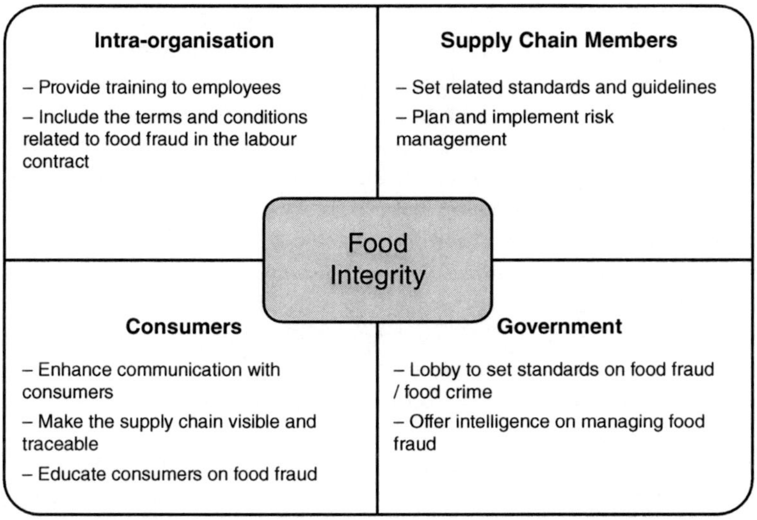

Figure 13.5 Calls to action.

difference between consumers' and managers' perceptions of quality risk in the food supply chain. We collected data from 279 UK consumers and 140 food industry practitioners to explore their risk perceptions and decision-making regarding the horsemeat scandal. The analysis of various scenarios in the psychometric model shows how consumers perceive the differences and similarities between the horsemeat scandal and other supply chain quality risk incidents, such as the melamine milk, dioxin pork and phthalate-plasticizer drink cases. In the analysis, we find that consumers perceive the horsemeat scandal as a newer and more uncontrollable risk than other food supply chain quality risk incidents. They also perceive the horsemeat incident as a fatal risk, even though horsemeat is less dangerous than dioxin pork. Following the psychometric paradigm, we adopt a seven-dimensions toolkit to investigate how managers perceive the risk posed by the horsemeat scandal. Like consumers, managers in the food industry also perceive the horsemeat incident as connected to dread, involuntary risk and highly new risk.

Our study also shows that compared with practitioners, consumers perceive higher risk with regard to food-related risks. This might be explained by the fact that consumers might underestimate the complicated process behind a food product; they have no idea of the complexity of the food chain. Once a food quality scandal is exposed, consumers might overestimate quality risk due to a shortage of knowledge. In addition, the impact of media reports on consumer attitudes toward the food industry is critical. With the rapid growth of social media, information transfers faster than ever before. For future research, exploring risk communication about food quality and safety between food companies and consumers on social media might show how to identify more resilience strategies for food industry.

We analysed the possible consumer response actions by adopting the product recall response action list proposed by Feng *et al.*, (2010). We find that 'talk with friends about their experience with the horsemeat issue' is the option people were most likely to choose when they heard about the scandal. Therefore, policymakers should consider approaches to disseminate relevant information about a food fraud to the local community. In that way, consumers could transfer accurate knowledge about the food fraud incident, such as product use, disposal and repurchase decisions, during the discussion with friends. We find that 'read/listen to news coverage' is the second top response action related to the horsemeat incident. This implies that consumers prefer to seek food fraud information via traditional media, such as newspapers, television and radio. We also investigated how managers respond to the horsemeat scandal via information-seeking, external consultancy and instant quality assurance. Based on the response actions of practitioners, we have suggested a set of managerial recommendations to the industry.

This study provides a detailed representation of the situation regarding UK food fraud, potentially contributing to the debate among policymakers and practitioners with particular regard to the theme of firms' resilience after a food fraud incident has occurred. Moreover, our research contributes to the area of risk communication (Tierney *et al.*, 2001). It includes investigation and examination of the public response to a potential hazard, activities related to the key stages of Mileti and Fitzpatrick's (1992) perception and response model. Thus, the findings gathered from this study represent a useful instrument for policymakers and practitioners to evaluate policies and provide a risk management strategy that sustains both firms' competitiveness and food industry resilience.

Future research could extend the current context to a different country. For instance, it may be valuable to compare consumers' food risk perceptions in developed countries and developing countries. Moreover, using Slovic's *et al.*'s (1985) risk matrix method, follow-on work could include more recent case scenarios to compare with the existing cases in our study. Due to a limited sample size, this survey research might not provide the whole picture of consumer perceptions towards food fraud scandals. Therefore, research that adopts a larger data source, such as social big data (data from social media platforms), could help to give a more comprehensive view of consumers' risk perception.

Acknowledgment

This research was supported by the Seed Corn Research Fund – CILT(UK) 2013/2014.

Notes

1 According to the FSA (2013, p. 11) testing report, on 1 March 2013 only 44 out of 5,430 products tested positive for horsemeat. A level of 1 per cent (DNA or meat) is the pragmatic level to distinguish between gross contamination and adulteration.
2 Food manufacturers were blamed by 39 per cent, and 9 per cent blamed companies delivering from manufacturer to retailer.
3 Europol is the European Union's law enforcement agency.
4 Interpol is the International Criminal Police Organization.
5 Melamine is a chemical compound used mainly in producing durable plastic, insulation and soundproofing materials.

References

BBC (2013), 'Horsemeat Scandal to be Reviewed, Government Announces'. 15 April. http://www.bbc.co.uk/news/uk-22149690. [Accessed 14/10/2015].

Berman, B. and K. Swani (2010), 'Managing Product Safety of Imported Chinese Goods', *Business Horizons*, 53, pp. 39–48.

Bogdanich, W. (2015), 'Toxic Toothpaste Made in China Is Found in U.S.', *Nytimes.com*. 2 June. Retrieved 7 February 2015, from http://www.nytimes.com/2007/06/02/us/02toothpaste.html

Bowman, A., J. Froud, S. Johal, A. Leaver and K. Williams (2013), 'Opportunist Dealing in the UK Pig Meat Supply Chain: Trader Mentalities and Alternatives', *Accounting Forum*, 37, pp. 300–314.

Christopher, M. and H. Peck (2004), 'Building the Resilient Supply Chain', *International Journal of Logistics Management*, 15, pp. 1–14.

Elliot, C. (2013), *Elliott Review into the Integrity and Assurance of Food Supply Networks: Interim Report*.

Elliot, C. (2014), *Elliott Review into the Integrity and Assurance of Food Supply Networks: Final Report*, Department for Environment, Food and Rural Affairs, UK Government.

Feng, T.J., L.R. Keller, L.Y. Wang and Y.T. Wang (2010), 'Product Quality Risk Perceptions and Decisions: Contaminated Pet Food and Lead-Painted Toys', *Risk Analysis*, 30, pp. 1572–1589.

Fischhoff et al. (1975), Hindsight is not equal to foresight: The effect of outcome knowledge on judgment under uncertainty. Journal of Experimental Psychology: Human perception and performance, 1(3), p. 288.

Frentrup, M. and L. Theuvsen (2006), 'Transparency in Supply Chains: Is Trust a Limiting Factor', No 7733, 99th Seminar, February 8-10, Bonn, Germany, European Association of Agricultural Economists, http://EconPapers.repec.org/RePEc:ags:eaae99:7733. Retrieved 13 March 2015.

FSA (2013). Report of the Investigation by the Food Standards Agency into Incidents of Adulteration of Comminuted Beef Products with Horse Meat and DNA. [online] Food Standards Agency, p. 11. Available at: https://www.food.gov.uk/sites/default/files/multimedia/pdfs/board/board-papers-2013/fsa-130704-fsa-investigation-report.pdf [Accessed 17 Nov. 2014].

Hovick, S., V.S. Freimuth, A. Johnson-Turbes and D.D. Chervin (2011), 'Multiple Health Risk Perception and Information Processing among African Americans and Whites Living in Poverty'. *Risk Analysis*, 31(11), pp. 1789–1799.

Lindgreen, A. and M. Hingley, M. (2003), 'The Impact of Food Safety and Animal Welfare Policies on Supply Chain Management,' *British Food Journal*, 105, pp. 328–349.

MAFF (1999), *Working Together for the Food Chain: Views from the Food Chain Group*, London: MAFF.

Marucheck, A., N. Greis, C. Mena and L.N. Cai (2011), 'Product Safety and Security in the Global Supply Chain: Issues, Challenges and Research Opportunities', *Journal of Operations Management*, 29, pp. 707–720.

Mcdaniels, T., L.J. Axelrod and P. Slovic (1995), 'Characterizing Perception of Ecological Risk', *Risk Analysis*, 15, pp. 575–588.

Mileti, D.S. and C. Fitzpatrick (1992), 'The Causal Sequence of Risk Communication in the Parkfield Earthquake Prediction Experiment', *Risk Analysis*, 12, pp. 393–400.

Roth, A.V., A.A. Tsay, M.E. Pullman and J.V. Gray (2008), 'Unraveling the Food Supply Chain: Strategic Insights from China and the 2007 Recalls', *Journal of Supply Chain Management*, 44, pp. 22–39.

Safefood (2008), 'A Review of the Beef Food Chain'. February. Cork, Ireland: Safefood.

Savadori, L., S. Savio, E. Nicotra, R. Rumiati, M. Finucane and P. Slovic (2004), 'Expert and Public Perception of Risk from Biotechnology', *Risk Analysis*, 24, pp. 1289–1299.

Slovic, P., B. Fischhoff and S. Lichtenstein (1985), 'Characterizing Perceived Risk', in R. Kates, C. Hohenemser and J. Kasperson (eds.), *Perilous Progress: Managing the Hazards of Technology*, Boulder, CO: Westview Press.

START (2012), *Understanding Risk Communication Theory: A Guide for Emergency Managers and Communicators. Report to Human Factors/Behavioral Sciences Division, Science and Technology Directorate*, U.S. Department of Homeland Security. College Park, MD.

Theuvsen, L. (2004), 'Transparency in Netchains as an Organizational Phenomenon: Exploring the Role of Interdependencies', *Journal on Chain and Network Science*, 4, pp. 125–138.

Tierney, K., M.K. Lindell and R.W. Perry (2001), *Facing the Unexpected: Disaster Preparedness and Response in the United States*, Washington: Joseph Henry Press.

Trienekens, J. and P. Zuurbieri (2008), 'Quality and Safety Standards in the Food Industry: Developments and Challenges', *International Journal of Production Economics*, 113, pp. 107–122.

Tse, Y.K., K.H. Tan, S.H. Chung and M.K. Lim (2011), 'Quality Risk in Global Supply Network', *Journal of Manufacturing Technology Management*, 22, pp. 1002–1013.

Van Heerde, H., K. Helsen and M.G. Dekimpe (2007), 'The Impact of a Product-Harm Crisis on Marketing Effectiveness', *Marketing Science*, 26, pp. 230–245.

Yang, Z.B., G. Aydin, V. Babich and D.R. Beil (2009), 'Supply Disruptions, Asymmetric Information, and a Backup Production Option', *Management Science*, 55, pp. 192–209.

14

Case study: Institutional work and embedded agency

The institutionalization of enterprise risk management in a large, global oil and gas company

Anita Meidell and Katarina Kaarbøe

Introduction

Enterprise-wide risk management (ERM) has lately become part of organizational practices, and it has been seen as one of the major changes in organizations in the past decade (Arena *et al.*, 2010; Hayne and Free, 2014; Mikes, 2009; Power, 2007; Spira and Page, 2003). At the macro level, risk management practices have been embraced by organizations around the globe and nourished by worldwide government regulations aimed at making corporate governance, internal control and risk management more effective—for example, Sarbanes-Oxley (SOX) regulation; corporate governance codes; the Basel banking accords; the ERM framework of the Committee of Sponsoring Organizations of the Treadway Commission (COSO); and the International Organization for Standardization's ISO 31000:2009. However, the fluidity of ERM and the extent to which it is coupled to organizational processes tend to be overlooked (Arena *et al.*, 2010), opening up the question of how ERM practices become institutionalized in organizations.

ERM can be different things in different organizations, or even in the same organization over time (Arena *et al.*, 2010). Previous case studies on ERM practices within organizations have mostly focused on describing the institutionalized ERM practice at a certain point in time (Arena *et al.*, 2010; Caldarelli *et al.*, 2016; Mikes, 2009; Palermo, 2014; Tekathen and Dechow, 2013; Woods, 2009). Only a few case studies (Giovannoni *et al.*, 2016; Hall *et al.*, 2015; Mikes, 2011; Vinnari and Skærbæk, 2014) have explored how new ERM practices—in which actors compete to make their frame of ERM resonate at a collective level—emerge over time.

Previous management accounting studies on changes in ERM practices have focused on the changing role a risk management function has over time (Giovannoni *et al.*, 2016); how toolmaking can lead to differences in influence (Hall *et al.*, 2015); the boundary work of risk experts (Mikes, 2011); and how the internal auditor changes framing efforts over time (Vinnari and Skærbæk, 2014). Our theoretical argument differs from existing theories of how ERM practices have been institutionalized because we are interested in understanding the process of creating a collective action frame of ERM within an organization, which we argue will influence the institutionalization of ERM practices.

Prior research acknowledges that multiple actors are involved in the process of institutionalizing ERM within organizations (Arena *et al.,* 2010; Giovannoni *et al.,* 2016; Hall *et al.,* 2015; Mikes, 2009, 2011; Vinnari and Skærbæk, 2014; Woods, 2011). However, the embeddedness of actors in existing institutions and their framing of ERM has received less focus, and we have only limited knowledge about how actors frame ERM and how differences in the framing of ERM influence how ERM practices become institutionalized in organizations.

However, there are some descriptions about actors' background, experience and framing of ERM that can give some guidance on different interpretations of ERM within organizations. Some actors that have been pictured as being embedded in the norms of auditing tend to draw on the COSO ERM framework when framing ERM (Arena *et al.,* 2010; Vinnari and Skærbæk, 2014), while others frame ERM as an integrated part of the budgeting process (Arena *et al.,* 2010). In banks, actors have been described as embedded either in quantitative norms or in the norms of banking business, and risk management has been framed as either a quantitative practice or a more holistic practice (Mikes, 2009, 2011). However, in order to understand how ERM practices become institutionalized differently in organizations, we need further knowledge about the actors involved in the institutionalization process.

Previous research accounts of political struggles have mostly described the political outcome and not the actual political work that took place (e.g. Arena *et al.,* 2010; Giovannoni *et al.,* 2016; Hall *et al.,* 2015; Mikes, 2009, 2011). The focus on outcome also applies to technical work, but previous research mostly describes what ERM technologies (i.e. complex sets of practices, procedures and tools) have been developed (e.g. Arena *et al.,* 2010; Giovannoni *et al.,* 2016; Hall *et al.,* 2015; Mikes, 2009, 2011) without scrutinizing their development over time and how technical work has influenced the institutionalization of ERM practices. Our analysis differs and will demonstrate the critical role time plays as well as how institutional work changes over time and thus constructs and reconstructs the existing practice.

The aim of this chapter is to explore how different actors conceptually interpret ERM along with the actions actors take to create a collective action frame of new ERM practices in an organization. We want to show that understanding individuals as institutionally embedded actors enables a more critical understanding of how actors frame ERM, and how different framing of ERM influences the development of ERM practices.

The theoretical lens through which these developments are examined is institutional work. Institutional work has been defined as 'the purposive action of individuals and organizations aimed at creating, maintaining and disrupting institutions' (Lawrence and Suddaby, 2006, p. 215). In our study, the focus is directed more towards the creation of institutions, as we seek to explore how collective action frames of new ERM practices are created.

There are three defining characteristics of institutional work, which will be addressed in our study: first, institutional actors as reflexive; second, different forms of institutional work; and third, actors as institutionally embedded in extant institutions (Lawrence and Suddaby, 2006; Lawrence *et al.,* 2013). Institutional work theory helps us to increase our understanding of how institutional levels influence the actions actors take and, at the same time, what types of actions actors use to create collective actions to form new institutions.

The institutional level is emphasized in our identification of how actors are embedded differently depending on education and experience. We consider the actor level by focusing on how actors frame ERM (Benford and Snow, 2000). In order to understand institutional work, we follow Perkmann and Spicer's (2008) typology of political, technical and cultural work to enhance our understanding of how key actors strive to establish and maintain ERM practices in organizations.

With the above as a background, we pose the following research question: how do actors create collective action frames to form institutionalized practices of ERM? To answer our overall research question, we need to address the following questions. First, who are the main actors and how are they institutionally embedded? Second, how do actors frame ERM? Third, how do different kinds of institutional work lead to collective actions and the formation of institutionalized practices?

The context for analyzing the institutionalization of ERM practices at the organizational level is a company within the oil and gas industry, which operates in a high-risk environment. In the Norwegian oil and gas company Statoil, risk management is high on the agenda, and the journey toward creating a well-functioning ERM system began 19 years ago. The company's rationale for ERM practice has not only been to avoid risks but also to dare to take risks to increase performance. However, the development of new ERM practices has not been without struggles, as several actors have had different interpretations on what risk management is and should be in the company.

In our study, we have three main findings. First, we find that multiple actors are involved in the process of creating new ERM practices in the organization and that actors are embedded in different norms of risk management. Second, we find that actors have different ways of framing ERM, which are influenced by the actors' embeddedness. Third, different framing of ERM can lead to struggles over the collective framing of ERM, where actors mobilize political, technical and cultural work to create a collective action frame of ERM in three different arenas: the academic, political and border guard arenas. With this study, we contribute to the literature (Giovannoni *et al.*, 2016; Hall *et al.*, 2015; Mikes, 2011; Vinnari and Skærbæk, 2014) by using a case study of how ERM practices developed over time in a private sector other than the banking sector.

The remainder of the paper is structured as follows. The next section presents the theoretical framework. After outlining our research method, the paper provides an empirical analysis of how the collective action frame of ERM practices was created in the case company. In the subsequent discussion and conclusion, we answer the research questions, and we conclude with implications of our findings, contributions and directions for further research.

Theoretical framework

Institutional theory has become a dominant theory for understanding organizations (Greenwood *et al.*, 2008). Early neo-institutional studies emphasized ways that institutions constrained organizational structures and activities, thereby explaining the convergence of organizational practices within institutional environments (Meyer and Rowan, 1977; DiMaggio and Powell, 1983; Tolbert and Zucker, 1983). This perspective assumed that individuals and organizations tend to comply, at least in appearance, with institutional pressures, and actors were often assumed to have a limited degree of agency (Battilana and D'Aunno, 2009). Several researchers criticized neo-institutional theory for not including agency in the explanation of organizational behaviour and introduced the concept of 'institutional entrepreneurs' engaged in creating or transforming institutions (DiMaggio, 1988; Leca *et al.*, 2008). However, this research has in turn been criticized for a 'heroic' image of the entrepreneurial actor who changes institutions and for ignoring the notion of the actor as embedded in an institutionally defined context (Lawrence, Suddaby and Leca, 2009).

The institutional work approach (Lawrence and Suddaby, 2006) offers a counterpoint to previous institutional studies with the aim of a balance between agency and institutions, highlighting three main aspects: 'It depicts institutional actors as reflexive, goal-oriented and capable, it focuses on actors' actions as the center of institutional dynamics, and it strives to capture the embedded agent by focusing on how the interrelations between structure and agent works' (Lawrence *et al.,* 2013, p. 1024). The institutional work approach focuses on what actors do rather than on the outcome of institutionalization efforts (Lawrence and Suddaby, 2006).

In the centre of all institutional approaches is the concept of institutions (Greenwood *et al.,* 2008). In this study, we use Lawrence and Suddaby's (2006, p. 216) understanding of institutions as those 'enduring elements of social life ... that have a profound effect on the thoughts, feelings and behavior of individual and collective actors'. Institutions exist across many levels, from micro-level institutions in groups and organizations to field-level institutions (Lawrence and Suddaby, 2006). Most institutional studies have focused on how the field level or organizational level enables conditions for institutional change and have neglected the individual as a level of analysis (Battilana and D'Aunno, 2009; Suddaby, 2010). What is lacking is an understanding of how institutional meaning systems are created within organizations influenced by broader social systems (Suddaby, 2010) and how institutions are developed under the influence of individual agents (Battilana and D'Aunno, 2009; Suddaby, 2010).

Institutional work (Lawrence and Suddaby, 2006; Lawrence *et al.,* 2009, 2011, 2013) constitutes a useful analytical lens since it addresses the interactions between actors with different interests in institutionalising new practices, recognizing that these interactions are conditioned by extant institutional structures. Rather than viewing institutional change as having a definite end point, institutional work conceives of institutionalization as an ongoing process in which individuals and collective actors purposefully attempt to create, maintain or disrupt institutions (Lawrence and Suddaby, 2006; Lawrence *et al.,* 2009).

To a large extent, previous research using institutional work has concentrated on how 'different categories of work, or agency, may influence the institutionalization of novel practices whilst paying little systematic attention to how such processes are conditioned by extant institutional structures' (Modell 2015, p. 780). The lack of attention to embedded agency in empirical research on institutional work is problematic, as it overemphasizes the possibility of agency (Chiwamitt *et al.,* 2014; Khagan and Lounsbury, 2011; Modell, 2015) and neglects the purpose of institutional work to balance structure and agency (Lawrence and Suddaby, 2006). Our theoretical approach aims at bridging this gap in the literature, including both actors' embeddedness and reflexivity in the analysis by mobilizing the concept of framing.

The first defining characteristic of institutional work is actors' embeddedness, as 'even action which is aimed at changing the institutional order of an organizational field occurs within sets of institutional rules' (Lawrence and Suddaby, 2006, p. 220). The institutional work approach sees actors engaging in institutional work as influenced by existing institutions but not deterministically conditioned by them, since actors still have the free will to choose their behaviour (Lawrence and Suddaby, 2006). Empirically, actors' embeddedness can be difficult to observe, and our study will use proxies for an individual's former experience such as education, career history and functional membership.

The second defining characteristic of the institutional work approach is actors' reflective purposefulness (Lawrence and Suddaby, 2006; Lawrence *et al.,* 2009). The institutional work approach does not provide a definition of actors' reflexivity, but reflexivity has been associated with 'level of cognitive effort' and 'self-controlled form of thought' (Lawrence *et al.,* 2009, p. 15). As reflective purposefulness is a cognitive thought process within individuals, it is difficult to observe empirically and define conceptually (Lawrence *et al.,* 2013; Zilber, 2013).

To empirically overcome the challenge of studying actors' reflexivity and to relate reflexivity to embeddedness, this study will draw on the concept of framing. Benford and Snow (2000,

p. 614) conceptualized framing as an active process of 'meaning construction' in which the outcome of the activity is referred to as 'collective action frames'. In a diversified world in which actors cognitively interpret new institutions differently, actors can battle over meaning and challenge each other's framing to generate a collective framework (Benford and Snow, 2000; Kaplan, 2008).

Core framing tasks have been referred to as 'diagnostic framing' (problem identification and attributions), 'prognostic framing' (solutions) and 'motivational framing' (Benford and Snow, 2000, p. 615). The idea of framing contests elucidates 'how actors attempt to transform their own cognitive frames into the organization's predominant collective frames through their daily interactions' (Kaplan, 2008, p. 730). Snow *et al.* (1986) directed attention to how processes of frame alignment could gradually lead to broader enacted beliefs and meanings, or collective action frames, which could be translated into social action. While framing has traditionally been used to study broader social phenomena, it has been suggested that framing can be useful for studying the 'complex interplay between emerging and extant frames within organizations' (Yang and Modell, 2015), which is what we do in this chapter.

The framing process is conceptualized as an institutionally embedded phenomenon, as 'framing processes are affected by a number of elements of the socio-cultural context in which they are embedded' (Benford and Snow, 2000, p. 628). In this paper, actors' embeddedness and the outcome of the actors' reflective process is reflected in actors' framing of ERM. The actors' embeddedness does not predetermine a framing of ERM but may suggest tendencies towards a preferred framing of ERM.

The third defining characteristic of institutional work is actors' actions (Lawrence and Suddaby, 2006). From Lawrence and Suddaby's (2006) initial classification of the different types of work involved in creating, maintaining and disrupting institutions, Perkmann and Spicer (2008) have gone one step further in distinguishing between political, technical and cultural work.

Political work involves 'generating social support for a practice by recruiting relevant actors into coalitions and networks and establishing rules and regulations' (Perkmann and Spicer, 2008, p. 825). Political work often includes actors' mobilization for a certain frame (Kaplan, 2008), counter-framing activities when frames are divergent (Kaplan, 2008), or political negotiations between actors to establish a social basis for a collective framework (Chiwamit *et al.*, 2014). Political work also includes defining boundaries to show status within a hierarchical structure or other memberships of a social system (Lawrence and Suddaby, 2006). While political work provides the social basis for a collective frame, *technical work* provides the design for translating the frames into practice. Technical work involves developing theoretical models that can be codified into 'templates, procedures, manuals or tools' (Perkmann and Spicer, 2008, p. 827). Finally, *cultural work* is the more symbolic action of framing practices to make them appeal to broader audiences beyond those with an immediate interest in an institution. Cultural work often entails mobilization of normative discourses and rhetoric, tailored to the institutional context in which it is introduced.

Perkmann and Spicer (2008) suggested that a practice is more likely to achieve coordinated, collective action and institutionalization when all these types of institutional work are combined; when institutional work draws on skills from multiple actors; and when institutional work is carried out over time in a cumulative manner.

Figure 14.1 summarizes the theoretical framework for this study. The study focuses first on understanding the actors, their embeddedness in extant institutions and how they frame ERM. Second, the focus is directed towards actors' actions in creating a collective action frame and forming institutionalized practices.

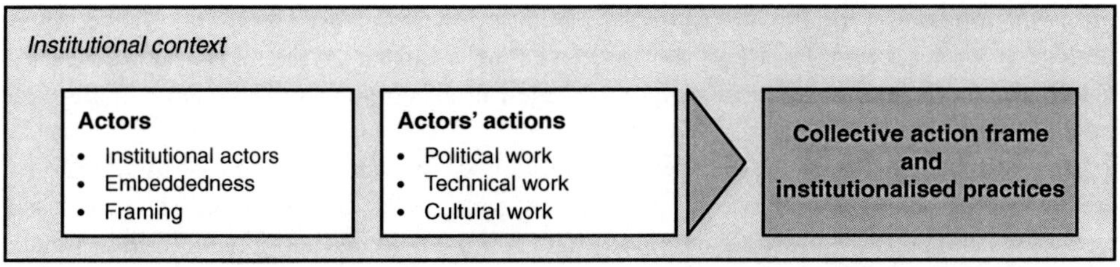

Figure 14.1 Theoretical framework.

Research methods

Our study builds upon an explanatory case study conducted in a single organization (Scapens, 1990; Yin, 1994). We adopt an understanding of field study research in which the main task of researchers is to inquire into a domain of practice and make sense of their observations by moving back and forth between empirical data and theory—an approach that is often called abduction (Ahrens and Chapman, 2006; Lukka and Modell, 2010). This requires closeness to the field site achieved through several visits that involve direct observations of actual ERM practices; interviews and informal conversations with members of the organization; and a study of secondary data.

The case company is Statoil, a Norwegian oil and gas company. The company has business operations in 30 countries, with more than 22,500 employees worldwide. During the case period, total revenue increased from NOK$107 billion in 1996 to NOK$623 billion in 2014. The corporate headquarters is located in Stavanger, Western Norway. In 2001, the company was listed on the stock exchanges in Oslo and New York.

We chose Statoil as a case study for two reasons. First, the organization is known for having a long history of developing ERM practices. Second, since we needed detailed information on how ERM practices developed over time, the study required both good access to personnel involved in the process and access to historical documentation. Statoil was open and accommodating in helping to set up interviews with the people to whom we needed to speak. In addition, one researcher was provided with office space and computer access that allowed her to participate in informal discussions. Furthermore, the company provided us with documentation of its historical development. This provided the opportunity to examine retrospectively the origins of risk-related activities and to investigate external pressure on ERM dimensions.

Data was collected through different methods from April 2013 to October 2015. First, we conducted 40 open-ended interviews with 33 different individuals. All interviews but one were recorded and transcribed. Second, we observed internal meetings where risk management was on the agenda (see the appendix for a full list of interviews and meetings). Third, we reviewed the company's internal documents—such as risk reports; risk project documentation; historical descriptions and presentations of risk management practice; and minutes from risk committee meetings—and finally, we reviewed public documents such as annual reports from the last 19 years. Field notes were written throughout the whole period of these field studies.

The historical data presented in this study is based on interviews over a much shorter time frame than the period of 19 years that we analyzed. This means that the informants refer to the past when they discuss the development of ERM practices. When interviewees talk about the past, their memory may be lacking or they may remember incorrectly. We have solved this by comparing memories with secondary data as well as by asking several people about the same event and comparing the descriptions. In addition, we have used temporal bracketing as a strategy to work around the risk of retrospective bias, focusing on the significant difference between events in time at the cost of more detailed understanding of the events (Yang and Modell, 2015).

Data collected in the field study was continuously analyzed through open-ended and thematic coding, using an abductive approach of going back and forth between empirical observations and possible theoretical explanations based on extant theory (Lukka and Modell, 2010). In the analytical process, the researcher with the most profound understanding of the context-specific meanings provided the analysis with an emic interpretation, while the other researcher took the role of a theoretically informed outsider providing a more etic perspective (Lukka and Modell, 2010; Yang and Modell, 2015).

All data material was read thoroughly by the researchers; notes were made, and the empirical data was organized and analyzed using several categories. First, we used information from field notes, transcripts of interviews, and archival material to construct a time line of events for how the ERM practice developed over a 19-year period (1996–2015). From the analysis, three main events were identified in which actors competed over the interpretation of ERM and worked to make their framing of ERM resonate at a collective level. As the internal struggles over the interpretation of ERM mainly happened during the last 10 years, this time period became the main focus of our research, while the story leading up to these events has been included as background information. A temporal bracketing approach (Langley, 1999) was used to cluster the three events in time, making it possible to compare them theoretically.

Second, we developed a general picture of the three main events and formed subcategories under each event according to our theoretical framework. From multiple readings of the data, we identified the main actors within each event. From statements in the interviews as well as interactions and documentations, we analyzed the institutional embeddedness of the actors; how the actors framed ERM; and, finally, what actions the actors took to make their interpretation predominant in efforts to gain a collective action frame of ERM practice. Sampling did at times lead to gathering new data, but sometimes it was enough to go back to old transcriptions and memos.

When presenting the findings of the analysis, we used first-order and second-order analyses inspired by Gioia and Chittipeddi (1991). The emic perspective of the insider (Lukka and Modell, 2010) was presented in a first-order analysis using the language of the informants. It is a rich description of the story that unfolded at Statoil, using citations to include the voices of the informants prominently in the reporting of the research. The second-order analysis took an etic, outsider perspective (Lukka and Modell, 2010), in which first-order themes were assembled into higher-order perspectives that allowed explanation of the social phenomena.

The development of collective action frames of ERM practices at Statoil

The first section will introduce the rise of ERM at Statoil from 1996 until 2006 as background information for the following section, in which we tell the story about how different actors competed over the interpretation of ERM in three events which we have named 'enterprise risk map', 'SOX' and 'ERM principles'. The events are struggles over different parts of the ERM practice. As collective action frames were formed around these parts of the ERM practice, the new understanding was integrated into the overall emerging ERM practice in the company and gradually became part of the institutionalized practice. An approximate timeline of the rise of ERM at Statoil and the three events is illustrated in Figure 14.2.

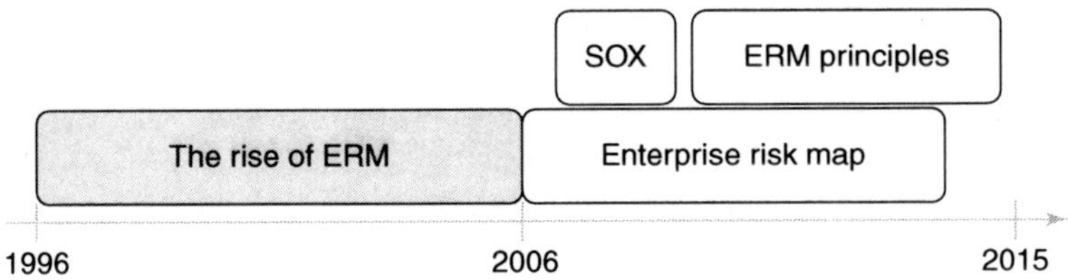

Figure 14.2 Timeline of the events.

The rise of ERM at Statoil

In 1996, Statoil's CEO initiated a project with the mandate to address risk management for the entire company and translate it into understandable, quantitative terms. A project was established to extend risk management ideas from the financial department to the whole company. A project manager, responsible for optimizing risk management in the financial department, was appointed project manager for the project. He was recently hired at Statoil, with 18 years of former trading experience in the banking industry. The project manager invited a corporate controller to join the project, since the two of them had worked together on a hedging project and found that they shared a common view on risk management. The corporate controller had worked in Statoil's corporate control function for 4 years, focusing on scenario modelling and how to simulate economic effects for Statoil. In addition, he was academically skilled, with a higher degree in finance. (For reasons of simplicity, in the following story the project manager and the controller will be named ERM managers 1 and 2).

The two ERM managers got the mandate to develop a holistic risk management approach for Statoil. They discussed, argued and found a common ground for understanding risk management based on four main principles. The first principle was a view of risks as both opportunities and threats. The second principle was to take a holistic approach to risk management in supporting the overall goals for Statoil. A third principle was that risk management should contribute to the creation of value for the company. A fourth principle was to quantify risks as much as possible in monetary terms.

Over the next 3 years, the ERM managers involved other internal and external actors in developing a market risk tool for aggregating market risks into portfolios and lifting hedging decisions to the corporate level. When the new market risk technology was put into practice in 1999, the numbers became so large that no single manager had the mandate to make hedging decisions. Under the leadership of the CFO, a Market Risk Committee (MRC) was formed, comprising senior executives from functions such as finance and trading as well as chief controllers from different business areas (BAs), corporate control and the ERM function. All the members of MRC had financial backgrounds, which resonated with the ERM managers' understanding of risk management. Since 1999, MRC has had 6–10 meetings a year to discuss risk issues. To prepare for the MRC meetings and calculate the market risk scenarios, a new corporate risk function (which we refer to as the ERM function) was formed, led by ERM manager 1 and with ERM manager 2 as the only employee. This function reported to the CFO.

Since the ERM function had gained legitimacy in risk management, it expanded its jurisdiction to a new area: calculating country risk. When making international investment decisions, the country risk assessment was based on a qualitative risk report developed by the country risk department, in addition to the requirement of an increased rate of return. The ERM function found the requirement of an increased rate of return imprecise and flawed, so it developed a country risk tool for quantifying the country risk directly in the cash flow. When the country risk tool was ready to be implemented, a requirement was incorporated into the investment handbook that international investments with medium-to-high risks should use the quantitative country risk approach, a requirement that has been valid since 2002. In 2002, the MRC changed its name to the Corporate Risk Committee (CRC), with a mandate to address risk from an enterprise perspective rather than focusing only on market risk.

From its beginning in 1996 until 2006, the ERM function had gained legitimacy in issues of risk management by introducing new risk technologies and by discussing risk management topics with senior executives on a monthly basis in MRC/CRC meetings. We shall now turn to internal struggles that occurred as risk management emerged as an enterprise-wide perspective.

First event: enterprise risk map

In the first main event in which actors started to struggle over the meaning of ERM, the ERM function developed a new enterprise risk map technology to be used by multiple actors throughout the organization. During this process, some actor groups had a competing understanding of what was important within risk management.

In 2005, the ERM function started developing a simple risk register in Excel, including a description of the main risks; the upside and downside consequences; actions; and possible high, medium or low impact for different BAs (see Figure 14.3a). Desiring to illustrate graphically the overall risks for Statoil in a risk map, the ERM function got in contact with the internal audit function, which had been using the audience response tool in risk workshops since 2001. The purpose for the internal audit's risk mapping had been to get input for the annual audit plan, focusing on the downside risks. The internal auditor described it as follows:

> We held risk workshops. … We went to the operational environments and challenged management in risk thinking; it was very simple … [discussions of] what can go wrong. We did this from 2001 until 2006 … and then we were asked to help [the ERM function] to develop the methods [for enterprise risk maps] around 2006.

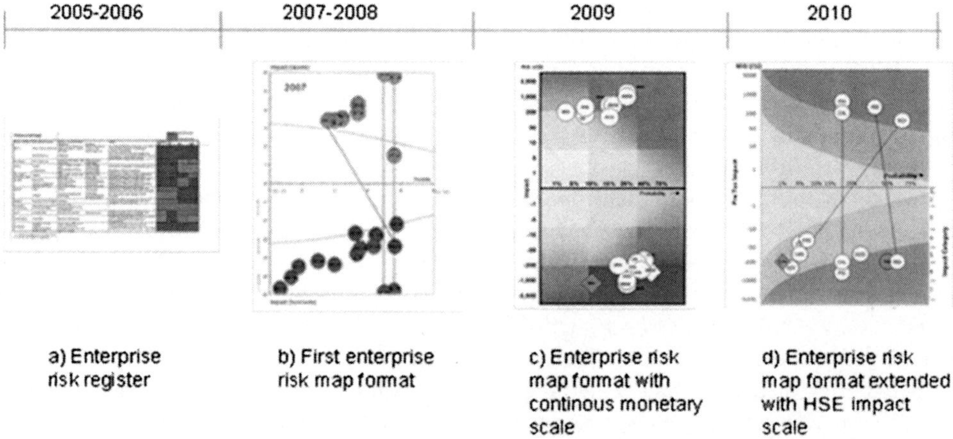

Figure 14.3 The historical development of the enterprise risk map format at Statoil.

Note: For reasons of confidentiality, the text in Figure 14.3 has been deliberately blurred at the request of the case study company.

The ERM function borrowed the audience response tool from the internal auditors and held risk workshops with the management team in each BA. With the audience response tool, managers voted on a scale of 1–6 on the impact and probability of different risks, viewing risks in terms of both the best and worst possible outcomes and the probability of the risk occurring (see Figure 14.3b). However, the ERM function was not satisfied with the approach. A scale of 1–6 was seen to be too inaccurate by the ERM managers; they wanted to calculate the risks using a continuous monetary scale, as ERM manager 2 recalled:

> The scale was from 1–6, and I thought it was fun to get started and to learn, but then I thought that this wasn't good enough. ... Here you can see the questions and look at all the differences. For instance, 'loss of several key personnel'—one votes very high, another one votes very low, and what is shown is an average of 2.7. You know, I think it was a bit difficult to analyze. The differences were too large. What we did instead of having the management teams answer everything, we asked different professional environments to evaluate the risks. Afterwards, management could approve or adjust it. ... We need to see the money and some numbers allowing us to calculate.

The ERM function started working directly with professionals in the BAs to quantify the risks in monetary terms instead of using the audience response tool. An enterprise risk map illustrating risks on a continuous monetary scale was developed and presented in 2009 (see Figure 14.3c).

In 2007, Statoil merged with the oil and gas division of Hydro, and the corporate risk functions in the two companies merged. The ERM function doubled in size, and the Hydro risk management group complemented the competence in Statoil's risk management group. Hydro's risk management group had individuals with an engineering education and experience in risk management from an operational perspective as well as familiarity with the international standards on risk management. The Hydro risk management group argued that there were important risks not included in the risk map because they could not be assessed in monetary terms—for instance, the loss of lives.

In cooperation with the safety function, the Hydro risk management group developed a health, safety and environment (HSE) impact scale, allowing for qualitative risk assessment in other terms than money. HSE risks were to be assessed on a predefined scale of 1–8—where, for instance, risks assessed at impact level 7 or 8 would be major accidents with large-scale fatalities and loss of installations. In 2010, the enterprise risk map format contained both risks assessed in monetary terms and HSE risks assessed in relation to the predefined impact scale (see Figure 14.3d). This was a solution that resonated with all actor groups, and the impact scale approach was later extended in cooperation with the legal function to include integrity risks. ERM manager 1 expressed his contentment with the solution:

> [The impact scale] was great, because we are concerned with what is the impact for Statoil, and then this predefined impact scale was good to have, because then you have articulated what are the consequences you are talking about. This was great work, and it was done in agreement with [the] safety [function].

From 2007, the enterprise risk map was presented annually to the Corporate Executive Committee (CEC). However, from 2009, top management decided to have a risk update as part of the quarterly business review meetings between the CEO, CFO and BA management, and an annual risk update to the board of directors. Later in 2013, the board of directors decided to have risk updates three times a year, which was changed to twice a year from 2014.

As the enterprise risk maps were to be used broadly, there was a need for a more advanced tool than the simple Excel version that was developed for internal use in the ERM function. The ERM function started searching internally and externally for a risk management tool that could support their needs; however, there were no tools available illustrating risk in a map with both upside and downside risks, and with a continuous monetary scale. The solution was to develop a more advanced Excel model internally.

The self-developed enterprise risk map tool was made available for all employees to download from the intranet. However, when risk maps became widely used in the organization, all kinds of risk map formats were developed. The top management team wanted to have one standard form of risk map, and they decided that the enterprise risk map format was required when presenting risks at higher levels in the organization. However, at lower levels, the organization could use whatever risk format was suitable. As an ERM employee explained, 'there is a jungle of risk map formats'.

As the BAs appointed risk coordinators to manage the quarterly BA risk updates, a risk network was established with biannual meetings. The risk network was administered by the ERM function, which comprised risk coordinators from the BAs. In addition, risk management training was given in risk courses three times a year. Despite efforts to make the enterprise risk map available and understandable to a broader audience, the parts of the organization with technical and operational backgrounds found the enterprise risk map less useful for operational needs. As an operational risk manager expressed:

> What happened was that the ERM function developed an enterprise risk map tool ... that no one in the BAs could use for operational risk management ... then someone came and said we have [the project management tool] PIMS, that is Statoil's way. ... The ERM function is right when they say that PIMS is only a project management tool, but for the rest of our business that is what it is all about. From PIMS it is actually possible to throw out the most important risks and aggregate them; that's no problem.

The ERM function found the PIMS tool to be suitable for operational risk management needs. However, according to ERM manager 2, the tool was too simple for the purpose of ERM:

> I don't think it is wrong to use PIMS risk as a project management tool. However, what is wrong is to use [PIMS] as a risk management tool for an enterprise. You have five numbers (5 x 5 matrix, with high, medium and low), and you don't think in terms of before and after tax, and the risks that are put in the same box can differ by ten times. Ten times is a pretty large difference. How do you then prioritize? ... Risk management is about making decisions.

When we asked how the ERM function would handle the contradiction, the ERM manager was reluctant to escalate the issue to a higher level, as there was a risk that decisions would be made that could backfire on the ERM approach. As ERM manager 2 expressed:

> I have been thinking that we can't escalate, because then you only get a clash, and it could go from bad to worse. ... You also risk that the ones making the decision don't know the consequences and it can turn out the wrong way. In addition, I am not the guy who escalates issues. I am the guy who works through arguments. If I have good arguments, then the right approach will win in the long run.

Instead, the ERM manager worked on how to theoretically distinguish between enterprise risks and task risks, determining that ERM is concerned with risks that would have major impacts on the company and task risk management (TRM) is about managing risks limited to a specific task. The ERM and TRM concepts were introduced with the updated function requirement to risk management published in 2014. A background memo for the function requirement was written and made available in the organization along with an academic paper that elaborated theoretically on the concepts of ERM and TRM (Aven and Aven, 2015). In addition, the concepts were included in risk management training and in risk committee and risk network meetings.

In this first event, we can identify a mix of collaboration and competition. In creating the enterprise risk map, the ERM managers used their four risk management principles to guide further development of the enterprise risk map format. The solution included a holistic risk map illustrated with both upside and downside risks and incorporating the use of a quantitative monetary scale. In collaboration with other professionals, new ideas were integrated into the enterprise risk map, since the suggestions fit with the ERM managers' framing of ERM. When the enterprise risk map was put into use, the enterprise risk map format did not fit with the framing of risk management in some of the operational environments. Both the ERM managers and the operational managers argued for their interpretation of risk management, and they could not agree on a collective framework. Lately, efforts have been taken to adjust the interpretation of what distinguishes ERM from TRM to allow for both frames of risk management to exist side by side.

Second event: SOX

In duration, the second event was only a short episode in the total history of ERM in the company. However, we have included it as an event because it was important to how ERM was understood and came in the wake of SOX implementation in the company. As an international company listed on New York Stock Exchange, Statoil was subject to SOX. New practices, routines and tools that were in line with SOX regulations were implemented in the company in 2006. To accomplish this change, a SOX project worked for 3 years to bring the internal control system into line with the SOX regulations in section 404, assisted by a large number of consultants from PwC.

The actors responsible for implementing SOX in the organization belonged to the internal audit function and were educated chartered accountants with previous experience from the Big Four accounting firms. With the introduction of SOX, the auditors took an approach to risk management focused on identifying risks and key controls, using COSO's ERM framework as a frame of reference. One of the internal auditors explained this as follows:

> In the beginning SOX was a bottom-up process, starting with the source of the transaction to verify that it was organized in a reassuring manner before it ended in the books. It was not risk-driven, just that everything that was going into the financial report needed to be controlled and documented. … Then there was a change from SEC [Securities and Exchange Commission] … and a switch to a top-down approach, where risks were identified and how to mitigate the risks, and a development of a control design from a risk-based approach … built on the COSO framework, as it still is.

Since the enterprise risk map had been put into use, the SOX project wanted to have the financial reporting risk plotted into the overall risk map for Statoil as the most important risk for the company. However, the ERM function did not agree with the importance of the financial reporting risk. The SOX project interpreted financial reporting risk as one of the most important risks for Statoil, referring to examples like Enron and noting that financial reporting errors could amount to several billions. The counterargument from the ERM function was that financial reporting errors would only have a minor direct cash-flow effect on the company in the form of a fine but could have additional reputation consequences. One employee in the ERM function who participated in discussions with the SOX project remembered it as follows:

> If you have a financial reporting error of several million dollars, then the SOX project wanted to have that amount plotted into the risk map ... Then we said, what is the consequence for Statoil if we have a financial reporting error of 20 million dollars in the financial statement? The bottom-line effect is not 20 million dollars; how much can it be? We can have fines of 1 or 2 million dollars. ... Over time there could also possibly be trust issues with the company; how much does that cost? It is serious enough to make a reporting error, but it is not as important as a major accident or the oil price risk.

In addition, the SOX project had a view that the SOX approach to risk management of identifying risks and key controls was the way forward for all risk management in the company, as expressed by one of the ERM managers:

> We were met with statements like, 'SOX is what risk management is about'. That, of course, triggered us to respond, and we said that SOX would be one of many elements, where SOX's focus is on financial reporting errors.

An actor from the internal audit function explained that the SOX is built on the COSO framework and that means that the focus on management signing off for their review of controls increased. While the ERM function acknowledged the need for compliance risk management within the company, this was not the preferred approach for managing enterprise risks in the company, as ERM manager 2 explained:

> If you just focus on compliance instead of thinking what is really driving the risks, whether you are compliant or not, then you limit yourself ... It is a job too [to become compliant], but it is not complete ERM thinking.

The ERM function and the SOX project spent several meetings arguing about how to understand the financial reporting risk and the possible impact for Statoil. As the two groups did not agree, the issue was escalated to the CFO. The principle that bottom line impacts mattered most for Statoil was supported by the CFO. ERM manager 2 described it as follows:

> There was heated discussion all the way up to the CFO, because we disagreed on how [financial reporting risk] was handled. We had a meeting with the CFO, together with the SOX project, and I felt we managed to put it in the right perspective. ... We were very analytical in what we did, and then we pulverized the huge impacts shown [by the opponents], because we said we have probabilities and impact, and we need to have an argument for the impact. ... However, [SOX] continued, because there was also a compliance job that had to be done. ... It was just that it was way out of proportion.

The ERM function acknowledged that the compliance approach was necessary for financial reporting errors; however, they argued that this had a limited amount to do with how to manage enterprise risks. One of the ERM managers explained it as follows:

> We fought against having [SOX] within our function, because this was about financial reporting errors, a responsibility that rests with the accounting function. [SOX] does not have to be within the ERM function. … It is the accounting function that needs to manage the SOX compliance and do the top-down risk assessment. We had nothing to do with it, and we saw that this was way out of all proportion.

In the second event, we can identify how two dissimilar professional groups framed ERM differently, which led to heated arguments and escalation of the issue to the CFO. At the CFO's table, a pragmatic solution was found: the ERM function and the SOX project continued the work within their own domains, and the bottom-line logic of how to assess risks was supported.

Third event: ERM principles

The final event was another example of how different actor groups struggled over the meaning of ERM. When Statoil merged with Hydro Oil & Gas in 2007, the corporate risk management functions in the two companies merged, revealing divergent interpretations of how to manage enterprise risks.

The difference in organizational cultures between Statoil and Hydro was used by respondents as one explanation for the difference between the two corporate risk groups. While Statoil was organized in a matrix with process and line responsibilities, Hydro was organized in a traditional hierarchical model, as explained by a former Hydro employee:

> The main difference, I guess, was the matrix model and management system in Statoil. … Hydro is more of a classical hierarchical model, with responsibility in the line organization.

Similarly, Statoil employees emphasized differences in culture between the two companies in terms of the role Statoil had (before it became a listed company) on behalf of the Norwegian government. For instance, Statoil had responsibility for selling not only their own gas but all gas produced in Norway. Statoil employees explained that they were used to taking holistic approaches to find the best solutions for the Norwegian continental shelf, while Hydro had long experience as a traditional company with a different mindset. Another employee stated that the differences were in how the hierarchy was used:

> Hydro had a general manager [on top], and they were streamlined from top to bottom, while Statoil had a more Norwegian culture in that everyone had a say, and that you could argue and discuss until the decision was made, while in Hydro decisions were made on top and then everyone followed.

Respondents also pointed to the different backgrounds of the actors as a reason for why the two risk management groups had different perspectives on ERM. While the Statoil risk managers had a financial background and had started by quantifying the most important risks for Statoil, the Hydro risk managers had more operational experience and followed the international risk management standards about how to manage enterprise risks by mitigating risks on objectives.

The difference in interpretation of principles for managing enterprise risks centred on what was going to be the object of the enterprise risk assessment. The risk group from Hydro focused on managing risks for not reaching goals as defined in the performance management system. The idea was to have risk management actions entered into the performance management system to assist managers in reaching their goals. One actor from the Hydro risk management group expressed it like this:

> What happened when Hydro and Statoil merged the two corporate risk functions was that there were almost two separate departments, with different approaches to risk management. Hydro was concerned with actions in the risk assessment, and that the identified risks had to be mirrored by the performance management system. If not, we would have two separate processes, and that does not work.

On the other hand, the risk group from Statoil viewed ERM as something more than 'risk management based on objectives', as the group did not necessarily believe in a performance management system in which all goals at lower levels of the organization were synchronized with the overall objectives of the company. The Statoil risk group argued that risk objectives were risks identified in the value chain that had to be tested in relation to Statoil's overall goals of creating value and avoiding incidents. One of the actors from Statoil's risk management group expressed it like this:

> Historically, people have had a view that if you only have risk management connected with performance management, then you are done with ERM, but that is too short-sighted. … Many people think that 'if I have a goal … then the goal is my risk'. I have had the question many times: 'If I don't have a goal, then I don't have a risk?' Then I have to tell them that risks don't appear because you have a goal, risks appear because you have an activity; we explore and produce oil, and we have risks whether we have a goal or not.

In addition, the Statoil risk group had a view that risks had to be assessed on a continuum from the best possible outcome to the worst likely outcome, not just that the most likely outcome and risks had to be assessed using a portfolio approach identifying correlations.

With the merger between Statoil and Hydro, a new operating model was defined in which the ERM function was appointed process owner of the risk management process in the company. As a result, function requirements had to be developed, and a risk management process had to be designed. The differences in interpretation of the ERM principles resulted in heated discussions within the ERM function in which both groups argued for their perspectives.

At the same time, the ERM function looked for an enterprise risk map tool that could support the ERM practice in the company. One option that was investigated was the possibility of integrating ERM with the performance management tool. This would allow risks to be connected with the objectives entered into the performance management system, with one tool for following up actions in relation to both risk management and performance management. However, the effort was stranded because the performance management tool was seen as too simple for the purpose of ERM. It would only allow for a risk register, not a visual illustration, and risks were only assessed as high, medium and low, which the ERM function viewed as too inaccurate. Those responsible for the performance management tool expressed it as follows:

> We genuinely made an effort to connect objectives and risk into one tool, and introduce it as one process in the organization. For every action you took, you connected it to a risk,

> and you had to define high, medium and low. Then you could have it on a scale and an impact. I believe that was the breaking point for the ERM manager that we could not get the system to plot bubbles in a risk map. However, we were able to make a list over all the actions, and calculate the risks as high, medium and low.

Because the ERM function had internal differences, not all ERM principles could be stated clearly to the rest of the organization. It was only after a reorganization of staffs and services at Statoil in 2013, including reallocation of some of the resources in the ERM function, that the ERM principle of managing risks in relation to the value chain could be explicitly stated in the function requirement to risk management as follows: 'All risks are related to activities in Statoil's value chain for a specific period of time in the future'.

With the reorganization in 2013, the ERM function merged with the performance management function, with one manager responsible for both processes. During the field study, we observed discussions on how to integrate the two processes. Participants in the discussion claimed that it had been important to develop risk management separately from performance management in order to train the organization in a holistic approach to risk management. However, as the organization matured in relation to both performance management and risk management, the ERM function and the performance management function found the timing was right to integrate the two processes more closely. In 2015, work was conducted to develop a new performance management and risk tool with an integrated action database.

In the third event, we can identify how enterprise risk managers from two different companies interpreted ERM differently—with one group following international risk management frameworks, in which ERM is concerned with 'uncertainty on objectives', and the other group following their own principles of ERM developed over a 10-year period. The differences in interpretation of ERM led to internal struggles in the ERM function as the two groups argued for their own views. The prevailing approach became that enterprise risks should be assessed holistically from the value chain and not just in terms of risk management based on objectives. However, as the use of the ERM process matured in the organization over almost a decade, the time came to create closer integration between the ERM and performance management processes by developing a common tool. At this time, the ERM function was not concerned that ERM would be reduced to risk management based on objectives, since the organization had been trained over a ten-year period in assessing enterprise risks from a holistic approach.

Discussion and conclusions

This chapter started with the concern that we have little knowledge about how ERM practices are institutionalized in organizations. The chapter explored how different actors conceptually interpret ERM, and the actions actors take to create a collective action frame of new ERM practices in an organization. To address this aim, we found it helpful to mobilize the institutional work approach to study how ERM practices emerge in an organization. This analytical framework enabled us to deconstruct the institutionalization process into a number of theoretical concepts and delineate how each concept influenced the creation of new ERM practices in the organization. The concepts included actors and their embeddedness in extant institutions; actors' framing of ERM; and actors' actions for gaining a collective action frame forming institutionalized practices. We outlined a set of research questions to address each of the concepts, and in the following sections we will answer these questions and provide a detailed understanding of how these concepts influenced the institutionalization process of ERM practices in the case company.

Actors and actors' embeddedness

The first research question was, 'Who are the main actors and how are they institutionally embedded?' In line with previous studies (e.g. Arena *et al.*, 2010; Mikes, 2009, 2011) we show that there are a number of actors involved in the construction of ERM practices. We have clustered the actor groups into three groups: uncertainty experts, other professional groups and board of directors and senior executives. In Table 14.1, we have illustrated which actor groups were involved in the three different events of framing the ERM practices.

Uncertainty experts include the actors responsible for overall risk management in the company as well as the risk management specialists in charge of traditional risk silo analysis—in this case, safety risk management—and the risk managers working with internal audit and the SOX project. In this case, other professional groups are professionals using risk management as part of their practice, either as controllers or within operational and project management. The third group of actors is the board of directors and senior executives with the power to support or change the framing of ERM.

The fluidity in the concept of risk management makes it possible for all professions to incorporate the concept into their daily work. In the case study, company risk management was incorporated into the values of the company and integrated in the way work was to be conducted. However, different actors had different perceptions of how risk management was to be interpreted and acted upon. Actors' embeddedness in existing institutional context and historical background influenced the way actor groups framed ERM. Table 14.2 gives an overview of the uncertainty experts and other professional groups' tendencies of embeddedness in different norms.

From previous studies of ERM in the management accounting literature, we have found actors tend to be embedded in norms of auditing (Arena *et al.*, 2010; Vinnari and Skærbæk, 2014); norms of management accounting (Arena *et al.*, 2010); quantitative norms (Mikes, 2009, 2011); and norms of banking business (Mikes, 2009, 2011). In our study, we found that there are multiple actors involved in the institutionalization of ERM and that they are embedded in a diversified social context, which may help explain the existence of different understandings and struggles over the meaning and use of ERM (see Table 14.2). In the next section, we will see how actors' embeddedness influenced the ways actors framed the concept of ERM and how risk should be managed.

Table 14.1 Actors and their involvement in the events

Actors	*Enterprise risk map*	*SOX*	*ERM principles*
Uncertainty experts			
ERM function	X	X	X
Internal audit and SOX	X	X	
Safety function	X		
Other professional groups			
Operational and project managers	X		
Controllers	X		X
Board of directors and senior executives			
Board of directors	X		
CEO, senior executives and risk committee	X		
CFO	X	X	

Table 14.2 Professional groups and their embeddedness

Professions	*Embeddedness*	*Norms*
Statoil ERM managers	Financial education; several with higher academic degrees Former experience as corporate controller at Statoil, focusing on corporate control, financial calculations and simulations for total effects for Statoil One ERM manager had almost 20 years' trading experience in the banking industry before he started at Statoil	Embedded in economic and finance norms of risk management
Hydro ERM managers	Some of the risk managers from Hydro had engineering degree, had experience in operational risk management and were well trained in international risk standards	Embedded in the international standardization norms of risk management
Internal audit and SOX	Financial accounting education, some as chartered accountants Previous experience at Big Four accounting firms Responsibility for internal audit and for SOX implementation	Embedded in auditing norms of risk management
Controllers	Financial education Corporate controllers with responsibility for financial calculations and simulation for Statoil BA controllers with responsibility for financial calculations and simulations for BAs	Embedded in management accounting norms of risk management
Safety function	Technical education, several with engineering degrees Responsible for safety risk management Focus on risk management in operations and on how to assess and mitigate risks for incidents in the company	Embedded in safety and technical norms of risk management
Operations/project engineering	The dominating background was technical education A large group of actors involved in the core operations of the company, including the project environment	Embedded in operational and project management norms of risk management

Actors' framing of ERM

The second research question focused on how actors frame ERM. To answer this question, we have used Benford and Snow's (2002) framing tasks of diagnostic (problem) and prognostic (solution) framing. In the following, we discuss how actors framed ERM differently for each of the three events.

In the first event, 'Enterprise risk map', the ERM managers from Statoil had developed an enterprise risk map tool in order to illustrate the total risk for the company in monetary terms, using both upside and downside risk. This way of framing ERM resonated with their economic and finance backgrounds, which led them to think about risks in relation to a portfolio and to see risk as something a company must take on in order to get a monetary return. The ERM managers from Hydro, in collaboration with the safety function, found that the enterprise risk map failed to illustrate the total risk for the company because important non-monetary risks were excluded—for instance, the loss of a life. A second scale was incorporated into the risk map format to include HSE incidents on a scale of 1–8. The Statoil ERM managers found the addition helpful in extending their goal of a holistic approach to risk management, and they supported the change in the risk map format.

However, when the enterprise risk map format was put into use, not everyone supported the new tool. Actor groups from the operational and project engineering environment found the tool of little use for their operational needs. Their focus was on what could go wrong, focusing on the downside of risks. A categorization of risks as high, medium or low was sufficient for their purpose, and they did not see the need to calculate risks in monetary terms before and after tax. A summary of the actors, their embeddedness and their framing of ERM in the first event of 'Enterprise risk map' is illustrated in Table 14.3.

In the second event, 'SOX', the Statoil ERM managers and the SOX project disputed the importance of financial reporting errors as well as the way risks should be managed in the company. The Statoil ERM managers, who were embedded in economic norms, focused on the cash-flow effect of risk impacts and argued against the importance of financial reporting error, while the SOX project used examples like Enron to demonstrate the importance of financial reporting errors and argued that their governance, risk and control approach was the way to manage risk. The Statoil ERM managers acknowledged that compliance was important but argued that it had to be handled in the risk silos, not as part of ERM. A summary of the actors, their embeddedness and their framing of ERM in the second event of 'SOX' is illustrated in Table 14.4.

In the third event, 'ERM principles', internal struggles in the ERM function surfaced as ERM principles were decided. The Hydro ERM managers, with their extensive knowledge about international risk management standards and experience in operational risk management, focused on managing risks in relation to the objectives stated in the performance management system. With a tight coupling to the performance management system, it would be possible for the company to follow up all actions using one process and one tool. The controllers also found this approach appealing, but without fighting for one solution or the other. The Statoil ERM managers did not support this approach, as in their view this would reduce ERM to what they called 'risk management based on objectives'—focusing only on managing the risks in relation to the key performance indicators and neglecting to assess all the relevant risks in the value chain. A summary of the actors, their embeddedness and their framing of ERM in the third event of 'ERM principles' is illustrated in Table 14.5.

Table 14.3 Actors, embeddedness and framing in the first event of 'Enterprise risk map'

Professional groups	*Embeddedness*	*Diagnostic framing*	*Prognostic framing*
Statoil ERM managers	Economic and finance norms	Need a risk map to illustrate total risks for Statoil in monetary terms	Holistic risk map using monetary scale, with both upside and downside risks
Hydro ERM managers Safety function	Safety and technical norms and international risk management standards	Not all safety risks can be assessed in monetary terms	Safety risks need to be assessed in qualitative terms
Operations/project engineering	Operational and project management norms	Need a risk map for operational needs and for project management	Project risk map, focusing on downside risk and using a scale of high, medium and low

Table 14.4 Actors, embeddedness and framing in the second event of 'SOX'

Professional groups	*Embeddedness*	*Diagnostic framing*	*Prognostic framing*
Statoil ERM managers	Economic and finance norms	The SOX approach to risk management was out of proportion	Financial reporting errors are most likely not significant for Statoil, and ERM is about value creation, not only compliance
SOX project	Auditing norms	The importance of financial reporting errors had to be acknowledged, and the SOX approach to risk management was the way forward for handling risk management in the company	Financial reporting risk was one of the most important risks for Statoil, and the governance, risk and control approach was the way to handle risks in the company

Table 14.5 Actors, embeddedness and framing in the third event of 'ERM principles'

Professional groups	*Embeddedness*	*Diagnostic framing*	*Prognostic framing*
Statoil ERM managers	Economic and finance norms	ERM is something more than risk management on objectives	Risks needs to be assessed in the value chain in relation to the overall goals for Statoil
Hydro ERM managers	International standardization of risk management	We need to have an approach that makes risk manageable	Risk assessment and risk-mitigating actions need to be connected to the goals in the performance management system
Controllers	Management accounting norms	It would be nice to have both actions in relation to risk management and performance management included in one register	Integrate ERM into the performance management tool

Three arenas of institutional work

The third research question focused on how different kinds of institutional work lead to collective actions and institutionalized practices. To answer this question, we have used Perkmann and Spicer´s (2008) typology of how actor groups mobilize different forms of political, technical and cultural work to make the actor groups' interpretations of ERM resonate at a collective level.

Findings showed that the actors used the three types of work differently in the three events, which can help to explain how actions shaped the collective framing of ERM. A summary of the work activities for each event is found in Table 14.6.

When theorizing different results of how the ERM function tried to create collective frames of ERM, we created three different arenas as metaphors—the academic, political and border guard arenas—to show how different clusters of political, technical and cultural work are put together (see Table 14.7).

Table 14.6 Actors' political, technical and cultural work in the three events

Event	*Political work*	*Technical work*	*Cultural work*
Enterprise risk map	Got support from senior executives and board of directors for the enterprise risk map format	Developed enterprise risk map methods, tools and practices	ERM was illustrated graphically in a risk map, using a monetary scale
	The risk map was developed in collaboration with several actor groups	Education through risk management training and risk network meetings with controllers in BAs	Enterprise risk map became a requirement when presenting risk maps at the top of the organization
	Struggles between actor groups on the use of risk map formats led to boundary work of reframing ERM versus TRM		
SOX	Struggle over the framing of ERM was escalated to the CFO for a decision		Each group argued to convince the other group that their framing should be the predominant framing
ERM principles	Differences in framing of ERM principles resulted in heated discussions within the ERM function	ERM principles were documented, but due to internal differences this took a long time	Due to internal differences, it was difficult to clearly present the ERM principles
	Re-organization of the ERM function ended the discussions		

Table 14.7 Summary of metaphors clustering the actors' political, technical and cultural work

Metaphor	*Political work*	*Technical work*	*Cultural work*
Academia	Convinced others and peers through argumentation	Developed risk methods, tools and practices to make the argument operational	Used a language based on logic and monetary terms to make the argument resonate with a wider group
	Mobilized coalitions to develop legitimacy	Trained other groups	
Political	Negotiated with peers	No work	No work
	Escalated to higher management level if agreement could not be reached		
Border Guards	Reframed the concept of ERM and tried to make the distinction between ERM and other practices more clear-cut in defining the borders from the inside and the outside	Made the concept of ERM clearer in writing and included the explanations in relevant documents, meetings and trainings	Elaborated on the meaning of different concepts and illustrated with practical examples to make concepts understandable for a wider group

Within the metaphor of academia, the work is clustered around *argumentation*. The involved professional groups use arguments to convince peers and get acceptance for their interpretation of ERM. Well-founded arguments are taken in, and poor arguments are excluded from the debate. The process can be a debate between different groups to co-create a stronger argument or a battle over competing arguments. In order to get their argument to predominate, actors mobilize coalitions at higher levels to get legitimacy and work with external partners to widen their knowledge and improve their arguments. While political work is concerned with ensuring an argument's social acceptance, technical work is concerned with integrating the argument into risk methods, tools and practices in order to convince others that the argument is solid. The line of reasoning is written down in functional requirements for ERM, and training is given so that the interpretations can be understood by and are homogeneous for all professional groups. Finally, the cultural work consists of how the ERM function argues using logical and monetary-based explanations. The metaphor is used since this process is similar to how academics work to get their findings accepted. The one with the best arguments, which are developed together with peers, wins, and then others accept the new truth.

Within the metaphor of politics, it is no longer just the argument that counts. The arena of politics appears when actor groups cannot agree on the arguments and there is a high degree of contradiction. The political arena differs from the academic arena because the work to be done is to *negotiate*. This is a mix between competition and collaboration. The groups try to find a solution in which the definition of ERM can become a synthesis between the two interpretations. In Hargrave and Van de Ven's (2009) terms, this is a 'both/and approach' where both actors acknowledge poles of contradiction, frame these poles as complementary and use the contradiction as a source of innovation.

If a negotiated 'both/and approach' is not found between the actor groups, the issue can be escalated to a higher management level. However, to escalate a disagreement over an argument can be a risk for actor groups, since they might lose control over the outcome of the negotiation. There is no further technical or cultural work within this metaphor because the problem is handed over to managers at higher levels who can decide what interpretation will be used. The empirical data shows that escalation was only used once at Statoil to find a pragmatic solution to the argument between the SOX project and ERM function. However, escalation was not seen as the preferred path to win an argument, since the outcome could be uncertain. This is in line with what Hargrave and Van de Ven (2009) called 'moderation', referring to the dividing of resources between contradictory poles. The actors' underlying view is that the poles are opposed, and therefore that trade-offs must be made between them. There are no further opportunities for synergies.

The final metaphor is the arena of border guards, where political, technical and cultural work clusters around *boundary work*. The border guard arena occurs when there is not only a disagreement between professional groups but a conflict between different groups. The aim of boundary work is to solve the conflict and enable the debate to get back to the academic arena, where argumentation work can again be used to reach a collective action frame.

The political dimension of boundary work is when professional groups redefine boundaries to make a clearer distinction between what is inside and what is outside the ERM definition, with the aim of making the redefinition socially acceptable for the opponents. An example from the case study is the conflicting views on risk management of the ERM function and some operational environments over the use of risk maps. To solve the issue, the ERM function made efforts to reframe ERM by making a distinction between enterprise risks and task risks to allow for different approaches to managing the risks. To make the different concepts of ERM and TRM operational and understandable, different forms of technical work were conducted. For instance, the concepts were included in newer versions of function requirements and in a memo that described the function's requirements in more detail, and the concepts were included in network meetings and in training. The cultural work required actors to be very precise in the use of language and concepts, and to illustrate the concepts with examples to make the different concepts of ERM and TRM resonate with a wider audience. This is in line with what Hargrave and Van der Ven (2009) called the 'either/or approach' which means that there are different poles of contradiction and one tends to deny one pole by proceeding as if the pole does not exist.

To sum up how different kinds of institutional work lead to collective actions and institutionalized practices, we have shown that individual actors' cognitive frames are influenced by actors' embeddedness in previous experiences and their professional backgrounds. As risk management has become an integrated practice within different professions, actors can have different interpretations of what ERM is within an organization. Actors' interpretation of ERM can be quite similar or can diverge, resulting in different degrees of the initial frame of resonance.

If the degree of the initial frame resonance is high, actors can concentrate on the political, technical and cultural work that is needed to develop an argument that resonates at the collective level, which over time becomes an institutionalized practice. The case study is an example of how the market risk and country risk practices were developed during the rise of ERM in the company.

However, if the degree of the initial frame resonance is low, more institutional work efforts need to be done, often over time, to reach a collective action frame. If institutional work efforts do not succeed in creating a collective action frame, divergent practices will be the outcome. Initially, the institutional work is done at the academic arena, where arguments are used to convince peers. Arguments in the academic arena can either change actors' initial frames to a higher degree of frame resonance or the initial contradicting frames can be upheld. When actors manage through argumentation to increase the degree of frame resonance, predominant collective frames can emerge that over time result in institutionalized practices.

However, if the degree of frame resonance is still low after arguments in the academic arena, institutional actors have three options: to move the discussion to the political arena or to the border guards arena, or to do nothing. Being in the political arena is related to excessive risks, since the issue is handed over to managers at higher levels to make decisions that can either result in decisions to take collective actions but also in decisions to uphold divergent practices. On the other hand, being in the border guards arena means substantial work must be done in order to reframe, outline, describe and demonstrate the boundaries to other close areas. If the boundary work succeeds, actors can go back to the academic arena to work on increasing the frame resonance in order to achieve a collective action frame that can be institutionalized over time. Figure 14.4 illustrates how actors work to reach a collective action frame of a new practice.

In our analysis, we have addressed the issue of conflation (Archer, 1982, 1995, Modell, 2015) in terms of how to balance between the structural and agency perspectives. Our study has shown that institutionalization of ERM has to be understood from both a structural perspective and an agency perspective. The structural perspective helps us to understand how actors' embeddedness influences the cognitive frames actors are predisposed to have and the options the actors are more likely to follow. The agency perspective, on the other hand, helps us to understand how actors are able to change cognitive frames through interaction with other actors, and how that work can be done in cooperation or in competition with multiple actor groups who together create the final collective frame that becomes institutionalized over time.

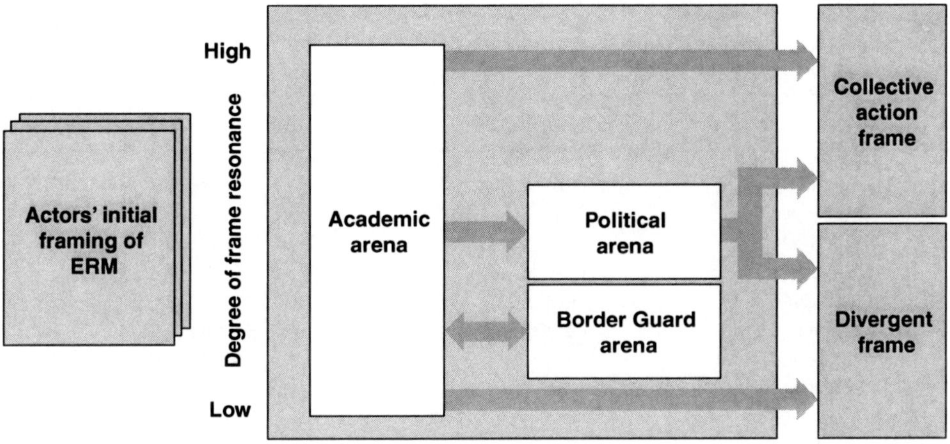

Figure 14.4 The process of gaining a collective action frame.

To conclude the chapter, we draw attention to our main contributions and suggestions for further research. First, we have contributed to the management accounting literature with a historical case study of a large, private company outside the banking sector, in which ERM practices were institutionalized over a 19-year period. Second, the paper has contributed by using a case study that demonstrates actors have multiple ways of framing ERM, influenced by actors' embeddedness in existing institutions. Different framings of ERM can lead to struggles in terms of reaching a collective action frame of ERM. Third, we have demonstrated how actors work in three different arenas—academic, political and border guard—to reach a collective action frame of ERM. The different arenas demand different types of institutional work in order to influence other actors' interpretation of ERM to reach a collective action frame and, finally, an institutionalized practice.

A future research agenda would include research on the edge of new ERM practices, with extreme cases related to how new ERM practices move the ERM agenda forward and how ERM practices are integrated with other management controls. Two examples of further research areas can be found in our case study, in which we observed efforts to integrate ERM and performance management—an integration that so far has been under-researched. In addition, we observed efforts to develop a risk appetite framework to integrate risk management with strategy work, which is another area that needs further exploration.

Appendix

Table 14.8 List of formal interviews

#	Role	Function	Date	Length
1	ERM manager (1)	ERM	23/04/2013	120 min
2	ERM employee	ERM	23/04/2013	105 min
3	ERM manager (1)	ERM	29/04/2013	120 min
	ERM manager (2)	trading		
4	ERM employee	ERM	30/04/2013	120 min
5	Performance manager	Performance management	30/04/2013	90 min
6	ERM employee	ERM	30/04/2013	60 min
7	ERM employee	ERM	07/05/2013	45 min
8	ERM employee	ERM	07/05/2013	60 min
9	ERM employee	ERM	04/06/2013	135 min
10	Safety risk manager	Safety management	05/06/2013	120 min
	Safety risk employee			
11	Trading employee	Trading	07/06/2013	45 min
12	Safety risk employee	Business continuity management	12/06/2013	120 min
13	Performance manager	Performance management	24/06/2013	60 min
14	Safety manager	Safety management	27/09/2013	30 min
15	Safety risk employee	Safety management	01/10/2013	300 min
16	Safety risk employee	Safety management	02/10/2013	90 min
17	Safety risk employee	Safety management	14/10/2013	75 min
18	Management system employee	Management system	18/10/2013	120 min
19	Risk coordinator	BA 1	30/10/2013	120 min
20	Safety risk coordinator	BA 2	08/11/2013	90 min
21	Safety risk coordinator	BA 3	08/11/2013	90 min
22	Internal audit manager	BA 3	11/11/2013	75 min
23	Risk coordinator	BA 3	11/11/2013	70 min
24	Safety manager	BA 3	13/11/2013	60 min
25	Finance controller	BA 3	13/11/2013	60 min
	Risk coordinator			
	Finance employee			
26	Finance and control manager	BA 1	21/11/2013	60 min
27	Safety manager	BA 2	21/11/2013	60 min
28	Safety risk employee	Safety management	22/11/2013	50 min
29	Finance and control manager	BA 3	18/12/2013	60 min
30	Risk coordinator	BA 2	15/01/2014	60 min
31	Two ERM employees	ERM	30/01/2014	60 min
32	ERM manager (2)	ERM	30/01/2014	90 min
	Performance manager	Performance management		
33	ERM manager (2)	ERM	30/01/2014	90 min
34	Two ERM employees	ERM	27/03/2014	120 min
35	ERM manager (2)	ERM	23/04/2014	150 min
	ERM employee			
36	ERM manager (2)	ERM	18/12/2014	120 min
	ERM employee			
37	Internal auditor (1)	Internal audit	12/02/2015	60 min
38	Internal auditor (2)	Internal audit	12/02/2015	60 min
39	Former ERM employee	BA1	23/03/2015	60 min
40	ERM manager (2)	ERM	12/10/2015	60 min

Table 14.9 List of observed meetings

Meeting	*Date*	*Length*
CRC meeting	16/05/2013	90 min
Risk improvement project meeting	02/10/2013	120 min
Internal meeting in safety and sustainability	04/10/2013	60 min
Risk improvement project group meeting	08/10/2013	350 min
Risk improvement project group meeting	09/10/2013	300 min
Risk improvement reference group meeting	18/10/2013	120 min
Risk improvement project group meeting	22/10/2013	120 min
Risk improvement project group meeting	09/12/2013	120 min
Risk improvement project group meeting	15/12/2013	120 min
Internal meeting in safety and sustainability	15/12/2013	60 min
Internal meeting in safety and sustainability	15/01/2014	60 min
Safety management—department meeting	03/02/2014	60 min
ERM—function meeting	23/04/2014	75 min
ERM—function meeting	23/04/2014	75 min
ERM—function meeting	26/06/2014	75 min
ERM—function meeting	20/08/2014	240 min
Risk network meeting	26/10/2015	120 min

References

Ahrens, T. and C.S. Chapman (2006), 'Doing Qualitative Research in Management Accounting: Positioning Data to Contribute to Theory', *Accounting, Organizations and Society*, 31(8), pp. 819–841.

Archer, M.S. (1982), 'Morphogenesis versus Structuration: On Combining Structure and Action', *British Journal of Sociology*, 33(4) pp. 455–483.

Archer, M.S. (1995), *Realist Social Theory: The Morphogenetic Approach*, Cambridge: Cambridge University Press.

Arena, M., M. Arnaboldi and G. Azzone (2010), 'The Organizational Dynamics of Enterprise Risk Management', *Accounting, Organizations and Society*, 35(7), pp. 659–675.

Aven, E. and T. Aven (2015), 'On the Need for Rethinking Current Practice That Highlights Goal Achievement Risk in an Enterprise Context', *Risk Analysis*, 35(9), pp. 1706–1716

Battilana, J. and T. D'Aunno (2009), 'Institutional Work and the Paradox of Embedded Agency', in T.B. Lawrence, R. Suddaby and B. Leca (eds.), *Institutional Work: Actors and Agency in Institutional Studies of Organizations*, Cambridge: University of Cambridge Press, pp. 31–58.

Benford, R.D. and D.A. Snow (2000), 'Framing Processes and Social Movements: An Overview and Assessment', *Annual Review of Sociology*, 26(1), pp. 611–639.

Bourdieu, P. (1977), *Outline of a Theory of Practice*, vol. 16, Cambridge: Cambridge University Press.

Caldarelli, A, Fiondella, C., Maffei, M., Zagaria, C. (2016). Managing risk in credit cooperative banks: Lessons from a case study. *Management Accounting Research*, 32, 1–15.

Chiwamit, P., S. Modell and C.L. Yang (2014), 'The Societal Relevance of Management Accounting Innovations: Economic Value Added and Institutional Work in the Fields of Chinese and Thai State-Owned Enterprises', *Accounting and Business Research*, 44(2), pp. 144–180.

DiMaggio, P.J. (1988), 'Interest and Agency in Institutional Theory', in L. G. Zucker (ed.), *Institutional Patterns and Organizations: Culture and Environment*, Ballinger, 1, pp. 3–22.

DiMaggio, P.J. and W.W. Powell (1983), 'The Iron Cage Revisited: Institutional Isomorphism and Collective Rationality in Organizational Fields', *American Sociological Review*, pp. 147–160.

Giovannoni, E., S. Quarchioni and A. Riccaboni (2016), 'The Role of *Roles* in Risk Management Change: The Case of an Italian Bank', *European Accounting Review*, 25(1), pp. 109–129.

Gioia, D. A., Chittipeddi, K. (1991), Sensemaking and sensegiving in strategic change initiation. *Strategic Management Journal*, 12(6), 433–448.

Goffman, E. (1974/1986), *Frame Analysis: An Essay on the Organization of Experience*, 2nd edn, Boston: Northeastern University Press.

Greenwood, R., C. Oliver, K. Sahlin and R. Suddaby (eds.) (2008), *The SAGE Handbook of Organizational Institutionalism*, London: Sage.

Hall, M., A. Mikes and Y. Millo, Y. (2015), 'How Do Risk Managers Become Influential? A Field Study of Toolmaking in Two Financial Institutions', *Management Accounting Research*, 26, pp. 3–22

Hargrave, T.J. and A.H. Van de Ven (2009), 'Institutional Work as the Creative Embrace of Contradiction', in *Institutional Work: Actors and Agency in Institutional Studies of Organizations*, pp. 120–140.

Hayne, C. and C. Free (2014), 'Hybridized Professional Groups and Institutional Work: COSO and the Rise of Enterprise Risk Management', *Accounting, Organization and Society*, 39, pp. 309–330.

ISO (2009), *ISO 31 000. Risk Management—Principles and Guidelines*. Geneva, ISO.

Jordan, S., L. Jørgensen and H. Mitterhofer (2013), 'Performing Risk and the Project: Risk Maps as Mediating Instruments', *Management Accounting Research*, 24(2), pp. 156–174.

Kaghan, W. and M. Lounsbury (2011), 'Institutions and Work', *Journal of Management Inquiry*, 20(1), pp. 73–81.

Kaplan, S. (2008), 'Framing Contests: Strategy Making under Uncertainty', *Organization Science*, 19(5), pp. 729–752.

Langley, A. (1999). Strategies for theorizing from process data. *Academy of Management Review*, 24(4), 691–710.

Lawrence, T. and R. Suddaby (2006), 'Institutions and Institutional Work', in S.R. Clegg, C. Hardy, T. Lawrence and W.R. Nord (eds.), *The Sage Handbook of Organization Studies*, London: Sage Publications, pp. 215–254.

Lawrence, T.B., R. Suddaby and B. Leca (eds.) (2009), *Institutional Work: Actors and Agency in Institutional Studies of Organizations*, Cambridge: Cambridge University Press.

Lawrence, T., R. Suddaby and B. Leca (2011), 'Institutional Work: Refocusing Institutional Studies of Organization', *Journal of Management Inquiry*, 20(1), pp. 52–58.

Lawrence, T.B., B. Leca and T.B. Zilber (2013), 'Institutional Work: Current Research, New Directions and Overlooked Issues', *Organization Studies*, 34(8), pp. 1023–1033.

Leca, B., J. Battilana and E. Boxenbaum (2008), *Agency and Institutions: A Review of Institutional Entrepreneurship*, Cambridge, MA: Harvard Business School.

Leca, B. and P. Naccache (2006), 'A Critical Realist Approach to Institutional Entrepreneurship', *Organization*, 13(5), pp. 627–651.

Lukka, K. and S. Modell (2010), 'Validation in Interpretive Management Accounting Research', *Accounting, Organizations and Society*, 35(4), pp. 462–477.

Lundqvist, S.A. (2014), 'An Exploratory Study of Enterprise Risk Management Pillars of ERM', *Journal of Accounting, Auditing & Finance*, 29(3), pp. 393–429.`

Meyer, J.W. and B. Rowan (1977), 'Institutional Organizations: Formal Structure as Myth and Ceremony', *American Journal of Sociology*, 83(2), pp. 340–363.

Mikes A. (2009), 'Risk Management and Calculative Cultures', *Management Accounting Research*, 20(1), pp. 18–40.

Mikes, A. (2011), 'From Counting Risk to Making Risk Count: Boundary-Work in Risk Management', *Accounting, Organizations and Society*, 36, pp. 226–245.

Millo, Y. and D. MacKenzie (2009), 'The Usefulness of Inaccurate Models: Towards an Understanding of the Emergence of Financial Risk Management', *Accounting, Organizations and Society*, 34(5), pp. 638–653.

Modell, S. (2015), 'Making Institutional Accounting Research Critical: Dead End or New Beginning?' *Accounting, Auditing & Accountability Journal*, 28(5), pp. 773–808.

Palermo, T. (2014), 'Accountability and Expertise in Public Sector Risk Management: A Case Study', *Financial Accountability & Management*, 30(3), pp. 322–341.

Perkmann, M. and A. Spicer (2008), 'How are Management Fashions Institutionalized? The Role of Institutional Work', *Human Relations*, 61(6), pp. 811–844.

Power M. (2007), *Organized Uncertainty: Designing a World of Risk Management*, Oxford: Oxford University Press.

Scapens, R.W. (1990), 'Researching Management Accounting Practice: The Role of Case Study Methods', *British Accounting Review*, 22(3), pp. 259–281.

Snow, D.A., E.B. Rochford Jr, S.K. Worden and R.D. Benford (1986), 'Frame Alignment Processes, Micromobilization, and Movement Participation', *American Sociological Review*, 51(4), pp. 464–481.

Spira, L.F. and M. Page (2003), 'Risk Management: The Reinvention of Internal Control and the Changing Role of Internal Audit', *Accounting, Auditing & Accountability Journal*, 16(4), pp. 640–661.

Suddaby, R. (2010), 'Challenges for Institutional Theory', *Journal of Management Inquiry*, 19(1), pp. 14–20.
Tekathen, M. and N. Dechow (2013), 'Enterprise Risk Management and Continuous Re-alignment in the Pursuit of Accountability: A German Case', *Management Accounting Research*, 24(2), pp. 100–121.
Tolbert, P.S. and L.B. Zucker (1983), 'Institutional Sources of Change in the Formal Structure of Organizations: The Diffusion of Civil Service Reform, 1880–1935', *Administrative Science Quarterly*, 28, pp. 22–39.
Vinnari, E. and P. Skærbæk (2014), 'The Uncertainties of Risk Management: A Field Study on Risk Management Internal Audit Practices in a Finnish Municipality', *Accounting, Auditing & Accountability Journal*, 27(3), pp. 489–526.
Woods, M. (2009), 'A Contingency Theory Perspective on the Risk Management Control System within Birmingham City Council', *Management Accounting Research*, 20(1), pp. 69–81.
Woods, M. (2011), *Risk Management in Organizations: An Integrated Case Study Approach*, London: Routledge.
Yin, R.K. (1994), *Case Study Research: Design and Method*, Thousand Oaks: Sage.
Zilber, T.B. (2013), Institutional logics and institutional work: Should they be agreed. *Research in the Sociology of Organizations*, 39, 77–96.

Part IV

Risk monitoring

15

Over-compliance and the conformity trap

Gregory B. Vit

Introduction

This chapter, using three brief case studies, will seek to explain why organizations were fooled by individuals making mammoth fraudulent and legal wagers that defied accounting judgement and common sense.

Compliance and over-compliance is viewed as a dynamic process, and a framework is presented that explains how very non-compliant bets happened and were tolerated due to the complicity of investigators and finance professionals. This framework illuminates the social activities of analytic in-groups (fraudsters, so-called investment bank equity 'analysts', accounting firms and so-called 'industry expert' consultants) that participated in speculation in highly risky 'assets'. The principal actors that suffered heavy losses in the case studies presented below (Madoff Investments, Lehman Brothers and the Sino-Forest Corporation) depended on routines that substituted for independent thought and action. This chapter presents preliminary research and outlines how the cognitive patterns and ideological pressures of a profession wove together within financial analyses to short-circuit economic rationality within these organizations. This social rationalizing behaviour masquerading as rational analysis and accounting compliance is explored by using descriptive organizational models. I call this the 'conformity trap'.

Compliance

Compliance is defined as 'the practice of obeying rules and requests made by people in authority' (*Oxford Advanced Learner's Dictionary*, 2015). The creation of and obeisance to rules is a cornerstone of social organization and organizational life (Mintzberg, 1979, 1983). In terms of accounting, compliance means making certain that a company's activities respect and follow existing laws and regulations. Who makes sure of this, and how is it done and undone?

Legal and illegal frauds perpetually surface that shock organizations and their auditors, analysts and investigators due to their inability to uncover glaring non-compliance. Ex-post, practioners and researchers refer to seemingly clear signs (Kindleberger, 1975; Lounsbury and Hirsch, 2010; Vit, 2013). How, then, is it possible that so many important compliance warning signs are missed a priori? The reassuring and unquestioning acceptance of legitimacy-building activities that are contrary to apparent technical-rational warning signs, and the illusion of control and confidence they create, can be conceptualized by what I call over-compliance and the conformity trap. Building upon recent theory (Vit, 2013), this chapter will seek to understand how this might happen by proposing several cases and a conceptual over-compliance framework that presents four compliance models. It is exploratory in nature and will require further research of its very preliminary conclusions. The chapter will focus upon processes within three cases of non-analysis and so-called fact-checking that resulted in the meteoric success, stock crash, delisting and bankruptcy, and fraud prosecution of Canada's largest listed forest products company, Sino-Forest Products, and the bankruptcy of two US investment firms, Madoff Investments and Lehman Brothers.

Method

This chapter presents empirical research on competing economic and non-economic social processes and forces that I call logics (Vit, 1997, 2013) in and around three firms. The overly compliant risk assessors of these three firms include actors whose livelihood and central activity hinged on the assumption that the firms were in compliance, including equity analysts, investors, creditors, auditors and regulators. To date, the data on Sino-Forest and surrounding actor logics and processes contained in this paper is taken from filings with the Ontario Securities Commission (2011); Ontario Supreme Court Bankruptcy proceedings; investment bank analyst reports before and after the company's demise; Ernst & Young audited financial statements and reports; and filings with the People's Republic of China State Administration for Industry and Commerce (SAIC). Madoff Investments data was collected from the US Securities and Exchange Commission (SEC)'s own investigation of its six failed investigations (SEC Office of Investigations, 2009, OIG-509) and Lehman data was from bankruptcy court judgements (US Bankruptcy Court, 2010).

Further reports by auditors, government authorities and legal authorities may provide more interesting data in the future. Although the data may forever be incomplete, particularly regarding the role of individuals, conclusions can begin to be noted regarding the manipulation and management of compliance that resulted in over-compliance by financial watchdogs.

Triangulation (Pettigrew, 1974) from interviews, primary and secondary data, external accountants, regulators, competitors, bank officials and other informants will continue in coming years as more data emerges.

Case 1: Sino-Forest

The Sino-Forest case involved alleged massive fraud over a period of 18 years by rainmaking senior management within the firm along with the manipulation of its auditors (Ernst & Young), investment bank equity analysts (Bank of Montreal (BMO), Credit Suisse (CS), Dundee Securities (Dundee), Merrill Lynch (ML), Morgan Stanley (MS), RBC Dominion Securities (RBC) and Scotia Capital (Scotia)) and a prestigious forest products consulting firm (Helsinki-based Poyry). At Canadian Sino-Forest, the alleged massive fraud appears to have existed from its inception in 1994 to its collapse in 2011. Sino-Forest's implosion resulted in the destruction of \$3 billion in equity value and a further \$3 billion in losses to bondholders and creditors.

The opacity of complex financial structures (i.e. 150 British Virgin Island subsidiaries) and a web of intricate and often fictive timber rights, questionable Chinese equity joint ventures and anonymous middlemen in China obfuscated economic analysis of what appeared to be a consistently growing and highly profitable enterprise. Consistent growth was illusory yet necessary for a Ponzi scheme to flourish. This is reminiscent of the Madoff Ponzi scheme described below, as investors were promised consistent high returns in an inconsistent market.

Sino-Forest Products started as a public company in 1994 and 1995 on the Alberta Stock Exchange and Toronto Venture Stock Exchange (ticker symbol: TRE) via a reverse takeover (RTO). From 2003 to 2011, it began to actively raise debt (over $2 billion) and equity (over $4 billion) via a complicated and opaque structure. On 8 June 2011, the Ontario Securities Commission (OSC) announced that it had begun an investigation into Sino-Forest Products due to a highly unfavourable research report by Muddy Waters LLC, which was made public on 2 June 2012. After reviewing documents submitted by an independent audit committee of Sino's board of directors, a cease trade order was issued by the OSC in respect of Sino-Forest shares and senior management on 26 August 2011. On 30 March 2012, the company commenced bankruptcy proceedings under Canada's Companies' Creditors Agreement Act. On 4 April 2012, Ernst & Young officially resigned as the company's auditor, and on 5 April 2012 the OSC filed an enforcement notice for activity contrary to the Ontario Securities Act. On 22 May 2012, the OSC decided to go ahead with a lawsuit accusing Sino-Forest's senior management of fraud.

Sino-Forest claimed that Chinese agents, or authorized intermediaries (AIs), bought logs, turned them into chips and sold them to customers on behalf of Sino-Forest. The identities of the AIs were not disclosed due to 'competitive' reasons. Sino-Forest's management claimed that the company could not engage in owning timber and rights in China as a foreign firm (although this was subsequently disputed, since it had Chinese subsidiaries and joint ventures). Throughout the value chain, Sino-Forest agreed to only be responsible for the asset risk between the transformation of raw timber into wood chips and the sale of the wood chips. The AIs apparently (often fictively and opaquely) owned timber assets and cutting rights with a multitude of Chinese government agencies, middlemen and partners at multiple levels and geographic locations. In exchange, Sino-Forest owned rights to the wood in process and bought and resold the rights for a profit. Money appears to have been raised in Canada and then moved into and tunnelled out of China (via over 150 subsidiaries in the British Virgin Islands, intercompany transactions, joint venture transactions and unidentified 'independent' AI's) without assets being verified and the volume of timber activity claimed actually being done, and without it being at arm's length. It appears that no outsiders were able to accurately verify who owned what and where. Sino-Forest's auditors had little concern for assets that the company did not own but rather would sample contracts and money movements (real and opaque). Revenues were inflated and rose consistently as more debt and equity was raised each year and funnelled in and out of China. Sino-Forest earned a 55 per cent gross margin for taking little risk and doing little. Financial statements were thus fabricated and looked better and better each year, fuelling successful capital raising. Auditors and investment bank analysts were for the most part non-Chinese and based in Canada, further complicating matters as transactions, joint venture partners, AIs, timber rights and assets were mainly in China. In order to build legitimacy, Sino-Forest used a highly reputable Finnish forest products consultancy (Poyri), giving them limited access to timber holdings for verification purposes (0.3% of inflated assets) and allegedly falsifying information regarding the size and nature of timber holdings and cutting rights. Investment analysts relied upon management assurances, audited numbers and Poyri's consulting reports to engage in armchair analysis that recommended buying the stock. It is interesting to note that Sino-Forest's stock was recommended by eight investment bank analysts prior to Muddy Waters's scathing negative analysis and allegations of fraud on 2 June 2011. Within one month, these banks all reversed their recommendations and halted coverage, except for one analyst that called the allegations groundless (Dundee

Capital). Two of the analysts belonged to firms that earned over $20 million in fees from capital-raising for Sino-Forest in 2010. A future stage of this research is envisaged that looks at how discourse built legitimacy for Sino-Forest stock via analyst reports in Canada and China before and after the firm's demise.

Case 2: Madoff and the SEC

On 29 June 2009, Bernard L. Madoff was sentenced to 150 years in prison by a US federal court judge for securities fraud charges brought forward by the SEC. In 1960, at the age of 22, Madoff founded a small independent trading firm, Madoff Investment Securities LLC. His business grew over several decades, and by 1989 Madoff's firm handled over 5 per cent of the volume of the New York Stock Exchange. In 1990 he became chairman of NASDAQ, the electronic stock exchange of the National Association of Securities Dealers. In 1992, Madoff was investigated for allegations related to a Ponzi scheme allegedly run by Frank Avellino, but no charges were laid. In private communications with the SEC since 1999 and publicly from November 2005, a private investigator, Harry Markopolos, and numerous others alleged that Madoff's returns were fictive and that he was running a giant Ponzi scheme. The SEC's very cursory investigations exonerated Madoff. In 2008, as a result of the stock market crash and a lack of new funds from which to pay illusory successful returns on investments, Madoff told his son, Peter, that his business was a massive fraud. His son contacted the police shortly thereafter, and Madoff was charged with fraud. It is estimated that Madoff's fraud cost investors over $65 billion over 20 years.

Since none of the numerous major red flags related to Madoff and dating back to 1975 were acted upon by the SEC, the SEC's Office of Inspector General (OIG) launched a far-reaching major investigation into the SEC's New York, Boston and Los Angeles offices, among others, on 18 December 2008. It carefully reviewed all investigative papers related to Madoff and his firms, family and associates between 1975 and 2009. In addition to 3.7 million emails and numerous documents, the OIG interviewed 122 individuals with knowledge of the SEC's previous investigations of Madoff. The OIG discovered that the SEC had received six major substantive complaints that raised massive red flags between 1992 and December 2008. It noted that even though the SEC conducted three examinations and two investigations, a 'thorough and competent' investigation or examination was never conducted. Also, the OIG confirmed that the SEC was aware of but ignored two 2001 articles in reputable publications regarding Madoff's highly questionable long-term track record of consistently positive and extraordinary returns. Table 15.1 in the appendix highlights some of these red flags and how Madoff and the SEC ignored them.

Case 3: Lehman Brothers

Lehman Brothers Holdings Inc. sought Chapter 11 protection in September 2008 in the largest ever bankruptcy of its kind. Lehman was highly leveraged, with assets of approximately $700 billion against capital of approximately $25 billion. In addition to its very high leverage, its long-term assets were funded primarily by short-term deposits. In fact, it had to make billions of dollars in daily borrowings to stay afloat. In 2006, Lehman decided to increase its exposure to sub-prime assets, and it exceeded its own risk limits and controls. The collapse of Bear Sterns in March 2008 put further stress on liquidity. Rating agency leverage and liquidity ratios became important to Lehman's senior management. Lehman did not disclose that it was both legally and allegedly illegally manipulating its numbers by using an accounting device known to Lehman as Repo 105, which temporarily removed $50 billion of assets (treated as asset sales rather than financings) on balance sheet snapshot dates at the end of the first and second quarters of 2008. According to the bankruptcy court examiner, Lehman's accountants, Ernst & Young, were aware but did not question the non-disclosure and use of this major balance sheet window-dressing accounting transaction (Repo 105). For example, at the second quarter 2008 balance sheet date, Lehman's reported net leverage was 12.1:1 using Repo 105 versus actual net leverage without Repo 105 of 13.9:1 times. In May 2008, a Lehman senior vice president wrote a letter to Ernst & Young alleging accounting improprieties, which was ignored. On 12 June 2008, while investigating the letter, Ernst & Young was informed by the executive that Lehman used $50 billion of Repo 105 transactions to temporarily remove this amount of assets from its balance sheet. The next day, Ernst & Young met with Lehman's audit committee but did not advise them of the executive's concerns, despite directions from the audit committee that it be advised of all allegations.

Why and how did these many risk detection and management systems fail in the face of the smoke and fire of large warning flares going off? This chapter will highlight the dialogue between economic, social and ideological logics and processes that helps to explain these failures.

Conceptualizing over-compliance: a dynamic view of two packages of processes

When viewing over-compliance that culminates in financial fraud and collapse, there are two processes that become apparent at an organizational level over time. These processes lead to two important outcomes. The first is the accumulation of non-compliant activities by an in-group of an organization, which at some point puts the survival of an organization at risk (e.g. rogue bankers). Somehow, rationality and control of internal and external compliance officers is undermined and overridden. The second is when those unaware of the facts realize that something is amiss. This often may cause a credit crisis and losses. This may end in a firm's demise and bankruptcy, as illustrated by the cases of Sino-Forest, Madoff and Lehman. Given the synchronous nature of most large financial institutions and markets, mimetic behaviour can threaten the entire financial system (see Vit, 2013, on the subprime crisis).

I have condensed these two processes—crisis building due to over-compliance and the crash—into two events (Event 1 and Event 2; see Figure 15.1). Within the three cases presented, the firms achieved fame and fortune based upon knowingly taking large risks that were not understood by internal and external compliance officers and regulators. Next, red flags warn that the company is at risk. These signals are ignored by compliance officers and denied by fraudsters (and legal risk-takers). Over-compliance and the comfort afforded when social

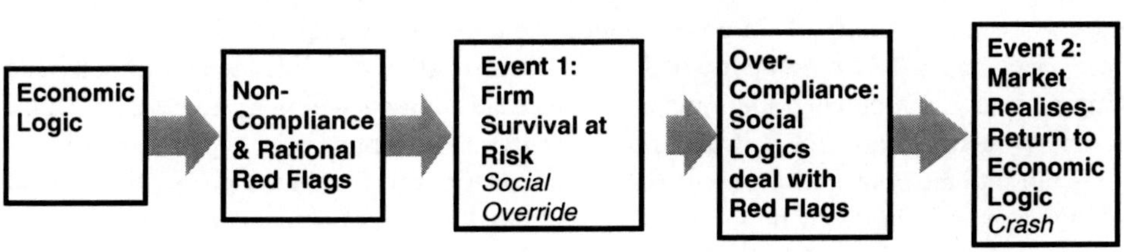

Figure 15.1 Social override of non-compliance by over-compliance (adapted from Vit, (2013)).

forces override technical rationality often move fictive assets and their prices even higher. The risks taken accumulate until they ultimately threaten the survival of the firm. Although a thorough investigation would tell a different rational-financial story, a highly profitable false money machine is rationalized by insiders (management and sometimes fraudsters) and enthusiastic outsiders (analysts, rating agencies) as self-evident. Event 1 occurs when the firm's survival is at risk. The focus of this chapter is on how social logics deal with contradictions thrown up by a management accounting system's loud warnings bells. Finally, managerial and market participants discover that there is a huge problem, which then results in Event 2: a financial collapse or crash. The non-economic logics that permit deviation from rules and regulations prior to Event 1 and temporarily reconcile contradictions (a state of nature I call 'over-compliance') prior to Event 2 are the central areas of interest of this chapter. These may be legal or illegal activities, but the underlying processes are identical.

If over-compliance can be better understood by examining processes around these events, frauds and crashes might be avoided. Over-compliance reinforces favourable conditions for fraudulent activity (Vit 1997, 2013). In the cases of Sino-Forest, Madoff and the SEC, and Lehman, it appears that management used this social space in order to profit from over-compliance. Opaque financial models and information provided to compliance officers, equity analysts and debt rating agencies further turbocharged the process.

Theory: economic and non-economic logics

Reason and economic logic are sometimes truncated by social forces and conformism. The over-reliance on social logics by internal and external compliance governors in the above-mentioned cases demonstrates the successful decoupling of economic rationality from analysis. For example, this chapter discussed facts related to the underlying technical and economic logic of risk analysis and compliance by Sino-Forest's and Lehman's managements, boards and accountants. The chapter also touched upon the different cognitive routines (taken-for-grantedness of accuracy and veracity of audited numbers) and cultural norms as well as the limited identification of the actors involved (auditors, directors and equity analysts), although further research is necessary in this regard. Recent compliance scholarship has married economics and sociology theory to examine the economic sociology of the 2008 US financial crisis via a recent collection of the writings of management theorists (Lounsbury and Hirsch, 2010). In a similar vein, and building upon the work of Merton (1933), Thompson and Tudon (1958) and Vickers (1965), I call these multiple packages of conformity-building processes eco-logics, socio-logics and ideo-logics, respectively (Vit, 2007). Economic logic operates under the assumption of some form of market efficiency and rationality (eco-logics). Sociology's institutional theory sheds light upon the invisible institutionalization and structuration of a field that results in unthinking conformity (socio-logics) and isomorphism (DiMaggio and Powell, 1983; Scott, 2005). Also, at an organizational and sub-organizational level of analysis, the norms, culture and ideology of 'in-groups' (ideo-logics) may be fragmented and in competition with one another to the point at which social identification overrides seemingly obvious warning signs (e.g. fraudulent traders and compliance accountants within an investment bank). Evolutionary theory is another body of knowledge that may explain why organizational participants fall into the conformity trap. If risk compliance governors do not deeply understand either the economic logics of how money is made or the institutional games organizations play, they open themselves up to being buffeted by chance and prearranged routines that may result in financial disaster. Evolutionary theory is a dialogue between these two unthinking processes: contingency and incumbency.

All of these logics manifested themselves at Sino-Forest, the SEC and Lehman within different groups. Figure 15.2, illustrates a risk governor's reliance upon economic theory (Quadrant 1), institutional and identification theory (Quadrant 2) or lack of understanding of both, resulting in the conformity trap and the effects of runaway evolutionary theory (Quadrant 4). The deep contrarian understanding of all of these dimensions in order to manage risk is desired (Quadrant 3). This framework can be used prospectively and retrospectively. Quadrant 1 presupposes that a compliance officer has expert knowledge related to economic logic, but ignores non-economic signals. In contrast, Quadrant 2 is rooted in the non-economic logics of institutional and identification theory and suggests that compliance officers are influenced by and manage risk using social ties, trust and social structure.

Quadrant 3 of Figure 15.2 represents a deep understanding of both economic and non-economic logics on the part of compliance officers who flag non-compliance and prevent fraud and possible massive losses. Quadrant 3 also represents a fraudster's insight into all logics that may be necessary to override technical rationality between Event 1 and Event 2 to create a fictive money machine. Thus, 'super-intelligence', or an ability to orthogonally see and understand economic and non-economic activity, is essential on the part of compliance officers as illustrated by Quadrant 3. Sino-Forest, Madoff and Lehman did not survive, but the SEC and other organizations (see Vit, 2013) were able to survive the manipulation of logics and an Event 2 crash. Quadrant 4 of Figure 15.2 presents an alternative accidental or evolutionary theoretic view that suggests that risk compliance officer non-awareness of

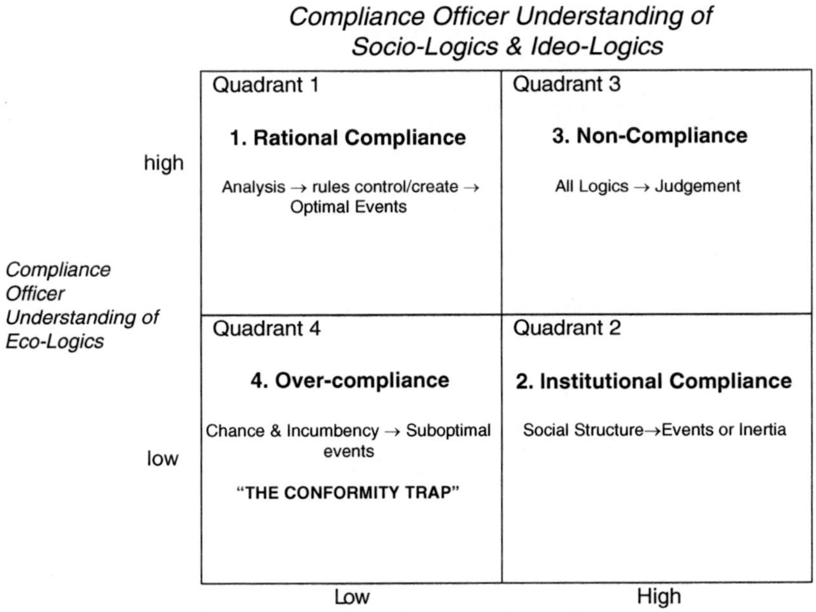

Figure 15.2 Sino-Forest, and the SEC re: Madoff and Lehman: multiple logics and compliance models (adapted from Vit, 2013).

both economic and non-economic pressures may allow small chance events to combine with organizational routines and algorithms to create big suboptimal events such as fraud that could threaten the survival of an organization. I call this the conformity trap. For example, Sino-Forest's auditors and investment bank equity analysts were locked in their day-to-day routines and did not detect the manipulation by management of Chinese joint ventures; fictive Chinese joint ventures and timber rights; needless opacity involving 150 Cayman Islands subsidiaries; and outright fraud. The appendix operationalizes these logics with respect to the Lehman and Madoff cases. The processes noted within these quadrants may be summarized by the models described below.

This dominant rational compliance model is prescriptive. It assumes that rigorous internal and external analysis is ongoing, and that this in turn results in optimal rules, decisions and action. It is driven by technical rationality (Thompson, 1967).

In fact, as outlined in the three cases discussed, facts were actually myths that were given life by non-economic manipulation.

Alternative micro process-based models

Figures 15.3–15.6 present alternative risk management and mismanagement models. The first model suggests that events happen, and organizations engage in manufacturing sense. The last two are evolutionary and institutional; they offer explanations of how firms are shaped by and shape approaches to understanding and managing risk. In the three cases discussed, these alternative organizational risk models provide perspectives that help to explain the social eclipse of technical rationality and numbers.

External ↘
Analysis → rules govern → control-> Optimal events
Internal ↗

Figure 15.3 Rational compliance model (adapted from Vit, 2013).

Deep Under standing of All Logics → Fraud Prevented (Compliance Governors)
Or Fraud (Fraudsters)

Figure 15.4 Non-compliance model (adapted from Vit, 2013).

chance ↘
suboptimal events & over-compliance
incumbency ↗

Figure 15.5 Over-compliance (conformity trap) model (adapted from Vit, 2013).

social structure → events or non-events

Figure 15.6 Institutional compliance model (adapted from Vit, 2013).

For example, the non-compliance model illustrated in Figure 15.4 can be used to explain risk-taking by fraudsters that leads to an Event 1. In a booming and opaque market, questionable facts that are never questioned by auditors or by expert analysts and consultants become praxis. Sino-Forest, Madoff and Lehman took on disguised but increasing levels of risk that produced attractive returns, which were attributed to these money machines. Fraudulent and manipulative senior managers and traders understood both economic and social logics in order to game compliance and risk systems.

The over-compliance model (see Figure 15.5) has its roots in evolutionary theory (Gould, 1990). It suggests that many small chance events may contribute to quantum change, and that routines and habits are obstacles to adaptation until an organization is faced with a big crisis (Miller and Friesen, 1985). For example, Sino-Forest's investment bank equity analysts and the SEC's Madoff investigators were locked into their narrowly defined incumbent routines, and chance events resulted in opportunities for manipulation of their processes that led to Event 1 and Event 2.

The institutional compliance model in Figure 15.6 suggests that—contrary to rational compliance model's assumption that analysis and rules drive the optimization of organizational action, as seen in Figure 15.3—the weight of social structures within an organization, and particularly its organizational field and peers, can also create risky action and inaction.

The same processes and logics treated at an organizational level of analysis in this chapter can be applied to a higher level of analysis in a way that is reinforcing. Within the accounting profession and the investment banking industry (particularly stock analysts and underwriters), institutional theory (DiMaggio and Powell, 1981, 1993; Scott, 1995; Holm, 1995; Vit, 2007) is useful in explaining how conformist-building forces and processes produce elites who appear to be infallible. Highly specialized professional groups (e.g. financial accountants, equity analysts and derivatives traders) in an organizational field manage to divorce themselves from the more certain economic routines of large organizations due to the over-compliance of regulators and of internal and external monitors. In the cases of Sino-Forest, Madoff and Lehman, external legitimating processes on the part of management consultants, bond-rating agencies, auditors, industry associations and journals built social legitimacy and assisted in the arrival of Event 1.

Conclusion

This exploratory chapter has begun to shed light upon the dynamics of over-compliance and the trap that is conformity. It has sought to demonstrate that the same logics that promote judgement within rational compliance management systems can also be used to explain processes that result in the abandonment of technical rationality and its consequences.

An important contribution of this paper is that different understandings of these multiple logics may be gained from viewing them in relation to different compliance models, as illustrated by the three cases presented. The cases presented were not isolated incidents of fraud. Rather, many internal and external risk analysts and compliance officers decoupled from the underlying technical and economic logic (Thompson, 1967) of these organizations. Rationalizing social forces of conformity trapped and incapacitated economic rationality.

This chapter and the three cases presented have demonstrated that compliance may be viewed in the context of compliance models that underscore the fact that nothing, except conformity, is a 'no-brainer'.

Appendix

Table 15.1 Compliance logics: Madoff/SEC and Lehman (adapted from Vit, 2006)

	Eco-logics	*Socio-logics*	*Ideo-logics*
Coordinating mechanisms	(a) Standardisation of work processes and outputs	(a) In-groups: standardization of skills—opaque models and specialists, reinforced by consultants and rating agencies	(A) Standardization of norms
Conformist mechanisms	(a) Rational rules (b) Economic models (c) Algorithms (d) Quantitative methods	(a) Cognitive routines (b) Recipes (c) Ceremonies	(a) Common values, norms/identification (b) Internalization/loyalty
Contrarian deviation in mechanisms	(a) Technology tampering (b) Alleged trader fraud and alleged forgery of confirmations, trades and reports	(a) Exploiting rules (b) Reinforcing ceremony (c) Navigation within rules and hierarchies (d) Soft social skills	(a) Cultural cleavages (b) In-groups vs outgroups (c) Limited identification

Madoff/SEC and Lehman

	Eco-logics	*Socio-logics*	*Ideo-logics*
Conformist mechanisms and over-compliance	**Madoff/SEC** • Madoff met with SEC and dealt with investigations related to six major complaints in 1992–2008	**Madoff/SEC** • Madoff was extremely well-connected and was chairman of NASDAQ in 1999 • Social pressures forced examiners to accept Madoff's responses at face value (SEC-OIG, p. 21) • Draft letter to National Association of Securities Dealers (NASD) to verify trade records was never sent due to investigators' worry over not being able to deal with the amount of trading data they were to get back • No third-party analysis of Madoff's trading inconsistencies	**Madoff/SEC** • SEC examiners in all cases were inexperienced attorneys and not from the financial broker/dealer community • Narrow framing of investigations done by SEC focused exclusively on front-running regardless of numerous serious complaints received

	Lehman • Lehman board, senior management, and finance and risk committees agreed to fund long-term high-risk assets with very short-term liabilities	**Lehman** • Despite publishing $2.8 billion loss on June 9, 2008, Lehman raises $6 billion in public offering on 12 June 2008, although Treasury Secretary warns of inadequate capital • 10 September 2008 public declaration of $41 billion in cash; liquidity was actually less than $2 billion	**Lehman** • Senior management ethos of long/short gap funding, and 'double-down' counter-cyclical 2006–2008 strategy (massively increasing risky bets and leverage) • Balance sheet manipulation viewed as normal
Contrarian deviation in mechanisms resulting in non-detection of non-compliance	**SEC/Madoff** • SEC consistently failed to contact third parties to confirm trades in 1994–2008 • SEC used inexperienced attorneys exclusively • Madoff engaged in elaborate Ponzi scheme with fictive trading since 1994 • Two reputable 2001 articles strongly questioned Madoff's consistently positive returns	**SEC/Madoff** • Madoff dealt with questions about never-ending positive returns and economic evidence of its impossibility by bullying questioners and stating that he uses 'gut-feel' to trade profitably over time	**SEC/Madoff** • Madoff alleged collusion with accountant and employees regarding Ponzi scheme • Madoff's niece Shana Madoff's romance with SEC-OCIE assistant director E Swanson disclosed, and SEC-OIG finds no evidence of conflict
	Lehman • Lehman used Repo 105 trick with no other purpose than to reduce leverage by removing $50 billion from balance sheet • Ernst & Young external auditors were aware of Repo 105 transactions • Ernst & Young did not report Lehman senior vice president's allegations of leverage ratio manipulation even though Lehman board audit committee ordered all allegations to be escalated to them	**Lehman** • Short-term bonus incentives drove long/short funding strategy; easy to increase assets and fund daily as rates fell in up-cycle • Pressure of rating agencies resulted in manipulation of leverage ratios	**Lehman** • Lehman's tight insiders did not disclose either the use or magnitude of Repo 105 to rating agencies, the government, investors or its own board of directors

Sources: US Bankruptcy Court, 2010; US Securities and Exchange Commission, 2009.

References

DiMaggio, P. and W.W. Powell (1983), 'The Iron Cage Revisited: Institutional Isomorphism and Collective Rationality in Organizational Fields', *American Sociological Review*, 48(2), pp. 147–160.
DiMaggio, P. and W.W. Powell (1991), *The New Institutionalism in Organizational Analysis*, Chicago: University of Chicago Press.
Holm, P. (1995), 'The Dynamics of Institutionalization: Transformation Processes in Norwegian Fisheries', *Administrative Science Quarterly*, 40(3), pp. 398–422.
Mintzberg, H. (1979), *The Structuring of Organizations: A Synthesis of the Research*, London: Prentice Hall.
Scott, W.R. (1995), *Institutions and Organizations*, Thousand Oaks: Sage.
Thompson, J.D. (1967), *Organizations in Action*, New York: McGraw-Hill.
Thompson, J.D. and A. Tudon (1959), 'Strategies, Structures and Processes of Organizational Decision', in J.D. Thompson *et al.* (eds.), *Comparative Studies in Administration*, Pittsburgh, PA: University of Pittsburgh Press.
US Bankruptcy Court (2010), Southern District of New York. Bank of America et al. vs. Lehman Bros. 08-1753.
US Securities and Exchange Commission (2009), 'Investigation of Failure of the SEC to Uncover Bernard Madoff's Ponzi Scheme', Report No. OIG-509, 31 August, Office of Investigations, US Securities and Exchange Commission. https://www.sec.gov/news/studies/2009/oig-509.pdf
Vickers, G. (1965), *The Art of Judgement: A Study of Policy Making*, New York: Basic Books.
Vit, G. (2007), 'The Multiple Logics of Conformity and Contrarianism: The Problem with Investment Banks and Bankers', *Journal of Management Inquiry*, 16(3), pp. 217–226.
Vit, G. (2013), *The Risk in Risk Management: The Problem of Conformity in Financial Institutions*, New York: Routledge.

Futher Reading

Asquith, P. and J. Mullins (1989), 'Original Issue High Yield Bonds: Aging Analyses of Defaults, Exchanges, and Calls', *Journal of Finance*, 44, pp. 923–952.
Astley, W.G. and C.J. Fobrum (1983), 'Collective Strategy: Social Ecology of Organizational Environments', *Academy of Management Review* 8(4), pp. 576–587.
Brealey, R. (1985), *An Introduction to Risk and Return*, London: Blackwell.
Covaleski, M. and M.W. Dirsmith (1988), 'An Institutional Perspective on the Rise, Social Transformation and Fall of a University Budget Category', *Administrative Science Quarterly*, 33(4), pp. 562–587.
Credit Suisse (2011a), 'Sino-Forest Corporation', A. Kuske, 16 May, research report.
Credit Suisse (2011b), 'The Long Road to Re-Rating', A. Kuske, 5 June, research report.
Dundee Capital Markets (2011a), 'Poyry Plantation 2010 Asset Valuation up 36% YOY Reiterate TOP PICK', R. Kelertas, 30 May, research report.
Dundee Capital Markets (2011b), 'Sino-Forest: Rating Under Review (Pending Further Information)', R. Kelertas, 3 June, research report.
Elsbach, K.D. (1999), 'An Expanded Model of Organizational Identification', in B.M. Staw and R.I. Sutton (eds.), *Research in Organizational Behaviour*, vol. 21, Greenwich, CT: JAI Press.
Galbraith, J.K. (2004), *The Economics of Innocent Fraud*, Boston: Houghton Mifflin.
Gimpl, M.L. and S.R. Dakin (1984), 'Management and Magic', *California Management Review*, 27(1), pp. 125–136.
Gould, S.J. (1987), 'The Panda's Thumb of Technology', *Natural History*, 96(1), p. 14.
Greenwood, R. and C.R. Hinings (1996), 'Understanding Radical Organizational Change: Bringing Together the Old and the New Institutionalism', *Academy of Management Review*, 21(4), pp. 1022–1054.
HSBC (2011a), 'Asia Credit Investment Daily', M. Olson, 31 May, research report.
HSBC (2011b), 'Asia Credit Investment Daily', M. Olson, 21 May, research report.
Martinet, A.-C. (1999), 'La lecture strategique du diagnostic global', in A. Marion (ed.), *Le diagnostic d'entreprise: Méthode et processus*, Paris: Economica.
Merton, R.K. (1936), 'The Unanticipated Consequences of Purposive Social Action', *American Sociological Review*, 1(6), pp. 894–904.
Merton, R.K. (1938), 'Social Structure and Anomie', *American Sociological Review*, 3(5), pp. 672–682.
Meyer, J.W. and B. Rowan (1977), 'Institutionalized Organizations: Formal Structures as Myth and Ceremony', *American Journal of Sociology*, 83, pp. 340–363.

Meyer, J., and W.R. Scott (1983), *Organizational Environments: Ritual and Rationality*, Beverly Hills: Sage.

Miller, D. (1987), 'The Genesis of Configuration', *Academy of Management Review*, 12(4), pp. 686–701.

Miller, D. (1996), 'Configurations Revisited', *Strategic Management Journal*, 17(7), pp. 505–512.

Miller, R. and D. Lessard (2000), *The Strategic Management of Large Engineering Projects*, Cambridge, MA: MIT Press.

Miller, C.C., L.B. Cardinal and W.H. Glick (1997), 'Retrospective Reports in Organizational Research', *Academy of Management Journal*, 40(1), pp. 189–204.

Mintzberg, H. (1991), 'The Effective Organization: Forces and Forms', *Sloan Management Review*, 32(2), p. 54.

Morison, E. E. (1966), 'Gunfire at Sea: A Case Study of Innovation', in *Men, Machines and Modern Times*, Cambridge, MA: MIT Press, pp. 17–44.

Perkins, T. and T. Kiladze (2011), 'Sino-Forest Controversy Puts Analysts in Spotlight', *Globe and Mail*, 10 June.

RBC Capital Markets (2011a), 'Concerns on Sino-Forest Could Represent a Significant Buying Opportunity', P. Quinn, 13 May, research report.

RBC Capital Markets (2011b), 'Sino-Forest Shares Halted; Significant Allegations Raised' P. Quinn, 3 June, research report.

Schwartz, N.D. and K. Bennhold (2008), 'Where the Heads No Longer Roll', *New York Times*, 17 February.

Selznick, P. (1949), *TVA and the Grass Roots*, Berkeley: University of California Press.

Selznick, P. (1957), *Leadership in Administration: A Sociological Interpretation*, New York: Harper and Row.

Shapira, Z. and D.J. Berndt (1997), 'Managing Grand Scale Construction Projects: A Risk-Taking Perspective', *Research in Organizational Behaviour*, 14, pp. 303–360.

Simon, H.A. (1945), *Administrative Behavior*, New York: Macmillan.

Simon, H.A. (1979), 'Rational Decision Making in Business Organizations', *American Economic Review*, 69, pp. 495–513.

Staw, B.M. and L.D. Epstein (2000), 'What Bandwagons Bring: Effects of Popular Management Techniques on Corporate Performance, Reputation, and CEO Pay', *Administrative Science Quarterly*, 45(3), pp. 523–556.

Suchman, M.C. (1995), 'Managing Legitimacy: Strategic and Institutional Approaches', *Academy of Management Review*, 20(3), pp. 571–610.

Tolbert, P.S. and L.G. Zucker (1996), 'The Institutionalization of Institutional Theory', in S. Clegg, C. Hardy and W. Nord (eds.), *Handbook of Organizations*, London: Sage.

UBS (2008), 'Shareholder Report on UBS's Writedowns', April 18, Zurich.

UBS (2009a), 10 F filing to United States Securities and Exchange Commission, Washington, D.C. 20549, SEC file no. 1-15060, March 11, 2009, p. 1–413 and appendices.

UBS (2009b), 'UBS Results in First Quarter 2009', UBS AG Zurich, restated May 20.

Vit, G. (1996), 'Financial Services Industry Mismanagement', *International Journal of Service Industry Management*, 7(3), pp. 6–16.

Vit, G. (2006), 'Organizational Conformity and Contrarianism: Regular Irregular Trading at National Australia Bank', *Corporate Governance*, 6(2), pp. 203–214.

Vit, G. (2009), 'Foreseeing the Problem of Conformity in Strategy Teaching, Research and Practice', in B. MacKay and L. Costanza (eds.), *The Handbook of Research on Strategy and Foresight*, Cheltenham: Elgar Press, pp. 518–527.

Weick, K.E. (1979), *The Social Psychology of Organizing*, 2nd edn, Reading, MA: Addison-Wesley.

Zald, M.N. and P. Denton (1963), 'From Evangelism to General Service: The Transformation of the YMCA', *Administrative Science Quarterly*, 8(2), pp. 214–234.

Zucker, L.G. (1987), 'Institutional Theories of Organization', *Annual Review of Sociology*, 13, pp. 443–464.

16

Monitoring Shariah non-compliance risk in Islamic banking institutions

Nunung N. Hidayah

Introduction

The objective of this chapter is to explore the concept and monitoring of Shariah compliance and Shariah non-compliance risk management in Islamic banking institutions and provide future research directions. The contrasts between the concept of risk-sharing and the shifting paradigm of risk-sharing in modern Islamic instruments are highlighted. In addition, this chapter discusses the three lines of defence in Islamic banking perspective, to the ideal religious compliance monitoring in Islamic banks. This chapter also explores the role of Shariah scholars and their function, and the interpretation and implementation of religious compliance risk management in every aspect of banking operations. Finally, in the UK setting, a case of Shariah compliance risk management and Shariah non-compliance risk monitoring gives an insight as to how it has been implemented at the bank level.

The original profit- and risk-sharing concept in Islamic banking institutions

The Islamic financial model originated out of the profit- and risk-sharing transactions of medieval traders known as *commenda*,[1] which were in the form of a joint venture[2] with proportionate profit and loss sharing (*mudharaba*). This partnership-based financial model was meant to encourage entrepreneurship. It, accordingly, expects to empower the active partner to have an equal position as the capital provider (*musharaka*). All participants engaged in this partnership investment bear equally distributed risks, and any increases in value are justified by the risks taken. From a theoretical perspective, the *mudharaba* and *musharaka* forms of pure investment vehicles will trigger real economic productive activity.

After the tenth century, Ahmad ibn ʻAlī al-Maqrīzī[3] (1364–1442) proposed a monetary reform in line with Islamic precedent and practices in Muslim society in the past (Meloy, 2003, p. 187). He published a book entitled *Helping the Community by Examining the Causes of Its Distress* (*Ighāthat al-umma bi-kashf al-ghumma*) in 1405 that was dedicated to examining famine and inflation since 1404 (Kato, 2012). Al-Maqrīzī addressed the economic crisis of the time, arguing that it was due to ‘political corruption, the rise of land prices and the circulation of copper money', which affected 'the distribution of income and wealth between social classes' (Kato, 2012, p. 36).

Al Maqrīzī thus proposed an idea for monetary reform in the Mamluk period in Egypt (1250–1517). He proposed the practice of risk-sharing through joint capital effort partnerships (*mudharaba*), which was one of the approved transactions during the caliphate of Umar bin Khattab (a very close companion of Prophet Muhammad), in addition to the development of a religious levy (*zakah*) and the creation of endowment (*waqf*) institutions to play a main role in funding public works (Diwany, 2010; Goitein, 1967; Meloy, 2003; Sabra, 2000). Risk-sharing and joint capital effort partnerships represent similar activities to modern banking practices that are performed in a Shariah-compliant way.

The Islamic banking institution (IBI) was reincarnated in a modern form when the Dallah al Barakah and Dar al Mal al Islami banking groups were founded in the 1970s. These groups sought to Islamize Western banking without changing its business model and institutional framework (Diwany, 2010, p. 250). Islamic principles (Shariah) govern IBIs, just as they govern individuals and their actions. Therefore, the Qur'an and the Sunnah, as the sources of the Islamic law (Shariah), govern the operations of IBIs. Those sacred references place emphasis on the importance of honesty, transparency, documentation, accountability and ethics (DiVanna *et al.*, 2009; Diwany, 2010; Iqbal and Mirakhor, 2007; Thomas *et al.*, 2005; Warde, 2010).

The religious imperative to infuse Shariah into financial institutions dictates the practices of IBIs in respect of avoiding exploitation and the unjust treatment of shareholders and customers (Shanmugam and Zahari, 2009). The religious imperative demands that IBIs be dedicated to empowering society through partnerships and philanthropic activities (Shanmugam and Perumal, 2006). A transaction in IBIs is deemed lawful and permissible under Shariah law as long as it avoids the involvement of interest (*riba*) in transactions; excessive uncertainty (*gharar*); and the taking of gain without either performing effort or accepting liability (Khir *et al.*, 2008).

The Shariah principles promote economic transactions based on real assets and an equal distribution of risks and obligations. The sacred rules also guide IBIs to avoid trading in respect of forbidden objects (for example, pig production, the sale and distribution of alcohol and the gambling business). The permissible contracts consist of transactional, financing, intermediation and social welfare contracts. The purpose of those contracts is to facilitate various forms of economic activity—including the sale and purchase of goods, exchanges, arrangement of credit and financing, collateral and guarantees—as well as to support society's development through investments and creation of opportunities (Diwany, 2010; Iqbal and Mirakhor, 2007; Vogel and Hayes, 1998).

When the risk-sharing paradigm shifts

In furthering the development of the Islamic banking instrument, a pioneer of modern Islamic banking and founder of the Jordan Islamic Bank, Dr Sami Hassan Homoud, in 1976 rediscovered the *murabaha* instrument, which represents sale with mark-up (Iqbal and Mirakhor, 2007). This vehicle was originally a sale contract for entrepreneurs to fulfil the needs of capital expansion of their business, under which the bank would provide commodities or raw materials. In a further development of practice, the sale contract turned into a financing contract, which was able to dominate the Islamic banking products portfolio.

In current banking practice, however, sales plus agreed margin—widely applied in the form of cost plus asset financing—are the dominant banking products. These products are akin to an interest-based loan in the interest-based banking system. Contracts that represent social welfare through a gratuitous loan and the collection of trust and endowment funds are gradually disappearing from banking products. Islamic bank products and services are relatively similar to their conventional counterparts. The deposits, financing and leasing products are merely mimicking the conventional banking products. As concluded by Hanif (2010), Islamic banks are very similar to modern conventional banks.

It is important to note, however, that as presented in a previous version of the Accounting and Auditing Organization for Islamic Financial Institutions (AAOIFI) standard (omitted in the newest version), loans are deemed to be rejected from the Islamic banks' investment vehicle:

> Islamic banks are founded on the principle of sharing profit and losses consistent with the Islamic concept of 'profit is for that who bears risk'. Islamic banks reject interest as a cost for the use of money and loans as investment vehicles (AAOIFI, 2009).

Along with the changes in the standard regarding loans, the practice of risk-sharing in Islamic banking products and services has changed as well. IBIs, under the guidance of Shariah, are unique compared to their conventional counterparts in their promotion of partnership through both risk-sharing and joint effort and equity partnerships. In the case of Islamic banks, customers are treated as partners or investment account holders in the partnership contract. In recent practice, *murabaha* is often combined with a leasing (*ijara*) contract with a deferred payment scheme, which appears Shariah-compliant in its structure, whilst also looking substantially like a standard loan. As a consequence, the concept that money should be created from productive activity in its ideal state turns into a result of debt-based transactions. The implication is that an Islamic bank that in theory is not highly leveraged and not susceptible to a liquidity crisis may not be quite as it appears.

The Shariah governance of Islamic banks

In a governance context, Chapra (1992, p. 234) has highlighted the concept of engaging stakeholder participation (*Shura*) in the affairs of IBIs, either directly or via representatives. The concept of *Shura* is represented by the existence of Shariah supervisory boards (SSB). Their role is to interpret and monitor the implementation of Islamic law (Shariah) in banking operations. The SSB plays a critical role in ensuring that all of a bank's activities are in line with Shariah principles, while shareholders also play a substantial role as active participants in the process of decision-making. Other stakeholders, including the community, should also cooperate to protect the interest of the bank as a whole and to stimulate the social well-being function that exists to meet social welfare needs. All of these processes are focused on fulfilling Islamic corporate governance's private and social goals by upholding the principle of distributive justice (Choudury and Hoque, 2004, pp. 85–88).

Therefore, it is clearly defined that the core attributes of IBIs are not restricted merely to ensuring that the actions of management are in line with the interests of shareholders and stakeholders; they must also fulfil religious values and Shariah requirements based on the Qur'an and Sunnah. In this way, the spirit of governance will be in accordance with the objective (*maqasid*) of Shariah, which is to bring about social welfare by upholding the principle of distributive justice for the organization and for society.

In view of the broader perspective and objective of corporate governance in IBIs, the conventional governance standards can be paired with Shariah requirements to create a corporate governance structure that is suited to IBIs. That is, there is another dimension to corporate governance in IBIs in addition to the conventional perspective. To add Shariah compliance assurance as an essential requirement of corporate governance in IBIs, the role and function of a Shariah committee or SSB is an important aspect of this governance.

In Islamic banks, there are two categories of owners: the shareholders, as in conventional institutions, and the investment account holders, or depositors. The relationship between investment account holders and the bank is similar to that of a collective investment scheme, in which participants (the investment account holders) have authorized their fund manager (the IBI) to manage their investments (Stanley, 2006). In a *mudharaba* contract, the depositors (investment account holders) are seen as the owners of capital (*rab-al-maal*), whilst the Islamic bank is the agent (*mudarib*). The depositors and the bank share the risks and rewards equally. Consequently, investment account holders are legally responsible for the incurrence of unexpected losses in the same way as shareholders. There is effectively no capital guarantee provided to shareholders/investments account holders.

To cope with such uncertainties, Islamic banks have adopted the use of a profit equalization reserve (PER) as a process of smoothing out returns to their unrestricted investment account holders. The Shariah-guided *mudharaba* contracts compete against the guaranteed returns offered by conventional banks, although in some jurisdictions the use of this guarantee scheme is effectively mandatory. The PER is a method to maintain a consistent level for Islamic banks' rates of return. The PER offsets the Islamic banks' poor performance when their profits are below the market return. However, the transparency of such practices is somewhat questionable from a good governance perspective. Therefore, corporate governance in IBIs must be customized to address such issues and protect the rights and needs of the investment account holders.

Three lines of defence in Islamic financial institutions

In January 2013, the Institute of Internal Auditors (IIA, 2013) proposed a position paper on the three lines of defence model, which provides a simple and effective way to help organizations delegate and coordinate essential control system, risk management and independent assurance duties in a systematic manner. This model was developed to enhance risk management, control and auditing as an independent assurance process by clarifying essential roles and duties. It provides a comprehensive way to help assure the ongoing success of control and risk management initiatives supported by the audit function, and it is appropriate for any organization regardless of size or complexity. Even in organizations in which a formal risk management framework or system does not exist, the three lines of defence model can enhance clarity regarding risks and controls and help improve the effectiveness of risk management systems.

The Committee of Sponsoring Organisations of the Treadway Commission (COSO) in the US has developed a well-known model of internal control that emphasizes the need for good corporate governance in organizations. The COSO model recommends that effective control systems contain the key elements of a control environment, which include the company's strategy for dealing with risk as well as its culture, codes of conduct, human resource policies and performance reward systems, and which should eventually support the business objectives. The company also needs to perform an assessment of risk and create controls to achieve its objectives.

The control activities should reflect, for example, the practices of segregation of duties, authorization and reconciliations. Moreover, communication and information are deemed important to ensure that all levels of management in the organization are made aware of any progress against objectives in a timely manner in the form of relevant and reliable reports. Additionally, monitoring and corrective action processes should be embedded in the organizational systems to ensure the effective application of policies and other control mechanisms (Norton and Hughes, 2009).

Based on the IIA (2013) paper on three lines of defence and the COSO framework of internal control, it is obvious that control, risk management assessment and monitoring are now seen as fundamental to an effective control system. These three important aspects will increase the likelihood of achieving objectives by ensuring that significant risks are addressed, that costs are reduced because the necessary controls are in place, and that continual monitoring through audit occurs as an independent assurance function. In the case of IBIs, the three lines of defence would be much more complex than in any other organization. Shariah law and the ethical culture attached to Islamic banking and finance provide underlying principles that shape the system of defence of IBIs. In addition, the three lines of defence need to be integrated into an IBI's operational and control system to achieve the business, ethical and social objectives that govern their operations.

Therefore, ideal corporate governance in IBIs in general and in Islamic banks in particular has a unique internalized stakeholders' perspective combined with Shariah compliance principles (Grais and Pellegrini, 2006). That is, IBIs should provide participation for all stakeholders, including investment account holders, combined with a strong fiduciary duty to both stakeholders and SSBs, to achieve the objective of complying with Shariah principles and providing excellent service to the community.

The way in which the three lines of defence can protect the values linked to IBIs and maintain their sustainability is illustrated in Figure 16.1. The framework provides a basis for understanding how an IBI can maintain its sustainability whilst instilling and integrating Shariah aspects into its operation. In the first line of defence, business unit and operational managers are the risk owners who are responsible for managing risks and implementing corrective actions to address inadequate processes and control deficiencies. They are responsible

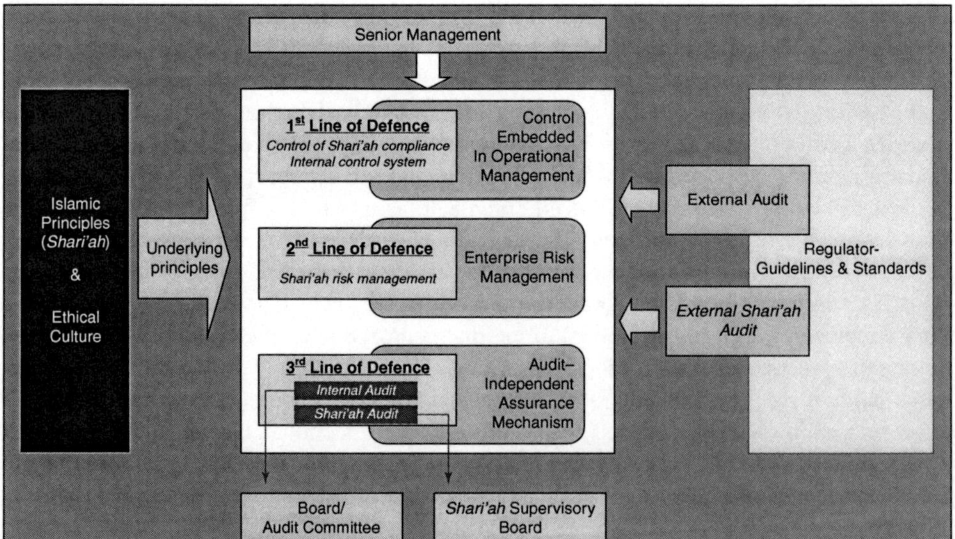

Figure 16.1 Modified three lines of defence in Islamic financial institutions (based on Ciorciari and Blattner, 2008; IIA, 2013; Norton and Hughes, 2009).

for maintaining effective internal and Shariah compliance controls, and for executing risk and control procedures on a day-to-day basis. Both general and Shariah compliance aspects of IBI operations need to be identified. IBIs should assess, control and mitigate risks, guiding the development and implementation of internal Shariah-compliance-driven policies and procedures and ensuring that activities are consistent with goals and objectives.

The second line of defence is the enterprise-wide risk management (ERM) function that provides independent oversight of the risk management activities of the first line of defence. Combined with the compliance functions, various risk management functions build and monitor the first line of defence controls. The specific functions will vary by organization and industry, but a typical function of risk management is to facilitate and monitor the implementation of effective risk management practices by operational management as the risk owners in defining the target risk exposure and reporting adequate risk-related information throughout the organization (IIA, 2013).

In IBIs, it is necessary to have important functions to monitor day-to-day Shariah compliance and the possibility of Shariah non-compliance risk occurrence. Shariah compliance review is required to provide direction and guidance in implementing Shariah pronouncements disseminated by the SSB. It is important to mitigate any unique risks within the operation, including any risks whereby customers may withdraw their funds, and to manage risks in respect of any aspects of non-compliance with the underlying principles.

The governance structures of an IBI are distinguished from conventional governance structures by the addition of an SSB. The SSB's role is as an in-house religious advisor with responsibility to ensure that the institution's business practices and products conform to Islamic law and to minimize the institution's exposure to fiduciary and reputational risks related to Islamic standards of compliance. Thus, in the third line of defence, independent assurance is required in respect of key controls that add value and enhance the effectiveness of the company's operation, including assurance of whether the IBI is Shariah-compliant.

This independent and objective assurance in Islamic financial institutions usually covers a broad range of objectives, including efficiency and effectiveness of operations; safeguarding of assets; reliability and integrity of reporting processes; and compliance with Islamic laws and other rules and regulations in all policies, procedures and contracts. It also covers all elements of the risk management and internal control framework, including the internal control environment and all elements of an organization's risk management framework (i.e. risk identification, risk assessment, risk response, information and communication, and monitoring).

The third line of defence should also examine the business processes of the overall entity and its divisions, subsidiaries, operating units and functions, including marketing, operations, accounting, human resources, asset management and information technology. Both an internal and external audit and a Shariah audit should be performed to challenge the level of assurances provided by the business unit and oversight functions, in respect of both operational and Shariah compliance perspectives. The reporting of risk will be forwarded to the ERM function for review.

Information on any Shariah non-compliance risk is collated with other risk reports, assessed and reported to the risk committee who are responsible for representing stakeholders in respect of risk issues. The internal audit findings should be reported to the board audit committee, who have the responsibility to maintain oversight and monitor the effectiveness of internal control processes, risk management processes and audit activities. At the same level, Shariah audit findings are reported to the SSB, which has a monitoring role and states an opinion based on the effectiveness of the Shariah compliance control system, Shariah non-compliance risk processes and Shariah audit activities.

With full support of senior management, the roles of the external auditor and the external Shariah auditor within the related regulatory environment complete the third line of defence by providing independent assurance on both business operations and Shariah oversights. For example, even though the practice of external Shariah audit is still under discussion there, the Sultanate of Oman produces through their central bank a very strict and robust framework for Shariah compliance. This framework requires that after three years of operations, Islamic banks operating in the jurisdiction must hire an independent body to perform an external Shariah review to ensure they are complying with Islamic principles.

Monitoring Shariah non-compliance risk in the Islamic banking industry in the UK

The UK became the first country in the European Union to allow stand-alone IBIs to offer Shariah-compliant products. It is now perceived to be the Western hub of Islamic finance, with the highest value of Shariah-compliant assets of any non-Muslim country (Morales and Shiblaq, 2013). The Financial Services Authority (FSA)[4] in the UK stated that its position as a secular regulator implied it had no mandate to cover any religious compliance requirements, as reiterated by the UK Treasury:

> The Government does not intend to adopt a state-led approach to improving standardisation in Islamic finance. The Government believes that such an approach would be inappropriate in the UK. … The UK Authorities are secular bodies, not religious regulators.
>
> *(HM Treasury, 2008, p. 24)*

This secular approach in the UK meant there was no space for a variation of regulations to address the uniqueness of Islamic finance contracts. In the case of a profit- and loss-sharing (*mudharaba*) deposit product, for example, the FSA required a deposit protection scheme. However, from an Islamic law perspective, customers, as investors, should bear any risk of loss as well as the potential profit generated. When operating in the UK market and within the UK regulatory framework, this contract cannot be fully applied. In effect, it forces an amendment of the basic Islamic financial contract to meet the regulatory requirements. In this sense, it appears that the Islamic principles operate below the UK standards and regulatory requirements.

> Shariah scholars interpret the principles of Shariah in light of community consensus and analogical reasoning, issuing a fatwa in order to give the go ahead to a product they deem to be permissible. Because the Shariah principles can be subject to varying interpretations … for Islamic finance there can be differences of opinion, either within or across national borders, on the permissibility of certain instruments.
>
> *(HM Treasury, 2008, p. 23)*

As the Treasury report explains, the nature of Islamic financial products is that they derive from an interpretation of Islamic law through consensus and analogical reasoning, which creates the possibility of different interpretations amongst Islamic scholars. For this reason, IBIs could have a range of opinions on the permissibility of certain products, either within or across different legal jurisdictions. From a regulator's perspective, the possibility of different interpretations of Islamic law is problematic. The FSA seemed to want to avoid potential arbitrage problems due to the uncertainty and ambiguities of Islamic law interpretations.

> What we don't want is a situation where firms undertake arbitrage because one form of regulatory treatment has favour over another. For example, if this Firm A does not care about Shariah compliance or not, [and] they just want to have a lower legal or regulatory build, then they may look at the regime, apply cost-benefit analysis, when actually it is more cost-effective for us to be Shariah-compliant than non-Shariah-compliant or vice versa (FSA officer—interview).

The regulator did not want to get involved in any Shariah aspect of Islamic products, as any conflicting Shariah opinion would create legal issues. It understood that the interpretation and implementation of Shariah principles has an ambiguity, with the result that Shariah principles are self-regulated in Islamic financial institutions. Concerned about the long process of Shariah certification and a lack of Shariah knowledge, the FSA consciously left the Islamic finance industry to decide on solutions.

As a result, Islamic finance in the UK faces the challenge of a lack of religious compliance rules due to this self-regulatory approach. The difficulties associated with defining what constitutes Shariah compliance ends with, as the FSA officer suggested in the above quotation, Shariah compliance assurance needing to be taken case by case, without a standardized approach.

This shapes the politically contested nature of religious rules in Islamic financial institutions, demonstrating Mahoney and Thelen's (2010) viewpoint that the lack of Shariah compliance enforcement opens a different degree of openness in the interpretation and implementation of these rules. Additionally, the lack of codification of the sacred rules due to different religious interpretations, the absence of globally accepted religious rules and the non-binding power of the existing standards add to the complexity and create ambiguity. Within this ambiguous rules environment, it will be interesting to explore the role religious principles play in the conception of the banking institution.

Shariah compliance risk management: the case of Ethical Trust Bank

Ethical Trust Bank (ETB),[5] our case organization, is one of four fully fledged Islamic banks in the UK. ETB has operated for almost ten years as a Shariah-compliant banking institution. Commencing business in the second half of 2004, ETB initially had seven branches in London, the Midlands and the North West. In its early days, ETB asserted that the purpose of its existence was to fulfil the religious needs of the 5 per cent of Muslims in the total UK population. It also aims to attract investors from Muslim countries, especially Middle Eastern investors who seek Shariah-compliant investment instruments. London, as a leading international financial centre, became an important selling point for this new industry.

Formed by Middle Eastern investors and FSA-approved,[6] this financial institution publicly states that five ethical and social values underpin its operations.[7] ETB declares that everything it does is in line with Islamic values. This development is inseparable from the development of Islamic finance in Muslim countries, and ETB defers to the religious imperative of having financial investment industry alternatives that suit minority religious values. As a consequence, the values demanded by the religious imperative dynamically shape and continuously reshape the identity and logic of ETB as it seeks to preserve its claim to be a Shariah-compliant institution.

ETB formally and informally addresses its vision to offer ethically and religiously based financial alternatives. ETB has made a commitment to fulfilling the religious imperative to provide alternative financial services in keeping with the principles and teaching of Islam. The different functions of the bank and the institution as a whole are aware of the need to address this imperative. The provision of alternative financial products and institutional arrangements based upon Shariah principles and with consequent ethical and social justice features is a specific ETB values commitment that in turn shapes its identity.

> The central operating capability [is] being rapidly expanded to enable the Bank to satisfy in a wholly Shariah compliant way the financial needs of the modern consumer. (anonymous, 2005)
>
> The Islamic bank offers an Islamic banking solution as a non-exploitative financial alternative for people. It still has to be competitive and at the same time be able to offer solutions for Muslims in the West. (senior Treasury manager—interview)

ETB's values commitment governs how the institution fulfils the religious imperative. ETB needs to present this religious commitment and a transcendental frame of reference to achieve institutional legitimacy. At the same time, it needs to secure an acceptable level of financial and economic performance. However, to combine these goals and balance them within the boundary of religious rules is not easy. Friedland and Alford (1991) explore five core institutions in society that bring their own logic to the creation of rules and constraints for individual, organizational and societal behaviours. The five institutions with different value spheres form various types of institutional logic that provide a cognitive frame of reference, an orientation for action and a sense of self and identity (Friedland and Alford, 1991; Glynn, 2013).

In this case, ETB is trying to combine the logic of both religion and the capitalist market, since a bank is a product of a capitalist market. At the same time, it cannot avoid the commercial logic embedded in financial institutions. ETB was established in order to provide an alternative for religious and ethical finance, thus requiring it to blend the two belief systems. ETB's values commitment, identity, operational frame of reference and orientation are formalized and have been documented in its Articles of Association since inception:

> It is intended that the business affairs of the Company shall be conducted in accordance with Shariah. Activities of the Company will at all times be supervised by the Shariah Supervisory committee. The Directors of the Company are obliged to ensure that the business of the Company is at all times Shariah compliant.

Formally, ETB frames the conduct of business and institutional actions so that it is obliged to comply with religious values. From the institutional perspective, the consequences are that the bank should infuse religious principles within its governance and control system as well as having its products and services follow the religious tenets. In the context of ETB, Shariah compliance is the unique value this Islamic bank has to offer to fulfil the need of the religious imperative from an economic and financial aspect. In terms of a Shariah-compliant aspect, ETB has created a values commitment in all of its activities. However, there are many factors, pressures and obstacles that might affect the way ETB delivers on its promises to offer Shariah-compliant banking solutions. Therefore, it would be interesting to investigate how the endogenous Shariah compliance principle works within the ambiguous rules of the ETB institutional environment.

Bracketing a symbolic Shariah compliance risk management

The role of the in-house scholars in the Shariah Supervisory Committee (SSC) is very important for ETB as an institution that declares Shariah as the values basis for its operation. The SSC is an independent body designed to perform the function of religious law translation and interpretation and to oversee the implementation of religious compliance principles in the operation of banks. ETB has three Shariah Middle Eastern scholars on its board of scholars. They have multiple board memberships in various Islamic banks globally.

> We are doing [the Shariah supervisory role/function] based on the current practices. For the current practices, the Shariah scholars set the rules, but the rules are to be executed and obeyed by the employees. So, the Shariah board is the writer of the rules, and they are themselves at the end of the year the verifier that those rules were observed or not. The internal officer helps them (SSC member 3—interview).

The Shariah board responsibility is delegated to the internal Shariah compliance officer (SCO) in the Shariah Compliance department for the day-to-day Shariah assurance process. The SCO's responsibility covers all of the process of the Shariah compliance review of every single transaction and includes an audit of Shariah compliance for all operational aspects of the bank. ETB confirms that the SCO's line of reporting in terms of Shariah compliance is solely to the SSC, as represented in the following statement: 'The SCO advises the Bank as an internal representative of the Bank's Shariah Supervisory Committee (SSC), and undertakes regular Shariah compliance audit and monitoring of the Bank's operations' (ETB, 2013).

As an internal Shariah compliance advisor and supervisor, the SCO receives a full delegation from the SSC to oversee the bank's Shariah compliance. His role as internal representative and as an assistant of the SSC is primarily to provide additional support for the SSC. The SCO's position and his relationship with the SSC are equal to the role and relationship of the audit manager and audit committee within the bank's governance system. Ideally, the SCO is responsible for reviewing religious compliance guidance codified by the in-house scholar and ensuring that it is implemented. In reality, however, the situation is the other way around.

The SCO plays the central role in the religious enactment process. He drafts and proposes religious policies and resolutions for any Shariah-related issues happening in the daily operation. SSC approval seals the religious policy in the form of Shariah pronouncements for operational activities. A lack of supervision from the SSC and the UK regulator's light-touch approach opens up space for differences in the enactment process between previous and current SCOs.

> The Arrow risk framework is the FSA version. We have our Shariah non-compliance risk in our risk framework. So there is a section … [discussing] Shariah and all the risk associated with Shariah. So we work to that. The FSA would not necessarily work for that. So what they would do is they have a copy of our risk management framework. So in there they would say that we are covering Shariah. The FSA does not require Shariah reporting. … They want to know about HPP sales. They never want to know anything [being reported] from Shariah perspectives (Manager of Compliance and Risk—interview).

In line with the risk management, governance and audit framework of the bank, the previous SCO classified the review and audit findings into four levels of rating. The rating is designed to note any improvement in the implementation of the Shariah control system and take into consideration the management response as well as the existing Shariah compliance control. The main concerns of Shariah non-compliance risk-monitoring, however, seem only to conform to both regulatory imperatives. This risk-monitoring concentrates on customer complaints related to Shariah, which in a sense is led by the FSA's customer protection rules. Any 'red' or 'amber' ratings disclosed are highlighted and discussed, and further action is needed to rectify non-Shariah-compliant action or activities. The SCO's tacit knowledge is also an important factor in the escalation of ambiguity in Shariah non-compliance risk interpretation as part of the processes of value maintenance.

Conclusion and future research directions

This chapter explains the underlying context and historical development of the risk-sharing concept in Islamic banking institutions. Shariah has guided IBIs to offer ethical investment alternatives that avoid interest-based transactions and avoid taking excessive risks. The chapter explains that Islamic banks have been replicating their non-Islamic counterparts' products and services. In addition, the issues of governance and religious compliance in Islamic banks in relation to Shariah scholars' roles and function have played an important role in the complexity of the interpretation and implementation of religious compliance principles in all aspects of banking operation.

The chapter reported findings from a case study of ETB, one of four recognized Islamic banks in the UK. This financial institution has publicly stated that as part of its five ethical and social values, its banking operation is based on Islamic values. The chapter explored the concept of religious compliance work represented in the process of Shariah compliance interpretation, enactment and implementation within the ETB institution. At the regulatory level, ETB faces the challenge of a lack of religious compliance rules. It needs to adapt and adopt existing regulatory imperatives into its operation, including it in the implementation of religious compliance.

The UK's regulators are reluctant to address religious compliance in their standards and guidelines, as they want to secure their identity as secular regulators and maintain regulation for everyone on a level playing field. This relates to their identity and values as regulators and their light-touch approach to regulation, which the regulator believes leaves the bank to self-regulate in respect of Shariah compliance (Tomasic, 2010). This regulatory identity, intended to prevent the country from losing the economic value of the business due to regulatory arbitrage (Black, 2010), facilitates institutional focus on the letter of the law rather than its spirit (Woods *et al.* 2013). The UK's self-regulatory approach creates competing regulatory imperatives for ETB, both from religious and local-authority perspectives. It leaves ETB to formalize its own religious compliance principles as an endogenous rule. This induces a symbolic monitoring of Shariah non-compliance risk.

Further research avenues in the implementation of religious compliance risk management in respect of product development will expand the existing research in this field. The impact of Shariah non-compliance risk on revenue recognitions and other banking operations would be another interesting research project. From a practitioner perspective, the concept and the implementation of Shariah risk management is still at an early stage. Joint research and collaboration between academics and banking practitioners to conduct further research could produce a strong impact for both current academic literature and the Islamic banking industry.

Notes

1 *Commenda* was one of five forms of business association practiced by Maghribi traders in the medieval era, alongside sea loans (with fixed interest upon arrival of a ship voyage), partnerships, formal friendships and commissions for services to absentee traders (e.g. representing a trader in court). *Commenda* was a joint capital and effort partnership in the form of selling and trading merchandise overseas (Çizakça, 2011; Greif, 1989, pp. 871–872).
2 This is an arrangement whereby a capital provider provides capital to an entrepreneur for a business activity. Any profits that accrue will be shared between the capital provider and the entrepreneur according to an agreed ratio, while losses are borne solely by the capital provider. In this case, the entrepreneur is considered to have lost the time and hard work they have invested in the partnership. However, if the entrepreneur is guilty of negligence or dishonesty, they will be liable for the loss caused by his or her negligence or misconduct (Iqbal and Mirakhor, 2007).
3 A scholar trained in the religious sciences whose area of research is public policy analysis and management of monetary affairs.
4 Note that the FSA no longer exists as the regulator for financial services in the UK, having been replaced in 2013 after a restructuring of banking regulation following the banking crisis.
5 The real name of the bank is not disclosed to maintain its anonymity.
6 The research conducted at ETB occurred when the FSA was the regulatory body. Therefore, reference to the FSA has not been altered in this case, even though the FSA is no longer the regulatory body responsible for bank regulation in the UK.
7 The five values of ETB include Shariah compliance and ethical/good values. The others have not been disclosed so as to preserve the anonymity of the case organization.

References

AAOIFI (Accounting and Auditing Organization for Financial Institutions) (2009), Financial Accounting Standards No 1, Kingdom of Bahrain.

Anonymous (2005), Ethical Trust Bank Annual Report, 2005. United Kingdom.

Black, J. (2010), 'The Rise, Fall and Fate of Principles-Based Regulation'. LSE law, society and economy working papers, 17-2010 . Department of Law, London School of Economics and Political Science, London, UK.

Chapra, M. U. (1992), *Islam and the Economic Challenge (No. 17)*, International Institute of Islamic Thought (IIIT).

Choudhury, M. A. and Hoque, M. Z. (2004), *An Advanced Exposition of Islamic Economics and Finance*. Mellen Studies in Economics (Book 25). Lewiston, NY: Edwin Mellen Press.

DiVanna, J.A., A. Sreih and M. Ainley (2009), *A New Financial Dawn: The Rise of Islamic Finance*, Cambridge: Leonardo and Francis Press.

Diwany, T.E. (ed.) (2010), *Islamic Banking and Finance: What It Is and What It Could Be*, Bolton: 1st Ethical Charitable Trust.

ETB (2013), Investor Information on Shariah Compliance, website. United Kingdom.

Friedland, R. and R.R. Alford (1991), 'Bringing Society Back In: Symbols, Practices and Institutional Contradictions', in W.W. Powell and P.J. Dimaggio (eds), *The New Institutionalism in Organizational Analysis*, Chicago: University of Chicago Press, pp. 232–265.

Glynn, M. A. (2013), "Patricia. Thornton, William Ocasio and Michael Lounsbury: The Institutional Logics Perspective: A New Approach to Culture, Structure, and Process', *Administrative Science Quarterly*, 58(3), pp. 493–495.

Goitein, S.D. (1967), *A Mediterranean Society*, Berkeley: University of California Press.

Grais, W. and M. Pellegrini (2006), Corporate Governance and Shari'ah Compliance in Institutions Offering Islamic Financial Services, World Bank Policy Research, World Bank.

Greif, A. (1989), 'Reputation and Coalitions in Medieval Trade: Evidence on the Maghribi Traders', *Journal of Economic History*, 49(4), pp. 857–882.

Hanif, M. (2010), 'Differences and Similarities in Islamic and Conventional Banking', *International Journal of Business and Social Sciences*, 2(2).

HM Treasury (2008), *The Development of Islamic Finance in the UK: The Government's Perspective*. HM Treasury.

IIA (2013), 'The Three Lines of Defense in Effective Risk Management and Control.' IIA Position Paper. The Institute of Internal Auditors. January.

Iqbal and Mirakhor (2007), *An Introduction to Islamic Finance: Theory and Practice*, Singapore: John Wiley & Sons.

Kato, H. (2012), 'Reconsidering al-Maqrīzī's View on Money in Medieval Egypt', *Mediterranean World* = 地中海論集, 21, pp. 33–44.

Khir, K., L. Gupta and B. Shanmugam (2008), *Islamic Banking: A Practical Perspective*, Pearson Malaysia.

Mahoney, J. and K. Thelen (2010), *Explaining Institutional Change: Ambiguity, Agency, and Power*, Cambridge: Cambridge University Press.

Meloy, J.L. (2003), 'The Merits of Economic History: Re-Reading al-Maqrīzī's Ighāthah and Shudhūr', *Mamlūk Studies Review*, 7(2), pp. 183–203.

Morales, R.A. and B. Shiblaq (2013), *Islamic Finance and Market 2014*, Lancaster: Law Business Research.

Norton, A. and J. Hughes (2009), *CIMA Official Learning System Enterprise Management*. CIMA Publishing.

Sabra, A. (2000), *Poverty and Charity in Medieval Islam: Mamluk Egypt, 1250–1517*, Cambridge: Cambridge University Press.

Shanmugam, B. and Perumal, V. (2006), Governance Issues and Islamic Banking. Eurekahedge. December. http://www.eurekahedge.com/NewsAndEvents/News/889/Governance_Issues_and_Islamic_Banking

Shanmugam, B. and Z.R. Zahari (2009), *A Primer on Islamic Finance*. The Research Foundation of CFA Institute

Stanley, M. (2008). Implementing Corporate Governance for Islamic Finance. *Finance Netwerk* (22 January): www.financenetwerk.nl/files/articles/90.pdf.

Thomas, A.S., S. Cox and B. Kraty (2005), *Structuring Islamic Finance Transactions*, London: Euromoney Books.

Tomasic, R. (2010), 'Beyond "Light Touch" Regulation of British Banks after the Financial Crisis', in I. MacNeil and J. O'Brien (eds), *The Future of Financial Regulation*, Oxford: Hart Publishing.

Vogel, F.E. and S.L. Hayes (1998), *Islamic Law and Finance: Religion, Risk, and Return*, London: Kluwer Law International.

Warde, I. (2010), *Islamic Finance in the Global Economy*, Edinburgh: Edinburgh University Press.

Woods, M., C. Humphrey and C.Y. Lim (2013), 'Risk Imbalances: In Search of an Alternative Risk Management Framework'. Conference Paper. British Accounting & Finance Association Conference.

17

Technology and business risks

Kirstin Gillon

Introduction

Most organisations today rely extensively on information technology (IT) systems throughout their operations and strategy. Consequently, technology has become an increasingly important component of organisational risk management, creating new risks and influencing existing operational and strategic risks.

This influence has grown as technology has shifted from being primarily a back-office support to a pervasive part of all organisational activities. IT systems have traditionally been associated with driving operational efficiencies and process improvements. However, digital technology increasingly underpins customer-facing and front-office tasks too. Products and services are bought and sold over the internet or on mobile devices. Marketing and advertising focus on digital channels such as social media. Indeed, digital content is becoming a key product or service for many businesses.

As a result, the organisational impact of system successes and failures has become more profound. Poor investment decisions or implementation projects can create competitive disadvantage and waste substantial organisational resources, leading to serious consequences for the sustainability of the business. Failures in cyber security can result in significant financial loss, reputational damage or business disruption. Therefore, when considering the risk environment of an organisation, whether through the lens of management, board oversight or audit activities, accountants need to be aware of the influence and impact of technology.

This chapter will outline some of the ways that technology is affecting the risk environment of businesses and highlight some of the particular challenges that accountants may encounter in their risk-based activities. It will focus on two areas that are having a growing practical impact:

- **Systems investment and deployment**—technology can represent substantial levels of capital or operational expenditure, and therefore decisions around new investments present major risks of wasted resources, poor value for money or competitive disadvantage. Furthermore, there is a long history of high-profile IT projects failing as well as a sense of underachievement in many cases, reflecting significant risks when delivering major IT-related projects.

- **Cyber security**—cyber risks have gone up the agenda of boards across the world as concern has grown about the impact of major cyberattacks and data breaches. While the need for information security is not new, the scale of the risk, in terms both of impact and likelihood, has qualitatively changed.

The chapter concludes by highlighting some opportunities to improve risk management more broadly through the use of new capabilities in data and analytics.

System investment and deployment

IT systems underpin many aspects of an organisation's strategy and operations today. As a result, making good investment decisions on new systems is extremely important to the future success of an organisation. And yet for many organisations, this is an area fraught with risks of poor decisions and implementations.

Strategic risks

Digital technology increasingly supports the creation and delivery of products and services, making it central to the economics and operation of many business models. As a result, technology investments present significant strategic opportunities and risks. Good decisions can enable competitive advantage and open up new markets. Bad decisions can result in competitive disadvantage and leave businesses vulnerable to new challengers. In this context, in which digital technology enables challenges to business models, the term commonly used is 'digital disruption'.

Growth of digital disruption

Risks of strategic failure based on technological innovation are not new. The economist Joseph Schumpeter's (1943) theory of creative destruction referred to the power of technological innovation to disrupt industries and destroy companies. This could be the result of technology enabling reduced costs, improved processes, more valuable products or services, or new models that destroy the value of existing assets.

'Digital disruption' is a term that updates this destructive idea. It describes the potential impact of digital technology on the value of products and services and on the sustainability of business models. It is important to recognise that this type of disruption has broad application across all industries and sectors of the economy, not just those immediately associated with digital products and services. Digital technology transforms the economics of information and enables many new ways of communicating and coordinating activities. Given that data and communication between stakeholders are at the heart of all organisations, it is to be expected that such developments can have radical implications for any business.

Digital disruption stems from a combination of many improvements in technology capabilities. First, disruption can stem from greatly improved capabilities in the capture, processing and analysis of data. These improvements are primarily a result of vastly increased computing power (Brynjolfsson and McAfee, 2014) as well as the increasing 'datafication' of our lives (Cukier and Mayer-Schonberger, 2013). This is reflected in an explosion of many new sources of data, including data from mobile phones, from the internet and social media, from images and from text. New data is coupled with more advanced analytics, which put greater emphasis on patterns, outliers, exceptions, profiling and predictive models. These developments enable businesses to find powerful new ways to create value, target activities and optimise operations through better use of data.

Alongside these data capabilities are new communications tools and platforms, which enable individuals and businesses to interact differently with one another. Cloud computing, mobile technology, social media and online platforms all enable greater flexibility, collaboration, social interaction, and the ability to share information, insights and images more quickly and easily. Businesses and individuals can connect across the world, find new business partners and associates, find new clients and join new communities.

Examples of digital disruption

Technology-based companies clearly face strategic risks of disruption from technical innovations. One of the first companies associated with the idea of digital disruption was Kodak, the camera and film manufacturer and processor. Although Kodak recognised the development of digital photography techniques, it failed to appreciate the significance for the economics of its business model—built around physical film and printing—or the emergence of new competitors. It made a series of decisions over a number of years that emphasised its core business of print and film and rejected moves towards a more digital strategy (Munir, 2012: Mui, 2012).

Another well-known example is Blockbuster, a business that hired out videos and DVDs to customers. It failed to foresee the new capabilities of streaming content online and downloading content, and it was left with a business model that no longer reflected the needs of the market (Downes and Nunes, 2013). This contrasts with Netflix, which also started with a business model of sending physical DVDs through the post but spotted the changing environment. By shifting to an online model built on streaming content, Netflix was able to respond successfully to disruptive changes and ultimately lead competitors through its innovative use of new technologies (Culp *et al*, 2012).

Businesses whose products and services are made up of information content, such as books, newspapers, music and film, have been heavily disrupted by digital technology. New distribution channels through the internet have created new competitors. Furthermore, the economics of digital information are radically different. When no longer tied to physical manifestations such as books and paper, information content becomes virtually free to replicate (Quah, 2003). The changing economics have led to heavy emphasis on providing content free of charge, requiring businesses to finding new ways of building revenue from such content. This has been reflected in greater reliance on advertising revenues; the building of new products and services alongside free content, such as events or merchandise; and the development of new models such as 'freemium', whereby some content is free but premium content is paid for (Anderson, 2009).

This shift is being acutely felt in the newspaper industry, where revenues have dropped substantially through the loss of sales of physical papers as well as the collapse in many advertising revenues, which have shifted to new competitors. Many newspapers have experimented with paywalls or freemium models on the basis that consumers are unlikely to pay for news but will pay to access specific commentators. They are using other sources of revenue such as advertising and events. Some papers have expanded internationally, making use of the global reach of digital technologies. But they are also facing new, digitally born competitors, such as Buzzfeed, which have highly agile and consumer-focused models (Andrews, 2015; Anthony, 2015).

The internet has also been very effective at challenging business models that are based on an intermediary or broker role. Travel agents, for example, have had to reshape their business models based on the ability of customers to book travel directly with providers. In addition, new models have emerged that act as platforms to connect the buyers and sellers of goods in particularly efficient or effective ways. Uber, for example, connects taxi drivers and passengers in a way that can be quicker and cheaper than hailing a cab on the street or booking a taxi through a dispatch service (Damodaran, 2014).

Responding to disruption risks

Established companies can face significant challenges to compete against such digital innovation and thereby manage the strategic risks. They have legacy systems and processes, and digital innovation will typically need to coexist with other existing products and services. This can result in complex multi-channel models, which raise costs. Established companies also have to undergo substantial change programmes to maximise the benefits of new technologies. Legacy systems can pose particular challenges in this context. They are often inflexible and have been built over years by adding pieces on as needed, leading to complex architectures that cannot be easily or quickly changed. They can also take up substantial amounts of IT budgets, leaving less for businesses to invest in innovation.

This presents many contrasts with start-ups that are built around digital technology. Business models in these cases can scale very quickly across the world, and they require few assets other than the technology infrastructure. Indeed, companies such as Airbnb and Uber make use of assets owned by others, providing a service that matches these assets together. Furthermore, most young companies make use of cloud infrastructures, enabling them to access computing power as a service when they need it rather than requiring them to invest in hardware themselves. They will usually make use of existing simple software or modules, rather than building things from scratch. As a result, new competitors can appear and scale very quickly. They can also benefit from the momentum created by the economic feature of network effects, which underpins many digital services and encourages dominant networks and providers. Most people want to be on the most popular platforms so that they can connect with more people, and therefore early momentum in products can be particularly powerful (Katz and Shapiro, 1985).

As a result of these conditions, the pace of disruption can be fast and often unpredictable, and the impact can be profound. These features make it particularly difficult to make good strategic decisions, manage the risks of disruption and take advantage of the opportunities presented by new technologies and business models.

Risk of poor return on investment

While some decisions on IT investments have strategic implications, others represent incremental improvements. Sometimes, investments may be required because technology has become obsolete and needs to be replaced, or systems no longer support operations or compliance requirements. In other cases, new systems may enable specific benefits, such as improved processes. However, many organisations struggle to apply good decision-making practices in this context, and therefore the risks of poor investment decisions and wasted resources are high.

Undisciplined investment decision practices

Surveys and anecdotal evidence show that many IT decisions are made without full financial justification or scrutiny (Ballantine and Stray, 1998; Capgemini Consulting, 2014). Management are frequently unable to pinpoint the financial impact of new systems and therefore cannot know whether or not investments are providing a clear return (Barua *et al.* 2010).

Articulating and measuring the financial value of IT investments has proved challenging at many levels. Solow's productivity paradox, whereby he could 'see computers everywhere except the productivity statistics' set the tone for many years and sparked substantial economic research into the value of IT systems (Solow, 1987). While evidence emerged in the 1990s of the link between US economic growth and IT investment, questions remain about the long-term economic impact (Brynjolfsson and Hitt, 2003; contrast with the assessment of US economic growth in Gordon 2012).

This is also reflected in difficulties in valuing businesses that are based on technology and data-based services. The dot-com boom and bust in the early 2000s demonstrated the risks of poor valuations of businesses based not on cash flows and profits but on features such as website user numbers (*Forbes*, 2008). While some businesses from that original bubble, such as Google, have gone on to be enormously successful, it still appears difficult to derive reliable valuations. Furthermore, there has been substantial growth of 'unicorn' businesses, which are private businesses valued at $1 billion or more. As venture capital money has continued to flood into many sectors of the technology market, there has been a marked growth in these highly valued businesses. However, many of these unicorn businesses continue to show little revenue or profit.

Linking IT with cash flows

At the heart of the problem of IT value is the difficulty of linking cash flows directly with IT systems. In most cases, IT systems contribute only indirectly to changes in cash flow by improving the quality, quantity or speed of information available to different organisational stakeholders. As a result, applying traditional discounted cash-flow techniques can result in seemingly arbitrary results.

These difficulties can be seen when examining in more detail the different ways in which benefits can be achieved from investments in IT (ICAEW, 2008). There can be specific and identified financial benefits from new systems—reduced headcount from the automation of processes or reduced working capital through better inventory management, for example. However, in many cases, benefits are more intangible and indirect. They may relate to enhanced customer satisfaction, greater collaboration across departments or improved management reporting capabilities. Even efficiencies can be hard to pinpoint in practice, especially where they are reflected in time freed up for other activities. In these cases, the financial benefits are one or more steps away from the actual IT investment, with many factors determining the outcome.

Investments may be creating or supporting new digital products or services, such as content-driven websites or platforms. Predicting the take-up of such services can be particularly difficult because success is often driven by the momentum of network effects. Platforms will also often be driven by the economics of two-way markets (Eisenmann *et al.* 2006). In these cases, it is not simply about finding a buyer for the product or service; it is about connecting buyers and sellers, and therefore the market is more complex. Then there is the question of monetisation of digital products and services. Gaining users is typically the first step of any digital service. Finding ways to monetise it is a second and often harder step for many businesses.

Furthermore, IT investment also frequently aims to provide organisations with new capabilities or with an infrastructure for other activities. This could include building global reach, achieving greater agility or speed to market and utilising new operating models such as outsourcing. In these cases, investment can build organisational options but may provide little direct benefit in itself.

There are no easy solutions to managing the risks of poor investments. While more sophisticated methods such as options theory may help to get a better handle on the economics of new technology, delivering value from investments will only improve when businesses get a better understanding of the specific benefits that they are trying to achieve. This means understanding how technology improves their information and communication capabilities, and how this can ultimately translate into financial benefits. Based on this understanding, businesses can then derive a range of measures, financial and non-financial, that can help them make good decisions and reduce their risks of wasted resources.

Deployment of systems

Once a decision has been made to invest in a new IT system, an organisation needs to engage in a process of change in order to implement it. But significant numbers of IT projects fail to be delivered on time, on budget or with the required functionality (NAO (National Audit Office), 2015; House of Commons Committee of Public Accounts, 2014). As a result, IT projects are typically viewed as particularly high-risk projects that require strong management and review throughout their lives.

Link to business change

The risks attached to IT projects stem from a number of their features. First, there is a close link between IT and business change, so business systems cannot be implemented in isolation. In order to achieve the desired benefits, they usually require some degree of process or operational change. At the minimum, this may involve communication of how the system works. Staff may need to be persuaded to use the new system, so communication of the benefits may be required.

More extensive process re-engineering may also be required. This could occur across departments and result in high levels of organisational change. Large-scale enterprise resource planning (ERP) system implementations, for example, could require changes across multiple departments, including finance, human resources and operations. Furthermore, information flows are often hardcoded into how an organisation operates, so changing those flows can require radical change.

This adds greater difficulty and complexity to the purely technical aspects of the project. As a result, research consistently shows that in order to achieve value from IT investments, businesses need a wide variety of complementary resources and capabilities (e.g. Nah *et al.*, 2001; Peppard *et al.*, 2007). These could relate to the skills available to the organisation, other aspects of the technology infrastructure, the ability of the organisation to learn and the extent to which the leadership is committed to business change.

Nature of project life cycle

All IT implementations start by defining the business requirements that the system has to meet. However, it can be difficult to define clear and comprehensive requirements for a system at the start of a project. Staff may not be able to envisage how things could be done differently. The internal and external environment may change over the course of the project so that the needs of the business and market change. This is especially the case with large projects, which typically take significant time.

As a result, IT projects often feature high levels of uncertainty, as requirements change and evolve through the process. IT projects also typically exhibit poor accuracy in estimation and prediction, especially around time frames and costs. Complexity is frequently underestimated.

The amount of business time and opportunity cost associated with change are not properly understood. As most organisations do not undertake major IT projects frequently, there is a lack of benchmarking as to previous projects. The unique nature of many projects also makes it hard to compare with other organisations. It is therefore hard to learn from previous experience—and while good practices may be clear, they can be difficult to implement effectively.

Furthermore, it remains culturally difficult in many organisations to stop projects and acknowledge failure, even when this would be the right decision. Management who have committed to the investment may be reluctant to cancel it, even when it appears to be failing.

Reducing project risks

Many businesses have changed their approach to IT projects in recent years to enable greater flexibility and reduce the risks associated with large IT investments in particular. For example, projects may be broken into a series of smaller projects to avoid the complexity of a single major project. This has been seen especially in the public sector, where 'big bang' IT projects have become actively discouraged.

Aligned to this shift are new project management techniques termed 'agile' (NAO, 2012). This approach recognises the difficulty of defining complex requirements up front and adopts a structure that is based on iterations and developing requirements through the practical use of systems. Users are engaged early on to pilot software, give feedback and shape future developments. Things often start small and then build on the basis of success. New developments are added on the basis of short, sharp pieces of work. If the system is not working as hoped, there is a greater emphasis on stopping projects quickly.

However, these more incremental approaches are not without their challenges. What does success look like, for example? How can a business judge whether the project has achieved its objectives when those are not set out clearly in advance? And, therefore, how can businesses make good decisions about investments based on this approach?

Good project management practices

There are well-established project management methodologies, such as Prince2, which provide a clear and structured approach to delivering highly complex projects. This includes processes to follow related to, for example:

- approval processes and business cases;
- agreeing the formal requirements for the project;
- planning, budgeting and reporting progress;
- identifying and managing dependencies between different projects or project streams;
- managing changes to the requirements, plan or budget.

Individuals can be certified as Prince2-qualified after completing the training course and passing an exam. This, which has traditionally been the standard method used for major projects, is commonly termed a 'waterfall' approach, as all the activities are planned in a sequential fashion. However, it is increasingly being replaced or supplemented by 'agile' methods, in which requirements are defined by small teams, or 'scrums', which operate in short windows such as two-week periods. This enables code to be delivered quickly and allows for greater flexibility in approach.

In conclusion, investing in IT systems has always been a risky endeavour, and the impact of failures is becoming more profound as digital technology becomes increasingly embedded in business models and all organisational activities. The risks of poor decision making are significant, especially given the high levels of uncertainty and the extent to which IT is entwined with other factors, both internal and external. Furthermore, the risks of project failure or under-delivery continue to be high, despite a wealth of established good practice. However, these challenges also provide substantial opportunities for those who make the right decisions and implement projects effectively.

Cyber risks

The need to secure and protect sensitive information has a long history. Principles of cryptology date back to Roman times, with the Caesar cipher being an early example of a substitution code. In a digitally-based economy, risks related to the security of data and systems are rapidly moving towards the top of corporate and government agendas (World Economic Forum, 2015). The impact of significant security failures on individual businesses and wider economies can be profound, which is reflected in high levels of concern about the ability of businesses to manage their cyber security risks.

This section summarises the changing nature of information security risks, outlines why they have become more important and highlights some of the specific challenges faced by businesses when trying to articulate and manage cyber risks.

Changing nature of security risks

Information security has always been an integral part of the business use of computers. Furthermore, as finance and accounting was the first area in most businesses to be computerised, accountants were at the forefront of new questions about the integrity, confidentiality and availability of computerised financial information. Consequently, audit activities over general IT and specific application controls strongly influenced the information security field for many years.

As the business environment has become increasingly digitised, though, the nature of security risks has changed. The impact of security breaches has become much greater. Businesses have become subjected to unrelenting levels of cyberattack from many different sources. New ways of working through the use of technology have also exposed businesses to greater risk (ICAEW, 2013).

Impact of breaches

Traditional concerns about security focused on back-office systems. While security breaches had a business impact, it was relatively confined to internal operations. Today, concerns about security have spread across many more aspects of business operations as digital technology has become central to customer-facing and critical operational tasks. Many businesses now hold large amounts of personal and financial data related to customers, for example. Many operations and supply chains are highly integrated and automated, based on IT systems. Customer-facing functions typically rely heavily on technology.

As a result, failures in security mean that a business can be severely impacted and even crippled in its operations, and its reputation can be seriously damaged. The speed with which news of failures travels around social media can exacerbate the impact of failures and make it impossible to contain and control the damage.

The extensive coverage of the data breach at TalkTalk in October 2015, for example, demonstrates the severe reputational impact that can occur in such cases. The company admitted a major data breach of its customer data, its third in less than a year, although it was unable to provide any detail about what had happened and how many customers were affected. The chief executive officer was featured on TV news on a number of occasions, trying to reassure customers, and it was a major media story for many days as well as the subject of a UK House of Commons select committee enquiry (House of Commons Culture, Media and Sport Committee, 2016). In the event, it was confirmed that only a small subset of customers were affected. However, the unsophisticated nature of the attack, the impression that TalkTalk had not invested sufficiently in security, and the confused public response meant that the impact on the company's reputation was substantial. One of the largest data breaches in the US, when the retailer Target had 27 million customer card details stolen, even resulted in senior board members losing their jobs, including the CEO and chief information officer (CIO) (Riley and Lawrence, 2014).

Nature of threats

The threats to businesses from cyberattacks have grown enormously in terms of source, variety and volume.

The archetypal 'teenager in a bedroom' who hacks purely for pleasure still exists, and indeed was behind the major TalkTalk attack highlighted in the previous section. However, cybercrime has also become a well-organised economic activity. This is reflected in widespread, fairly unsophisticated hacking using cheap tools that are easily accessible on the internet. All businesses and individuals can be subject to indiscriminate and untargeted attacks on this basis, including ransomware, viruses, phishing and social-engineering techniques,. Attackers are typically looking to access systems and extract money through extortion, fraud and theft.

Some businesses may also be attacked by more sophisticated groups with the aim of acquiring specific information, such as intellectual property. Often referred to as advanced persistent threats (APTs), these are more targeted efforts in which many different tools or techniques may be used in order to gain access to networks. Attackers could include criminals, competitors and governments.

A new source of threat is the 'hactivist', who may target specific companies with whom they have political, ethical or other disagreements. Groups such as Anonymous have particularly targeted governments to demonstrate disapproval of issues ranging from copyright laws to censorship of websites. In such attacks, hackers typically deface or bring down websites and publish sensitive emails or other information to embarrass the organisation and publicise their specific agenda (for a list of recorded operations, see the Anonymous entry on Wikipedia).

Finally, while attention may often focus on external attacks, it has always been the case that many security breaches are caused by employees, and the 'insider threat' remains important today as source of attack. Bitter or fraudulent employees or ex-employees can cause considerable damage by taking copies of data for personal use or to post online, or by helping external attackers to gain access to systems or data.

New areas of vulnerability

There are also new vulnerabilities in the business environment that can be exploited by attackers. In particular, organisational boundaries have become much less clear and are often described as porous. Business data is increasingly being held or being accessed by other organisations and businesses may have limited control over this process. Therefore, traditional thinking about security, which was focused on defending organisational boundaries and keeping data within that perimeter, no longer reflects business reality in many cases.

For example, supply chains have become more integrated, and it is common for other companies in a supply chain to have access to a business's systems or data, or even to store data themselves. This creates new weaknesses as attackers get into businesses through the systems of others (Shackleford, 2015). The most well-documented example of this concerns the major data breach at the US retailer Target, whereby the credit card details of 27 million customers were accessed by hackers. Access to Target's systems was gained through a supplier of air-conditioning systems, who were linked into the Target billing system and enabled attackers to get into Target's network. From there, the hackers were able to place malware on point-of-sale systems and harvest credit card details.

The use of IT outsourcing or cloud-computing providers is another change. This shifts the location of data into the provider's data centre rather than the organisation's own premises. As a result, businesses are dependent on the controls and security provided by the supplier and are likely to have little influence or even visibility over the controls in place. While this is not inherently any less secure—and indeed, cloud suppliers often argue that their specialist data centres will be far more secure than a typical small- or medium-sized business—it moves the control over data into the management of contracts and service-level agreements.

A new area of particular weakness is mobile technology, as employees increasingly use devices such as smart phones and tablets. These devices may have weaker security in the first place, which is exacerbated by the trend of 'bring your own device' (BYOD) whereby the device is owned by the employee but used for business purposes. This approach further reduces the level of control over the security of devices and often leads to a mix of personal and business data on the employee's personal device. While sophisticated solutions can manage the associated risks and separate business and personal data, many businesses have not yet adopted such tools.

For these reasons, businesses are experiencing greater impact from security failures. At the same time, there are both greater threats to security and new areas of vulnerability. However, many of these are far beyond the traditional remit of accountants. Specifically, financial statement audits do not consider security risks to non-financial data and systems other than in the context of general organisational risk management. Instead, these risks are the subject of broader assurance or advisory activities.

Articulating cyber risks

Cyber security has three broad aims—confidentiality, integrity and availability of data and systems. Failures in security therefore have three potential effects:

- Data can be accessed or stolen by those without authority. When this happens, it is termed a data breach.
- Data can be changed or corrupted by attackers or through other means. Examples include when banking details are changed so that money is paid to an attacker and when information on websites is defaced.
- Systems can be deliberately disrupted or taken down. Denial of service attacks, for example, specifically target and take down websites by overwhelming them with web traffic.

When looked at in this context, the impact of security failures is essentially technical and measured by elements such as stolen records and system downtime. However, such technical failures can also have significant impacts on a business. Articulating the meaning of cyber risks to a business, therefore, must incorporate both the technical failures and the business impact.

Business impact

The impacts on a business of a cyber security failure are varied and fall into a number of broad areas:

- *Recovery costs*—there will almost certainly be some direct costs incurred as a result of a breach. External experts may be required to rectify any issues and improve the security in place. Significant internal staff time will be involved in response and remediation. If personal data has been stolen, the business may need to provide credit-monitoring services for affected individuals for a period of time.
- *Reputational damage*—the incidents likely to cause greatest reputational damage concern the hacking and theft of customer data. If this is made public, it typically creates substantial concern in the affected individuals and suggests that the business is not sufficiently careful about protecting its customers' data. A poor response to a breach can be particularly damaging. If the business is slow to respond, especially in an environment dominated by social media and real-time customer reactions, the damage can be severe. eBay, for example, was strongly criticised for its response to a major breach of customer data in 2014, when it took three months for the company to uncover the breach and then over two weeks to notify customers. eBay were also seen to downplay the significance of the breach and provide poor information to customers on actions to take (Greenberg, 2014).
- *Loss of competitive advantage*—many of the concerns about cyber security at government level focus on industrial espionage and the theft of intellectual property from companies in sectors such as pharmaceuticals, technology and defence. Professional service companies can also be targeted for commercially sensitive data in the course of merger and acquisition (M&A) deals and other bidding processes. This could lead to long-term loss of competitive advantage for individual companies and for economies more broadly.
- *Business disruption*—many types of cyber security failure, such as viruses or distributed denial of service (DDoS) attacks on websites, can lead to the disruption of operations or customer service. The impact of this on the business will vary depending on the exact circumstances. In January 2016, for example, HSBC blamed a DDoS attack for bringing down access to its online banking services for customers (Peachey, 2016). DDoS attacks can also be used to hide and distract attention from other types of attack.
- *Fines*—the regulatory framework around cyber security is patchy, but there are clear regulatory duties around the protection of personal data, especially across the European Union. Businesses that are deemed to have failed in their duty of care over personal data can be fined by regulators such as the UK Information Commissioner. Industry bodies, such as in financial services, may also impose fines where appropriate. In 2014, for example, the online travel company Think W3 was fined £150,000 after hackers stole customer data (Information Commissioner's Office, 2014).

Furthermore, it is not just the business itself that can suffer damage in the event of security failures—other parties can also suffer losses. When hackers get hold of financial and other personal information, for example, individuals can become particularly susceptible to fraud. Financial institutions may pick up liability for paying money without the correct authorisation. However, in many cases in which the individual has been fooled into authorising a payment to a criminal or has given out sensitive information such as a PIN number, the institution can argue that the individual was at fault and is therefore liable for their own losses. Identity theft based on stolen data can also cause individuals significant harm. For example, criminals can take out debt in the name of the individual, reducing credit ratings and forcing the individual to prove that they did not take out the debt, which can be a difficult process.

In addition, businesses within sectors termed the 'critical national infrastructure', such as energy, transport, communications and financial services, present risks of far more serious societal consequences in the event of major security failures and terrorist attacks. Power stations or communications could be disrupted, for example. There are fears that terrorists could take control of vital systems, such as air traffic control or nuclear power stations, and create massive physical damage. While no incidents of such magnitude have happened to date, the risks exist.

Predicting impact and likelihood

The broad range of business effects means that the precise impact from security failures will vary substantially depending on a specific context. The theft of intellectual property, for example, could have a catastrophic impact if a competitor can take it to market more quickly or cheaply. In that case, the breach could severely undermine the long-term sustainability of the business. On the other hand, if the competitor fails to make use of it, the impact on the business of the theft could be minimal. This variability was reflected in the discussion surrounding the UK government's report on losses to the UK economy as a result of cyber-crime. The headline figure of £27 billion per annum was heavily based on estimated losses from intellectual property theft but was disputed by many critics (Detica, 2011; contrast with analysis by Anderson *et al.*, 2012).

Similarly, the impact of business disruption will vary depending on the systems involved, the time of the disruption and many other factors. Reputational impact is particularly hard to predict and is dependent on many external factors, such as the quality and speed of the organisation's responses to the failure. The networked nature of systems also means that incidents such as viruses can spread across different organisations quickly.

As a result, predicting the specific impact of security failures is difficult. This is compounded by a lack of data surrounding previous incidents and impacts. Internal data is often poor. Major catastrophic breaches are rare. Many businesses may not even realise that they have been breached. Most businesses do not wish to share information publicly, although they are increasingly doing it in private communities. These factors all severely limit the data available to model scenarios and predict the potential impact of specific failures.

Similarly, predicting the likelihood of incidents is problematic. Major failures can be seen in the context of 'black swan' incidents, as they are rare but can be catastrophic when they occur. Businesses need to consider the extent to which they can prepare for such incidents, given that their occurrence is likely to be impossible to predict.

Managing cyber risks

Getting basic security right

There is a lot of good practice that can be implemented to prevent security failures. Much of this involves simple processes and standard software, such as anti-malware and firewall software. Indeed, the UK intelligence agency Government Communications Headquarters (GCHQ) is frequently quoted saying that 80 per cent of breaches could be prevented by having basic measures such as these (e.g. Cabinet Office, 2010).

Basic cyber security measures

There are many sources that define good security practices. These include the following:

- The UK government's Cyber Essentials standard specifies the five technical controls that would stop most unsophisticated attacks. These focus on firewalls, keeping all software up to date, changing all default passwords, anti-malware software and access control.
- ICAEW's ten steps to cyber security features ten basic good practices aimed particularly at smaller organisations. The steps extend beyond technical controls into management controls such as training and allocating responsibility (ICAEW, 2016a).

However, all the evidence shows that most businesses do not have good basic security measures in place (ICAEW 2013a, 2014, 2015a). There are many reasons for this. Smaller businesses may lack the knowledge, skills and resources to implement good security measures. In particular, they will often treat security as a second-order priority in running a business, unless the business suffers a breach directly. For larger businesses, the IT environment can be extremely complex, with multiple suppliers and many versions of software and hardware, making even basic security expensive to keep up with. The sheer volume of suppliers makes effective supply chain cyber risk management potentially arduous and unmanageable.

Furthermore, most security breaches in practice can be linked to human behaviour. While technology has got more sophisticated, people continue to be referred to as the weakest link in security. Many incidents of hacking are enabled by staff allowing attackers into systems using their accounts, whether through poor password discipline, through clicking on links and infecting their machines or by giving away relevant information over the phone or on social media.

Inevitability of security breaches

The number of security incidents and breaches being experienced by many businesses is leading to a growing acceptance that data compromises are an inevitable part of operating in a digital environment. Businesses cannot protect all the data that they own, and attackers will always be able to get into systems if they want.

This shift in thinking has a number of implications. It means that businesses need to focus more on detecting breaches, monitoring systems and building response capabilities. Traditional security practices have focused on preventing breaches. In this new world, while prevention is still important, it is not enough. Resilience becomes the key aim (World Economic Forum, 2014).

As a result, boards in particular need to consider new questions about their response capability. For example, what information should be communicated to customers if their data has been breached, and when should it be communicated? When should access to systems be stopped, and who will make that decision?

Further questions arise. What is the level of risk appetite and tolerance in the business? If a certain level of compromise is to be expected, what level is acceptable to the business? And how can a board get comfort that it is doing enough? When breaches happen, how will the company demonstrate to regulators, investors and others that it was doing all that could be reasonably expected of it?

Concepts such as risk tolerance and risk appetite are common across risk management practice. However, they have not been considered specifically in the context of cyber security, which has traditionally viewed any breach as a failure. Accepting that breaches are inevitable, no matter how good a business's security is, requires a big shift in thinking and culture about security.

Lack of clear standards

One of the underlying difficulties in terms of governance and oversight of cyber risks is the lack of clear standards on what constitutes good practice. While there are many information security standards, none of them are viewed as particularly satisfactory (UK Department for Innovation and Skills and PwC, 2013).

Because the risks vary so much between businesses, it is impossible to define a one-size-fits-all prescriptive standard. A prescriptive standard would also have to change quickly to respond to changes in the technology. While a principles-based approach would therefore appear to be more appropriate, it would potentially be so high level as to be fairly meaningless in practice.

There are also concerns that too much focus on standards could create a compliance and tick-box mentality around security that would be counterproductive. It could lead to a false sense of security, as breaches would still happen even to companies compliant with the standard. It could also equate security with process compliance rather than making it an integral way of thinking about how to do business. As businesses increasingly have to innovate with new technology, they need to embed security into their cultures, business models and ways of operating. A strong focus on standards, processes and compliance may hinder that shift.

However, the lack of clear standards causes significant practical difficulties. Managing supply chain cyber risks, for example, is problematic without an agreed standard against which assurance can be sought. While the financial statement audit includes an assessment of IT controls, it is specific to financial systems and the associated environment, and it therefore does not consider the wider systems environment other than in the context of general risk management and governance by the board. As a result, big businesses are developing their own cyber-assurance questionnaires for suppliers to complete, creating significant work and not necessarily improving cyber risk management across the supply chain (ICAEW, 2015).

The lack of standards also hinders the development of a strong insurance market for cyber security. This is not the only barrier; lack of data to price premiums is possibly the biggest barrier in many jurisdictions. However, lack of clear standards makes it harder for insurers to ensure that policyholders are taking appropriate steps to protect themselves. Consequently, the established approach of transferring risk through insurance is not widespread in this area, and businesses cannot rely on insurance so readily in this context. This means that they have to take full responsibility for the risks presented by cyberattacks.

Finally, the lack of standards makes it hard for governments and regulators to create a stronger regulatory environment around cyber security risk management, if they wish to do so. While it can be argued that businesses can live with the consequences of their own poor security, failures can have a wider impact. The networked nature of systems can enable poorly performing businesses to spread viruses to supply chain partners, for example. People can suffer losses when their data is accessed and used in fraudulent activities. Attacks on businesses in the critical national infrastructure could have a catastrophic impact on wider society. Consequently, regulators and governments have a legitimate interest in ensuring businesses do manage their cyber risks appropriately.

This is reflected in a variety of measures, particularly in the US and Europe. For example, breach notification laws are widespread in the US and will be increasingly implemented across the EU through new data protection and cyber security legislation. This requires businesses to report breaches to relevant authorities and aims to provide more data about breaches as well as to act as an incentive for businesses to improve their security and prevent breaches.

Using data to improve risk management

While technology presents new risks to organisations, it also presents opportunities to better manage many kinds of risks—technology-based and otherwise. In particular, through the use of new data sets and more sophisticated modes of analysis, such as risk analytics, there are a variety of ways in which IT can help risk management (ICAEW, 2013b).

Big data and analytics

In the first instance, businesses may be able to utilise new sources of data to get better understanding of the past and present and thereby increase the transparency around risks. This could involve external sources of data to improve understanding of external factors, markets, competitors and suppliers. Data on locations, demographics, political factors and weather, for example, can be integrated into existing risk management frameworks. The 'internet of things' enables tagging of individual stock items and granular analysis of status or location.

By analysing large data sets, businesses may be able to get new insights from identifying patterns, exceptions and outliers. Visualisation tools may help to spot anomalies and present key messages to management.

Management may also be able to use predictive models more effectively to understand the potential impact and likelihood of different risks occurring. While businesses have used predictive models for many years, models have generally become more accurate as more data has become available to use in them and methods have become more applied (Haghighi, 2012). This enables greater reliance on the output. In addition, developments in artificial intelligence may lead to greater automation of risk management activities, allowing more sophisticated and real-time responses to exceptions.

As a result, there is extensive use of analytics in many areas of risk management—but especially in financial services, including credit risk, fraud, capital requirements and investment portfolios. Auditors are also integrating these techniques into their audit process to enable better understanding of the risks in the business and to therefore focus audit activities in the right areas (ICAEW, 2016b). The ability to examine all the transactions of the business rather than focusing on sampling opens up new opportunities to identify unusual activities and profile transactions on the basis of risk.

Limits of new approaches

However, care needs to be taken in this context. Models can be wrong, and there are limits to our ability to predict things. It is possible to contrast, for example, the tremendous improvements to our ability to predict short-range weather with the lack of progress in predicting earthquakes (Silver, 2012).

The path of Hurricane Sandy was very accurately predicted, which enabled effective mitigating actions and greatly reduced the insurance payouts involved. The enormous amount of data now available in this context means that models around short-term weather activities are much better, although they are by no means perfect. By contrast, we have seen very little improvement in our ability to predict earthquakes, either by location or time frame. The level of data required is still not captured, and scientists do not have a good enough understanding of the variables and how they interact to build a more accurate model.

Similarly, complex systems such as economics remain highly unpredictable. The ability of experts to predict the next crash may not be markedly better despite the enormous amounts of data available to them. The complexity of the interactions between variables, the pace of change and other factors continue to hamper our ability to predict.

Furthermore, technologies are not always helpful in an organisational context (ICAEW, 2015b). People can over-rely on technology, which can be fallible. Human judgement is still a vital part of risk management. The 'black box' nature of technology and models can also alienate non-experts and subdue effective discussion of risks. Good risk management benefits from discussion and knowledge-sharing, which may be discouraged by an overemphasis on technology. Reliance on technologies also raises questions about who really understands what is in models and whether risks are being properly managed—consider the use of complex models in the run up to the 2008 financial crisis. Therefore, while technology can play a useful role, its limits must be clearly understood.

Conclusion

Technology is changing the business environment profoundly and therefore also changing the risk environment in which accountants operate. This works at all levels—from the highest strategic risks faced by businesses to the everyday actions required to protect data and systems. The purchase and implementation of new IT systems creates significant risks in terms of value for money as well as strategic failure. Traditional information security risks have gone up corporate agendas as cyber security failures make front-page news and even threaten the very existence of some companies.

Technology also represents important opportunities to manage risks better in the future. Controls and assurance activities will increasingly be automated and embedded in software. Audit activities will focus on sophisticated data analysis. Predictive models can be powerful tools in managing many types of operational risk, from the prevention of system failures to the presence of fraudulent activities.

A common theme in making the most of new technology and managing the associated risks is the ongoing difficulty of connecting technology with the business. Technology in many cases continues to be a 'black box' and an area in which people do not have intuitive knowledge. It continues to be dominated by technical specialists with their own language. While this is a familiar feature of many specialist business areas, it does seem to represent particular difficulties in IT—the failure of businesses to understand the investment case for IT systems, the failure to change business operations to exploit new systems, and the failure to articulate the specific cyber risks the business faces.

Roles such as the CIO and newer roles such as chief information security officer (CISO) and chief digital officer (CDO) aim to provide a bridge between technical specialists and business leaders. These officers should be able to communicate effectively with both communities and have a combination of technical and business skills. However, in many cases, these roles continued to be performed by technical specialists, and it remains hard in practice to find individuals who can bridge the gap effectively.

Accountants, in the different roles they play in the business environment, have many opportunities to engage with technology specialists and build better understanding and communication. They should be involved in the process of IT investment, ensuring that the full benefits, costs and risks of projects are understood. They should always be aware of the security risks of new technology, challenging business areas to ensure that appropriate risk management actions are being taken. They should also look to make use of technology to improve the ways that they do things.

It is noted, finally, that academic research into technology-related risks has been predominantly undertaken by specialist technology communities such as accounting information systems researchers and the broader information systems community. Little research has taken place in more generalist areas, and the gap between technology and other business topics is as wide here as it is in practice. Furthermore, this is an area that lends itself to multi-disciplinary research that can consider the economic, organisational, psychological, ethical and sociological aspects of technology. To support more integrated thinking, greater research from a variety of disciplines into the impact of technology on business risks would be very welcome.

References

Anderson, C. (2009), *Free: The Future of a Radical Price*, New York: Hyperion.

Anderson, R., C. Barton, R. Bohme, R. Clayton, M. van Eeten, M. Levi, T. Moore and S. Savage (2012), 'Measuring the Cost of Cybercrime'. *11th Annual Workshop on the Economics of Information Security*. Berlin, 25–26 June. Available from: http://www.econinfosec.org/archive/weis2012/papers/Anderson_WEIS2012.pdf.

Andrews, R. (2015), 'Old Media's Prospects Have Improved but the New Media Threat Looms Large', *Guardian*, 20 March. Available from: http://www.theguardian.com/media-network/2015/mar/20/new-media-threat-buzzfeed-vice.

Anthony, S. (2015), 'What the Media Industry Can Teach Us about Digital Business Models', *Harvard Business Review*, June 10. Available from: https://hbr.org/2015/06/what-the-media-i ndustry-can-teach-us-about-digital-business-models.

Ballantine, J. and S. Stray (1998), 'Financial Appraisal and the IS/IT Investment Decision Making Process', *Journal of Information Technology*, 13(1), pp. 3–14.

Barua, A., L. Brooks, K. Gillon, R. Hodgkinson, R. Kohli, S. Worthington and B. Zukis (2010), 'Creating, Capturing and Measuring Value from IT Investments: Could We Do Better?' *Communications of the Association for Information Systems*, 27, article 2.

Bharadwaj, A., O.A. El Sawy, P. Pavlou and N. Venkatraman (2013), 'Visions and Voices on Emerging Challenges in Digital Business Strategy', *MIS Quarterly*, 37(2), pp. 633–661.

Brynjolfsson, E. and L. Hitt (2003), 'Computing Productivity: Firm Level Evidence', *Review of Economics and Statistics*, 85(4), pp. 793–808.

Brynjolfsson, E. and A. McAfee (2014), *The Second Machine Age: Work, Progress, and Prosperity in a Time of Brilliant Technologies*, New York: W.W. Norton & Company.

Cabinet Office (2011), *The UK Cyber Security Strategy Protecting and Promoting the UK in a Digital World*, London: Cabinet Office.

Capgemini Consulting (2014), *Measure for Measure: The Difficult Art of Quantifying Return on Digital Investments*, Paris: Capgemini Consulting.

Cukier, K. and V. Mayer-Schonberger (2013), *Big Data: A Revolution That Will Transform How We Live, Work and Think*, London: John Murray.

Culp, C., M. Friedman, G. Lincoln, Q. Reeve and M. Zepernick, (2012) Netflix: Past, Present, and Future Innovation, working paper, Dartmouth College. Available from: http://faculty.tuck.dartmouth.edu/images/uploads/faculty/ron-adner/11EIS_Main_Project_-_Netflix_Paper.pdf.

Damodaran.A.(2014),'ADisruptiveCabRidetoRiches:TheUberPayoff',*Forbes*,10June.Availablefrom:http://www.forbes.com/sites/aswathdamodaran/2014/06/10/a-disruptive-cab-ride-to-riches-the-uber-payoff.

Detica and the Cabinet Office (2011), *The Cost of Cyber Crime*, London: Cabinet Office.

Downes, L. and P. Nunes (2013), 'Blockbuster Becomes a Casualty of Big Bang Disruption', *Harvard Business Review*, 7 November. Available from: https://hbr.org/2013/11/blockbuster-becomes-a-casualty-of-big-bang-disruption.

Eisenmann, T., G. Parker and M. W. Van Alstyne (2006), 'Strategies for Two-Sided Markets', *Harvard Business Review*, 84(10), pp. 92–101.

Forbes, W. (2008), *The Boys in the Bubble: Searching for Intangible Value in Internet Stocks*, Edinburgh: Institute of Chartered Accountants of Scotland.

Greenberg,A.(2014),'eBayDemonstratesHowNottoRespondtoaHugeDataBreach',*Wired*,23May.Available from: http://www.wired.com/2014/05/ebay-demonstrates-how-not-to-respond-to-a-huge-data-breach.

Gordon, R. (2012), *Is U.S. Economic Growth Over? Faltering Innovation Confronts the Six Headwinds*, Cambridge, MA: National Bureau of Economic Research.

Haghighi, A. (2012), 'What It Takes to Build Great Machine Learning Products', *O'Reilly*, 16 April. Available from: http://radar.oreilly.com/2012/04/great-machine-learning-products.html [Accessed 13 October 2014].

House of Commons Culture, Media and Sport Committee (2016), Cyber Security: Protection of Personal Data Online, First Report of Session 2016–17, HC 148, 20 June. Available from: http://www.publications.parliament.uk/pa/cm201617/cmselect/cmcumeds/148/148.pdf

House of Commons Committee of Public Accounts (2014), *BBC Digital Media Initiative Fifty-Second Report of Session 2013–14 Report*, London: House of Commons.

ICAEW (Institute of Chartered Accountants in England and Wales) (2008), *Measuring IT Returns*, London: ICAEW.

ICAEW (Institute of Chartered Accountants in England and Wales) (2013a), *Audit Insights: Cyber Security*, London: ICAEW.

ICAEW (Institute of Chartered Accountants in England and Wales) (2013b), *Big Data and Analytics: What's New?* London: ICAEW.

ICAEW (Institute of Chartered Accountants in England and Wales) (2014), *Audit Insights: Cyber Security 2015*, London: ICAEW.

ICAEW (Institute of Chartered Accountants in England and Wales) (2015a), *Audit Insights: Cyber Security—Closing the Cyber Gap*, London: ICAEW.

ICAEW (Institute of Chartered Accountants in England and Wales) (2015b), *Risk Management: Mindfulness and Clumsy Solutions*, London: ICAEW.

ICAEW (Institute of Chartered Accountants in England and Wales) (2016a), *10 Steps to Cyber Security for the Smaller Firm*, London: ICAEW.

ICAEW (Institute of Chartered Accountants in England and Wales) (2016b), *Data Analytics: International Auditing Perspectives*, London: ICAEW.

Breach Watch (2014), *Think W3 Limited*. 23 July. Available from: http://breachwatch.com/2014/07/23/think-w3-limited/.

Katz, M. and C. Shapiro (1985), 'Network Externalities, Competition and Compatibility', *American Economic Review*, 75(3), pp. 424–440.

Mui, C. (2012), 'How Kodak Failed', *Forbes*, 18 January. Available from: http://www.forbes.com/sites/chunkamui/2012/01/18/how-kodak-failed/#2b75a6efbd6a.

Munir, K. (2012), 'The Demise of Kodak: Five Reasons', *Wall Street Journal*, 26 February. Available from: http://blogs.wsj.com/source/2012/02/26/the-demise-of-kodak-five-reasons.

Nah, F., J. Lau and J. Kuang (2001), 'Critical Factors for Successful Implementation of Enterprise Systems', *Business Process Management Journal*, 7(3), pp. 285–296.

NAO (2012), *Governance for Agile Delivery*, London: NAO.

NAO (2015), *E-borders and Successor Programmes*, London: NAO.

Peachey, K. (2016), 'HSBC On-line Banking is "Attacked"', *BBC News*, 29 January. Available from: http://www.bbc.co.uk/news/business-35438159.

Peppard, J., J. Ward and D. Elizabeth (2007), 'Managing the Realization of Business Benefits from IT Investments', *MIS Quarterly Executive*, 6(1), pp. 1–11.

Quah, D. (2003), *Digital Goods and the New Economy*, LSE Centre for Economic Performance, discussion paper no. 563.

Riley, M. and D. Lawrence (2014), 'As Data Breach Woes Continue, Target's CEO Resigns', *Bloomberg*, 5 May. Available from: http://www.bloomberg.com/bw/articles/2014-05-05/as-data-breach-woes-continue-targets-ceo-resigns.

Schumpeter, J. (1943), *Capitalism, Socialism and Democracy*, London: G. Allen & Unwin.

Shackleford, D. (2015), *Combatting Cyber Risks in the Supply Chain*, Cardiff: SANS Institute.

Silver, N. (2012), *The Signal and the Noise: The Art and Science of Prediction*, London: Allen Lane.

Solow, R. (1987), 'We'd Better Watch Out', *New York Times Book Review*, 12 July, p. 36.

UK Department for Business Innovation and Skills and PwC (2013), *UK Cyber Security Standards: Research Report*.

World Economic Forum (2015), *Global Risks Report 2015*, Geneva: World Economic Forum.

World Economic Forum and McKinsey (2014), *Risk and Responsibility in a Hyperconnected World*, Geneva: World Economic Forum.

18

Case study: Failed decision-making at Dexia?

A lack of integrated risk culture

Peter Verhezen and Marie Gemma Dequae

> Strategy that lacks alignment to risk management is not only insufficient but downright dangerous. … Risk management is pointless unless it is closely tied to the company's strategic objectives.
>
> *T. Nagumo, Bank of Tokyo-Mitsubishi*

Introduction: gained or lost value? Or failed decision-making?

Most analysts focus on companies whose stock price has proven to be steady and increasing; however, most companies' stock price is quite volatile. A lot of underperforming companies have destroyed shareholder value as a result of the mismanagement of strategic risks. The Dexia group is a case in point.

We claim that an appropriate risk culture, integrated into the corporate strategy, helps organisations to create and gain sustainable organisational value instead of destroying it. In others words, the hypothesis is that an integrated risk culture, embedded throughout the whole organisation and aligned with a clear risk appetite with respect to what the firm strategically wants to achieve, will help management to make better strategic decisions (see Figure 18.1).

Prior to making a final decision, strategic leaders find common ground and align the different interests of the relevant stakeholders who may have disparate and distinctive views and agendas. Strategic leaders map the positions of the different stakeholders and pinpoint any possible misalignment of interests. For this reason, the success of a reasonable and acceptable decision on a strategic bet not only depends on the alignment of the different perspectives through proactive communication, dialogue and frequent engagement but also on the ability to sell an overall common ground within the broader purpose and vision of the organisation. Ultimately, CEOs and top management need to make tough calls with incomplete information and choose between well-formulated options, taking both short- and long-term goals into account based on a robust decision process (Lafley *et al.* 2012; Sull and Eisenhardt, 2012; Sull, 2009; Simons, 2010). Dexia's management and its board failed this test. The strategic choice often needs to refer to pilot projects and stage the commitments to retain the flexibility to adapt where necessary.

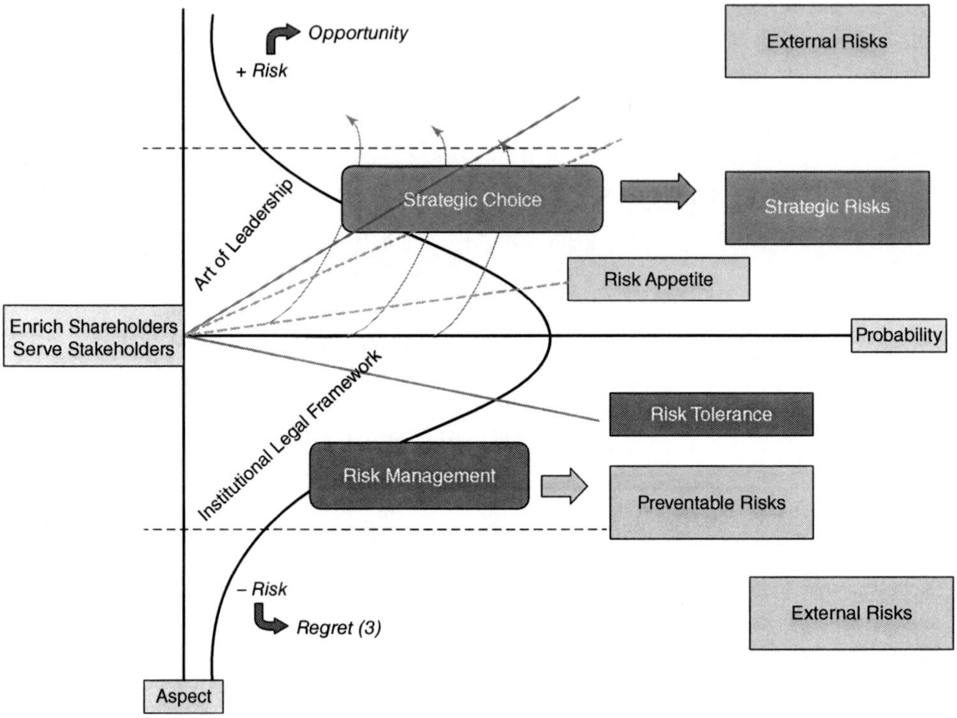

Figure 18.1 Risk, risk culture and risk appetite: creating and preserving value (based on Verhezen, 2010, 2015a,b).

This case study is structured as follows. We begin by defining a framework that can be used to audit a 3-by-3 matrix as a risk tool to enable boards and top executives to make better decisions. Beside overconfidence, biasedness, ethical barriers and herd behaviour, a lack of risk culture is one of the major factors that can generate poor executive decision-making.

Secondly, we analyse how Dexia's board and top executives managed to lose enormous organisational value, not only because of bad decision-making resulting from a weak or non-existent risk culture but also because of overconfidence in their strategic choices and opaque—if not outright unethical—behaviour that was aggravated by herd behaviour or groupthink.

Finally, we suggest some crucial steps that could have been taken by Dexia to prevent such a disaster. These recommendations can realistically reduce the probability of destroying enterprise value and improve the chance of creating value for shareholders and stakeholders alike.

Risk culture to improve decision-making: a new fad?

In times of high volatility and uncertainty, one could argue in hindsight that value destruction in firms is often a result of mismanagement of strategic risks that is rooted in an inappropriate or non-aligned risk culture. Indeed, contrary to conventional wisdom that non-compliance is primarily responsible for destroying shareholder value, research seems to indicate that bad evaluation of strategic risks causes the biggest losses (Dann *et al.*, 2012). A risk management team may draw attention to the possible risks associated with doing business in a particular context, but it is the CEO, supported and monitored by an engaged board and chairperson, who makes the final decision.

The risk leader needs to focus on a number of components within any organisation: strategic partnership linked to strategic risks; executive partnership that is related to operational responsibilities and risks; organisational capabilities that can help to reduce operational risks; and culture that allows the organisation to better prepare for external threats or prevent potential operational risks from taking place. Understanding these components of risk management requires the risk person in charge to have certain characteristics and key qualities. Particularly, that person will need to be able to navigate stakeholders' sometimes contradictory and politically inspired organisational concerns. Courage and communication skills will be extremely useful in being an effective risk officer. Without credibility in terms of capabilities and competence, and without the necessary ethical values and high level of integrity, it will be hard to be effective in optimising organisational or enterprise value.

Decision-making experts have argued that most failures in allocating resources in an organisation can be explained by the following factors: overconfidence, bias and ethical blindness, herd behaviour and groupthink, and certain risk aversions (Malkiel, 2015; Heath and Heath, 2013; Kahneman, 2011). Others have added nuance to this mainstream criticism of weak decision-making by distinguishing between cognitive, deliberate and affirmative decision-making processes, the latter of which requires high confidence from senior executives to execute the decision after reasonable deliberation of all scenarios and possibilities (Rosenzweig, 2014).

Enterprise or shareholder value destruction can be caused by major strategic blunders, major operational problems, fraud, ethics violations, accounting problems and other compliance violations (Dann *et al.*, 2012). In addition, not being prepared for rare but impactful external events can have a dramatic impact on a firm.

For this reason, a generic risk management approach distinguishes three main kind of risks, each following their own approach. *Strategic risks* need to be evaluated through dialogue and discussion, whereas *operational or compliance-oriented risks* can and should be prevented, and finally *external risks* may be difficult to forecast but firms need to be prepare themselves for such rare but dramatic risks (Kaplan and Mikes, 2012). Having determined that risks can be characterised in terms of three categories and that decision-making usually fails because of three main issues, we developed a 3-by-3 risk matrix.

Some strategic risks are deliberately taken to achieve superior strategic returns known in finance as 'idiosyncratic alpha returns', which are in excess of industry-related returns. Booz & Company research argues that this category of strategic risks accounts for 81 per cent of organisational value destruction (Dann *et al.*, 2012). In such cases, top managers and CEOs can be held responsible for the biggest strategic blunders, such as new market failures or being caught flat-footed by a major industry shift. Most value is lost because of a new product launch failure, because of entering a new (emerging) market at the wrong time or with the wrong partner, or because of often-quoted mergers and acquisitions failures. In more than 50 per cent of such cases, the loss occurred gradually, but the company took too long to react. In the remaining cases, the lost value was caused by a sudden sharp shock, such as in the case of strategic failure to anticipate the introduction of a new and superior product by a competitor. These ideas are applicable to the case of Dexia, as analysed below.

Strategic risks imply that leadership will need to allocate scarce resources to mitigate critical risk events. Dexia failed to do so. Maps of likelihood and the expected impact of some identified risks could help leadership to determine the strategic choices needed for sustainable performance.

An additional question is whether there is scope for certain operational risks to also be prevented. Some sudden losses of shareholder value can be explained by operational problems such as supply chain disruptions, customer service breakdowns and operational accidents. The Deepwater Horizon offshore rig explosion and subsequent leak in the Gulf Coast in April 2010 wiped more than US$50 billion off BP's shareholder value over just a couple of weeks, taking down its CEO in the process. Other important risks are those of fraud, ethical violations, accounting problems and other violations or failures to comply to the law or standards. The prominent examples of Tyco's accounting lawsuits in 2002 and Enron's demise in the same year demonstrate that such risks could have been prevented. Indeed, one could question whether leadership would have addressed an organisational culture and related procedures that condoned creative and extremely aggressive organisational behaviour—presumably resulting in 'superior' short-term performance—if it could have anticipated the resulting consequences. We would suggest that most of these preventable risks can be avoided or eliminated through an integrated culture-and-compliance model (Kaplan and Mikes, 2012). Internal controls and audits, mission statements, values and belief systems and standard operating procedures should help firms to reduce or avoid these preventable risks. The board and its top management should focus on building a robust risk culture. Again, we will argue that Dexia did not have a well-functioning integrated risk culture and flagrantly failed to prevent the crystallisation of operational risks, with disastrous consequences.

A final generic risk category is that of external shocks originating from natural, political or regulatory unforeseen events. These external risks—the 'black swans' described by Nassim Taleb (2007, 2005)—cannot be prevented, but one can prepare oneself in case such events occur. These external events are usually defined as 'tail' risks and can be tested through assessments, scenario-planning and even war-gaming. When the global financial crisis with its toxic mortgage-collateralised securities hit the American subsidiary of Dexia, Financial Security Assurance (FSA), these external risks were internalised as a Trojan horse through the American-acquired entity, thereby aggravating the situation for Dexia shareholders.

Most organisations and leaders are quite poor at detecting threats and opportunities in the ambiguous and often complex data they gather. Challenging business assumptions and anticipating new trends remains more of an art than a scientific discovery process. Nonetheless, strategy requires leaders to become more systematic in approaching strategic decisions (Lafley *et al.*, 2012). Questioning and analyzing the current business model as regards new trends requires leaders to talk to relevant and important stakeholders, customers, employees and suppliers to better understand the challenges ahead.[1] Market research and business simulations can show how competitors may react to certain trends, gauge likely reactions by competitors to new product launches and predict potential disruptive offerings (Schoemaker *et al.*, 2013). Scenario-building has been used as a tool to imagine different potential futures that can prepare the firm for the unexpected. Looking at fast-growing competitors or customers who switched to competitors may indicate which trends may prevail in the near future. Once it has become clear that changes are underway, leaders need to focus on the root causes of the imminent strategic challenge and ask why a customer is dissatisfied or why a product does not sell well. Strategic leaders usually encourage debate through open dialogues in which conflict between different thoughts can be managed within a reasonably safe haven of organisational openness. Leaders allow those in the organisation who are immediately affected by a decision into the process of making tacit knowledge more explicit. Workshops are organised to identify and quantify anticipated trends (Mikes and Kaplan, 2014).

Managing risks—usually by focusing on possible threats and failures—is quite different from managing strategy. It is usually a tough process that should be undertaken by experienced executives who have a good risk understanding and have implanted a proper risk culture and risk appetite within the organisation they are managing—something Dexia executives and their supervising board apparently failed to achieve.

Dexia: failed decision-making and misunderstood risk management

Did Dexia's top management or its board follow any of the above recommendations? Let us briefly go through a historical review of what did go wrong at Dexia from a risk perspective. We focus on a period pre- and post-2011. Why 2011? It was the moment Dexia was nationalized and taken over by the Belgian–French and Luxembourg governments after the board and top management failed to save the bank.

The structure of the Dexia group slightly changed as a result of this takeover by the government, as shown in Figures 18.2 and 18.3.

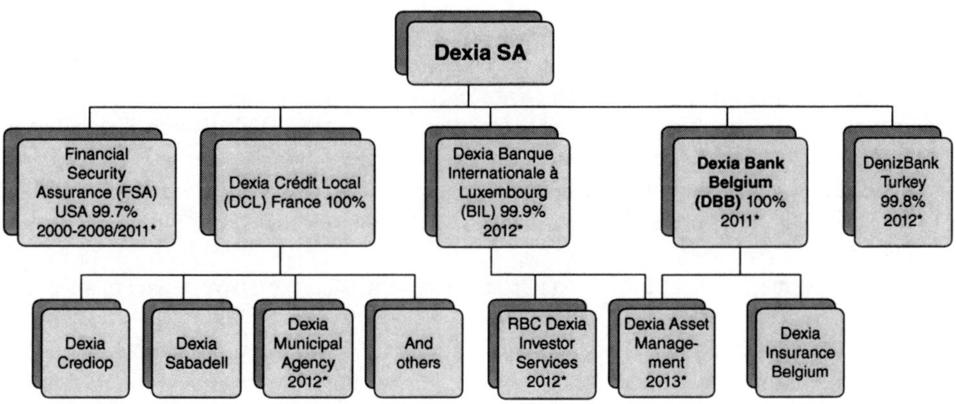

* Year of leaving Dexia Group

Figure 18.2 Corporate structure of the Dexia group before 2011.

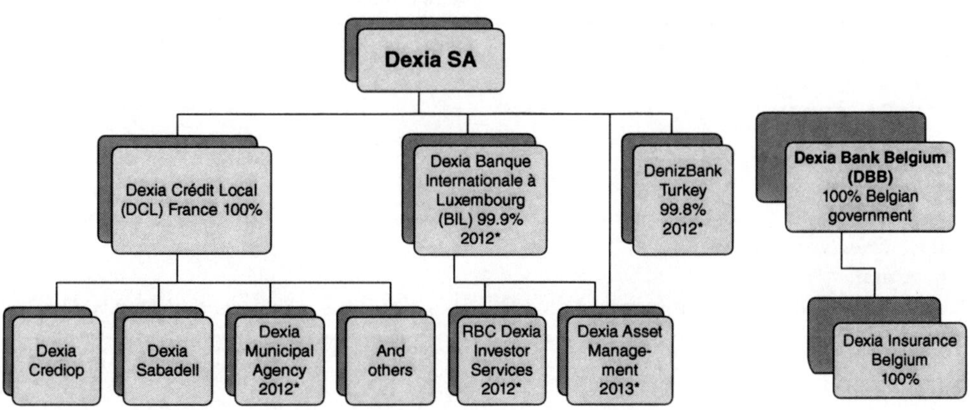

* Year of leaving Dexia Group

Figure 18.3 Corporate structure of the Dexia group after 2011.

The period before 2011

Risks before the crisis of 2008

Following the merger of Gemeentekrediet van België/Crédit Communal Belgique (GKB/CCB) and Crédit Local de France (CLF) in 1996, the Dexia group became one of the first pan-European financial institutions to pursue an aggressive growth strategy. In the early years of the growing Dexia group, the acquisition of the BACOB bank (working-class clients) and the Paribas Belgium bank (middle-class clients) within one group caused considerable cultural frictions. Combining these very different company cultures was overshadowed by a forced decision process, resulted in herd behaviour and groupthink within the merged bank that was reflected in how strategic risks were addressed (see Table 18.1: 1c).

The ambition of the most infamous CEO of GKB/CCB, François Narmon, who led the bank from 1979 until 2006, was to change the public credit institution into a full bank. On the other hand, Pierre Richard, the overzealous CEO of CLF, was convinced that CLF alone would not survive within the eurozone. Consequently, he made a presumably conscious decision to grow out of the 'old man's reputation' of CLF. For CLF, this would mean that the sources of financing loans were from Belgian savings, which became an important windfall if not a competitive advantage (for the French at least) of this merger.

Moreover, some restructuring followed the merger. In late 2005, Richard was elevated from CEO to chairman of the new board of directors, and Axel Miller, his *poulain* and former Dexia general counsel, was appointed CEO of the new Dexia bank. Obviously, we could question the integrity of this decision, and overconfidence definitely played a role in this process of appointment.

The 10-year strategic plan of the Dexia group in 2006 was built on 'two pillars of success':

1 Dexia would develop its universal banking activity beyond its traditional markets (GKB/CCB in Belgium and CLF in France) to become a leading European banking institution. This aim seemed at first a good project, but it was also one the causes of the subsequent problems. CLF had no real office network and was dependent on the money sources of savings that GKB/CCB collected.[2]

Table 18.1 What kind of risk categories are used in decision-making?

Risks in decision-making Risk categories	*a. Strategic risks*	*b. Operational risks*	*c. External risks*
1. Overconfidence and lack of risk culture	1a	2a	3a
	Over-optimism in risk approach	Silos and superficial risk understanding	Unintegrated and lacking professional risk culture
2. Biasedness and ethical barriers	1b	2b	3b
	Profit maximisation at all costs	Focus on positive consequences only	Inward-looking and unprofessional risk management
3. Herd behaviour or groupthink	1c	2c	3c
	Uncritical followers in risk understanding	Unfocused and unaware blindness	Non-reflective risk thinking

2 Dexia aimed to become the largest credit provider for local governments in the world, in this way maintaining its leadership position in public and project finance. The goal was to strengthen its position through 'geographic expansion, based on innovative scope of products'. Pierre Richard, now the chair of the merged bank, announced that Dexia would become the number one bank in financing public authorities and public investments, elevating this mantra to its core business model, 'growth without limit'. (Ardaen, 2012; Piffaretti, 2013)

Unfortunately, a fast-changing external environment was completely ignored. Moreover, the chairman was blinded by his own ambition for Dexia to become one of the biggest banks. Companies were acquired without good due diligence, and little time or effort was devoted to integrating the different acquired companies. The ultimate French ambition was to become the largest bank for public finance of local municipalities in the world (using the cheap money that Dexia Crédit Local (DCL) could source from Dexia in Belgium)—a typical example of overconfidence (see Table 18.1: 1a) and misaligned strategic objectives.

In pursuing this expansion strategy, Dexia made a number of acquisitions,[3] of which the acquisition of FSA in the USA in 2000 was undoubtedly the most significant. Unfortunately, hardly any internal control was implemented at the organisational and reporting levels (see Table 18.1: 1b), which resulted in unqualified risk-taking without appropriate checks and balances by either the top management or the board. This was due to the absence of a real risk management tool to guide management at CLF. One could easily argue that aggressively pursuing this growth strategy at any cost looked like casino banking: the core business (public financing) became a hedge fund in which structured long-term loans financed solar panels and windmills, which had a much higher risk profile than the direct loans to local municipalities. The lack of internal challenges to Richard's autocratic management style aggravated the lack of risk profiling, and Richard was hardly restrained by best corporate governance practices. Moreover, dangerous operational risks rooted in overconfidence, inappropriate risk aversion and an inappropriate risk culture—misaligned to an improperly defined risk appetite—aggravated the situation (see Table 18.1: 2a).

Dexia never became an integrated bank but rather remained a juxtaposition of separate entities without any embedded group culture or risk culture. In addition, as indicated above, there was a complete lack of good governance.

Dexia's blatant bias and ethical blindness in pursuing an ambitious growth strategy was exemplified by the acquisitions of the Labouchere and Kempen banks in 2000. These acquisitions of Labouchère and Kempen did not follow the required purchase procedures, as the bank had sold lease contracts to clients without the right information and promising unrealistic gains. This could easily be perceived as a case of fraud (see Table 18.1: 1b and 2b), although Dexia could argue that it was not actively involved in but rather had inherited the scandal. Nonetheless, it badly hurt Dexia's reputation, and the bank lost €2 billion in the process.

Looking at the strategic risks with a focus on herd behaviour and groupthink, we see that above all, the merger with Artesia Bank Corporation (ABC) between 2001 and 2002 caused a serious additional cultural clash between the different entities of the Dexia group. The more public management orientation in GKB/CCB and CLF did not fit the worker-focused cultural approach within BACOB. Moreover, this new merger was completely misaligned with the more investor-focused orientation at Paribas Belgium (see Table 18.1: 1c). The bank—across these national borders—was characterized by two distinctive cultures. In addition, these different cultures were enhanced by two significantly different compensation programs, which complicated the ability to address operational risks in an aligned manner at Dexia's headquarters.

In France, for instance, it can be argued that the management was overconfident and did not have a proper risk culture, which allowed executives to get involved in some excessive risk taking (see Table 18.1: 2a). Despite these cultural misalignments, the Belgian–French institution tripled its total assets from €152 billion to €567 billion between 1996 and 2006, and it nearly tripled its number of employees from 12,000 to 33,321 during the same period. It was known that Dexia was very ambitious and active in public finance, providing retail and commercial banking services to individuals and small- and medium-sized enterprises as well as serving its customers with asset management and insurance.

The lack of a proper industry analysis, however, was aggravated by a growth strategy without the appropriate financing. In other words, there was no focus on long-term financing, nor on guaranteeing enough short-term liquidity (see Table 18.1: 1a). One could argue that during that period of 1999–2006, the board committees hardly challenged management and the other consenting board members; one could call it a 'paper' or passive board that was far removed from the fiduciary duties that a board is supposed to perform.

Nonetheless, Dexia's risk manager mentioned financial risk and increasing liquidity problems from 2007 onwards. The executive committee, however, only made some minor changes and did not take the urgent decisions that were needed. Huge risks were still taken without embedding these strategic and operational risks into a coherent risk culture (see Table 18.1: 2a and 2b). In that same period, a strong growth of structured finance products in the portfolio of the Dexia group took place, dramatically changing the risk profile of the group and spreading it over the whole world. With such structured risks linked to the financial market, Dexia became much more dependent on the external market without the proper tools to monitor it (see Table 18.1: 3a and 3c).

Risks during the crisis of 2008

The demise of Lehman Brothers on 15 September 2008 made clear that this fallen investment bank had hidden, shifted and shared its financial risks with other international banks, resulting in complete distrust between those banks. In addition, the interbank market swiftly faded away as result of a complete lack of confidence between these banks. As a consequence of this strangled evolution, Dexia struggled with the short-term refinancing of their long-term loans (see Table 18.1: 3a and 3c).

Dexia's problem in 2008 was probably not capital and solvency but rather liquidity. The presumed solution to recapitalise in 2008 was therefore done to enable Dexia to retain control, albeit in vain.

Credit decisions were very quickly pushed through the credit committee (see Table 18.1: 1a and 1c). In the USA, however, Dexia had a New York banking office (FSA) and was therefore eligible for various bailouts from the US Federal Reserve. At its peak, Dexia had borrowed US$58.5 billion. Attention therefore was refocused on Dexia's loss-making FSA and the sub-prime mortgage crisis. The problems at FSA were minimised by the executive committee in 2008 (see Table 18.1: 2a and 2b). On June 23, 2008, Dexia was forced to announce that it was providing a US$5 billion credit line (for a minimum of 5 years and without any guarantees) to its American subsidiary, but this credit line was still dwarfed by the unit's distressed assets. Overconfidence and a lack of proper risk culture caused this enormous challenge (see Table 18.1: 2a and 2c). Splitting FSA from Dexia became impossible, meaning that FSA's large toxic risks were now fully the responsibility of Dexia. This meant that the external risk of the US sub-prime crisis was now imported into Dexia's European activities (see Table 18.1: 3c and 3a).

In 2008, when inter-bank lending rates were coming down, the majority of the board did not see the construction error in their business model in which long-term financing was sourced with short-term borrowing, as was done in FSA. Worse still, the board approved another US$5 billion standby line of credit for FSA. This is an example of a complete misunderstanding of strategic risk, with herd behaviour and groupthink (see Table 18.1: 1c) resulting in incompetence. The Dexia group's board of directors was poorly informed about the implications of the global outlook for the Dexia group, and it didn't ask the right questions. Local regulators only checked local activities rather than looking into the foreign US-based activities that were extremely risky (see Table 18.1: 1c).

Whereas most banks limited their loans, Dexia was still aggressively growing these in 2008 when 48 per cent more credit was provided compared to 2007. No correction of this misaligned strategy took place, suggesting that the strategic risk reflected misplaced confidence (see Table 18.1: 1a) and misunderstanding of the fast-approaching external risks (see Table 18.1: 3a and 3c).

Dexia's many investments in the period up to 2008 created a disproportionate balance sheet structure (bond portfolio versus equity) within the Dexia group. By the summer of 2008, debt stood at more than €600 billion without FSA (and about €1 trillion with FSA), compared to an equity level of only €20 billion. We could speak of taking too many strategic risks based on misguided overconfidence and a lack of proper risk culture (see Table 18.1: 1a). The Dexia group now also started to face solvency challenges.

At the end of September 2008, Dexia came under enormous pressure. Lenders worldwide became wary of lending to each other. Other banks and financial institutions refused to provide further credit to Dexia because of potential losses at its US subsidiary, FSA. In addition, Dexia faced a multi-billion loan to a troubled German bank DEPFA,[4] which had a comparable business model as a daughter of the French DCL, Dexia Municipal Agency (DMA). Again, overconfidence and a lack of risk culture to align Dexia's strategic risk started to pay a toll (see Table 18.1: 1a).

In addition, there was also a design error in Dexia's risk management, as the risk of defaulting on bought loans and bonds was considered but not the risk of refinancing in a difficult market in which the inter-bank market was swiftly disappearing. This could be described as an operational risk caused by overconfidence and, once more, a lack of proper risk culture.

In DCL France, there also was a lack of follow-up on the different risks. For instance, interest rate risks, liquidity and portfolio risks were hardly discussed in the asset liability committee (ALCO) due to the fact that they seemed to be too difficult to understand. Herd behaviour and groupthink were embedded in the mismanagement of operational risks (see Table 18.1: 3c).

On 30 September 2008, Dexia's chairman, Pierre Richard, and CEO, Axel Miller, were sacked. They were replaced on 7 October 2008 by former Belgian prime minister Jean-Luc Dehaene and by Pierre Mariani respectively. Dexia had to refocus on its core countries and core activities. The US risk had to be immunised and the bond portfolio aggressively reduced. International divisions were closed in Australia, Mexico, India, London and New York. Dexia was not able to sell either Crediop in Italy or Sabadell in Spain. In 2009, less risky and shorter term bonds worth €16.5 billion were sold, reducing the balance sheet but increasing the average duration and the volatility of the portfolio. To aggravate the situation, an accounting change—reclassifying items from assets for sale (AFS) to loans and receivables—reduced the value of the public-sector portfolio from €255 billion to €164 billion.

At the end of 2008, Dexia sold the healthy parts of FSA, ceased its trading activities in Paris and ceased trading on its own account in the financial markets. In June 2009, the mother holding of FSA, without the bad Financial Products division, was sold to Assured

Guaranty (a US insurer) for US$722 million, corresponding to one third of the purchase price. Dexia was forced to sell a performing company and to keep all the bad parts. The loss for Dexia was a €1 billion reduction in US participation and a loss of €1.9 billion in FSA Financial Products.[5]

The bank announced net losses of €3 billion in February 2009. Dexia's 2008 annual report mentions, among others, losses of €1.6 billion from selling FSA, €600 million on portfolios and €800 million on counterparties (including Lehman Brothers, Icelandic Banks, Washington Mutual and Madoff).

Dexia was financing most of its banking activities via interbank market transactions or with the help of bond investors, often on a very short-term basis Table 18.2. Most important functions—treasury, finance, risk, human resources, communication and legal—were centralised, reducing further integration and transparency and creating a strategic risk and lack of risk culture as the distance to operations increased and cooperation disappeared. The problems for Dexia were located in this gigantic bond portfolio, although the Dexia bank in Belgium did not seem to be aware of any of the potential huge risks.

Mariani's decision shortly after his nomination to generalise the purchase of interest swaps to cover the risk of rising interest costs carried a high price for Dexia: lower profit, reduced size and a less flexible balance sheet. On 5 March 2009, Dexia's share price fell to an all-time low of €1.21 per share, a loss of over 90 per cent in 1 year. A further restructuring plan aimed to concentrate on Dexia's primary activities and avoid risks on the financial markets. A total of 1,500 job cuts were announced, of which more than half were in Belgium, 260 in France and the rest worldwide. Dexia's share price subsequently increased over the rest of 2009, largely varying between €4 and €7.50.

Did Dexia become a hedge fund? DCL and some of its subsidiaries had misrepresented their balance sheets to the public at large. Their business model aimed to work with the money of the local municipalities and banks that had deposited into the French Treasury. But DCL did not have its own deposits, so it had to look for liquidity elsewhere. When the financial markets dried up, DCL had trouble finding enough money to refinance its enormous balance in the money markets. Consequently, the long-term loans were financed with short-term credit, without even considering the possibility that this market could dry up.

Downsizing and reorganising, and the eurozone debt crisis in 2010–2011

In early 2010, the European Commission approved a restructuring plan to justify government support for Dexia and to prevent unfair competition. First, some acquisitions had to be undone—Dexia Crediop, Dexia Sabadell and Dexia Banka Slovensko needed to be sold—while the banking activities that were highly promising in Turkey (DenizBank) could continue; second, by the middle of 2011, the state guarantee had to be abandoned; and third, Dexia had to downsize by more than a third by 2014.

Vintage retail activities represented a bigger share in profits again in 2010. Apart from Belgium and France, Turkey became very promising in this area. Predictions suggested that Turkish staff would account for half of Dexia's employees by 2014. At the same time, outgoing cash flows were diminished by reducing the bonds portfolio—even selling bonds at a loss if necessary, which explains to a large extent the lesser profits in 2010.

More incoming funds from private savings accounts and less outgoing capital through bonds and loans to public institutions meant that Dexia could already worry a bit less about finding sufficient short-term funding. Greater international trust in the company was shown when the bank announced an early retirement from the state guarantee on 30 June 2010.

Table 18.2 Financials of the Dexia Group until 2011, and Dexia (Holding) S.A. and Belfius Bank and Insurance after 2011

Year	*Revenue***	*Profits (after tax*)*	*Profit/ revenues*	*Assets**	*Equity**	*Equity/Assets*	*Employees*	*CETI*
DEXIA GROUP								
2005	5.976	2.038	34,1%	508.800	11.500	2.3%	24.4 IX	10,3%
2006	7.005	2.750	39,3%	566.700	14.400	2,5%	33.321	9,8%
2007	6.8%	2.533	36.7%	604.600	16.100	2.7%	35.202	9,1%
2008	3.556	–3.326	N.A.	651 000	17.500	2,7%	36.760	10,6%
2009	6.184	1.010	16,3%	577.600	l8.500	3,2%	35.234	12,3%
2010	5.310	723	13,6%	566.700	19.200	3,4%	35.200	13,1%
2011	–4.383	–11.639	N.A.	412.800	7.600	1,8%	22.461	7,6%
DEXIASA								
2012		–2.866		357	3,31	0.9%	3.373	19,9%
2013		– 1.083		223	3,96	1,8%	1.885	21,4%
2014		–606		247	3,13	1,3%	1.265	16,4%
2015		163		230	4.55	2.0%	1.173	15,9%
BKLFILS BANK & INSURANCE								
2011	66	– 1.367	N.A.	233	3.28	1,4%		11,8%
2012	2.458	416	16,9%	213	5*32	2,5%	7.113	13.3%
2013	1.834	445	24.3%	183	6,60	3.6%	7.323	13,8%
2014	2.071	462	22.3%	194	7,93	4.1%	6.941	14,7%
2015	2.184	506	23,2%	177	8,66	4.9%	6.703	15,9%

*all numbers in mio E
Source: Dexia, Dexia SA and Belfius Annual Reports 2005–2015

Since December 2008, the Dexia group had considerably reduced its risk profile and refocused its commercial franchises on its historical business lines and markets, in line with the restructuring plan validated by the European Commission. Dexia had thus principally organised its activity portfolio around retail banking, grasping opportunities for growth in Turkey. In the field of public banking, the group chose to remain a selective, profitable and recognised specialist, offering a diversified range of products. This plan was implemented in line with the objectives fixed until mid-2011.

DCL offered structured loans at a low interest rate but linked with a financial product (often an exchange rate) to a lot of mutual funds and municipalities, which became a big problem in 2010–2011 as interest rates were high. At the end of 2011, nearly 1,000 public organisations and communities in France had in one form or another a 'sensible loan' on the Dexia balance sheet, presenting a considerable strategic risk with potential biasedness in decision-making (see Table 18.1: 1a and 2a).

While problems in the USA prompted the first intervention, the eurozone debt crisis was at the root of Dexia's difficulties in 2011. Although the European Commission urged Dexia to speed up the execution of the restructuring plan, this plan was not really embedded in the group's risk approach. In fact, we could speak of a continuous lack of risk culture. In May 2011, the liquidity gap at €90 billion was expected to broaden, increasing the need for new financing.

Standard & Poor's (S&P) suggested that Dexia risked paying more interest for its financing activities than the interest receivable on loans, causing profits to completely melt down. And Dexia also risked incurring very high losses in selling its government bonds at fire prices as required. It was therefore not difficult to understand why S&P put DCL and Banque Internationale à Luxembourg (BIL) under credit watch—a step that implies a potentially reduced rating. This was shocking news for Dexia, since a reduced rating would cause funding costs to increase.

Between 2008 and 2010, cheap money loaned from the central bank was reduced from €54.4 billion to €25.5 billion. The National Bank in Belgium started working on a 'will' for Dexia by preserving some healthy parts—Dexia Bank Belgium (DBB), BIL, DenizBank and DMA—and bringing bad parts under state guarantee.

Dexia had €4 billion of exposure to potentially very toxic Greek government bonds. Analysts estimated Dexia to have a further €17.5 billion of exposure to sovereign debt issued by Italy, Spain, Portugal and other troubled eurozone economies. Dexia was in dire straits caused by bad risk management and weak board oversight and aggravated by a global financial crisis.

The period after 2011 and Dexia's second bailout

Alleged differences of opinion were reported at the top of Dexia. More specifically, tensions between Belgian directors and the French CEO, Pierre Mariani, were mounting, since the investments with losses were mostly caused by the French division of Dexia while the liquid funds were mainly sourced from the Belgian side.

On 15 July 2011 as part of its European bank stress tests, the European Banking Authority (EBA) surprisingly gave Dexia a clean bill of health, reporting that its tier 1 capital was 12.1 per cent and would fall to 10.4 per cent in 2012 under its 'adverse scenario'. This would make it one of Europe's safest banks. Subsequently, the bank issued a press release on 15 July 2011 entitled '2011 EU-wide Stress Test Results: No Need for Dexia to Raise Additional Capital'. (see Dexia website: Regulated information* – Brussels, Paris, 15 July 2011 – 6:05 pm) The problem was that the tests (and the models) did not take into account a scenario in which Greece might default on its bonds (see Table 18.1: 2a and 2c).

As a consequence of the aggravation of the sovereign crisis in the eurozone and more generally of the hardening of the macroeconomic environment, Dexia was confronted by renewed pressure on its liquidity during the summer of 2011. Dexia posted a €4 billion loss for the second quarter of 2011, the biggest in its history, after writing down the value of its Greek debt. On 4 October, Dexia's shares fell 22 per cent to €1.01 in Brussels, cutting its market value to €196 billion.

Having become one of the first casualties of the 2011 European sovereign debt crisis, Dexia lost €15 billion in deposits between August and October 2011, and it was estimated that the bank was losing €50–100 million per week. Dexia decided to sell the rest of FSA and some other portfolios, booking a loss of €8 billion.

There was no full information, no real discussion nor any good decision possible at board level. Between all partners—Belgium, France and Luxembourg—there was a lack of transparency in that period in 2011. The downgrading by Moody's in October 2011—due to loss of deposits of €15 billion in 2 months—created panic and finally led to some serious discussions amongst the French and Belgian board members, showing how an external risk creates biasedness and herd behaviour (see Table 18.1: 3b and 3c). Discussions focused on a possible breakup, with a plan to place Dexia's legacy division into a 'bad-debt bank' with government guarantees.

On 10 October 2011, it was announced that the Belgian banking arm would be sold for €4 billion to the Belgian federal government. The 49 per cent participation in DMA was halted, and DBB became responsible for the social liabilities in Dexia (Holding) S.A. (323 employees), a legacy portfolio of €19.5 billion and a government guarantee of €90 billion. This was a very high price to pay for previously mismanaged strategic risks and bias in the decision-making of management and board (see Table 18.1: 2a). The sale of DBB to the Belgian state was finalised on 20 October 2011.

Some units, such as DenizBank and BIL, were put up for sale in 2012. Some of Dexia's French operations were purchased by Caisse des Dépôts et Consignations and La Banque Postale.

October 2011 was a turning point. The Dexia group was split into two separate legal entities: Belfius Bank and Insurance, focusing on Belgian activities and core businesses,[6] and Dexia (Holding) S.A., a bad-debt bank that promised to clean up past failures and was to be dismantled over 5 years. The holding is earning interest income of only 0.3 per cent on its fixed income portfolio and is already dependent on the state, since more than 1 per cent needs to be paid as a result of the state guarantee and a risk premium on Euribor tariffs.[7]

These measures, comprising a definitive liquidity guarantee scheme, are part of a new restructuring plan that the states submitted to the European Commission in 2012. On 27 July 2012, Dexia confirmed the sale of its 50 per cent share in RBC Dexia Investor Services. The business went under the sole ownership of the Royal Bank of Canada (RBC) and was renamed RBC Investor Services.

The remaining troubled assets, including a 95 billion EUR bond portfolio, would remain within the Dexia Holding S.A., However, Dexia itself would only receive funding guarantees of up to 90 billion EUR, which would be provided by the governments of Belgium (60.5%), France (36.5%) and Luxembourg (3%). At the end of 2011, the historical shareholders of Dexia, Holding Communal and the ARCO holding, were declared bankrupt. Ethias had to book losses on their Dexia shares. The broad public and political world was crying out, 'How could this happen?

Recommended risk governance and concluding remarks

It can be argued that several interrelated crises and internal problems occurred almost simultaneously and were combined with dreadful management and indecisive board decisions: first, the bank crisis of 2008, aggravated by a global sub-prime mortgage crisis and the sovereign European debt crisis of 2011; second, a major bank crisis due to unaligned growth with a short-term financing strategy; and third, an almost complete absence of good governance, a lack of proper transparency and a very weak risk culture.

When organisations do not have a proper risk culture, the chances that something will go wrong are high. The case of Dexia is an obvious example that has cost shareholders dearly and had a huge negative effect on the economy as well as on the psyches of bank executives and bank customers, not to mention the citizens who had to pick up the bill. From this case, managers, executives and board members can learn a lesson about how to avoid such disasters.

Setting up a coherent risk management system

An analysis of the ambiguity and complexity of the uncertain future and trends may lead to different reactions to this uncertainty. During this analysis, the organisation promotes a culture of inquiry and searches for lessons in both successful and unsuccessful outcomes. In other words, a learning organisation attempts to identify new initiatives that turn the ambiguous and complex uncertainty into a possible opportunity to create business. Mistakes are valued and viewed as learning opportunities. Strategic leaders focus on finding patterns that push through the ambiguity and complexity of certain events and trends. They search for new insights and new interpretations of the 'noisy' uncertainty. For each unexplained event that is uncertain and thus potentially risky, leaders observe, invite perspectives from different stakeholders and actively look for missing information and evidence that disconfirms the firm's traditional hypothesis. Where possible, these observations are quantified, and an open mind is required to grasp some unexpected interpretations. Leaders need to overcome conflicting information and avoid the trap of making either/or decisions. Great strategic breakthroughs are often based on opposing ideas that are integrated into a new business model (Martin, 2007). A synthesising mind can more easily overcome apparently conflicting information or opposing ideas. Through a dialectical process of synthesis, new ideas are created and rigorously tested. Through this hypothesis-testing process, a leader will synthesise all relevant strategic bets or options from which a choice will need to be made.

Consolidating Dexia's activities into an integrated treaty: aligning strategy and risk

Dexia—which literally means 'treaty' in Greek—is a consolidated bank headquartered in Brussels and listed on the Euronext in Brussels and Paris as well as on the Luxembourg Stock Exchange. At first, consolidation seemed to be a good strategy to form a full bank, but differing cultures led to clashes and ultimately caused the unravelling of the group.

The first restructuring in 2008, organised by Pierre Mariani, focused on the following action plan: first, try to get a solid bank ratification for Dexia Holding in the hope that it would be easier to directly finance CLF; second, solve the problems of the FSA in the USA; third, restructure the bank; and fourth, find new management. Concretely, this meant that Mariani's recovery plan was a '3F' plan: first, financing (reject all activities that were not profitable);

second, funding (cut back on short-term financing); and third, franchising (focus on relationships with all clients).

Unfortunately, this plan was not realised according to expectations. Moreover, recent revelations about the Panama Papers under Miller's management did not help to improve the reputation of Dexia's management and board as regards their competence. It appears that BIL, a subsidiary of the Dexia group, did help clients to set up accounts in Panama, which functions as a tax haven that allows companies to legally or illegally reduce tax liabilities.

As mentioned earlier, a turning point for Dexia was in October 2011 when DBB was fully nationalised and put under state guarantee. The first priority for Belfius Bank and Insurance in 2012 was to increase its liquidity. Once this was acceptable, solvency became the priority,[8] followed by profitability and solving the legacy inherited from Dexia.

Is there a future for what is left of the Dexia group?

Considering the company's actual and future challenges, the historically low interest-rate environment facing Dexia is at the forefront of its uncertain future. Indeed, the way interest rates will evolve in the near future—external to management and depending on the US Federal Reserve and European Central Bank's monetary policies—will determine the severity of the problem. The bank's profitability may well be at risk under these stringent low interest rates, forcing the bank to search for other sources of income like commission fees on particular investment portfolios. Obviously, disruption in current activities and new innovative technologies—like FinTech and the Bitcoin block chain technology—will have to be further examined and possibly considered in relation to potential strategic moves. All banks are subject to these challenges.

Belfius Bank and Insurance, now 100 per cent in the hands of the Belgian government, will need to prepare serious actions to survive the expected consolidation in the European banking sector. Does Belfius have a chance to survive this competition after the enormous debacle described in this chapter? We believe a professional and competent board and top management is a condition sine qua non to address these future challenges. Cleaning up the past is one thing, but preparing for the future is quite another.

It concretely implies that the bank's strategy was not fully aligned to a clear risk management. It can be clearly questioned whether the risk management philosophy and risk appetite were discussed within the bank at a senior executive level or with the board that monitors and advises senior management. Second, there was hardly any regular review of the risk portfolio that focused on the evolution of risks—especially emerging risks. Consequently, the bank hardly knew how to respond to those emerging risks when they occurred. Third, we can also question whether the organisation was a well-oiled and functioning risk management system, whereby the organisation understood and implemented top-of-the-bill risk management, with advisory audit and risk committees to keep the board reasonably well informed Fourth, the organisation was hardly a transparent (both top-down and bottom-up). Fifth, enterprise-wide risk management practices were hardly implemented at all levels in the organisation. Finally, the bank did not have a proper supporting human resources management that consistently focuses on training personnel about key risk indicators and the potential effects of those risks.

We only can hope that Dexia's new senior management and board members will have learnt to avoid a similar disaster. Banks play a crucial role in any economy and should function as gatekeepers rather than speculators in this context. Rules and regulations—as recently upgraded and clearly defined under Basel II and Basel III regulations—should be implemented. Moreover, the board should have taken this risk management job more seriously by continuously monitoring and advising senior management to turn Dexia into a manageable and therefore more healthy organisation, which could have deserved the trust and confidence of its clientele and the public at large.

Notes

1 Strategists need to question the assumptions of the current business model and then analyse the current and new trends that may appear through the complexity and ambiguity of the prevailing uncertainty. After such a questioning and analysing exercise, leaders need to synthesise all the different options and their pros and cons. Finally, after conducting the necessary tests, a choice needs to be made. In other words, a strategic decision to take a bet will need to be taken.

2 Notwithstanding a majority Belgian shareholding (60.5%), the board was composed in parity, with an equal number of French and Belgian representatives. As well as the passionate public banker François Narmon, a hyper-ambitious French manager, Pierre Richard, joined the old GKB/CCB. Dexia would feel the over-representation of French interests quite quickly.

3 The Dexia group took a 40 per cent participation in Crediop in 1997. In 2000, the Dexia group acquired FSA in the USA for €2.6 billion. In 2000, Dexia took over Bank Labouchere; in 2001, Bank Kempen; and in 2001, ABC.

4 DEPFA Bank plc is a Dublin-based German-Irish bank that specialises in providing financing to the public sector and larger infrastructure projects. (The name derives from *Deutsche Pfandbriefbank.*) The bank ran into liquidity problems in 2008 as a result of economic and financial turmoil in the USA.

5 Further losses are still possible on the remaining FSA portfolio. On 19 January 2009, Moody's lowered the credit rating for Dexia's long-term bonds and saving accounts of the three banking parts of Dexia (DCL, DBB and BIL) from A3 to A1. The rating agency also downgraded the Bank Financial Strength Rating for the three banks from C− to D+.

6 Belfius Bank and Insurance's mission is first, to become a locally anchored relationship bank and insurer. Being a relationship-based bank with its roots in the local community also implies that it has to be accessible 24/7. With 804 branches, Belfius's presence is equally strong in Flanders, Brussels and Wallonia. Second, its mission is to become a bank that offers added value to society. From a financial point of view, Belfius seeks solutions to the major challenges in society, such as the ageing population, sustainable development and social integration. And, of course, Belfius aims to be the preferred financial partner in the public and social profit sectors. Finally, its mission is to become a bank that supports clear and transparent communication. Belfius's commercial activities focus on retail and commercial banking, public and wholesale banking, and insurance.

7 The Dexia (Holding) S.A. will be marked by the completion of pending divestment processes, subject to approval by the European Commission of the group's new restructuring plan. After completion of those disposals, the Dexia group's new activities will focus on public-sector services through its international subsidiaries and on managing a portfolio of assets in run-off.

8 At the end of 2012, Dexia reached an agreement to sell Dexia Asset Management to GCS Capital (later renamed Candriam). At an extraordinary general meeting (EGM) on 21 December 2012, the shareholders (the Belgian and French states) decided to increase the capital by another €5.5 billion, presumably strengthening Dexia (Holding) S.A. Consequently, Dexia (Holding) S.A. continues its activity of further cleaning up the past and dismantling the company. The mission of Belfius Bank and Insurance is to be a locally anchored relationship bank and insurer that offers added value to society and supports clear and transparent communication, with a focus on digital services.

References

Ardaen, B. (2012), *Tijdbom Dexia: De inside story*, Antwerp: Periscoop Producties.

Dann, C., M. Le Merle and C. Pencavel (2012), 'The Lesson of Lost Value', *Strategy + Business* 69, reprint 00146

Heath, D. and D. Heath (2013), *Decisive: How to Make Better Decisions*, London: Random House.

Kahneman, D. (2011), *Thinking, Fast and Slow*, London: Penguin-Pearson

Kaplan, R.S. and A. Mikes (2012), 'Managing Risks: A New Framework', *Harvard Business Review*, June, pp. 48–60.

Kaplan, R.S. and Mikes, A. (2014), 'Towards a Contingency Theory of Enterprise Risk Management', working paper 13-063, Harvard Business School, 13 January, p. 45.

Lafley, A.G., R. Martin, J.W. Rivkin and N. Siggelkow (2012), 'Bringing Science to the Art Strategy', *Harvard Business Review*, September, pp. 56–66.

LeMerle, M. (2011), 'How to Prepare for a Black Swan', *Strategy + Business*, Autumn (64), reprint 11303

Malkiel, B.G. (2015/1973), *A Random Walk Down Wall Street: The Time-Tested Strategy for Successful Investing*, New York: Norton & Company.

Martin, R. (2007), *The Opposable Mind: How Successful Leaders Win through Integrative Thinking*, Cambridge, MA: Harvard Business School Press.

Martin, R. and A. Kemper (2012), 'Saving the Planet: A Tale of Two Strategies', *Harvard Business Review*, April, pp. 48–46.

Piffaretti, A. (2013), *Enquête sur la plus grosse faillite bancaire Européenne: Le scandale DEXIA*, Paris: Nouveau Monde Editions.

Rosenzweig, P. (2015), *Left Brain, Right Stuff*, London: Public Affairs.

Simons, R. (2010), 'Stress-Test Your Strategy: The 7 Questions to Ask', *Harvard Business Review*, November, pp. 92–100.

Schoemaker, P.J.H., S. Krupp and S. Howland (2013), 'Experience: Strategic Leadership—The Essential Skills', *Harvard Business Review*, January–February, pp. 131–134.

Sull, D. (2009), *The Upside of Turbulence: Seize Opportunities in an Uncertain World*, New York: HarperCollins.

Sull, D. and K.M. Eisenhardt (2012), 'Simple Rules for a Complex World', *Harvard Business Review*, September, pp. 68–74.

Taleb, N.N. (2005), *Fooled by Randomness*, New York: Random House.

Taleb, N.N. (2007), *The Black Swan: The Impact of the Highly Improbable*, London: Allen Lane.

Bibliography

Verhezen, P. (2010), 'Giving Voice to a Culture of Silence: From a Culture of Compliance to a Culture of Integrity', *Journal of Business Ethics*, 96(2), pp. 187–206.

Verhezen, P. (2015a), 'Fear, Regret or Trust? Transparency to Control or Transparency to Empower', International Finance Corporation World Bank Paper, no. 38, Washington. Available from: http://www.ifc.org/wps/wcm/connect/topics_ext_content/ifc_external_corporate_site/corporate+governance/publications/private+sector+opinion/fear+and+regret_or+trust.

Verhezen, P. (2015b), *The Vulnerability of Corporate Reputation: Leadership for Sustainable Long-Term Value*, Berkshire: Palgrave Pivot Publishing.

19

Future research in accounting and risk

Margaret Woods and Philip Linsley

Introduction

The publication of this research text in accounting and risk marks something of a milestone in the evolution of a new area of study. Around the year 2000, as a young academic at Loughborough, I became interested in the way in which companies reported their exposure to financial derivatives, and I found that useful information was hard to come by. More importantly, nobody else seemed really interested in the topic, despite the fact that it raised serious questions about the quality of disclosure and levels of compliance with the conceptual framework. The topic could clearly be described as addressing the link between accounting and risk, but it took three years for an academic journal (*European Accounting Review*) to be willing to firstly review and subsequently publish a paper on the theme (Woods and Marginson, 2004). The core accounting journals rejected the paper without review on the grounds that it was not mainstream and was 'really finance'. The finance journals were similarly unwilling to review because it was 'too accounting-focused'.

The interface between accounting and finance issues remains a challenge, as researchers have become tightly focused on increasingly narrow themes, but this book is confirmation that academic thinking about risk and accounting has moved on substantially in the last decade. A search in June 2016 in the *European Accounting Review* for papers that included 'risk' in their title yielded a total of 648 results covering topics as diverse as risk management credibility within boardrooms (Gendron *et al.*, 2015), enterprise-wide risk management adoption, and the role of rules versus principles in accounting scandals (Ravenscroft and Williams, 2005). A similar search within the *British Accounting Review* generated 381 hits that were rather less diverse. Examples included several on risk reporting, including environmental risk disclosures (Elshandidy *et al.*, 2015; Abraham and Shrives, 2014; Campbell and Slack, 2011; Abraham and Cox, 2007) as well as the risks in public–private partnerships (Khadaroo, 2014; Demirag *et al.*, 2011). A more detailed search and analysis of other accounting journals could prove interesting in revealing other emerging areas of interest and could shed some light on the true extent to which accounting and risk is emerging as a mainstream theme within the academic literature.

The structure of this book clearly illustrates how risk is pertinent to many aspects of governance and to financial and management accounting, and the aim of this concluding chapter is to discuss the great scope for future research in the area of accounting and risk. We will therefore suggest ideas for both fundamental and empirical research in each of the areas of financial accounting, management accounting, governance and auditing. Our suggestions are in no respect intended to constitute a complete list of possibilities but rather merely to stimulate ideas for new research projects, with the aim of both adding to knowledge and potentially impacting upon corporate and regulatory practices. Notwithstanding the topics already raised in antecedent papers, however, we take the same approach as Ohlson (2011, p. 7), who observed that 'the best research questions derive from an acute sense of how the world works'. Undoubtedly, there is much still to learn about how the world of risk works.

Risk and financial accounting

Magnan and Markarian (2011, p. 215) concluded that the financial crisis revealed that:

> Accounting exhibited shortcomings in its structural foundation and in its application. Salient is its failure to account for uncertainty and to adequately capture, measure and disclose the impact of risk-taking on the financial statements, thus undermining their reliability and, potentially, their relevance as indicators of economic performance.

Readers of this book should perhaps, therefore, be grateful for the global financial crisis and successive corporate scandals that have served to highlight the challenges faced by accountants in dealing with risk and uncertainty.

The quote from Magnan and Markarian (2011) provides a useful starting point for identifying research ideas in relation to financial accounting, as these authors suggest shortcomings in both the *structural foundation* and the *application* of accounting in relation to uncertainty and risk. Central to the structural foundation of accounting is the conceptual framework. The joint conceptual framework project of the IASB and FASB, which began in 2004 and is currently being managed by the FASB, focuses on the objectives, components and qualitative features of financial statements as well as fundamental elements such as recognition and measurement. Such topics provide huge research opportunities in relation to risk. For example, in addition to the question of what information should be disclosed (and how) about many different types of risks—environmental, financial, legal, and so on—there are issues about the wider economic consequences of such disclosures. In the case of company pension liabilities, for example, transparency in respect of how they are valued and the size of the liability may affect the livelihoods of not just current and future employees but the wider public if bankruptcy results in the pension responsibility being transferred to the public purse. The recent demise of the UK retailer British Home Stores (BHS) illustrates this point clearly as well as highlighting the threats to potential mergers or takeovers when pension liabilities become very high. The administrators were unable to find a buyer for BHS because of the sheer scale of the pension deficit. In a different context, the study of transparency about risk exposure and risk transfers in public–private partnerships also has widespread economic consequences.

Other structural fundamentals in accounting that have a risk dimension include principles versus rules and the exercise of professional judgement in both the preparation and auditing of financial reports. Do rules encourage a compliance-based mindset that reduces risks, or do they instead increase risk because areas not covered by rules get ignored or missed? Similarly, as bodies such as the Committee of Sponsoring Organizations of the Treadway Commission (COSO) in the US set standards for risk management, and as regulators such as the Basel committee rewrite corporate governance regulations, there are questions to be asked about the subsequent implications for the accounting profession. An interesting paper by Carnegie and Napier (2010) considered the impact on the accounting profession and on the future of financial reporting of negative media coverage following the Enron scandal. The idea that the accounting profession per se may be at risk if financial scandals persist is one of significant interest to us all.

In terms of the application of accounting, key consideration needs to be given to the governance mechanisms (auditing, boards of directors and executive compensation schemes) that are dependent upon financial reports (Magnan and Markarian, 2011). For example, to what extent do auditors have the power, skills and expertise to evaluate highly technical risk exposures, such as complex financial instruments? These are issues that are already being debated within the academic literature (see, for example, Geiger *et al.*, 2014; Beattie *et al.*, 2013; Humphrey *et al.*, 2011; Woods *et al.*, 2009) but there is still much to explore. Other questions include, 'What are the consequences, in terms of risks, of auditors (both internal and external) using a risk-based approach to audit planning?'

The evolution of international governance regulations and the associated implications for risk management and risk-taking is another area worthy of analysis and debate. Media and academic concerns about excessive levels of executive compensation, often in the form of share options, raise questions about the extent to which equity-based forms of pay may encourage short-term thinking amongst senior managers. Researchers have suggested that this may lead to manipulation of share prices that breaks the owner–manager link the equity compensation was intended to provide (see, for example, Dong *et al.*, 2010; Bebchuk and Fried, 2010). We would also suggest a need for academics to question and evaluate the extent to which the figures reported in financial statements incorporate the underlying risks. For example, given the UK's vote for exit from the European Union, to what extent do UK company balance sheet asset values truly reflect the risks associated with huge currency fluctuations? Is there an argument for sensitivity analysis on balance sheets and increased access for users to interactive financial statements? The growth in use of XBRL would suggest that there is a demand for such interaction, and there is also debate about the extent to which it improves governance, transparency and the quality of financial reporting (see, for example, Efendi *et al.*, 2011). Risk considerations may generate changes to the traditional model of financial reporting.

In summary, financial accounting and auditing researchers can access a wealth of risk-related themes that provide opportunities for both quantitative and qualitative research. The priority is to get out and see what is happening inside organisations.

Risk and management accounting

Management accountants are trained in the design and maintenance of internal control systems. Their professional body, CIMA, defines risk management as 'the process of understanding and managing the risks that the entity is inevitably subject to in attempting to achieve its corporate objectives' (CIMA, 2005, p. 53). If risk management is about achievement of objectives, then it is also about performance and the associated internal control, remuneration systems and corporate governance mechanisms that drive an organisation. All of these areas fall within the remit of the management accountant, but a study by Collier *et al.* (2007) suggested that management accounting and risk management were only weakly integrated in practice. The evidence presented in Chapters 9, 10, 12 and 14 of this book suggest that this situation may be changing, but it remains an interesting area of research. Who is responsible for risk management in major organisations, and to what extent (if at all) are management accountants directly involved in risk identification, assessment and the design of risk control systems? The possible contrast between private and public sector organisations in this regard is also worthy of study.

Linked to the question of the role of accountants in risk management is the broader issue of how exactly risks are managed within organisations. There are still only a limited number of case studies of day-to-day practice, and limited analysis of how risk boundaries are defined and how interlinked risks are managed. Are corporate risks treated as a form of portfolio that is clearly structured and managed, or is the process more haphazard and ill-defined? How many firms say they use enterprise-wide risk management (ERM) when they really mean just risk management? The term ERM remains open to abuse, as the former is a very specific system but the latter is much more open to contextual interpretation.

Despite the encouragement of narrowly focused research agendas and increased specialisation amongst academics, it is also useful to note the strong interdependencies between research themes in financial and management accounting. This link was clearly expressed by Van der Stede (2011) in his analysis of the implications of the financial crisis for management accounting research. He presented the case for studies of change in management accounting practice post-crisis, and he argued that the increased demand for external disclosures that have emerged in response to risk management failures and crises will have a consequential impact on internal reporting practice. His arguments echoed those made by Power (1997) over a decade earlier in relation to auditing and corporate governance regulations (e.g. the Cadbury Code in the UK) that required directors to report on the effectiveness of the company's systems of internal control. How do auditors define internal controls, and what is meant by the term 'effective'? External regulations have internal control implications that affect the management accountant and provide potentially fruitful lines of research.

In a similar vein, the calls for links between pay and risk-taking that were made after the financial crisis also offer research potential, as highlighted by Van der Stede (2011). The design of incentive schemes, the introduction of clawback clauses and the resulting impact of such changes on managerial behaviour are all of interest to researchers. Questions about the relationship between risk culture or risk-taking and remuneration system design are relevant to organisations, academics and regulators. Risk culture and the interface between risk culture and corporate culture remains little understood, but the work of Power *et al.* (2013) in financial organisations provides a useful starting point for researchers looking to learn about this topic. The authors emphasised the contextual nature of risk culture and suggested that organisations are likely to exhibit multiple cultures rather than just one. They also noted the existence of strong tensions between operational staff and risk management staff in respect of what are deemed acceptable levels of risk-taking.

We conclude that, as with financial accounting, the research topics that are of potential relevance to management accounting researchers and also incorporate risk considerations are very extensive. The need is to address them in a manner that makes for good-quality research that will get published in the best peer-reviewed accounting journals.

What constitutes successful research?

There are a vast number of references that could be cited in answer to this question, and we also wish to avoid falling into the trap of defining successful research as only that which gets published in three- or four-star journals. Research is successful if it proves useful—to academics, practitioners, regulators or the wider public. We would therefore like to conclude this book by listing a set of criteria to consider before setting out on a new research project:

1 Ensure you are personally interested in the topic. Doing something just because it has been suggested by a supervisor or fellow academic is unlikely to work. Research is hard work, and good research is especially hard. You will only succeed if you are excited by the idea.
2 Read everything you can on the topic, and try to identify the limitations and unanswered questions in the research to date. For example, would a qualitative approach to an issue shed new light on something that has traditionally been analysed using quantitative methods?
3 Use your contacts. Research access can be difficult, so spend time making contacts and using them to full effect.
4 Leave time to play as well as work. Our brains process information in the background when we are occupied doing other things. Research benefits from such thinking and processing time, and you don't get stale from overwork.
5 Ask about who will find the research helpful or useful, and then pose questions and design the research to target that audience.
6 Get lots of feedback en route through the process. However much criticism you might face, you will learn from it.
7 Write in a simple and straightforward style. Just remember how many academic papers you have read that were close to incomprehensible, so you don't finish reading them!
8 Be patient. Sometimes it can take years to really understand something well, but that doesn't mean you are not a successful researcher.

We hope you have found this book both interesting and useful, and that it inspires many more people to undertake research into accounting and risk. We look forward to reading the papers and books that result from this work.

References

Abraham, S. and P. Cox, 'Analysing the Determinants of Narrative Risk Information in UK FTSE 100 Annual Reports', *British Accounting Review*, 39(3), pp. 227–248.

Abraham, S. and P. Shrives (2014), 'Improving the Relevance of Risk Factor Disclosure in Corporate Annual Reports', *British Accounting Review*, 46(1), pp. 91–107.

Beattie, V., S. Fearnley and T. Hines (2013), 'Perceptions of Factors Affecting Audit Quality in the Post-SOX UK Regulatory Environment', *Accounting and Business Research*, 43(1), pp. 56–81.

Bebchuk, L. and J. Fried (2010), 'How to Tie Equity Compensation to Long-Term Results', *Journal of Applied Corporate Finance*, 22(1), pp. 99–106.

Campbell, D. and R. Slack (2011), 'Environmental Disclosure and Environmental Risk: Sceptical Attitudes of UK Sell-Side Bank Analysts', *British Accounting Review*, 43(1), pp. 54–64.

Carnegie, G.D. and C.J. Napier (2010), 'Traditional Accountants and Business Professionals: Portraying the Accounting Profession after Enron', *Accounting, Organizations and Society*, 35(3), pp. 370–396.

CIMA (2005), *Official Terminology*, Oxford: CIMA Publishing.

Collier, P.M., A.J. Berry and G.T. Burke (2007), *Risk and Management Accounting: Best Practice Guidelines for Enterprise-Wide Internal Control Procedures*, Amsterdam: Elsevier.

Demirag, I., L. Khadaroo, P. Stapleton and C. Stevenson (2011), 'Risks and the Financing of PPP: Perspectives from the Financiers', *British Accounting Review*, 43(4), pp. 294–310.

Dong, Z., C. Wang and F. Xie (2010), 'Do Executive Stock Options Induce Excessive Risk Taking?' *Journal of Banking and Finance*, 34(10), pp. 2518–2529.

Efendi, J., L.M. Smith and J. Wong (2011), 'Longitudinal Analysis of Voluntary Adoption of XBRL on Financial Reporting', *International Journal of Economics and Accounting*, 2(2), pp. 173–189.

Elshandidy, T., I. Fraser and K. Hussainey (2015), What Drives Mandatory and Voluntary Risk Reporting Variations across Germany, UK and US? *British Accounting Review*, 47(4), pp. 376–394.

Geiger, A.M., K. Raghunandan and W. Riccardi (2014), 'The Global Financial Crisis: U.S. Bankruptcies and Going-Concern Audit Opinions', *Accounting Horizons*, 28(1), pp. 59–75.

Gendron, Y., M. Brivot and H. Guénin-Paracini (2015), 'The Construction of Risk Management Credibility within Corporate Boardrooms', *European Accounting Review*, DOI:10.1080/09638180.2015.1064008.
Humphrey, C., A. Loft and M. Woods (2011), 'Regulating Audit beyond the Crisis: A Critical Discussion of the EU Green Paper', *European Accounting Review*, 20(3), pp. 431–457.
Khadaroo, I. (2014), 'The Valuation of Risk Transfer in UK School Public Private Partnership Contracts', *British Accounting Review*, 46(2), pp. 154–165.
Magnan, M. and G. Markarian (2011), 'Accounting, Governance and the Crisis: Is Risk the Missing Link? *European Accounting Review*, 20(2), pp. 215–231.
Ohlson, J. A. (2011), 'On Successful Research', *European Accounting Review*, 20(1), pp. 7–26.
Paape, L. and R.F. Speklé (2012), 'The Adoption and Design of Enterprise Risk Management Practices: An Empirical Study', *European Accounting Review*, 21(3), pp. 533–564.
Power, M. (1997), *The Audit Society: Rituals of Verification*, Oxford: Oxford University Press.
Power, M., S. Ashby and T. Palermo (2013), *Risk Culture in Financial Organisations*, London: London School of Economics.
Ravenscroft, S. and P.F. Williams (2005), 'Rules, Rogues, and Risk Assessors: Academic Responses to Enron and Other Accounting Scandals', *European Accounting Review*, 14(2), pp. 363–372.
Van der Stede, W.A. (2011), 'Management Accounting Research in the Wake of the Crisis: Some Reflections', *European Accounting Review*, 20(4), pp. 605–623.
Woods, M. and D. Marginson (2004), 'Accounting for Derivatives: An Evaluation of Reporting Practice by UK Banks', *European Accounting Review*, 13(2), pp. 373–390.
Woods, M., C. Humphrey, K. Dowd and Y.L. (2009), 'Crunch Time for Bank Audits? Questions of Practice and the Scope for Dialogue', *Managerial Auditing Journal*, 24(2), pp. 114–134.

Index